THE TOP 10 OF SPORT

ABOUT THE AUTHORS

Russell Ash has written and contributed to more than 50 books on a diverse range of topics, including art, real and fictitious animals (he is the official biographer of Paddington Bear!), humour and popular reference subjects. He has also contributed to numerous publications, among them the *Sunday Times*, the *Observer* and *Punch*, and for several years had two weekly columns, 'The Week That Was' and 'Strange But True', in the London magazine *Midweek*.

Since 1989 Russell Ash has produced *The Top 10 of Everything*, an annual compendium of Top 10 lists on an immense array of subjects. The book has become an international bestseller, and *The Top 10 of Sport* is the first in a series of specialist titles derived from the Top 10 concept.

Ian Morrison has been an author of sports books since 1983 when he drifted away from the world of finance and into the seclusion of writing. Since then he has written in excess of 70 books, all but two of them on sport. He has covered everything from boxing to rugby league and American football to wrestling, and he has written or co-written some of the leading sports encyclopedias of the last few years. His *Encyclopedia of Snooker* (first published in 1985) is one of the biggest-selling books of its kind in the last decade.

Ian Morrison has now retired from writing and lives on the Mediterranean island of Mallorca. *The Top 10 of Sport* was one of his last works before embarking on his 'new life'.

THE TOP 10 OF SPORT

RUSSELL ASH
— AND —
IAN MORRISON

HEADLINE

First published in 1992
by HEADLINE BOOK PUBLISHING PLC

10   9   8   7   6   5   4   3   2   1

British Library Cataloguing in Publication Data

Ash, Russell
Top 10 of Sport
I. Title II. Morrison, Ian
796

ISBN 0-7472-0714-3

Additional material supplied by Stamp's Sporting Statistics Ltd

Cover photographs
Front (clockwise from top left): Mark Spitz, 1972 Olympics (*Colorsport*);
Graham Gooch, Lord's Test *v* India, 1990 (*Allsport*); Stephen Hendry, 1990
World Championship (*Professional Sport*); Ingemar Stenmark, 1987 World
Championships (*Colorsport*); Daley Thompson, 1984 Olympics (*Bob
Thomas*); Michael Lynagh (*Colorsport*); Gary Lineker (*Colorsport*); Peter
Scudamore on Beau Ranger, 1989 Cheltenham Festival (*Colorsport*);
James 'Buster' Douglas *v* Evander Holyfield, 1990 (*Allsport*)

Back (left to right): 1990 Boat Race (*Allsport*); Ian Woosnam (*Bob
Thomas*); 100m final, 1991 Tokyo World Championships (*Empics*)

Designed and produced by
The Pen & Ink Book Co. Ltd, Huntingdon

Printed and bound in Great Britain by
Butler and Tanner Limited, Frome

HEADLINE BOOK PUBLISHING PLC
Headline House
79 Great Titchfield Street
London W1P 7FN

CONTENTS

ACKNOWLEDGEMENTS

Thanks go to all those governing bodies who helped in the preparation of lists. The following deserve special mention for their prompt, efficient and friendly assistance:

Edward Abelson
Dominic Allom
Caroline Ash
Michael A. Berger of the National Hockey League (NHL)
The British Paralympic Association
Steve Catton
Sarah Dawson
Paul Dickson
Clive Everton
Ken Fiore of the National Football League (NFL)
Forbes Magazine
Christopher Forbes
Robert Gates
Lennie Gessler of the Professional Bowlers Association (PBA)
Mike Getty of the British Darts Organisation
Richard Gibbs
Ken Henhouse
The International Tennis Federation
Arthur Jones
Robert Treharne Jones

Kathy of the US Ladies Professional Golf Association (LPGA)
Ken Kneely of the Thoroughbred Racing Association of America
Barry Lazell
Richard Lockwood
Amanda Lovejoy
Terry Lyons of the National Basketball Association (NBA)
Ian Marshall
Peter Matthews
Media Department of the US Trotting Association
National Anglers' Council
Anikó Németh-Móra of the International Weightlifting Federation
Jack Rollin
Tanya Seton
Linda Silverman
Peter Went
Pat Williams

Ian Morrison would also like to thank Barrie Weekes and David Wright for casting an eye over certain parts of the manuscript, and Vincent Camroux who provided some invaluable croquet information. Ann Morrison deserves her usual praise for helping to check the manuscript, as always without remuneration.

PICTURE CREDITS

Action-Plus: 49
Allsport: 57, 68, 70–71, 73 (left), 76, 78, 178, 196–7, 213, 220, 221, 251, 252
Associated Sports Photography: 62, 207, 212, 226, 232
Michael Cole Camera-Work: 182–3
Colorsport: 22, 24, 28, 40–41, 42 (top), 47, 53, 65, 82, 99, 138, 175, 195, 201, 219, 229, 234, 236, 240, 247
Jim Connolly: 140 (top), 173
Peter Dazeley: 143
Patrick Eagar: 107, 108, 112, 129
David Frith Collection: 110, 113, 130–31
Hobbs Golf Collection: 140 (bottom), 145, 149, 154
The Hulton-Deutsch Collection: 58, 73 (right), 83, 86–7, 89 (top), 116, 120–21, 156, 180, 210–11, 249
Illustrated London News: 18
Kobal: 191
Kos Photos: 254
Roger Mann Collection: 115
David Muscroft: 241

Natural History Museum: 155
Peter Newark's Western Americana: 179
NFL: 10, 11, 14
Popperfoto: 161, 167 (bottom)
Professional Bowlers Association: 81
Professional Sport: 42 (bottom), 135
Alastair Scott: 192
Richard Sellers/Sportsphoto Agency: 242
Phil Sheldon: 152
Split Second: 164
Sport and General: 101, 168
Sporting Pictures (UK) Ltd: 89 (bottom), 95
Sutton Photographic: 204
Syndication International: 167 (top)
Bob Thomas: 19, 23, 36, 54
Topham: 80, 172
Andrew Varley: 227
Eric Whitehead: 79
Wimbledon Lawn Tennis Museum: 187
John Wood: 250

INTRODUCTION

Following the success of *The Top 10 of Everything* it was almost inevitable that we should decide to branch out into an area that lent itself to the style and format of the main book. The area that immediately sprang to mind was sport, a subject perfectly suited to a book of lists, charts and records.

When we composed our initial contents list, coming up with ideas for lists was an easy task because sport is such a wide and varied subject. Once we started compiling the lists themselves, even more ideas occurred to us and we could have gone on and on. It soon became clear to us that sport fitted the Top 10 concept so well that we could have compiled separate books on cricket and football alone, but we were compelled to make a number of difficult decisions about what to leave in and take out. We hope you are pleased with our choice, which we believe offers entertaining and informative reading.

The book is full of lists that will prove useful to those of you devising quizzes or wishing to settle the sort of arguments that can happen whenever two or more sports fans meet. But some of the entries are pure trivia, designed to be a little bit of fun. Both of us enjoy digging up those pieces of 'useless' information which people find fascinating and we have shared some sporting trivia with you.

As with all books of records and statistics, and especially in an area as dynamic as sport, there will inevitably be a few lists which are already out of date. 'Definitive' lists are much easier with subjects such as the world's highest mountains or longest rivers, but when it comes to the the capacities of football grounds or the top run-makers in Test cricket, for example, the lists are subject to constant change. However, for all the sports in the book we have chosen a logical cut-off point, normally coinciding with the end of that sport's last season.

We hope you enjoy *The Top 10 of Sport* and if you have any comments or suggestions for future lists we would be delighted to hear from you.

Russell Ash and Ian Morrison

American Sports **1** Harness racing. **2** Rodeo. **3** The Preakness Stakes. **4** Wade Boggs. **5** Ice hockey. **6** Chicago (White Sox, Cubs, Blackhawks, Bears, Bulls). **7** Joe Montana. **8** Three. **9** Wayne Gretzky (ice hockey). **10** Soap Box Derby.

Sporting Venues **1** Norway (Oslo). **2** Madison Square Garden. **3** Stamford Bridge, Chelsea. **4** Shea Stadium (home of the New York Mets). **5** Gatwick (staged the Grand National during World War I). **6** Swiss Grand Prix (motor racing is banned in Switzerland). **7** Isle of Man TT course. **8** Badminton (Three-Day Event). **9** No. 17. **10** Benson and Hedges Irish Masters.

FA Cup **1** Nottingham Forest. **2** 1935, when the game was refereed by A. E. Fogg of Bolton. **3** Blackburn (Rovers in 1882, 1884–86; Olympic 1883). **4** Queen's Park Rangers (1982). **5** Everton. **6** Chelsea (beat Leeds in 1970). **7** He was the first man sent off in a semi-final. **8** Millwall (1937). **9** Wimbledon. **10** They were the first team in a Wembley final to score first and end up as losers.

Football's World Cup **1** Italy (1934 and 1938). **2** Yes – he played in three games. **3** Wembley Stadium and White City. **4** He is the only one of the 66 whose surname does *not* end in a 'v'. **5** Fiji. **6** Franz Beckenbauer (West Germany). **7** Republic of Ireland, Costa Rica and United Arab Emirates. **8** Argentina (1978). **9** Emilio Butragueño (Spain). **10** Arthur Ellis.

Award Winners **1** Golden Boot Award (presented by Adidas). **2** Ice hockey (to the most valuable player in the NHL play-offs). **3** Anita Lonsbrough. **4** Bobby Moore (1966). **5** Stanley Matthews. **6** The jockey with the most wins at Royal Ascot. **7** Steve Cauthen. **8** Tessa Sanderson. **9** Kevin Keegan. **10** The scorer of the fastest first-class century.

World Heavyweight Boxing Champions **1** Trevor Berbick (WBC champion 1986, born in Jamaica). **2** Jess Willard (v Jack Johnson). **3** Just one (v Sonny Liston, 1964). **4** A million-dollar gate. **5** Floyd Patterson and Ingemar Johansson. **6** Bob Fitzsimmons. **7** James 'Bonecrusher' Smith (1987). **8** Tony Tucker (IBF). **9** Jack Johnson (v Tommy Burns, 26 December 1908). **10** Jimmy Ellis and Greg Page.

Test Cricket **1** 45 runs (Australia won both matches). **2** Headingley (Leeds). **3** 10 days (43 hours 16 minutes). **4** It was achieved on his Test debut. **5** Tony Greig (1973–74). **6** Bob Taylor. **7** John Edrich (1965). **8** South Africa. **9** The Hadlees (Dale and Richard). **10** The Ashes (he was the young journalist who wrote the 'obituary' to English cricket that appeared in the *Sporting Times*).

County Cricket Championship **1** Essex. **2** Glamorgan (1921). **3** 16. **4** Tom Moody (Warwicks v Glamorgan). **5** Taunton (Archie MacLaren [424] Lancashire v Somerset, 1895 and Graeme Hick [405 not out] Worcestershire v Somerset, 1988). **6** Middlesex and Kent (1977). **7** Jimmy Cook. **8** Cambridgeshire. **9** Essex. **10** Worcestershire (1988–89).

Sporting Nicknames **1** Ian Botham. **2** Twickenham. **3** Ty Cobb. **4** Craig Stadler. **5** Widnes v Warrington . **6** Billy Aird. **7** Rod Laver. **8** The Refrigerator. **9** Stoke-on-Trent (Port Vale v Stoke City). **10** Hannes Kolehmainen.

British Golfing Champions **1** Max Faulkner (1951). **2** Henry Cotton (1934, 1937 and 1948). **3** Ted Ray. **4** Ian Woosnam (1991). Despite his total loyalty to the 'Red Dragon', Woosnam was born at St Martins, in Shropshire, just over the Welsh border. **5** Ian Woosnam (1987). **6** Laura Davies (1987). **7** Dick Burton (1939). **8** Nick Faldo (1990, British Open and US Masters). **9** David Llewellyn. **10** Howard Clark.

The Grand National **1** Corbière. **2** Tommy Stack. **3** Six years. **4** Maghull. **5** Fulke Walwyn. **6** Garage proprietor. **7** Nicolaus Silver (1961). **8** Rubstic (1979). **9** Seagram. **10** Manifesto (1897–1903). He also appeared in a record eight races.

Winter Sports **1** Biathlon. **2** Nordic skiing. **3** Iditarod Trail (dog sled race). **4** Bobsleighing and tobogganing (Fédération Internationale de Bobsleigh et de Tobogganing). **5** Curling. **6** Ice hockey. **7** Fife. **8** Alexandr Zaitsev. **9** Plasterer. **10** Andreas and Hanni Wenzel (Liechtenstein).

Grand Slam Tennis **1**. Zina Garrison. **2** Frank Sedgman and Ken McGregor. **3** Steffi Graf (1988). **4** Great Britain (Fred Perry and Dorothy Round). **5** John and Tracey Austin. **6** Chris Evert-Lloyd. **7** Michael Chang (French Open). **8** Stefan Edberg. **9** Donald Budge (in 1937). **10** They were held in New Zealand.

A Little Bit of the Unusual **1** Mount Kilimanjaro. **2** Grape catching (Porter threw the grape which Dyomm caught in his mouth 219 feet away). **3** Pigeon racing. **4** Dung throwing. **5** Reginald Bosanquet's father, Bernard. **6** Reginald Bosanquet. **7** Literature (under the pseudonym Georg Hohrad and M Eschbach he won the literature prize for his *Ode to Sport*. **8** A rare Swiss postage stamp. **9** Angling (they are names of flies). **10** Subbuteo.

Formula One Grand Prix Racing **1** Lotus. **2** Stirling Moss. **3** Jackie Stewart. **4** Larousse. **5** Mike Hawthorn (French Grand Prix). **6** European Grand Prix. **7** Alain Prost. **8** Derek Warwick. **9** Tom Pryce. **10** Win races on their Grand prix debut.

Olympic Greats **1** Mark Spitz. **2** Vera Čáslavská (Czechoslovakia). **3** Beth Heiden (sister of Eric). **4** Carl Lewis. **5** Jesse Owens. **6** Dawn Fraser (100 metres freestyle). **7** Wilma Rudolph. **8** John Kelly (father of the late Princess Grace of Monaco). **9** Middleweight. **10** Abebe Bikila.

Water Sports **1** Angling (world freshwater champions). **2** Admiral's Cup. **3** Didier Pironi. **4** Diamond Sculls (at Henley). **5** Water skiing (by Andy Mapple). **6** 1500 metres (men). **7** Chris Snode. **8** Seven. **9** Matt Biondi (USA, 1988). **10** At 13 years 9 months she became the youngest ever swimming and diving gold medallist.

Rugby League Record-Breakers **1** Central Park, Wigan (Wigan v St Helens). **2** Eric Batten. **3** Anfield (Liverpool FC). **4** George West (Hull Kingston Rovers) or Lionel Cooper (Huddersfield). **5** Castleford. **6** Steve Carroll. **7** David Watkins. **8** Papua New Guinea. **9** Keith Elwell. **10** Wigan (28) and Hull (24) – 1985.

Rugby Union Record-Breakers **1** New South Wales. **2** Australia (21–9). **3** *1* Wales (32); *2* England (28); *3* Scotland (21); *4* Ireland (18); *5* France (17) Figures include shared wins. **4** Phil Bennett. **5** Jean-Pierre Rives (France). **6** Fiji. **7** Peter Butler. **8** Edinburgh Academicals. **9** Nottingham and Leicester. **10** Cyril Brownlee (New Zealand, 1924).

AMERICAN FOOTBALL

THE TOP 10 SUPER BOWL ATTENDANCES

	Match	Venue	Year	Attendance
1	Pittsburgh *v* Los Angeles	Pasadena	1980	103,985
2	Washington *v* Miami	Pasadena	1983	103,667
3	Oakland *v* Minnesota	Pasadena	1977	103,438
4	New York Giants *v* Denver	Pasadena	1987	101,063
5	Miami *v* Washington	Los Angeles	1973	90,182
6	San Francisco *v* Miami	Stanford	1985	84,059
7	San Francisco *v* Cincinnati	Pontiac	1982	81,270
8	Dallas *v* Miami	New Orleans*	1972	81,023
9	Pittsburgh *v* Minnesota	New Orleans*	1975	80,997
10	Kansas City *v* Minnesota	New Orleans*	1970	80,562

At the Tulane Stadium.

THE 10 MOST SUCCESSFUL TEAMS*

	Team	Wins	Runners-up	Pts
1=	Pittsburgh Steelers	4	0	8
1=	San Francisco 49ers	4	0	8
1=	Washington Redskins	3	2	8
4=	Dallas Cowboys	2	3	7
4=	Miami Dolphins	2	3	7
4=	Oakland/Los Angeles Raiders	3	1	6
7=	Denver Broncos	0	4	4
7=	Green Bay Packers	2	0	4
7=	Minnesota Vikings	0	4	4
7=	New York Giants	2	0	4

Based on two points for a Super Bowl win, and one for runner-up.

THE 10 BIGGEST WINNING MARGINS IN THE SUPER BOWL

	Winners	Runners-up	Year	Score	Mgn
1	San Francisco	Denver	1990	55–10	45
2	Chicago	New England	1986	46–10	36
3	Washington	Denver	1988	42–10	32
4	LA Raiders	Washington	1984	38–9	29
5	Green Bay	Kansas City	1967	35–10	25
6	San Francisco	Miami	1985	38–16	22
7	Dallas	Miami	1972	24–3	21
8=	Green Bay	Oakland	1968	33–14	19
8=	New York Giants	Denver	1987	39–20	19
10	Oakland	Minnesota	1977	32–14	18

The closest Super Bowl was in 1991 when the New York Giants beat the Buffalo Bills 20–19. Scott Norwood missed a 47-yard field goal eight seconds from the end of time to deprive the Bills of their first-ever Super Bowl win.

THE 10 COLLEGES WITH THE MOST BOWL WINS

	College	Wins
1	Alabama	24
2	University of Southern California (USC)	23
3	Oklahoma	19
4=	Georgia Tech	17
4=	Penn State	17
4=	Tennessee	17
7	Texas	16
8	Georgia	15
9	Nebraska	14
10	Mississippi	13

Bowl games are end-of-season college championship games, played at the end of December or beginning of January each year. The 'Big Four' Bowl games are: Rose Bowl, Cotton Bowl, Sugar Bowl and Orange Bowl. The Rose Bowl dates to 1902 when the leading Eastern and Western teams met at Pasadena as part of the Tournament of Roses floral celebration, which was first held in 1890 and by the turn of the century had become a major attraction. Originally called the 'East–West Bowl', it became known as the Rose Bowl when the new 100,000-plus capacity Rose Bowl Stadium was opened in 1923.

THE 10 COLLEGES WITH THE MOST HEISMAN TROPHY WINNERS

	College	No. of winners
1	Notre Dame	7
2	Ohio State	5
3	University of Southern California (USC)	4
4=	Army	3
4=	Oklahoma	3
6=	Auburn	2
6=	Georgia	2
6=	Navy	2
6=	Nebraska	2
6=	Yale	2

Originally known as the DAC Trophy, this prize was first launched in 1935 and the following year became known as the Heisman Trophy in memory of John W. Heisman, the first athletic director of the Downtown Athletic Club of New York. The club makes the award annually based on a poll of journalists who nominate the top college player of the year. The only dual winner of this coveted award is Archie Griffin of Ohio State who won it in 1974 and 1975.

THE 10 MOST SUCCESSFUL COACHES IN AN NFL CAREER

	Coach	Games won
1	George Halas	325
2	Don Shula	306
3	Tom Landry	271
4	Curly Lambeau	229
5	Chuck Noll	209
6	Chuck Knox	178
7	Paul Brown	170
8	Bud Grant	168
9	Steve Owen	153
10	Hank Stram	136

Correct to the end of the 1990–91 season.

THE 10 MOST SUCCESSFUL PASSERS IN AN NFL CAREER

	Player	Yards gained
1	Fran Tarkenton	47,003
2	Dan Fouts	43,040
3	Johnny Unitas	40,239
4	Dan Marino	35,386
5	Joe Montana	34,998
6	Jim Hart	34,665
7	John Hadl	33,513
8	Ken Anderson	32,838
9	Sonny Jurgensen	32,224
10	John Brodie	31,548

If the All-American Football Conference (1946–49) is also considered, then Y. A. Tittle would figure in 8th place with 33,070 yards.

Miami Dolphins coach Don Shula, after winning his 300th game in September 1991.

THE 10 CURRENT NFL PLAYERS WITH THE LONGEST CAREERS

	Player	Club	Years
1	Pat Leahy	New York Jets	18
2	Jackie Slater	Los Angeles Rams	16
3=	Ezra Johnson	Houston Oilers	15
3=	Raymond Clayborn	Cleveland Browns	15
3=	Steve DeBerg	Kansas City Chiefs	15
6=	Matt Bahr	New York Giants	14
6=	Blair Bush	Green Bay Packers	14
6=	Matt Cavanaugh	New York Giants	14
6=	Ken Clarke	Minnesota Vikings	14
6=	Mike Kenn	Atlanta Falcons	14
6=	James Lofton	Buffalo Bills	14
6=	Clay Matthews	Cleveland Browns	14
6=	Mickey Shuler	Philadelphia Eagles	14
6=	Doug Smith	Los Angeles Rams	14
6=	Mosi Tatupu	Los Angeles Rams	14

THE 10 PLAYERS WITH THE MOST TOUCHDOWNS IN AN NFL CAREER

	Player	Touchdowns
1	Jim Brown	126
2	Walter Payton	125
3	John Riggins	116
4	Lenny Moore	113
5	Don Hutson	105
6	Steve Largent	101
7	Franco Harris	100
8	Jerry Rice	97
9	Marcus Allen	94
10	Jim Taylor	93

THE TOP 10 POINTS-SCORERS IN AN NFL CAREER

	Player	Points
1	George Blanda	2,002
2	Jan Stenerud	1,699
3	Pat Leahy	1,470
4	Jim Turner	1,439
5	Mark Moseley	1,382
6	Jim Bakken	1,380
7	Fred Cox	1,365
8	Lou Groza	1,349
9	Nick Lowery	1,268
10	Chris Bahr	1,213

If points scored in the shortlived All-American Football Conference (1946–49) are also considered, then Lou Groza would be in 3rd place with a total of 1,608 points. Top-scorer George Blanda's career was spent with the following clubs: Chicago Bears (1949 and 1950 – 58); Baltimore Colts (1950); Houston Oilers (1960 – 66); Oakland Raiders (1967–75).

San Francisco's Joe Montana in action in Super Bowl XXIV. He is the 5th most successful passer in an NFL career.

THE 10 MOST SUCCESSFUL RUSHERS IN AN NFL CAREER

	Player	Yards gained
1	Walter Payton	16,726
2	Tony Dorsett	12,739
3	Eric Dickerson	12,439
4	Jim Brown	12,312
5	Franco Harris	12,120
6	John Riggins	11,352
7	O. J. Simpson	11,236
8	Ottis Anderson	10,242
9	Earl Campbell	9,407
10	Jim Taylor	8,597

If figures from the All-American Football Conference (1946–49) are taken into account, Joe Perry would rank 9th with 9,723 yards.

THE TOP 10 POINTS-SCORERS IN AN NFL SEASON

	Player	Team	Year	Points
1	Paul Hornung	Green Bay	1960	176
2	Mark Moseley	Washington	1983	161
3	Gino Cappelletti	Boston	1964	155
4	Chip Lohmiller	Washington	1991	149
5	Gino Cappelletti	Boston	1961	147
6	Paul Hornung	Green Bay	1961	146
7	Jim Turner	New York Jets	1968	145
8=	John Riggins	Washington	1983	144
8=	Kevin Butler	Chicago	1985	144
10	Tony Franklin	New England	1986	140

THE TOP 10 AVERAGE HOME ATTENDANCES IN THE NFL, 1990–91

	Team	Average attendance
1	Buffalo Bills	77,691
2	New York Giants	76,019
3	New York Jets	75,456
4	Denver Broncos	74,845
5	Cleveland Browns	72,874
6	Kansas City Chiefs	72,369
7	Detroit Lions	67,464
8	New Orleans Saints	66,084
9	Chicago Bears	66,067
10	Philadelphia Eagles	65,678

Figures are based on paying spectators.

THE 10 OLDEST CURRENT NFL STADIUMS

	Stadium	Home team	Year built
1	Memorial Coliseum	Los Angeles Raiders	1923
2	Soldier Field	Chicago Bears	1924
3	Cleveland Stadium	Cleveland Browns	1932
4	Mile High Stadium	Denver Broncos	1948
5	County Stadium, Milwaukee	Green Bay Packers*	1953
6	Lambeau Field, Green Bay	Green Bay Packers*	1957
7	Sun Devil Stadium	Phoenix Cardinals	1958
8	Candlestick Park	San Francisco 49ers	1960
9	Robert F. Kennedy Stadium	Washington Redskins	1961
10	The Astrodome	Houston Oilers	1965

Green Bay Packers are the only NFL team to play at two venues.

The smallest NFL stadium is the Robert F. Kennedy Stadium, home of the Washington Redskins, with a capacity of 55,672. Between 1946 and 1979 the capacity of the Los Angeles Memorial Coliseum was 92,604 – the largest-ever capacity of any stadium in the NFL.

THE 10 LARGEST NFL STADIUMS

	Stadium	Home team	Capacity
1	Memorial Coliseum	Los Angeles Raiders	92,488
2	Pontiac Silverdrome	Detroit Lions	80,494
3	Rich Stadium	Buffalo Bills	80,290
4	Cleveland Stadium	Cleveland Browns	80,098
5	Arrowhead Stadium	Kansas City Chiefs	78,067
6	Giants Stadium	New York Giants/Jets	77,311
7	Mile High Stadium	Denver Broncos	76,274
8	Sun Devil Stadium	Phoenix Cardinals	74,865
9	Tampa Stadium	Tampa Bay Buccaneers	74,315
10	Joe Robbie Stadium	Miami Dolphins	73,000

AMERICAN FOOTBALL IN EUROPE

The newly launched World Football League in 1991, which brought the highest level of gridiron football to Europe, was a great success. But American football in Europe is nothing new. Britons got their first glimpse of this 'strange' new game in 1910 when sailors from the USS *Georgia* and USS *Rhode Island* played a game at the Stonebridge Sports Ground at Northfleet, Kent. The crowd of 4,000 was fascinated by this form of football which *Georgia* won 12–0.

Because many servicemen stayed in Britain after World War II the game continued to be played by the troops, but no Brits were prepared to take up the gridiron game. They were quite happy with the more sedate rugby form of football.

However, after Channel 4 television started covering action from the top American NFL games in the 1980s, the sport's popularity boomed beyond all expectations. Many of the armchair fans felt inspired to try their hand at gridiron football and as a result teams sprang up all over the country. London, initially, was the hotbed of the British game and at Stamford Bridge in 1983, home of Chelsea FC, the newly formed London Ravens played and beat a team from the USAF base at Chicksands. It was the first-ever match between a British and an American team. Later that year the first game between two NFL teams in Europe took place at Wembley Stadium, when St Louis met Minnesota. By then teams had started appearing in the Midlands and northern England as well as north of the border.

Elsewhere in Europe, Italy is probably one of the keenest converts to the game, having had a league since 1983, but Germany, Spain, France and Holland are all devotees of the sport on the Continent, and Finland is home to the Helsinki Rooster team, one of the best in Europe.

The British, German and Spanish fans had the chance to get the feel of top-class gridiron with the arrival of the World League of American Football which kicked off on 23 March 1991 after two years on the drawing-board. The League consisted of 10 teams, largely made up of American players. Seven teams were based in the United States while three, the London Monarchs, Barcelona Dragons, and Frankfurt Galaxy, were Europe's representatives.

The championship play-off was held at Wembley Stadium, home of the Monarchs, who played Barcelona in the final, with the home team winning 21–0 in front of 61,108 fervent fans who proved that American football in Europe was alive, well, and – provided its commercial viability can be established – here to stay.

THE 10 BIGGEST WINNING MARGINS IN CHAMPIONSHIP GAMES

	Winners	Runners-up	AFC/NFC	Year	Score	Margin
1	Chicago Bears	Washington	NFC	1940	73–0	73
2	Buffalo	Los Angeles Raiders	NFC	1991	51–3	48
3	Cleveland	Detroit	NFC	1954	56–10	46
4	Detroit	Cleveland	NFC	1957	59–14	45
5	San Diego	Boston	AFC	1963	51–10	41
6	New York	Chicago Bears	NFC	1956	47–7	40
7	Green Bay	New York	NFC	1961	37–0	37
8	Baltimore	Cleveland	NFC	1968	34–0	34
9	Oakland	Houston	AFC	1967	40–7	33
10	Washington	Detroit	NFC	1992	41–10	31

QUIZ

AMERICAN SPORTS

1 What popular US sport contests The Hambletonian each year?
2 Bull riding, calf roping and team roping are just three of the six disciplines at what national finals held in Las Vegas each year?
3 Which of America's Triple Crown horse races is run at Pimlico each year?
4 Name the Boston Red Sox player who was the American League baseball batting champion from 1985 to 1988.
5 What is the Philadelphia Flyers' sport?
6 Which is the only US city to have two pro baseball teams, a pro ice hockey team, a pro football team and a pro basketball team?
7 Which quarterback helped the 49ers to three Super Bowl triumphs between 1985 and 1990?
8 How many points are awarded for a field goal in American football?
9 Who moved from Edmonton to Los Angeles in 1988 in his sport's record transfer?
10 Eleven-year-old Robert Turner from Muncie, Indiana, was the first winner of what popular annual US championship in 1934?

William Perry of the Chicago Bears, equal 6th heaviest player in the NFL in 1991.

THE 10 HEAVIEST PLAYERS IN THE NFL IN 1991

	Player	Club	Weight kg	Weight lb
1	Zefross Moss	Indianapolis Colts	153	338
2	Jeff Zimmermann	Dallas Cowboys	151	332
3=	James FitzPatrick	Los Angeles Raiders	150	330
3=	Ben Jefferson	Cleveland Browns	150	330
3=	Pat Tomberlin	Indianapolis Colts	150	330
6=	Howard Ballard	Buffalo Bills	147	325
6=	William Perry	Chicago Bears	147	325
8=	Nate Newton	Dallas Cowboys	146	322
8=	Tootie Robbins	Phoenix Cardinals	146	322
10=	Lorenzo Freeman	Pittsburgh Steelers	145	319
10=	Derek Kennard	Phoenix Cardinals	145	319

THE 10 BEST-PAID NFL PLAYERS IN 1991*

	Player/club	Years in contract	Salary and bonus ($)
1	Dan Marino (Miami)	5	25,000,000
2	Jim Kelly (Buffalo)	7	20,000,000
3	Randall Cunningham (Philadelphia)	6	15,400,000
4	Jeff George (Indianapolis)	6	15,000,000
5	Bernie Kosar (Cleveland)	6	14,000,000
6	Joe Montana (San Francisco)	4	13,000,000
7	Howie Long (LA Raiders)	7	9,700,000
8	Chris Doleman (Minnesota)	5	8,750,000
9	Barry Sanders (Detroit)	6	8,600,000
10=	Keith Millard (Minnesota)	4	8,000,000
10=	Warren Moon (Houston)	4	8,000,000

Based on current contracts.

THE TOP 10 SALARIES IN 1990 BY POSITION

	Position	Average salary ($)
1	Quarterback	1,250,000
2	Running back	666,000
3=	Linebacker	494,000
3=	Wide receiver	494,000
5	Defensive line	444,000
6	Defensive back	395,000
7	Offensive line	387,000
8	Tight end	345,000
9	Kicker	252,000
10	Punter	233,000

ANGLING

THE 10 LARGEST SPECIES OF FRESHWATER FISH CAUGHT IN GREAT BRITAIN

	Species	Angler/location/date	Weight kg	Weight g	Weight lb	Weight oz
1	Salmon	Miss G.W. Ballantine, River Tay, Scotland, 1922	29	029	64	0
2	Carp	Chris Yates, Redmire Pool, Herefordshire, 1980	23	410	51	8
3	Pike	Tommy Morgan, Loch Lomond, Scotland, 1945	21	680	47	11
4	Catfish	R. J. Bray, Wilstone Reservoir, Tring, Hertfordshire, 1970	19	730	43	8
5	Rainbow trout	Geoff Barnes, Avington Fishery, Hampshire, 1991	11	163	24	10
6	Grass carp	Gary Wallis, Honeycroft Fisheries, nr Canterbury, Kent, 1991	10	910	24	0
7	Brown trout	Richard Faulds, Dever Springs, Hampshire, 1991	10	255	22	9
8	Sea trout	Samuel Burgoyne, River Leven, Scotland, 1989	10	205	22	8
9	Zander	R.N. Meadows, Roswell Pits, Cambridgeshire, 1988	8	409	18	8
10	Common bream	Mark McKeown, Englefield Lagoon, nr Reading, 1991	7	528	16	9

THE 10 LARGEST SPECIES OF FRESHWATER FISH CAUGHT IN THE WORLD

	Species	Angler/location/date	Weight kg	Weight g	Weight lb	Weight oz
1	White sturgeon	Joey Pallotta III, Benicia, California, USA, 1983	212	472	468	0
2	Alligator gar	Bill Valverde, Rio Grande, Texas, USA, 1951	126	666	279	0
3	Nile perch	Kurt M. Fenster, Tende Bay, Entebbe, Uganda, 1989	69	036	152	1
4	Chinook salmon	Les Anderson, Kenai River, Arkansas, USA, 1985	44	152	97	4
5=	Blue catfish	Edward B. Elliott, Missouri River, South Dakota, USA, 1959	44	038	97	0
5=	Tigerfish	Raymond Houtmans, Zaïre River, Kinshasa, Zaïre, 1988	44	038	97	0
7	Lake sturgeon	James M. DeOtis, Kettle River, Montana, USA, 1986	41	882	92	4
8	Flathead catfish	Mike Rogers, Lake Lewisville, Texas, USA, 1982	41	428	91	4
9	Atlantic salmon	Henrik Henrikson, Tana River, Norway, 1928	35	923	79	2
10	Carp	Leo van der Gugten, Lac de St Cassien, France, 1987	34	362	75	11

THE 10 LARGEST SPECIES OF SALTWATER FISH CAUGHT IN GREAT BRITAIN

	Species	Angler/location/date	Weight			
			kg	g	lb	oz
1	Tunny	L. Mitchell Henry, Whitby, Yorks, 1933	385	989	851	0
2	Mako shark	Mrs J. M. Yallop, off Eddystone Light, Cornwall, 1971	226	786	500	0
3	Porbeagle shark	J. Potier, off Padstow, Cornwall, 1976	210	910	465	0
4	Thresher shark	S. Mills, off Portsmouth, Hants, 1982	146	504	323	0
5	Halibut	C. Booth, Dunnet Head, off Scrabster, Highland, 1979	106	136	234	0
6	Common skate	R. Banks, off Tobermory, Mull, 1986	102	961	227	0
7	Blue shark	N. Sutcliffe, Looe, Cornwall, 1959	98	878	218	0
8	Opah	A. R. Blewett, Mounts Bay, Penzance, Cornwall, 1973	58	057	128	0
9	Conger	Nial Ball, South Devon, off Dartmouth, 1992	51	075	112	8
10	Sunfish	T. F. Sisson, off Saundersfoot, Dyfed, 1976	48	986	108	0

THE 10 LARGEST SPECIES OF SALTWATER FISH CAUGHT IN THE WORLD

	Species	Angler/location/date	Weight			
			kg	g	lb	oz
1	Great white shark	Alfred Dean, Ceduna, South Australia, 1959	1,208	390	2,664	0
2	Tiger shark	Walter Maxwell, Cherry Grove, Southern California, USA, 1964	807	410	1,780	0
3	Greenland shark	Terje Nordtvedt, Trondheimsfjord, Norway, 1987	775	000	1,708	9
4	Black marlin	A. C. Glassell jr, Cabo Blanco, Peru, 1953	707	620	1,560	0
5	Bluefin tuna	Ken Fraser, Aulds Cove, Nova Scotia, Canada, 1979	678	590	1,496	0
6	Pacific blue marlin	Jay W. de Beaubien, Kaaiwi Point, Kona, Honolulu, 1982	624	150	1,376	0
7	Atlantic blue marlin	Larry Martin, St Thomas, Virgin Islands, 1977	581	520	1,282	0
8	Swordfish	L. Marron, Iquique, Chile, 1953	536	160	1,182	0
9	Mako shark	Patrick Guillanton, Black River, Mauritius, 1988	505	760	1,115	0
10	Hammerhead shark	Allen Ogle, Sarasota, Florida, USA, 1982	449	520	991	0

Miss Georgina Ballantine with her record catch.

THE TOP 10 COUNTRIES AT THE WORLD FRESHWATER CHAMPIONSHIPS

	Country	Individual	Team	Total
1	France	9	12	21
2	England	9	4	13
3	Belgium	5	6	11
4	Italy	4	5	9
5	West Germany	4	1	5
6	Holland	2	2	4
7=	Wales	1	1	2
7=	Luxembourg	0	2	2
9=	Ireland	1	0	1
9=	East Germany	0	1	1
9=	Romania	0	1	1

ARCHERY

THE 10 MOST SUCCESSFUL OLYMPIC COUNTRIES

	Country	Medals gold	silver	bronze	Total
1	USA	12	8	7	27
2	France	7	9	6	22
3	Belgium	10	7	2	19
4	South Korea	6	4	2	12
5	USSR/CIS	1	3	5	9
6	Great Britain	2	2	4	8
7	Finland	1	1	2	4
8=	Japan	0	1	1	2
8=	Italy	0	0	2	2
8=	China	0	2	0	2

Archery was first seen at the Olympics at the Paris Games in 1900 when it included a live pigeon shooting contest. However, many sources do not regard this as an official event and it is not included in most historians' records – and in view of the rather unsporting nature of this part of the competition we will not beg to differ. After appearing at three successive Games, archery was dropped in 1912, then was reinstated at Antwerp in 1920 but disappeared again until its re-emergence in 1972. It has maintained its place in the Olympic programme ever since.

ASSOCIATION FOOTBALL

THE 10 WEALTHIEST CLUBS IN EUROPE, 1989–90

	Club/country	Income (£)
1	AC Milan (Italy)	29,800,000
2	Barcelona (Spain)	21,000,000
3	Napoli (Italy)	20,800,000
4	Inter Milan (Italy)	19,000,000
5	Juventus (Italy)	17,000,000
6	Real Madrid (Spain)	16,000,000
7	AS Roma (Italy)	14,000,000
8	Bordeaux (France)	12,000,000
9	Fiorentina (Italy)	11,900,000
10	Marseille (France)	11,800,000

George Best cuts through the Benfica defence as Manchester United beat the Portuguese side 4–1 in the 1968 European Cup final to become England's first winners of the competition.

THE TOP 10 TEAMS IN THE THREE MAJOR EUROPEAN CLUB COMPETITIONS

	Club/country	EC	ECWC	UEFA*	Total
1	Real Madrid (Spain)	6	0	2	8
2	Barcelona (Spain)	1	3	3	7
3=	AC Milan (Italy)	4	2	0	6
3=	Liverpool (England)	4	0	2	6
5	Ajax Amsterdam (Holland)	3	1	1	5
6=	Bayern Munich (Germany)	3	1	0	4
6=	Juventus (Italy)	1	1	2	4
8=	Anderlecht (Belgium)	0	2	1	3
8=	Inter Milan (Italy)	2	0	1	3
8=	Tottenham Hotspur (England)	0	1	2	3
8=	Valencia (Spain)	0	1	2	3

*EC = European Champions' Cup; ECWC = European Cup-winners' Cup; UEFA = UEFA/Fairs Cup.

Five of Real Madrid's six European Champions' Cup successes were in the first five years (1956–60) of the tournament. They were Europe's most dominant team of that era and their reign eventually came to an end in the 1960–61 competition when they were eliminated by local rivals Barcelona.

THE 10 COUNTRIES WITH THE MOST WINNERS OF THE THREE MAJOR EUROPEAN CLUB COMPETITIONS

	Country	EC	ECWC	UEFA*	Total
1	England	8	6	9	23
2	Spain	7	5	8	20
3	Italy	7	5	5	17
4	Germany/West Germany	4	4	4	12
5	Holland	5	1	3	9
6=	Belgium	0	3	1	4
6=	Portugal	3	1	0	4
8=	Scotland	1	2	0	3
8=	USSR	0	3	0	3
10=	Sweden	0	0	2	2
10=	Yugoslavia	1	0	1	2

*EC = European Champions' Cup; ECWC = European Cup-winners' Cup; UEFA = UEFA/Fairs Cup.

While Liverpool have been England's most successful club side in Europe, the honour of being the first English team to win a major European title went to Tottenham Hotspur who beat Atletico Madrid 5–1 in the Cup-winners' Cup in Rotterdam in 1963. Two of Spurs' goals were scored by Jimmy Greaves. The first English side to appear in a European final was the representative London team that reached the final of the Inter Cities Fairs Cup in 1958. They were beaten 8–2 over two legs by a team representing the city of Barcelona. Jimmy Greaves also scored in that final.

THE 10 BIGGEST WINS BY BRITISH CLUBS IN EUROPE

	Match	Competition*	Date	Score
1	Chelsea v Jeunesse Hautcharage	ECWC	29 Sep 1971	13–0
2=	Derby County v Finn Harps	UEFA	15 Sep 1976	12–0
2=	Swansea City v Sliema Wanderers	ECWC	15 Sep 1982	12–0
4	Liverpool v Stromgodset	ECWC	17 Sep 1974	11–0
5=	Manchester United v Anderlecht	EC	26 Sep 1956	10–0
5=	Ipswich Town v Floriana	EC	25 Sep 1962	10–0
5=	Dunfermline Athletic v Apoel Nicosia	ECWC	18 Sep 1968	10–0
5=	Liverpool v Dundalk	FC	16 Sep 1969	10–0
5=	Leeds United v Lyn Oslo	EC	17 Sep 1969	10–0
5=	Rangers v Valetta	ECWC	28 Sep 1983	10–0

*EC = European Champions' Cup; ECWC = European Cup-winners' Cup; UEFA = UEFA Cup; FC = Fairs Cup.

Liverpool scored double figures for record third time on 1 October 198 when they beat OPS Oula 10–1 in the Champions' Cup. In the first leg of the Cup-winners' Cup tie with Jeunesse Hautcharage, Chelsea won 8–0. Consequently they won 21–0 on aggregate to establish a European reco which was equalled by Feyenoord in t UEFA Cup 12 months later. Peter Osgood, who scored a hat-trick in the first leg, added five in the second for a match aggregate of eight.

THE TOP 10 ATTENDANCES IN THE EUROPEAN CHAMPIONSHIP

	Match	Venue	Date	Attendance
1	Scotland v England	Glasgow	24 Feb 1968	134,461
2	USSR v Italy	Moscow	13 Oct 1963	102,358
3	USSR v Hungary	Moscow	28 Sep 1958	100,572
4	USSR v Sweden	Moscow	27 May 1964	99,609
5	England v Scotland	London	15 Apr 1967	98,283
6	England v West Germany	London	29 Apr 1972	96,766
7	East Germany v Yugoslavia	Leipzig	9 May 1971	94,876
8	England v Spain	London	3 May 1968	94,586
9	Scotland v Spain	Glasgow	20 Nov 1974	94,331
10	England v Northern Ireland	London	7 Feb 1979	91,224

All were in the qualifying stages of the championship. The biggest attendance in the final rounds was for the 1964 final between Spain and the USSR in Madrid when 79,115 watched the game. The lowest paying attendance for any match is 651 for the Greece v Hungary qualifying match at Salonika on 3 December 1983. The Holland v Cyprus match at Amsterdam on 9 December 1987 was played behind closed doors following an edict by UEFA, and the attendance is therefore officially given as 'none'.

THE 10 EUROPEAN CLUBS WITH THE MOST DOMESTIC LEAGUE TITLES*

	Club/country	Titles
1	Glasgow Rangers (Scotland)	42
2	Linfield (Northern Ireland)	40
3=	Benfica (Portugal)	29
3=	Rapid Vienna (Austria)	29
5	CSKA Sofia (Bulgaria)	27
6=	Olympiakos (Greece)	25
6=	Real Madrid (Spain)	25
8=	Floriana (Malta)	24
8=	Shamrock Rovers (Republic of Ireland)	24
8=	Ferencvaros (Hungary)	24

*To end 1991–92 season.

The top English club is Liverpool with 18 League titles.

THE 10 PLAYERS WITH THE MOST FOOTBALL LEAGUE APPEARANCES*

	Player	Years	Appearances
1	Peter Shilton	1966–92	968
2	Terry Paine	1957–77	824
3	Tommy Hutchison	1968–91	795
4	Alan Oakes	1959–84	777
5	John Trollope	1960–80	770
6	Jimmy Dickinson	1946–65	764
7	Roy Sproson	1950–72	762
8=	Billy Bonds	1965–88	758
8=	Ray Clemence	1966–87	758
10=	Pat Jennings	1963–84	757
10=	Frank Worthington	1967–88	757

*To end 1991–92 season.

Trollope's total of 770 is a record for one club. He spent his entire career with Swindon Town. Shilton's career has been spent with Leicester City (286 appearances), Stoke City (110), Nottingham Forest (202), Southampton (188), Derby County (175) and Plymouth Argyle (7).

Billy Wright leads out the England team on the occasion of his 100th cap in 1959. Their opponents were Scotland, whom they beat 1–0.

THE 10 MOST-CAPPED ENGLAND GOALKEEPERS*

	Player	Caps
1	Peter Shilton	125
2	Gordon Banks	73
3	Ray Clemence	61
4	Chris Woods	34
5	Peter Springett	33
6	Harry Hibbs	25
7	Bert Williams	24
8	Gil Merrick	23
9	Sam Hardy	21
10=	Frank Swift	19
10=	Vic Woodley	19

*At 26 June 1992.

Shilton played his first game for England in the 3–1 win against East Germany at Wembley on 25 November 1970. His 125th and last game was in the 2–1 defeat by Italy in the play-off for 3rd place in the 1990 World Cup finals. During his international career he conceded only 80 goals, and managed to keep a clean sheet in 65 of his 125 games. Only one man, Marco van Basten of Holland, scored a hat-trick past him. Had Shilton been selected for every England game played between his first and last appearances he would have won 216 caps; as it was, he missed 91 games in that period.

THE 10 MOST-CAPPED ENGLAND PLAYERS*

	Player	Years	Caps
1	Peter Shilton	1971–90	125
2	Bobby Moore	1962–74	108
3	Bobby Charlton	1958–70	106
4	Billy Wright	1947–59	105
5	Bryan Robson	1980–91	90
6	Kenny Sansom	1979–88	86
7	Ray Wilkins	1976–87	84
8	Gary Lineker	1984–92	80
9	Terry Butcher	1980–90	77
10	Tom Finney	1947–59	76

*At 26 June 1992.

The most-capped players for the other British Isles countries are: Northern Ireland – Pat Jennings 119; Scotland – Kenny Dalglish 102; Republic of Ireland – Liam Brady 72; Wales – Joey Jones and Peter Nicholas 72.

THE 10 MOST-CAPPED FOOTBALLERS IN THE WORLD

	Player/country	Caps
1	Peter Shilton (England)	125
2	Pat Jennings (Northern Ireland)	119
3	Heinz Hermann* (Switzerland)	117
4	Björn Nordqvist (Sweden)	115
5	Dino Zoff (Italy)	112
6	Oleg Blochin (USSR)	109
7=	Ladislav Bölöni (Romania)	108
7=	Bobby Moore (England)	108
9	Bobby Charlton (England)	106
10	Billy Wright (England)	105

Still playing international football 1991–92.

Swiss international Heinz Hermann, 3rd most-capped footballer in the world.

THE TOP 10 TRANSFER FEES IN THE WORLD*

	Player	From	To	Year	Fee (£)
1	Gianluigi Lentini	Torino	AC Milan	1992	13,000,000
2	Gianluca Vialli	Sampdoria	Juventus	1992	12,000,000
3	Jean-Pierre Papin	Marseille	AC Milan	1992	10,000,000
4	Igor Shalimov	Foggia	Internazionale	1992	8,000,000
5	Roberto Baggio	Fiorentina	Juventus	1990	7,700,000
6	David Platt	Bari	Juventus	1992	7,000,000
7	Diego Maradona	Barcelona	Napoli	1984	6,900,000
8=	Ruud Gullit	PSV Eindhoven	AC Milan	1987	5,500,000
8=	Thomas Hässler	FC Cologne	Juventus	1990	5,500,000
8=	Karl-Heinz Reidle	Werder Bremen	Lazio	1990	5,500,000
8=	David Platt	Aston Villa	Bari	1991	5,500,000
8=	Paul Gascoigne	Tottenham Hotspur	Lazio	1992	5,500,000

At 31 July 1992.

The world's first £1,000,000 footballer was Guiseppe Savoldi who moved from Bologna to Napoli in 1975.

THE TOP 10 TRANSFER FEES BETWEEN TWO FOOTBALL LEAGUE CLUBS*

	Player	From	To	Year	Fee (£)
1	Alan Shearer	Southampton	Blackburn Rovers	1992	3,600,000
2	Dean Saunders	Derby County	Liverpool	1991	2,900,000
3=	Keith Curle	Wimbledon	Manchester City	1991	2,500,000
3=	Ian Wright	Crystal Palace	Arsenal	1991	2,500,000
5=	Gary Pallister	Middlesbrough	Manchester United	1989	2,300,000
5=	Paul Stewart	Tottenham Hotspur	Liverpool	1992	2,300,000
7=	Gordon Durie	Chelsea	Tottenham Hotspur	1991	2,200,000
7=	Mark Wright	Derby County	Liverpool	1991	2,200,000
9=	Tony Cottee	West Ham United	Everton	1988	2,000,000
9=	Paul Gascoigne	Newcastle United	Tottenham Hotspur	1989	2,000,000
9=	Teddy Sheringham	Millwall	Nottingham Forest	1991	2,000,000
9=	David Rocastle	Arsenal	Leeds United	1992	2,000,000
9=	Darren Anderton	Portsmouth	Tottenham Hotspur	1992	2,000,000

*At 31 July 1992.

Paul Ince, who joined Manchester United from West Ham in 1989, was valued at £2,000,000. However, because of a doubt over his fitness, United paid £800,000 plus £5,000 a match.

Since arriving at Old Trafford in November 1986, manager Alex Ferguson has spent more than £15,000,000 on players to the end of the 1991–92 season.

MANCHESTER UNITED'S TOP 10 SIGNINGS

	Player	Transferred from	Year	Fee (£)
1	Gary Pallister	Middlesbrough	1989	2,300,000
2	Paul Parker	Queen's Park Rangers	1991	1,700,000
3=	Bryan Robson	West Bromwich Albion	1981	1,500,000
3=	Mark Hughes	Barcelona	1988	1,500,000
3=	Neil Webb	Nottingham Forest	1989	1,500,000
6	Garry Birtles	Nottingham Forest	1980	1,250,000
7	Danny Wallace	Southampton	1989	1,200,000
8	Andrei Kanchelskis	Shakhtyor Donetsk	1991	1,000,000
9=	Brian McClair	Celtic	1987	850,000
9=	Jim Leighton	Aberdeen	1988	850,000

THE FIRST 10 £1 MILLION FOOTBALLERS IN BRITAIN

	Player	From	To	Fee (£)	Date
1	Trevor Francis	Birmingham City	Nottingham Forest	1,150,000	Feb 1979
2	Steve Daley	Wolverhampton Wanderers	Manchester City	1,450,000	Sep 1979
3	Andy Gray	Aston Villa	Wolverhampton Wanderers	1,470,000	Sep 1979
4	Kevin Reeves	Norwich City	Manchester City	1,000,000	Mar 1980
5	Clive Allen	Queen's Park Rangers	Arsenal	1,200,000	Jun 1980
6	Ian Wallace	Coventry City	Nottingham Forest	1,250,000	Jul 1980
7=	Clive Allen	Arsenal	Crystal Palace	1,250,000	Aug 1980
7=	Kenny Sansom	Crystal Palace	Arsenal	1,350,000	Aug 1980
9	Garry Birtles	Nottingham Forest	Manchester United	1,250,000	Oct 1980
10	Justin Fashanu	Norwich City	Nottingham Forest	1,000,000	Aug 1981

The first British player to be involved in a £2,000,000 transfer was Mark Hughes when he went from Manchester United to Barcelona in May 1986. But the first £2,000,000 transfer between British clubs was in July 1988 when Paul Gascoigne joined Spurs from Newcastle. Rangers were the first Scottish club to pay over £1,000,000 for a player when they paid Spurs £1,500,000 for Richard Gough in October 1987.

Left Dean Saunders, who moved from Derby County to Liverpool in 1991 for the then record sum of £2,900,000.

THE SPIRALLING TRANSFER MARKET

Such was the craziness of the football transfer market in the 1970s that managers were paying hundreds of thousands of pounds for little-known players. It gave rise to the joke that Malcolm Allison, then manager of Manchester City, walked into a tailor's shop to enquire about the price of a suit in the window. When told it was £150 he immediately offered the salesman £250! Stories of the crazy money that changed hands for uncapped and untested players were certainly not apocryphal. That same situation returned in 1991 and, despite the country's economic gloom, somehow football clubs can still manage to find millions of pounds for footballers.

What a far cry it all is from that day in February 1905 when Middlesbrough paid £1,000, the first four-figure fee, for Sunderland's Alf Common. But even then the League was alarmed at such a spiralling increase in transfer fees. Common's fee had doubled in the three years since Sunderland bought him from Sheffield United and it was only 10 years before that Aston Villa had paid the then staggering sum of £100 for West Brom's Willie Groves.

The League clamped down after Common's £1,000 move and imposed a limit of £350 on all transfers, but the clubs responded by selling two players for £700, one being 'dead-weight'. Consequently the League had to lift the restriction.

Seven years after Common's move to Middlesbrough, Blackburn became the first club to fork out £2,000 when they bought Danny O'Shea from West Ham. The British record was upped to £5,000 in 1922 when Falkirk bought Syd Puddefoot from West Ham and six years later the magical figure of £10,000 was breached when Arsenal paid £10,890 for Bolton's David Jack, the scorer of the first goal at Wembley in 1923.

Tommy Lawton became the first £20,000 footballer in 1947 when he moved from Chelsea to Notts County, then in the Third Division (South). Bob Brennan holds a unique place in those days of transfer deals by becoming the first man to move for £20,000 on two occasions, when he went from Luton to Birmingham in 1949 and to Fulham a year later.

Denis Law became Britain's first £50,000 footballer when he moved from Huddersfield to Manchester City in 1960, and when he was sold to Torino of Italy in 1961 he became the first Briton to be involved in a six-figure move.

The first £100,000 between British clubs was not far away, but when Spurs' manager Bill Nicholson signed Jimmy Greaves from AC Milan in November 1961 he did not want the striker to be stuck with the tag of being Britain's first £100,000 player so he paid £99,999 for him! The honour of becoming Britain's first six-figure player fell to Alan Ball when he moved from Blackpool to Everton in 1966, shortly after he had made his mark in the World Cup final.

From that time the transfer market seemed to rise at an alarming rate. Martin Peters became the first £200,000 player when he went from West Ham to Spurs in 1970; Ball increased the record to £220,000 when he moved to

Arsenal in 1971; and in less than eight years David Mills had become the first player to cost half a million pounds when he joined West Brom from Middlesbrough in January 1979. Just a month later Trevor Francis became Britain's first £1 million player when he joined Nottingham Forest from Birmingham. Before the year was out the record had been broken twice again when Manchester City paid Wolves £1,450,277 for Steve Daley and Wolves in return increased the record a few days later when they bought Andy Gray from Aston Villa for £1,469,000.

Bryan Robson joined Manchester United from West Brom for £1,500,000 in 1981 and the transfer market seemed to stabilize and return to some form of normality after that. But it started all over again in 1987 when Liverpool bought Peter Beardsley from Newcastle for a record £1,900,000. The Geordies then sold Paul Gascoigne for £2 million; it is hardly surprising that Newcastle ended up in the Second Division, albeit with cash in the bank!

In 1988 Ian Rush became the most expensive player ever to be bought by an English club when Liverpool brought him back from Juventus for £2,800,000, a year after selling him for £3,200,000. And in 1991 the transfer market went crazy again when Liverpool bought Derby County and Wales striker Dean Saunders for £2,900,000. It was part of a £5,100,000 package that also brought England defender Mark Wright from the Midlands club.

The close-season spending spree in 1991 saw First Division clubs splash out more than £30,000,000 on the transfer market. Manchester City bought Wimbledon's uncapped defender Keith Curle for £2,500,000. Nottingham Forest joined the £2 million club when they bought Teddy Sheringham from Millwall, and Spurs did little to ease their own financial problems when paying Chelsea £2,200,000 for Gordon Durie.

In the 1992 close season the British record was broken by Southampton and England striker Alan Shearer, who was bought by newly promoted Blackburn Rovers for £3,600,000. Paul Stewart went from Spurs to Liverpool for £2,300,000, and two players moved with a £2 million price tag: David Rocastle (from Arsenal to Leeds) and Darren Anderton (from Portsmouth to Spurs).

However, these figures pale into insignificance compared with the sums Continental clubs are able to spend on the best players. The world's first £100,000 transfer was in 1957, five years before Britain's first six-figure deal, when Omar Sivori joined Juventus from River Plate, and it was another Italian club, Napoli, that paid the first seven-figure fee when they bought Guiseppe Savoldi from Bologna in 1975, this time four years before Britain's first £1 million player. Roberto Baggio's world record of £7,700,000 established in 1990 was shattered in 1992 by Gianluigi Lentini, who moved from Torino to AC Milan for the incredible sum of £13,000,000. All 10 most expensive players in the world (including David Platt and Paul Gascoigne) have been bought by Italian clubs.

THE 10 BRITISH CLUBS TO HAVE SIGNED THE MOST £1 MILLION PLAYERS*

	Club	Signings
1	Rangers	11
2	Liverpool	8
3=	Manchester United	7
3=	Manchester City	7
3=	Arsenal	7
6=	Nottingham Forest	6
6=	Everton	6
8=	Leeds United	5
8=	Aston Villa	5
8=	Tottenham Hotspur	5

*At 31 July 1992.

Rangers' 11 £1,000,000 signings have been: Richard Gough (from Spurs); Gary Stevens (Everton); Trevor Steven (Everton); Mo Johnston (Nantes); Oleg Kuznetsov (Dynamo Kiev); Andy Goram (Hibernian); Alex Mikhailichenko (Sampdoria); Stuart McCall (Everton); Dale Gordon (Norwich); Dave McPherson (Hearts) and Trevor Steven (Marseille).

At the end of the 1991–92 season, the only English First Division clubs *not* to have bought a £1,000,000 player were: Coventry City, Luton Town, Norwich City, Notts County, Oldham Athletic, Sheffield United and Wimbledon.

THE 10 BIGGEST SPENDERS IN THE FOOTBALL LEAGUE DURING THE 1991 CLOSE SEASON

	Club	Expenditure (£)
1	Liverpool	6,350,000
2	Leeds United	4,150,000
3	Aston Villa	3,840,000
4	Nottingham Forest	3,400,000
5	Manchester United	3,200,000
6	Manchester City	2,500,000
7	Chelsea	2,400,000
8	Everton	2,380,000
9	Tottenham Hotspur	2,000,000
10	Sheffield Wednesday	1,950,000

The 1991 close season saw a return to those 'lazy, hazy, crazy days of summer' transfers, when seemingly inflated prices were paid for players, many of whom had little or no proven track record at the highest level. Arsenal, the reigning champions, ignored all this activity and did not fork out any money on new signings, but they were the exception rather than the rule.

THE TOP 10 GOALSCORERS IN A FOOTBALL LEAGUE SEASON

	Player/club	Division	Season	Goals
1	Dixie Dean (Everton)	1	1927–28	60
2	George Camsell (Middlesbrough)	2	1926–27	59
3=	Ted Harston (Mansfield Town)	3N	1936–37	55
3=	Joe Payne (Luton Town)	3S	1936–37	55
5	Terry Bly (Peterborough United)	4	1960–61	52
6=	'Pongo' Waring (Aston Villa)	1	1930–31	49
6=	Clarrie Bourton (Coventry City)	3S	1931–32	49
8	Harry Morris (Swindon Town)	3S	1926–27	47
9=	Peter Simpson (Crystal Palace)	3S	1930–31	46
9=	Alf Lythgoe (Stockport County)	3N	1933–34	46
9=	Derek Dooley (Sheffield Wednesday)	2	1951–52	46

In the same season that Dean established the English record, Jimmy Smith of Ayr United established the Scottish League record of 66 goals in a season which, like Dean's, still stands. The post-war First Division record is 41 by Jimmy Greaves (Chelsea) in 1960–61.

THE PROGRESSION OF THE FIRST DIVISION GOALSCORING RECORD

Player	Club	Season	Goals
John Goodall	Preston North End	1888–89	21
Jimmy Ross	Preston North End	1889–90	24
Jack Southworth	Blackburn Rovers	1890–91	26
John Campbell	Sunderland	1891–92	32
Bert Freeman	Everton	1908–09	36
Fred Morris	West Bromwich Albion	1919–20	37
Joe Smith	Bolton Wanderers	1920–21	38
Ted Harper	Blackburn Rovers	1925–26	43
Dixie Dean	Everton	1927–28	60

The best First Division total since Dean's 60 goals is 49 by 'Pongo' Waring of Aston Villa in 1930–31.

DIXIE DEAN'S 60 GOALS

In the 1926–27 season Middlesbrough's George Camsell set a League record by scoring 59 goals in a season. Twelve months later he was deprived of the record when William Ralph Dean, known affectionately as 'Dixie' (although he personally disliked the nickname), scored 60 goals in Everton's title-winning campaign, but how close he came to *not* breaking the record.

Dean played in 39 of Everton's 42 matches and scored seven hat-tricks, including hauls of five goals against Manchester United and four against Burnley in the penultimate match of the season. Going into that game, Dean's tally of goals stood at 53 and he needed seven in the last two games to break the record. As a result of netting four against Burnley it meant he still had to score a hat-trick in the last game, at home to Arsenal.

With the title already assured, the Everton players created as many scoring opportunities for 'Dixie' as they could and in the third minute he opened his account when he scored Everton's 100th goal of the season. Three minutes later he converted a penalty to draw level with Camsell's record but, despite Everton players giving the ball to Dean at every opportunity, that record-breaking goal seemed to be eluding him. But, with eight minutes to go he rose high above the Arsenal defence to head home his record-breaking goal from a corner kick.

The match ended 3–3 but the 60,000 Everton fans were not interested in the outcome of the game – only in seeing 'Dixie' break the League record.

Everton's Dixie Dean, who holds the long-standing record for most goals scored in a League season: 60 in 1927–28.

THE TOP 10 GOALSCORERS IN A FOOTBALL LEAGUE CAREER

	Player	Seasons	Goals
1	Arthur Rowley	1946–65	434
2	Dixie Dean	1923–37	379
3	Jimmy Greaves	1957–71	357
4	Steve Bloomer	1892–1914	352
5	George Camsell	1923–39	346
6	Vic Watson	1920–36	317
7	John Atyeo	1951–66	315
8	Joe Smith	1908–29	314
9=	Henry Bedford	1919–34	309
9=	Harry Johnson	1919–36	309

Dean scored 349 goals for Everton, a record for a single club. All Atyeo's 315 goals were for Bristol City, his *only* League club.

THE TOP 10 CURRENT* GOALSCORERS

	Player	Club	Goals†
1	Tommy Tynan	Doncaster Rovers	254
2	John Aldridge	Tranmere Rovers	213
3	Luther Blissett	Watford	205
4	Mick Quinn	Newcastle United	203
5	Kerry Dixon	Chelsea	198
6	Ian Rush	Liverpool	197
7	Gary Lineker	Tottenham Hotspur	192
8	Gordon Davies	Wrexham	177
9	Trevor Francis	Sheffield Wednesday	175
10=	Lee Chapman	Leeds United	168
10=	Simon Garner	Blackburn Rovers	168

Those who appeared in the League in 1991–92.
†Football League only.

THE TOP 10 GOALSCORERS IN THE FOOTBALL LEAGUE, 1991–92

	Player	Club/Division	Goals
1	Ian Wright	Arsenal (1)	29*
2	Gary Lineker	Tottenham Hotspur (1)	28
3=	Dave Bamber	Blackpool (4)	26
3=	Phil Stant	Mansfield Town (4)	26
5=	Mike Conroy	Burnley (4)	24
5=	Dean Holdsworth	Brentford (3)	24
5=	Iwan Roberts	Huddersfield Town (3)	24
8=	Duncan Shearer	Blackburn Rovers (2)	23†
8=	David Speedie	Blackburn Rovers (2)	23
10=	John Aldridge	Tranmere Rovers (2)	22
10=	Wayne Biggins	Stoke City (3)	22
10=	Dave Crown	Gillingham (4)	22
10=	Carl Dale	Cardiff City (4)	22

Including 5 for former club Crystal Palace.
†Including 22 for former club Swindon Town.

The top scorer in all matches (League and Cup games) was Aldridge with 40 goals.

QUIZ

SPORTING VENUES

1 In which country is the famous Bislett Stadium?
2 The site of which American sporting venue was once owned by circus proprietor P.T. Barnum?
3 Which ground staged the last FA Cup final before Wembley became its new home in 1923?
4 In which famous baseball stadium did the Beatles perform a live concert in the 1960s?
5 The site of which current British airport was once used as the venue for one of Britain's great sporting events?
6 Which motor racing Grand Prix was last staged around the Dijon circuit in France in 1982?
7 Before appearing at which British sporting venue is it advisable to 'talk to the fairies' first for good luck?
8 Where can Luckington Lane be found?
9 The Road Hole at St Andrews' Old Course is one of the most famous, or infamous, in golf. What numbered hole is it?
10 Which snooker tournament is played in the sales ring of Goff's, County Kildare, each year?

THE TOP 10 ENGLAND GOALSCORERS AT WEMBLEY*

	Player	Goals
1	Bobby Charlton	24
2	Gary Lineker	22
3	Jimmy Greaves	17
4	Geoff Hurst	16
5=	Mick Channon	10
5=	Kevin Keegan	10
7=	Martin Peters	9
7=	Tommy Taylor	9
9=	Johnny Haynes	8
9=	Nat Lofthouse	8
9=	Bryan Robson	8

Full internationals; at May 1992.

England's first international at Wembley was the 1–1 draw with Scotland on 12 April 1924. The scorer of England's first goal on the hallowed turf was Billy Walker, who later found fame as the manager of FA Cup winning teams Sheffield Wednesday (1935) and Nottingham Forest (1959).

THE TOP 10 ENGLAND GOAL-SCORERS IN FULL INTERNATIONALS*

	Player	Goals
1	Bobby Charlton	49
2	Gary Lineker	48
3	Jimmy Greaves	44
4=	Tom Finney	30
4=	Nat Lofthouse	30
6	Vivian Woodward	29
7	Steve Bloomer	28
8	Bryan Robson	26
9	Geoff Hurst	24
10=	Stanley Mortensen	23
10=	Own goals	23

At 26 June 1992.

THE FIRST 10 ENGLAND PLAYERS TO SCORE HAT-TRICKS IN FULL INTERNATIONALS

	Player*	Opponents	Date
1	Oliver Vaughton (5)	Ireland	18 Feb 1882
2	Arthur Brown (4)	Ireland	18 Feb 1882
3	Clem Mitchell	Wales	3 Feb 1883
4	Henry Cursham	Ireland	25 Feb 1884
5	Ben Spilsbury (4)	Ireland	13 Mar 1886
6	Tinsley Lindley	Ireland	5 Feb 1887
7	Albert Allen	Ireland	31 Mar 1888†
8	John Yates	Ireland	2 Mar 1889†
9	Fred Geary	Ireland	15 Mar 1890
10	Walter Gilliat	Ireland	25 Feb 1893†

Figures in brackets indicate where more than three goals were scored.
†Player's only match for England.

There is some uncertainty about whether Vaughton or Brown scored the first hat-trick in England's record 13–0 win over Ireland in 1882. Contemporary newspaper reports of the game are very vague, but there is every indication that Vaughton was the first to score three goals in one game. Perhaps remarkably, the first player to score a hat-trick against Scotland was Dennis Wilshaw (four goals) at Wembley on 2 April 1955, 83 years after the two countries first played each other. The first man to score two England hat-tricks was Steve Bloomer. He scored five against Wales on 16 March 1896 and four against Wales, again, on 18 March 1901. He is the only man to score hat-tricks for England in two different centuries.

THE 10 BIGGEST WINS BY ENGLAND

	Opponents	Year	Venue	Score
1	Ireland	1882	Belfast	13–0
2	Ireland	1899	Sunderland	13–2
3	Austria	1908	Vienna	11–1
4=	Portugal	1947	Lisbon	10–0
4=	USA	1964	New York	10–0
6=	Ireland	1895	Derby	9–0
6=	Luxembourg	1960	Luxembourg	9–0
6=	Luxembourg	1982	Wembley	9–0
9=	Ireland	1890	Belfast	9–1
9=	Wales	1896	Cardiff	9–1
9=	Belgium	1927	Brussels	9–1

England have scored nine goals on two other occasions: 9–2 *v* Ireland at Maine Road in 1949, and 9–3 *v* Scotland at Wembley in 1961. On successive days, on 31 May and 1 June 1909, England scored 16 goals in two matches. First, they beat Hungary 8–2 in Budapest, and then Austria 8–1 in Vienna. Vivian Woodward scored seven goals in the two games.

THE 10 BIGGEST DEFEATS FOR ENGLAND

	Opponents	Year	Venue	Score
1	Hungary	1954	Budapest	1–7
2	Scotland	1878	Glasgow	2–7
3	Scotland	1881	Kennington Oval	1–6
4	Hungary	1953	Wembley	3–6
5	Yugoslavia	1958	Belgrade	0–5
6=	Scotland	1882	Glasgow	1–5
6=	Scotland	1928	Wembley	1–5
6=	Brazil	1964	Rio de Janeiro	1–5
9=	France	1931	Paris	2–5
9=	France	1963	Paris	2–5

The 5–2 defeat by France in a European Championship qualifier in 1963 was Alf Ramsey's first game as England manager. However, from that inauspicious start he went on to guide the team to World Cup glory three years later.

While England's biggest defeat in terms of goals is the 7–1 thrashing by Puskas' 'Mighty Magyars' at Budapest in 1954, the most embarrassing defeat the English national side has ever suffered was in the 1950 World Cup finals. At the Mineiro Stadium, Belo Horizonte, on 29 June, England's team, littered with famous names including Bert Williams, Alf Ramsey, Billy Wright, Jimmy Dickinson, Tom Finney and Stan Mortensen, were humbled by the unfancied United States team that won thanks to a 37th-minute goal from Joseph 'Larry' Gaetjens. When the result was flashed around the world, newspaper offices could not believe it, thinking England's score should have read '10' instead of '0'.

THE 10 HIGHEST-SCORING FOOTBALL LEAGUE GAMES

	Match	Div.	Season	Score	Goals
1	Tranmere Rovers v Oldham Athletic	3N	1935–36	13–4	17
2=	Aston Villa v Accrington	1	1891–92	12–2	14
2=	Manchester City v Lincoln City	2	1894–95	11–3	14
2=	Tottenham Hotspur v Everton	1	1958–59	10–4	14
5=	Stockport County v Halifax Town	3N	1933–34	13–0	13
5=	Newcastle United v Newport County	2	1946–47	13–0	13
5=	Barrow v Gateshead	3N	1933–34	12–1	13
5=	Sheffield United v Cardiff City	1	1925–26	11–2	13
5=	Oldham Athletic v Chester	3N	1951–52	11–2	13
5=	Hull City v Wolverhampton Wanderers	2	1919–20	10–3	13
5=	Middlesbrough v Sheffield United	1	1933–34	10–3	13
5=	Stoke City v West Bromwich Albion	1	1936–37	10–3	13
5=	Bristol City v Gillingham	3S	1926–27	9–4	13
5=	Gillingham v Exeter City	3S	1950–51	9–4	13
5=	Derby County v Blackburn Rovers	1	1890–91	8–5	13
5=	Burton Swifts v Walsall Town Swifts	2	1893–94	8–5	13
5=	Stockport County v Chester	3N	1932–33	8–5	13
5=	Charlton Athletic v Huddersfield Town	2	1957–58	7–6	13

Gillingham have figured in the only two League games to finish 9–4 and have been on both ends of the scoreline.

THE 10 CLUBS TO CONCEDE THE MOST GOALS IN A FOOTBALL LEAGUE SEASON

	Club	Season	Division	Goals conceded
1	Darwen	1898–99	2	141
2	Nelson	1927–28	3N	136
3=	Merthyr Town	1929–30	3S	135
3=	Rochdale	1931–32	3N	135
5	Newport County	1946–47	2	133
6	Blackpool	1930–31	1	125
7	Accrington Stanley	1959–60	3	123
8	Bradford Park Avenue	1955–56	3N	122
9	Ipswich Town	1963–64	1	121
10	Charlton Athletic	1956–57	1	120

The record for the Fourth Division is 109 conceded by Hartlepool United in 1959–60. The last team to concede 100 goals was Newport County (105) in the Fourth Division in 1987–88. Darwen's total of 141 came from 34 League games. At home they conceded just 32 goals while their performance away from home was not far short of abysmal. They played 17 away games, won 0, drew 1, and lost 16. They scored six goals and conceded 109. They were beaten 10–0 on three occasions, by Loughborough, Manchester City and Walsall. Grimsby Town and Manchester United both scored nine goals against them, while Birmingham and Luton Town scored eight. The only team they took a point off away from home was Gainsborough in a 2–2 draw.

QUIZ

THE FA CUP

1 Which is the only team to have been drawn against opponents from England, Ireland, Scotland and Wales?

2 'Who won the Cup and never scored a goal?' is one of those trick questions, we're sorry to say, that hasn't an answer – nobody called 'Never' has ever scored a goal in a Cup final – but when did Fogg stop a Cup final?

3 London, between 1978 and 1982, was the second town or city to have a team appear in five successive FA Cup finals. Which was the first town nearly 100 years earlier?

4 Before Sunderland in 1992, who were the last Second Division FA Cup finalists?

5 Which team has appeared in a record 22 semi-finals?

6 Who won the first Wembley Cup final to require a replay?

7 What distinction befell Arthur Childs of Hull City in 1930?

8 Which was the first Third Division team to reach the semi-final?

9 Name the non-League team that beat First Division Burnley 1–0 in the 1974–75 competition.

10 What was achieved for the first time by Arsenal in the 1932 final when beaten 2–1 by Newcastle United?

THE 10 HIGHEST-SCORING FA CUP FINALS*

Teams/year	Scores	Total gls
1= Tottenham Hotspur v Sheffield United (1901)	2–2, 3–1	8
1= Manchester United v Brighton and Hove Albion (1983)	2–2, 4–0	8
3= Blackburn Rovers v Sheffield Wednesday (1890)	6–1	7
3= Blackpool v Bolton Wanderers (1953)	4–3	7
3= Chelsea v Leeds United (1970)	2–2, 2–1	7
3= Tottenham Hotspur v Manchester City (1981)	1–1, 3–2	7
3= Manchester United v Crystal Palace (1990)	3–3, 1–0	7
8= Bury v Derby County (1903)	6–0	6
8= Sheffield Wednesday v West Bromwich Albion (1935)	4–2	6
8= Manchester United v Blackpool (1948)	4–2	6

Including replays.

THE FIRST 10 PENALTY KICKS IN AN FA CUP FINAL

	Player	Match	Year
1	Albert Shepherd	Newcastle United v Barnsley*	1910
2	Charlie Wallace†	Aston Villa v Sunderland	1913
3	Billy Smith	Huddersfield Town v Preston North End	1922
4	George Mutch	Preston North End v Huddersfield Town	1938
5	Eddie Shimwell	Blackpool v Manchester United	1948
6	Ronnie Allen	West Bromwich Albion v Preston North End	1954
7	Danny Blanchflower	Tottenham Hotspur v Burnley	1962
8	Kevin Reeves	Manchester City v Tottenham Hotspur*	1981
9	Glenn Hoddle	Tottenham Hotspur v Queen's Park Rangers*	1982
10	Arnold Muhren	Manchester United v Brighton and Hove Albion*	1983

Replay.
† Penalty kick missed.

THE TOP 10 VENUES FOR THE FA CUP FINAL*

	Venue	Year first used	No. of times used
1	Wembley Stadium	1923	68
2	Kennington Oval	1872	22
3	Crystal Palace	1895	21
4=	Old Trafford	1911	3
4=	Stamford Bridge	1920	3
6	Goodison Park	1894	2
7=	Lillie Bridge	1873	1
7=	Baseball Ground	1886	1
7=	Fallowfield	1893	1
7=	Burnden Park	1901	1
7=	Bramall Lane	1912	1

Including replays.

Since the first FA Cup final at Kennington Oval in 1872 a total of 11 grounds have been used to stage the most famous cup competition in the world.

Bramall Lane, home of Sheffield United, stands alone as the only present-day League ground to have played host to both the FA Cup final and a cricket Test match.

THE 10 HIGHEST RECORD ATTENDANCES OF FOOTBALL LEAGUE CLUBS

	Club	Year	Attendance
1	Manchester City	1934	84,569
2	Chelsea	1935	82,905
3	Everton	1948	78,299
4	Aston Villa	1946	76,588
5	Sunderland	1933	75,118
6	Tottenham Hotspur	1938	75,038
7	Charlton Athletic	1938	75,031
8	Arsenal	1935	73,295
9	Sheffield Wednesday	1934	72,841
10	Manchester United	1920	70,504

Because of drastic reductions in ground capacities over the last 20 years or so as a result of safety precautions, these records are likely to stand for all time. The last club to establish a new record attendance at its ground, other than clubs moving to new grounds in recent years, was Crystal Palace whose record of 51,801 at their Selhurst Park ground was set in a League game against Burnley on 11 May 1979.

THE 10 LOWEST RECORD ATTENDANCES OF FOOTBALL LEAGUE CLUBS

	Club	Year	Attendance
1	Maidstone United*	1979	10,591
2	Barnet*	1952	11,026
3	Scarborough*	1938	11,130
4	Cambridge United*	1970	14,000
5	Hartlepool United	1957	17,426
6	Wimbledon*	1935	18,000 †
7	Hereford United*	1958	18,114
8	Shrewsbury Town	1961	18,917
9	Aldershot	1970	19,138
10	Crewe Alexandra	1960	20,000

Not in the Football League at the time.
† *At Plough Lane, their old ground.*

While most Football League clubs established their record attendances in either the Football League or FA Cup, Wimbledon and Barnet stand alone establishing theirs in the FA Amateur Cup.

THE TOP 10 AVERAGE FOOTBALL LEAGUE ATTENDANCES SINCE WORLD WAR II

	Club	Season	Average attendance
1	Manchester United	1967–68	57,552
2	Newcastle United	1947–48	56,283
3	Tottenham Hotspur	1950–51	55,509
4	Arsenal	1947–48	54,982
5	Manchester United	1947–48	54,890
6	Manchester United	1975–76	54,750
7	Tottenham Hotspur	1949–50	54,111
8	Newcastle United	1948–49	53,992
9	Manchester United	1976–77	53,709
10	Manchester United	1958–59	53,258

Manchester United have topped 50,000 a record nine times and were the last club to have an average home attendance of over 50,000 (51,608 in 1979–80). In addition to the clubs in this list, the only other team to have a post-war average of more than 50,000 is Everton (51,460 in 1962–63).

THE 10 LOWEST AVERAGE FOOTBALL LEAGUE ATTENDANCES SINCE WORLD WAR II

	Club	Season	Average attendance
1	Workington	1973–74	1,173
2	Torquay United	1985–86	1,239
3	Rochdale	1977–78	1,275
4	Workington	1975–76	1,276
5	Halifax Town	1986–87	1,327
6	Workington	1976–77	1,338
7	Hartlepool United	1982–83	1,368
8	Halifax Town	1984–85	1,381
9	Halifax Town	1985–86	1,405
10	Halifax Town	1983–84	1,412

THE TOP 10 AVERAGE FOOTBALL LEAGUE ATTENDANCES, 1991–92

	Club	Average attendance
1	Manchester United	44,984
2	Liverpool	34,799
3	Arsenal	31,905
4	Sheffield Wednesday	29,560
5	Leeds United	29,459
6	Tottenham Hotspur	27,761
7	Manchester City	27,690
8	Aston Villa	24,818
9	Nottingham Forrest	23,721
10	Everton	23,143

All were First Division clubs. The highest averages for the other three divisions were: Division 2 – Newcastle United 21,148; Division 3 – Stoke City 13,007; Division 4 – Burnley 10,521.

MANCHESTER UNITED'S 10 BIGGEST HOME CROWDS, 1991–92

	Opponents	Date	Attendance
1	Nottingham Forest	20 Apr 1992	47,576
2	West Ham United	23 Nov 1991	47,185
3	Sheffield Wednesday	8 Feb 1992	47,074
4	Manchester City	7 Apr 1992	46,781
5	Everton	11 Jan 1992	46,619
6	Arsenal	19 Oct 1991	46,594
7	Luton Town	21 Sep 1991	46,491
8	Crystal Palace	22 Feb 1992	46,347
9	Notts County	17 Aug 1991	46,276
10	Middlesbrough	11 Mar 1992	45,875

All the matches in this list were Football League matches, except the game against Middlesbrough (League Cup semi-final second leg). United played 26 home games in the League and domestic cup competitions, and the lowest attendance was 29,543 for the visit by Portsmouth in the third round of the League Cup. Their lowest League attendance was 38,554 for the visit by Queen's Park Rangers.

THE TOP 10 AVERAGE HOME ATTENDANCES IN NON-LEAGUE FOOTBALL, 1991–92

	Club	League	Average attendance
1	Wycombe Wanderers	GMVC*	3,606
2	Colchester United	GMVC	3,418
3	Yeovil Town	GMVC	2,118
4	Woking	Diadora	1,880
5	Kettering Town	GMVC	1,806
6	Dover Athletic	Beazer Homes	1,367
7	Kidderminster Harriers	GMVC	1,306
8	Barrow	GMVC	1,249
9	Boston United	GMVC	1,202
10	Telford United	GMVC	1,039

* GM Vauxhall Conference.

The highest non-League attendance in the 1991–92 season was 7,193 for the GMVC match between Colchester United and Barrow on 2 May 1992.

The Estadio Maracana in Rio de Janeiro, Brazil, has a capacity of 165,000, making it the largest football ground in the world.

THE 10 LARGEST FOOTBALL GROUNDS IN THE WORLD

	Ground/location	Capacity
1	Estadio Maracana, Rio de Janeiro, Brazil	165,000
2	Rungnado Stadium, Pyongyang, South Korea	150,000
3	Estadio Maghalaes Pinto, Belo Horizonte, Brazil	125,000
4=	Estadio da Luz, Lisbon, Portugal	120,000
4=	Estadio Morumbi, São Paulo, Brazil	120,000
4=	Senayan Main Stadium, Jakarta, Indonesia	120,000
4=	Yuba Bharati Krirangan, nr Calcutta, India	120,000
8	Estadio Castelão, Fortaleza, Brazil	119,000
9=	Estadio Arrudão, Recife, Brazil	115,000
9=	Estadio Azteca, Mexico City, Mexico	115,000
9=	Nou Camp, Barcelona, Spain	115,000

THE 10 LARGEST FOOTBALL GROUNDS IN ENGLAND AND SCOTLAND

	Ground/club	Capacity
1	Wembley Stadium	78,421
2	Hampden Park (Queen's Park)	64,110
3	Celtic Park (Glasgow Celtic)	52,000
4	Old Trafford (Manchester United)	50,726
5	Highbury (Arsenal)	45,000
6	Ibrox Stadium (Glasgow Rangers)	44,500
7	Maine Road (Manchester City)	44,055
8	Stamford Bridge (Chelsea)	43,900
9	Goodison Park (Everton)	41,366
10	Elland Road (Leeds United)	40,176

These capacities are subject to change at any time.

Contrary to popular belief, the capacity of Wembley Stadium is *not* 80,000.

THE 10 SMALLEST LEAGUE GROUNDS IN ENGLAND AND SCOTLAND*

	Club	Ground	Capacity
1	Brechin City	Glebe Park	3,091
2	Alloa Athletic	Recreation Park	3,100
3	Stenhousemuir	Ochilview Park	3,480
4	Albion Rovers	Cliftonhill Stadium	3,496
5	Stranraer	Stair Park	4,000
6	Cowdenbeath	Central Park	4,778
7	East Fife	Bayview Park	5,150
8	Berwick Rangers	Shielfield Park	5,235
9	Maidstone United	Watling Street	5,250
10	Torquay United	Plainmoor	5,539

* Based on 1991–92 capacities.

THE 10 FOOTBALL LEAGUE GROUNDS HIGHEST ABOVE SEA LEVEL

	Ground	Club	Height above sea level m	ft
1	The Hawthorns	West Bromwich Albion	165	541
2	Vale Park	Port Vale	160	525
3	Boundary Park	Oldham Athletic	155	509
4	Spotland	Rochdale	145	476
5	Molineux	Wolverhampton Wanderers	131	430
6	St Andrews	Birmingham City	123	404
7	Turf Moor	Burnley	119	390
8	Field Mill	Mansfield Town	118	387
9	Valley Parade	Bradford City	117	384
10	Kenilworth Road	Luton Town	116	381

THE 10 MOST WESTERLY FOOTBALL LEAGUE GROUNDS

	Ground	Club
1	Home Park	Plymouth Argyle
2	Vetch Field	Swansea City
3	St James Park	Exeter City
4	Plainmoor	Torquay United
5	Ninian Park	Cardiff City
6	Bloomfield Road	Blackpool
7	Prenton Park	Tranmere Rovers
8	Racecourse Ground	Wrexham
9	Goodison Park	Everton
10	Anfield	Liverpool

THE 10 MOST NORTHERLY FOOTBALL LEAGUE GROUNDS

	Ground	Club
1	St James' Park	Newcastle United
2	Roker Park	Sunderland
3	Brunton Park	Carlisle United
4	Victoria Ground	Hartlepool United
5	Ayresome Park	Middlesbrough
6	Feethams	Darlington
7	Seamer Road	Scarborough
8	Bootham Crescent	York City
9=	Bloomfield Road	Blackpool
9=	Valley Parade	Bradford City

THE 10 MOST EASTERLY FOOTBALL LEAGUE GROUNDS

	Ground	Club
1	Carrow Road	Norwich City
2	Portman Road	Ipswich Town
3	Layer Road	Colchester United
4	Roots Hall	Southend United
5	Priestfield Stadium	Gillingham
6	Watling Street	Maidstone United
7	Abbey Stadium	Cambridge United
8=	Upton Park	West Ham United
8=	The Valley	Charlton Athletic
10	Brisbane Road	Leyton Orient

THE 10 MOST SOUTERLY FOOTBALL LEAGUE GROUNDS

	Ground	Club
1	Home Park	Plymouth Argyle
2	Plainmoor	Torquay United
3	St James Park	Exeter City
4	Dean Court	AFC Bournemouth
5	Fratton Park	Portsmouth
6	Goldstone Ground	Brighton and Hove Albion
7	The Dell	Southampton
8	Recreation Ground	Aldershot
9	Twerton Park	Bristol Rovers
10=	Priestfield Stadium	Gillingham
10=	Selhurst Park	Crystal Palace/ Wimbledon

THE 10 OLDEST ENGLAND INTERNATIONALS

	Player	Year of last match	Age yrs	days
1	Stanley Matthews	1957	42	103
2	Peter Shilton	1990	40	292
3	Leslie Compton	1950	38	71
4	Sam Hardy	1920	36	227
5	Tom Finney	1958	36	200
6	Dave Watson	1982	35	240
7	Jesse Pennington	1920	35	230
8	Frank Hudspeth	1925	35	207 *
9	Ian Callaghan	1977	35	185
10	Ted Hufton	1929	35	171

Hudspeth was born in April 1892, exact date unknown. He was thus 35 years and from 177 to 207 days old.

Compton, at 38 years 64 days, is the oldest England debutant. Pennington and Hardy both played their last matches in the same game, against Scotland on 10 April 1920. The youngest international is almost certainly James Prinsep; he was 17 years 252 days old when he made his only appearance, against Scotland in 1879. However, the age of Edward Johnson has never been established and it is possible that he was younger than Prinsep when he made his debut in 1880.

THE 10 YOUNGEST ENGLAND GOALSCORERS

	Player	Year	Opponents	Age* yrs	Age* days
1	Tommy Lawton	1938	Wales	19	16
2	Jimmy Greaves	1959	Peru	19	86
3	Joe Baker	1959	Northern Ireland	19	123
4	Jimmy Brown	1882	Ireland	19	172
5=	Jackie Robinson	1937	Finland	19	238
5=	Duncan Edwards	1956	West Germany	19	238
7	Stanley Matthews	1934	Wales	19	240
8	Tom Galley	1937	Norway	19	283
9	Joe Lofthouse	1885	Ireland	19	320
10	Johnny Haynes	1954	Northern Ireland	19	358

If a player would appear in the list twice, only the youngest age at which he played is included.

Billy Mosforth scored against Scotland in 1879 and his age has never been accurately established. He was either 19 or 20 at the time. All players in this list scored just one goal in the match, with the exception of Brown who scored two.

When Stanley Matthews scored against Northern Ireland in 1956 he was 41 years 248 days old, making him the only man to score for England beyond his 40th birthday.

THE 10 YOUNGEST FOOTBALL LEAGUE CLUBS

	Club	Year formed
1	Colchester United	1937
2	Peterborough United	1934
3	Wigan Athletic	1932
4	Hereford United	1924
5	York City	1922
6=	Cambridge United	1919
6=	Leeds United	1919
8	Swansea Town (now City)	1912
9	Halifax Town	1911
10=	Mansfield Town	1910
10=	Torquay United	1910

Scotland's youngest club is Meadowbank Thistle, formed in 1974.

THE 10 OLDEST FOOTBALL LEAGUE PLAYERS, 1991–92

	Player	Club	Date of birth
1	Peter Shilton*	Plymouth Argyle	18 Sep 1949
2	Kenny Swain	Crewe Alexandra	28 Jan 1952
3	Ian McDonald	Aldershot	10 May 1953
4	Brian Talbot	Aldershot	21 Jul 1953
5	Steve Sherwood*	Grimsby Town	10 Dec 1953
6	Trevor Francis	Sheffield Wednesday	19 Apr 1954
7	Jimmy Case	AFC Bournemouth	18 May 1954
8	Graham Barrow	Chester City	13 Jun 1954
9	Barry Siddall*	Chester City	12 Sep 1954
10	Jack Ashurst	Doncaster Rovers	12 Oct 1954

* Goalkeeper.

THE 10 OLDEST FOOTBALL LEAGUE CLUBS

	Club	Year formed
1	Notts County	1862
2	Stoke City	1863
3	Nottingham Forest	1865
4	Chesterfield	1866
5	Sheffield Wednesday	1867
6	Reading	1871
7	Wrexham	1873
8=	Aston Villa	1874
8=	Bolton Wanderers	1874
10=	Birmingham City	1875
10=	Blackburn Rovers	1875

Scotland's oldest club is Queen's Park, formed in 1867. They remain the only amateur team in League soccer in England and Scotland.

THE 10 OLDEST POST-WAR FOOTBALL LEAGUE PLAYERS

	Player	Last club	Last appearance	Age yrs	Age days
1	Neil McBain	New Brighton	15 Mar 1947	51	120
2	Stanley Matthews	Stoke City	6 Feb 1965	50	5
3	Alf Wood	Coventry City	29 Nov 1958	43	199
4	Tommy Hutchison	Swansea City	12 Mar 1991	43	171
5	Michael Burns	Ipswich Town	6 Oct 1951	43	121
6	Alex Ferguson	Swindon Town	15 Nov 1947	43	103
7	Ted Sagar	Everton	15 Nov 1952	42	281
8	John Oakes	Plymouth Argyle	1 May 1948	42	230
9	Peter Shilton	Plymouth Argyle	4 May 1992*	42	229
10	Matt Middleton	York City	6 May 1950	42	195

* Still playing 1992–93.

Matthews is the oldest First Division player. The second oldest is Sam Bartram (Charlton Athletic), who was 42 years 47 days when he played his last game on 10 March 1956.

The Spurs side of 1960–61, who achieved the League and Cup double under the captaincy of Danny Blanchflower (front row, third from left).

THE TOP ENGLISH TEAMS OVER THE DECADES

The following lists have been compiled by allocating a team winning the League, FA Cup or League Cup two points, and one point to teams who were runners-up in each competition. Because the Football League did not start until 1888–89, some 16 years after the birth of the FA Cup, the first decade chosen is the 1890s. All subsequent decades, with the exception of the 1910s and 1940s, because of war interruptions, have been included. League Cup performances are taken into account from 1961 when the tournament was launched.

	1890s	
1	Aston Villa	13
2	Sunderland	8
3	Everton	6
4=	Preston North End	5
4=	Sheffield United	5
6	Blackburn Rovers	4
7=	Derby County	3
7=	Notts County	3
7=	Sheffield Wednesday	3
7=	West Bromwich Albion	3
7=	Wolverhampton Wanderers	3

1900s

1	Newcastle United	9
2=	Aston Villa	6
2=	Everton	6
2=	Sheffield Wednesday	6
5=	Bury	4
5=	Liverpool	4
5=	Manchester United	4
5=	Sheffield United	4
9=	Manchester City	3
9=	Sunderland	3

1920s

1	Huddersfield Town	12
2	Bolton Wanderers	6
3=	Cardiff City	4
3=	Liverpool	4
3=	Newcastle United	4
6=	Aston Villa	3
6=	Burnley	3
6=	Tottenham Hotspur	3
6=	West Bromwich Albion	3
10=	Arsenal	2
10=	Blackburn Rovers	2
10=	Everton	2
10=	Manchester City	2
10=	Sheffield United	2
10=	Sheffield Wednesday	2

1930s

1	Arsenal	16
2	Everton	6
3=	Manchester City	5
3=	Sunderland	5
5	Sheffield Wednesday	4
6=	Huddersfield Town	3
6=	Portsmouth	3
6=	Preston North End	3
6=	West Bromwich Albion	3
6=	Wolverhampton Wanderers	3

1950s

1	Manchester United	10
2	Wolverhampton Wanderers	8
3	Newcastle United	6
4	Arsenal	5
5=	Blackpool	4
5=	Tottenham Hotspur	4
7=	Bolton Wanderers	3
7=	Manchester City	3
7=	Preston North End	3
7=	West Bromwich Albion	3

1960s

1	Tottenham Hotspur	9
2	Manchester United	8
3=	Leeds United	7
3=	Liverpool	7
5	Leicester City	6
6=	Everton	5
6=	West Bromwich Albion	5
8=	Burnley	4
8=	Manchester City	4
10=	Aston Villa	3
10=	Chelsea	3
10=	West Ham United	3
10=	Wolverhampton Wanderers	3

	1970s	
1	Liverpool	16
2=	Arsenal	9
2=	Leeds United	9
4	Nottingham Forest	7
5	Manchester City	6
6	Aston Villa	5
7=	Derby County	4
7=	Manchester United	4
7=	Tottenham Hotspur	4
10=	Chelsea	3
10=	Everton	3
10=	Southampton	3

The 1897 FA Cup winners Aston Villa, the most successful club of that decade.

Liverpool celebrate their victory in the 1986 FA Cup final after beating Merseyside rivals Everton 3–1.

1980s

1	Liverpool	29
2	Everton	11
3	Manchester United	7
4=	Arsenal	6
4=	Tottenham Hotspur	6
6=	Luton Town	3
6=	Nottingham Forest	3
6=	West Ham United	3
9=	Aston Villa	2
9=	Coventry City	2
9=	Ipswich Town	2
9=	Norwich City	2
9=	Oxford United	2
9=	Queen's Park Rangers	2
9=	Watford	2
9=	Wimbledon	2
9=	Wolverhampton Wanderers	2

I n the 1980s, Liverpool won 12 of the 30 domestic trophies on offer.

THE 10 CLUBS WITH THE MOST FOOTBALL LEAGUE TITLES IN AGGREGATE

	Club	Division						Total
		1	**2**	**3**	**4**	**3N**	**3S**	
1	Liverpool	18	4	–	–	–	–	22
2=	Arsenal	10	–	–	–	–	–	10
2=	Everton	9	1	–	–	–	–	10
2=	Aston Villa	7	2	1	–	–	–	10
5=	Manchester United	7	2	–	–	–	–	9
5=	Sheffield Wednesday	4	5	–	–	–	–	9
7=	Sunderland	6	1	1	–	–	–	8
7=	Wolverhampton Wanderers	3	2	1	1	1	–	8
7=	Manchester City	2	6	–	–	–	–	8
10	Derby County	2	4	–	–	1	–	7

W olverhampton Wanderers have uniquely won the title in five divisions.

THE 10 CLUBS WITH THE MOST WINS IN THE FOOTBALL LEAGUE*

	Club	Year of first win	Total wins
1	Liverpool	1893	1,650
2	Manchester United	1892	1,568
3	Aston Villa	1888	1,557
4=	Everton	1888	1,537
4=	Arsenal	1893	1,537
6	Wolverhampton Wanderers	1888	1,504
7	Sunderland	1890	1,489
8	Manchester City	1892	1,463
9	Derby County	1888	1,454
10	Newcastle United	1893	1,443

*To end 1991–92 season.

T he first of Liverpool's record 1,650 wins was at Middlesbrough Ironopolis on 2 September 1893, their first-ever Football League game. A Second Division game, Liverpool won 2–0 thanks to second-half goals from Malcolm McVean, scorer of Liverpool's first-ever League goal, and Joe McQue. The match was watched by little more than 2,000 fans.

LIVERPOOL'S 10 BIGGEST CHAMPIONSHIP-WINNING MARGINS

L iverpool have won the Football League Championship a record 18 times, which is eight more than their nearest rivals, Arsenal. This is a list of their 10 best Championship seasons. Because of the change to three points awarded for a win in 1981–82, all margins since then have been converted back to the old two-points-for-a-win system.

	Season	Runners-up	Margin
1	1978–79	Nottingham Forest	8
2=	1982–83	Manchester United*	7
2=	1989–90	Aston Villa	7
4=	1921–22	Tottenham Hotspur	6
4=	1922–23	Sunderland	6
4=	1965–66	Leeds United	6
4=	1987–88	Manchester United	6
8=	1905–06	Preston North End	4
8=	1963–64	Manchester United	4
8=	1981–82	Ipswich Town	4

*Watford actually finished in 2nd place, but if the old points system is used, Manchester United finished runners-up.

LIVERPOOL'S 10 BIGGEST DEFEATS UNDER KENNY DALGLISH

	Opponents (home/away)	Competition	Date	Score
1=	Luton Town (a)	Football League	25 Oct 1986	1–4
1=	West Ham United (a)	Littlewoods Cup	29 Nov 1988	1–4
1=	Southampton (a)	Football League	21 Oct 1989	1–4
4=	Luton Town (a)	FA Cup	28 Jan 1987	0–3
4=	Arsenal (a)	Football League	2 Dec 1990	0–3
6=	Manchester United (a)	Football League	1 Jan 1989	1–3
6=	Manchester United (a)	Rumbelows League Cup	31 Oct 1990	1–3
8=	Arsenal (a)	Football League	14 Dec 1985	0–2
8=	Everton (h)	Football League	22 Feb 1986	0–2
8=	Watford (a)	Football League	6 Dec 1986	0–2
8=	Arsenal (h)	Football League	26 May 1989	0–2
8=	Sheffield Wednesday (a)	Football League	29 Nov 1989	0–2

Kenny Dalglish took over as Liverpool manager in the aftermath of the Heysel disaster in 1985. He made the shock announcement of his retirement on 22 February 1991, shortly after his team had engaged in a memorable 4–4 draw with Everton in the FA Cup.

THE 10 CLUBS WITH THE MOST FIRST DIVISION TITLES

	Club	Years of first and last titles	First Division titles
1	Liverpool	1901–1990	18
2	Arsenal	1931–1991	10
3	Everton	1891–1987	9
4=	Manchester United	1908–1967	7
4=	Aston Villa	1894–1981	7
6	Sunderland	1892–1936	6
7=	Newcastle United	1905–1927	4
7=	Sheffield Wednesday	1903–1930	4
9=	Huddersfield Town	1924–1926	3
9=	Wolverhampton Wanderers	1954–1959	3

THE 10 CLUBS WITH THE MOST SEASONS IN THE FIRST DIVISION*

	Club	Seasons
1	Everton†	89
2	Aston Villa†	81
3	Liverpool	77
4	Arsenal	75
5	Sunderland	70
6=	Manchester City	68
6=	West Bromwich Albion†	68
8	Manchester United	67
9	Newcastle United	63
10	Bolton Wanderers†	60

To end 1991–92 season.
† Founder members of the Football League in 1888.

THE 10 CLUBS TO HAVE SPENT THE LONGEST IN THE FIRST DIVISION WITHOUT WINNING THE TITLE

	Club	Seasons in First Division
1	Bolton Wanderers	60
2	Stoke City	52
3	Birmingham City	50
4	Middlesbrough	46
5=	Leicester City	38
5=	West Ham United*	38
7	Notts County*	30
8	Blackpool	27
9	Coventry City*	25
10=	Bury	18
10=	Charlton Athletic	18

In First Division in 1991–92.

Of these clubs, only Leicester City, Blackpool and Charlton Athletic have managed to finish runners-up in the table. However, Stoke City should have won the title in 1946–47. Needing to beat Sheffield United in their last game of the season to win the title on goal average from Liverpool, they lost 2–1 and managed to finish only 4th in the table. It is, nevertheless, their best-ever finish in the top division.

THE 10 CLUBS WITH THE CURRENT LONGEST CONTINUOUS SPELL IN THE FIRST DIVISION

	Club	Last season not in First Division	Continuous seasons in First Division*
1	Arsenal	1914–15	66
2	Everton	1953–54	38
3	Liverpool	1961–62	30
4	Coventry City	1966–67	25
5	Manchester United	1974–75	17
6	Nottingham Forest	1976–77	15
7=	Southampton	1977–78	14
7=	Tottenham Hotspur	1977–78	14
9	Luton Town†	1981–82	10
10	Queen's Park Rangers	1982–83	9

* To end 1991–92 season.
† Relegated.

THE 10 CLUBS TO HAVE SPENT THE MOST SEASONS IN THE SECOND DIVISION WITHOUT WINNING PROMOTION

	Club	Seasons in Second Division
1	Barnsley*	56
2	Hull City	50
3	Port Vale*	35
4=	Lincoln City	34
4=	Plymouth Argyle*	34
6	Rotherham United (formerly Rotherham Town)	26
7	Stockport County	21
8	Chesterfield	20
9	Bristol Rovers*	18
10	Gainsborough Trinity	16

* In Second Division in 1991–92.

Of the above, only Barnsley, Hull City, and Rotherham United have finished 3rd and just missed out on promotion. All three have been deprived of a place in the First Division by goal average; Barnsley in 1921–22, Hull City in 1909–10 and Rotherham in 1954–55 when they finished with the same points as the champions Birmingham City and runners-up Luton Town.

THE 10 MOST-RELEGATED FOOTBALL LEAGUE CLUBS

	Club	Times relegated
1	Notts County	12
2=	Birmingham City	10
2=	Bolton Wanderers	10
2=	Grimsby Town	10
2=	Preston North End	10
6=	Cardiff City	9
6=	Sheffield Wednesday	9
8=	Bristol City	8
8=	Burnley	8
8=	Derby County	8
8=	Doncaster Rovers	8
8=	Leicester City	8
8=	Manchester City	8
8=	Sheffield United	8
8=	Wolverhampton Wanderers	8

Among other famous clubs that have been relegated are Arsenal (once), Everton (twice), Liverpool (three times), Tottenham Hotspur (four times) and Manchester United (five times).

Apart from Barnet, the only clubs never to have been relegated are Scarborough, Maidstone and Wigan Athletic.

THE 10 CLUBS TO SCORE THE MOST GOALS IN A FOOTBALL LEAGUE SEASON

	Club	Season	Division	Goals
1	Peterborough United	1960–61	4	134
2=	Bradford City	1928–29	3N	128
2=	Aston Villa	1930–31	1	128
4=	Millwall	1927–28	3S	127
4=	Arsenal	1930–31	1	127
6	Doncaster Rovers	1946–47	3N	123
7	Middlesbrough	1926–27	2	122
8=	Everton	1930–31	2	121
8=	Lincoln City	1951–52	3N	121
10	Chester	1964–65	4	119

The highest figure in the Third Division (formed 1958) is 111 by Queen's Park Rangers in 1961–62. Peterborough's all-time record haul was in their first season in the Football League. Sunderland, in 1892–93, was the first team to score 100 goals in a season and Northampton Town, in 1986–87, the last. Tottenham Hotspur in 1962–63 was the last First Division club to reach treble figures. Lincoln City, Sheffield Wednesday and Wolverhampton Wanderers have each scored a record 100 goals or more on five occasions.

THE 10 CLUBS TO HAVE DRAWN THE MOST GAMES IN A FOOTBALL LEAGUE SEASON

	Club	Division	Season	Matches played	Matches drawn
1=	Norwich City	1	1978–79	42	23
1=	Exeter City	4	1986–87	46	23
3=	Tranmere Rovers	3	1970–71	46	22
3=	Aldershot	4	1971–72	46	22
3=	Chester	3	1977–78	46	22
3=	Carlisle United	3	1978–79	46	22
7=	Plymouth Argyle	3	1920–21	42	21
7=	Halifax Town	3	1973–74	46	21
7=	Halifax Town	4	1977–78	46	21
7=	Leeds United	2	1982–83	42	21
7=	Oldham Athletic	2	1988–89	46	21

The first-ever drawn game was on the Football League's first day, 8 September 1888, when Wolverhampton Wanderers and Aston Villa drew 1–1.

THE TOP 10 DEFENSIVE RECORDS OF FOOTBALL LEAGUE CHAMPIONS

	Club	Season	Goals conceded*
1	Preston North End	1888–89	15 (22)
2	Liverpool	1978–79	16 (42)
3	Arsenal	1990–91	18 (38)
4=	Nottingham Forest	1977–78	24 (42)
4=	Liverpool	1987–88	24 (40)
6	Leeds United	1968–69	26 (42)
7=	Sheffield Wednesday	1903–04	28 (34)
7=	Huddersfield Town	1924–25	28 (42)
9=	Everton	1890–91	29 (22)
9=	Arsenal	1970–71	29 (42)

Figures in brackets indicate matches played.

THE 10 CLUBS WITH THE MOST SEASONS UNDEFEATED AT HOME

	Club	No. of seasons undefeated
1	Liverpool	9
2	Sunderland	6
3=	Grimsby Town	5
3=	Manchester United	5
3=	Millwall	5
6=	Arsenal	4
6=	Blackburn Rovers	4
6=	Leeds United	4
6=	Manchester City	4
6=	Mansfield Town	4
6=	Plymouth Argyle	4
6=	Reading	4
6=	Sheffield Wednesday	4

Leeds United in 1991–92 was the last club to go through a League season without defeat at home.

THE 10 LONGEST-SERVING FOOTBALL LEAGUE MANAGERS*

	Manager	Club	Div.	Appointed
1	Brian Clough	Nottingham Forest	1	Jan 1975
2	Joe Royle	Oldham Athletic	1	Jul 1982
3	Dario Gradi	Crewe Alexandra	4	May 1983
4	Harry Redknapp	AFC Bournemouth	3	Oct 1983
5	Arthur Cox	Derby County	2	Jan 1984
6	John Rudge	Port Vale	2	Mar 1984
7	Steve Coppell	Crystal Palace	1	May 1984
8	Harry McNally	Chester City	3	Jun 1985
9	Phil Neal	Bolton Wanderers	3	Dec 1985
10	George Graham	Arsenal	1	May 1986

To end of 1991–92 season.

The League's longest-serving manager, Brian Clough of Nottingham Forest.

THE 10 LONGEST-SERVING FIRST DIVISION MANAGERS*

	Manager	Club	Appointed
1	Brian Clough	Nottingham Forest	Jan 1975
2	Joe Royle	Oldham Athletic	Jul 1982
3	Steve Coppell	Crystal Palace	Jun 1984
4	George Graham	Arsenal	May 1986
5	Alex Ferguson	Manchester United	Nov 1986
6	Dave Stringer	Norwich City	Dec 1987
7	Dave Bassett	Sheffield United	Jan 1988
8	Howard Wilkinson	Leeds United	Oct 1988
9	Neil Warnock	Notts County	Jan 1989
10	Billy Bonds	West Ham United	Feb 1990

*To end 1991–92 season.

Despite being in charge at Nottingham Forest for 17 years, 'Cloughie' has still got a few years more to do before he overtakes Matt Busby as the longest-serving manager at one Football League club. Busby spent a total of 24 years 3 months at Manchester United during his two spells as team boss. The longest-serving British manager is Willie Struth who was Glasgow Rangers' manager for nearly 33 years from August 1920 to April 1953.

THE LAST 10 CLUBS TO JOIN THE FOOTBALL LEAGUE

	Club	Club replaced	Season joined
1	Colchester United* †		1992–93
2	Barnet	†	1991–92
3	Darlington*	Colchester United	1990–91
4	Maidstone United	Darlington	1989–90
5	Lincoln City*	Newport County	1988–89
6	Scarborough	Lincoln City	1987–88
7	Wigan Athletic	Southport	1978–79
8	Wimbledon	Workington	1977–78
9	Hereford United	Barrow	1972–73
10	Cambridge United	Bradford Park Avenue	1970–71

*Rejoined.
†No club relegated.

Scarborough was the first team to benefit from the automatic promotion/relegation between the Fourth Division of the Football League and the GM Vauxhall Conference. Wigan was the last club to be voted into the League at the Annual General Meeting.

THE 10 MOST SUCCESSFUL ENGLISH LEAGUE CLUBS*

	Club	League	FA Cup	League Cup	Total
1	Liverpool	18	5	4	27
2	Aston Villa	7	7	3	17
3	Arsenal	10	5	1	16
4	Manchester United	7	7	1	15
5	Everton	9	4	0	13
6	Tottenham Hotspur	2	8	2	12
7	Newcastle United	4	6	0	10
8	Wolverhampton Wanderers	3	4	2	9
9=	Blackburn Rovers	2	6	0	8
9=	Manchester City	2	4	2	8
9=	Sheffield Wednesday	4	3	1	8
9=	Sunderland	6	2	0	8

*Based on success in the three main domestic competitions: Football League Division One, FA Cup and Football League Cup.

THE 10 CLUBS WITH THE MOST FA CUP WINS

	Club	Wins
1	Tottenham Hotspur	8
2=	Aston Villa	7
2=	Manchester United	7
4=	Blackburn Rovers	6
4=	Newcastle United	6
6=	Arsenal	5
6=	Liverpool	5
6=	The Wanderers*	5
6=	West Bromwich Albion	5
10=	Bolton Wanderers	4
10=	Everton	4
10=	Manchester City	4
10=	Sheffield United	4
10=	Wolverhampton Wanderers	4

The Wanderers were formed by Old Havonians as Forest FC in 1859 and were based at Snaresbrook in Epping Forest. They disbanded in 1863 but re-formed in the same year as The Wanderers – so called because they had no official ground. It was not until 1870 that they acquired a home ground, Kennington Oval, thanks to the efforts of their secretary, C.W. Allcock, who was also secretary of both Surrey CCC and the FA.

The oldest soccer competition in the world, the first FA Cup competition was started in 1871 and the following spring The Wanderers became the first holders of the most coveted club trophy in the world. They went on to win the Cup five times and were never beaten in the final. Tottenham Hotspur had a modern-day equivalent until beaten by Coventry City in the 1987 final. It was their eighth appearance in the final, and their first defeat. They have since gone on to win the trophy for a record eighth time. Arsenal, Everton, Manchester United and Newcastle have all appeared in a record 11 finals.

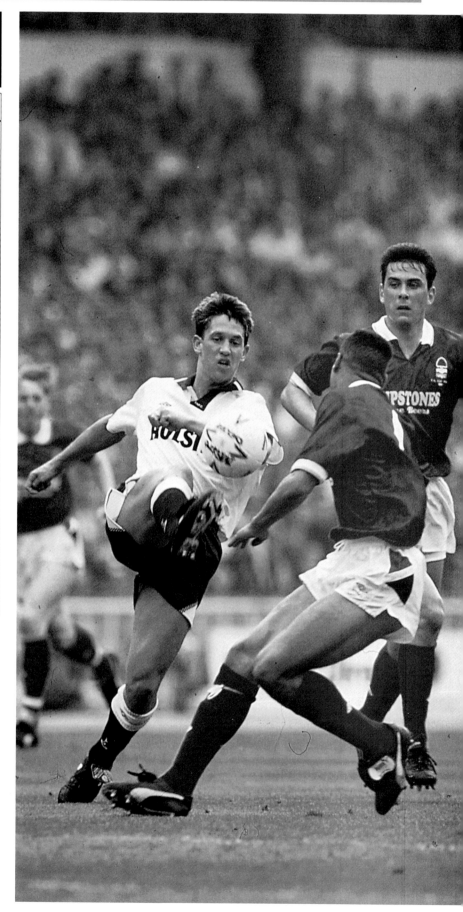

Tottenham's Gary Lineker does battle with Des Walker and the Nottingham Forest defence in the 1991 FA Cup final, which the London side won 2–1 (aet) to notch up their record eighth victory in the competition.

THE 10 COMMONEST REASONS FOR CAUTIONS IN FOOTBALL LEAGUE MATCHES

	Offence	Total
1	Foul tackle	1,609
2	Showing dissent	435
3	Tripping	368
4	Persistent infringement of the laws of the game	318
5	Adopting an aggressive attitude	189
6	Ungentlemanly conduct	136
7	Dangerous play	132
8	Time wasting	131
9	Shirt pulling	120
10	Foul play	61

In addition to these cautions (recorded during League matches in the 1989–90 season) there were smaller numbers of sendings-off for a variety of reasons, led by 'Persistent misconduct' (56 instances), 'Striking' (35), 'Serious foul play' (29) and 'Foul language' (17), followed by a variety of examples of 'Violent conduct' including elbowing, kicking and butting.

THE 10 ENGLISH FOOTBALL LEAGUE CLUBS WITH THE MOST IN-GROUND ARRESTS, 1990–91

	Club	Arrests
1	Aston Villa	219
2=	Wolverhampton Wanderers	195
2=	Charlton Athletic	195
4	Coventry City	149
5	Arsenal	143
6	Newcastle United	141
7	West Bromwich Albion	128
8	West Ham United	126
9	Bristol City	124
10	Liverpool	121

How some of the other well-known clubs fared: Manchester City 33; Manchester United 39; Leeds United 87; Everton 91; Tottenham Hotspur 100; Nottingham Forest 115.

Chester City and Scarborough had the best records with no arrests, while Chester had two ejections and Scarborough just one.

THE 10 LONGEST-NAMED FOOTBALL LEAGUE CLUBS IN ENGLAND AND SCOTLAND

	Club	Letters
1	Wolverhampton Wanderers	22
2	Brighton and Hove Albion	21
3	Dunfermline Athletic	19
4=	Hamilton Academical	18
4=	Peterborough United	18
4=	Sheffield Wednesday	18
4=	West Bromwich Albion	18
8=	East Stirlingshire	17
8=	Heart of Midlothian	17
8=	Meadowbank Thistle	17
8=	Queen's Park Rangers	17

THE 10 COMMONEST TYPES OF FOOTBALL INJURY

	Type of injury	% of injuries
1	Twist, sprain, etc	52
2	Bruise	7
3=	Fracture	8
3=	Tear	8
5	Inflammation	6
6	Cut, laceration	4
7=	Concussion	2
7=	Dislocation	2
7=	'Other'	2
10	Abrasion	less than 1

Research carried out by Dr Klim McPherson and the late Sir Norman Chester during the 1984–85 football season studied reports of 1,364 injuries during training and matches. They found that more than a third of injuries occurred during training sessions, and that injuries caused without contact with another player were commonest (387 cases), with tackles second (288). There were 809 injuries caused by 'twists, etc'. Injuries to the upper leg are commonest (24 per cent of the total), the knee second (20 per cent) and ankle third (18 per cent). They calculated that there is a 29 per cent chance of one player being injured during a match and a 16 per cent risk of any player being injured during a season.

THE 10 CLUBS WITH THE MOST FWA/PFA PLAYER OF THE YEAR AWARDS

	Club	FWA	PFA	Total
1	Liverpool	10	4	14
2	Tottenham Hotspur	6	2	8
3	Manchester United	3	3	6
4	Leeds United	4	1	5
5	Everton	2	2	4
6=	Manchester City	3	–	3
6=	Arsenal	2	1	3
8=	Blackpool	2	–	2
8=	Preston North End	2	–	2
8=	Stoke City	2	–	2
8=	Wolverhampton Wanderers	2	–	2
8=	Derby County	1	1	2
8=	Ipswich Town	1	1	2
8=	Nottingham Forest	1	1	2
8=	Aston Villa	–	2	2

Only the main awards are taken into consideration. The PFA Divisional Awards and Young Player of the Year Award are not included.

The Football Writers' Award (FWA) was first made in 1948 and won by Stanley Matthews (Blackpool). Matthews is one of five men to have won the award twice. The others are Tom Finney (Preston) – the first to do so – Danny Blanchflower (Tottenham Hotspur), Kenny Dalglish and John Barnes (both Liverpool). The Professional Footballers' Association (PFA) awards were launched in 1974 and the winner is elected by his fellow professionals. Norman Hunter of Leeds United was the first winner. Mark Hughes (Manchester United) became the first person to win the award a second time when he was honoured in 1991.

THE TOP 10 PROGRAMMES ACCORDING TO *MATCH WEEKLY*, 1991–92

1	Aston Villa
2	Everton
3=	Derby County
3=	Tottenham Hotspur
5	West Ham United
6	Leeds United
7	Manchester City
8	Norwich City
9	Chelsea
10	Ipswich Town

Every year the soccer magazine *Match Weekly* assembles a panel of experts who decide which are the season's best programmes. They take into account presentation, picture quality, colour quality, editorial content and value for money. All the above programmes were for First Division clubs with the exception of Derby and Ipswich (Second Division). The programmes voted the best in the Third and Fourth Divisions were, respectively, West Bromwich Albion and Wrexham.

THE 10 BIGGEST WORLD CUP ATTENDANCES

	Match	Venue	Year	Attendance
1	Brazil v Uruguay	Rio de Janeiro*	1950	199,854
2	Brazil v Spain	Rio de Janeiro	1950	152,772
3	Brazil v Yugoslavia	Rio de Janeiro	1950	142,409
4	Brazil v Sweden	Rio de Janeiro	1950	138,886
5	Mexico v Paraguay	Mexico City	1986	114,600
6	Argentina v West Germany	Mexico City*	1986	114,590
7=	Mexico v Bulgaria	Mexico City	1986	114,580
7=	Argentina v England	Mexico City	1986	114,580
9	Argentina v Belgium	Mexico City	1986	110,420
10	Mexico v Belgium	Mexico City	1986	110,000

* Final tie.

The biggest crowd outside Mexico or Brazil was that of 98,270 at Wembley in 1966 for England's game against France. The attendance for the Brazil–Uruguay final in 1950 is the world's highest for a soccer match.

THE 10 COUNTRIES THAT HAVE PLAYED THE MOST MATCHES IN THE FINAL STAGES OF THE WORLD CUP

	Country	Tournaments	Matches played
1	Germany/ West Germany	12	68
2	Brazil	14	66
3	Italy	12	54
4	Argentina	10	48
5	England	9	41
6	Uruguay	9	37
7	France	9	34
8	Yugoslavia	8	33
9=	Hungary	9	32
9=	Spain	8	32

Mexico have also appeared in nine tournaments, while Belgium, Czechoslovakia and Sweden have all appeared in eight tournaments. Brazil is the only country to have appeared in the final stages of all 14 competitions.

THE TOP 10 GOALSCORERS IN THE FINAL STAGES OF THE WORLD CUP

	Player/country	Years	Goals
1	Gerd Müller (West Germany)	1970–74	14
2	Just Fontaine (France)	1958	13
3	Pelé (Brazil)	1958–70	12
4	Sandor Kocsis (Hungary)	1954	11
5=	Helmut Rahn (West Germany)	1954–58	10
5=	Teófilio Cubillas (Peru)	1970–78	10
5=	Grzegorz Lato (Poland)	1974–82	10
5=	Gary Lineker (England)	1986–90	10
9=	Leónidas da Silva (Brazil)	1934–38	9
9=	Ademir Marques de Menezes (Brazil)	1950	9
9=	Vavà (Brazil)	1958–62	9
9=	Eusebio (Portugal)	1966	9
9=	Uwe Seeler (West Germany)	1958–70	9
9=	Jairzinho (Brazil)	1970–74	9
9=	Paolo Rossi (Italy)	1978–82	9
9=	Karl-Heinz Rummenigge (West Germany)	1978–86	9

Fontaine's 13 goals in the 1958 finals is a record for one tournament.

THE TOP 10 INDIVIDUAL APPEARANCES IN THE FINAL STAGES OF THE WORLD CUP

	Player/country	Years	Appearances
1=	Uwe Seeler (West Germany)	1958–70	21
1=	Wladislaw Zmuda (Poland)	1974–86	21
3	Grzegorz Lato (Poland)	1974–82	20
4=	Wolfgang Overath (West Germany)	1966–74	19
4=	Hans-Hubert Vogts (West Germany)	1970–78	19
4=	Karl-Heinz Rummenigge (West Germany)	1978–86	19
4=	Diego Maradona (Argentina)	1982–90	19
8=	Franz Beckenbauer (West Germany)	1966–74	18
8=	Sepp Maier (West Germany)	1970–78	18
8=	Mario Kempes (Argentina)	1974–82	18
8=	Gaetano Scirea (Italy)	1978–86	18
8=	Antonio Cabrini (Italy)	1978–86	18
8=	Pierre Littbarski (West Germany)	1982–90	18

While Seeler and Zmuda have both played in 21 matches, the West German's career is slightly longer at 1,980 minutes as opposed to 1,807 minutes. The most appearances by a British player is 17 by Peter Shilton (England), 1982–90.

The legendary Pelé celebrates after scoring Brazil's first goal in their 4–1 victory over Italy in the 1970 World Cup final.

THE 10 HIGHEST-SCORING WORLD CUP FINALS

	Year	Games	Goals	Average per game
1	1954	26	140	5.38
2	1938	18	84	4.66
3	1934	17	70	4.11
4	1950	22	88	4.00
5	1930	18	70	3.88
6	1958	35	126	3.60
7	1970	32	95	2.96
8	1982	52	146	2.81
9=	1962	32	89	2.78
9=	1966	32	89	2.78

The lowest-scoring World Cup was Italia '90 which produced 115 goals from 52 matches at an average of 2.21 per game.

THE 10 TEAMS GIVEN THE MOST YELLOW CARDS IN THE FINAL STAGES OF THE 1990 WORLD CUP

	Country	Cards*
1	Argentina	22 (3)
2	Cameroon	15 (2)
3	Czechoslovakia	13 (1)
4	Austria	11 (1)
5=	Uruguay	9 (0)
5=	Yugoslavia	9 (1)
7=	South Korea	8 (1)
7=	West Germany	8 (1)
9=	Brazil	7 (1)
9=	Romania	7 (0)
9=	United Arab Emirates	7 (1)
9=	USA	7 (1)

* Figures in brackets indicate sendings-off.

The fewest number of yellow cards was two, issued to Belgium. England were given six, the Republic of Ireland four, and Scotland three.

THE 10 LEAST SUCCESSFUL WORLD CUP COUNTRIES

	Country	Tournaments	Matches played	won
1	Bulgaria	5	16	0
2	South Korea	3	8	0
3	El Salvador	2	6	0
4	Republic of Ireland	1	5	0
5	Egypt	2	4	0
6=	Bolivia	2	3	0
6=	Canada	1	3	0
6=	Haiti	1	3	0
6=	Iraq	1	3	0
6=	New Zealand	1	3	0
6=	United Arab Emirates	1	3	0
6=	Zaïre	1	3	0

THE 10 MOST-FOULED PLAYERS IN THE FINAL STAGES OF THE 1990 WORLD CUP

	Player/country	Fouls
1	Diego Maradona (Argentina)	53
2	Paul Gascoigne (England)	27
3=	Roberto Donadoni (Italy)	22
3=	Salvatore Schillaci (Italy)	22
3=	Dragan Stojkovic (Yugoslavia)	22
6	Carlos Valderrama (Colombia)	21
7=	Claudio Caniggia (Argentina)	19
7=	Lothar Matthäus (West Germany)	19
7=	Tomas Skuhravy (Czechoslovakia)	19
10=	Roberto Baggio (Italy)	18
10=	Jurgen Klinsmann (West Germany)	18

Many of Maradona's 'fouls' were, of course, Oscar-winning performances by the 'Master of the Dive'. Sadly, referees gave him the benefit of the doubt all too often and, because the referee's decision is final, his acrobatics and downright deceptions were recorded as 'fouls'. His total of 53 represents an average of 7.57 per game. 'Gazza' was fouled 4.5 times per game.

The Republic of Ireland's most-fouled player was Kevin Moran (11), while Mo Johnston and Maurice Malpas, with five each, were Scotland's most fouled duo.

THE 10 TEAMS THAT COMMITTED THE MOST FOULS IN THE FINAL STAGES OF THE 1990 WORLD CUP

	Country	Fouls
1	Argentina	177
2	Cameroon	136
3	Czechoslovakia	120
4	Italy	115
5	West Germany	114
6	Republic of Ireland	112
7	England	106
8	Yugoslavia	89
9=	Colombia	88
9=	South Korea	88

South Korea effectively had the worst record because they played only three matches and committed a foul once every 3.07 minutes, whereas Argentina did so every 5.77 minutes. England had the best record, committing a foul only once every 6.79 minutes.

QUIZ

FOOTBALL'S WORLD CUP

1 Which was the first country to win the Jules Rimet Trophy twice?
2 Did Jimmy Greaves appear for England in the final stages of the 1966 World Cup?
3 Of all the grounds used for the final stages of the 1966 World Cup, which two were not Football League grounds at the time?
4 Bulgaria has played in 16 matches in the final stages of the World Cup and used a total of 66 players. But why is one of their 1970 stars, Milko Gaidarski, unique among his fellow Bulgarians?
5 Who lost 10–0 to Australia in a qualifying match in August 1981 and the following day conceded 13 goals to New Zealand?
6 Who is the only man to captain and manage World Cup winning teams?
7 Name the three countries that made their World Cup debuts in the final stages in 1990.
8 Which was the last country to win the World Cup on home soil?
9 Who, in 1986, was the last man to score four goals in a single match in the final stages?
10 Name the former referee on the television programme *It's A Knockout* who is also one of just three officials to have sent off three players in the final stages of the World Cup.

Diego Maradona of Argentina, the most-fouled player of the 1990 World Cup, is unfairly challenged by Brazil's Jorginho. The Argentinians won the match 1–0.

ATHLETICS

THE TOP 10 OLYMPIC TRACK AND FIELD GOLD MEDAL WINNING COUNTRIES

	MEN Country	Gold medals		WOMEN Country	Gold medals
1	USA	249	1	USA	36
2	Finland	47	2	USSR/CIS	34
3	Great Britain	42	3	East Germany	25
4	USSR/CIS	37	4	Germany/West Germany	14
5	Sweden	17	5	Australia	11
6	East Germany	14	6	Romania	9
7	Italy	13	7=	Poland	6
8=	Germany/West Germany	12	7=	Holland	6
8=	Kenya	12	9	Great Britain	5
10	Canada	10	10	France	4

THE 10 LONGEST-STANDING CURRENT OLYMPIC RECORDS

	Event	Winning time/distance	Competitor/ nationality	Date
1	Men's long jump	8.90m	Bob Beamon (USA)	18 Oct 1968
2	Men's javelin	94.58m	Miklos Nemeth (Hun)	25 Jul 1976
3	Women's shot	22.41m	Ilona Slupianek (GDR)	24 Jul 1980
4	Women's 800 metres	1min 53.43sec	Nadezhda Olizarenko (USSR)	27 Jul 1980
5	Women's 4 x 100 metres relay	41.60sec	East Germany	1 Aug 1980
6	Women's marathon	2hr 24min 52sec	Joan Benoit (USA)	5 Aug 1984
7	Men's 800 metres	1min 43.00sec	Joaquim Cruz (Bra)	6 Aug 1984
8	Decathlon	8,847 points	Daley Thompson (GB)	9 Aug 1984
9	Men's 100 metres	9.92sec	Carl Lewis (USA)	24 Sep 1988
10	Women's 100 metres	10.54sec	Florence Griffith-Joyner	24 Sep 1988

Bob Beamon's record-breaking jump in 1968 is regarded as one of the greatest achievements in athletics. Admittedly he was aided by Mexico City's rarefied atmosphere, but to add a staggering 55.25cm/21¾in to the old record, and win the competition by 72.39cm/28½in was no mean feat. Beamon's jump of 8.90m/29ft 2½in was the first beyond both 28 and 29 feet (8.53 and 8.84m).

THE TOP 10 INDIVIDUAL OLYMPIC GOLD MEDAL WINNERS*

	Athlete/nationality	Years	Gold medals
1	Ray Ewry (USA)	1900–08	10
2	Paavo Nurmi (Fin)	1920–28	9
3	Carl Lewis (USA)	1984–92	8
4=	Martin Sheridan (USA)	1906–08	5
4=	Ville Ritola (Fin)	1924–28	5
6=	Alvin Kraenzlein (USA)	1900	4
6=	Myer Prinstein (USA)	1900–06	4
6=	Archie Hahn (USA)	1904–06	4
6=	James Lightbody (USA)	1904–06	4
6=	Erik Lemming (Swe)	1906–12	4
6=	Mal Sheppard (USA)	1908–12	4
6=	Hannes Kolehmainen (Fin)	1912–20	4
6=	Jesse Owens (USA)	1936	4
6=	Fanny Blankers-Koen (Hol)	1948	4
6=	Harrison Dillard (USA)	1948–52	4
6=	Emil Zatopek (Cze)	1948–52	4
6=	Betty Cuthbert (Aus)	1956–64	4
6=	Al Oerter (USA)	1956–68	4
6=	Lasse Viren (Fin)	1972–76	4
6=	Bärbel Wöckel (GDR)	1976–80	4

Track and field.

All Ewry's 10 gold medals were in the now discontinued standing jumps (high jump, long jump and triple jump). The most gold medals won at one Olympics is five by Paavo Nurmi in 1924 when he won the 1500 metres, 5000 metres, 3000 metres team race, and team and individual cross-country.

THE 10 LONGEST ATHLETICS EVENTS EVER CONTESTED AT THE OLYMPIC GAMES

	Event	Year(s)	Distance
1	Walk	1932–88	50,000 metres *
2	Marathon	1920	42,750 metres
3	Marathon	1908, 1924–88	42,295 metres
4	Marathon	1906	41,860 metres
5	Marathon	1900	40,260 metres
6	Marathon	1912	40,200 metres
7	Marathon	1896, 1904	40,000 metres
8	Walk	1958–88	20,000 metres
9	Walk	1908	10 miles †
10	Cross-country	1912	12,000 metres

Equivalent to 31.06856 miles.
†*Equivalent to 16.09344 kilometres.*

THE TOP 10 SCORING EVENTS BY DALEY THOMPSON AT THE 1984 OLYMPICS

	Event	Time/distance	Points
1	Pole vault	5.00m	1,052
2	Long jump	8.01m	1,022
3	400 metres	46.97sec	950
4	100 metres	10.44sec	948
5	110 metres hurdles	14.33sec*	923
6	High jump	2.03m	882
7	Shot put	15.72m	831
8	Javelin	65.24m	824
9	Discus	46.56m	810
10	1500 metres	4min 35.00sec	556

Thompson's time for the hurdles was originally given as 14.34 seconds and worth 922 points, but this was subsequently amended by the IAAF in 1986.

Daley Thompson carried off his second successive Olympic decathlon title at Los Angeles in 1984 and in the process equalled Jürgen Hingsen's world record of 8,798 points. However, new tables were introduced in 1985 and when Thompson's figures were recalculated they came out at 8,847 points, which gave him the world record outright. These are his top 10 events at the 1984 Olympics according to points earned in each discipline.

The first over the line in 1908 was Dorando Pietri of Italy who came home 32 seconds ahead of John Hayes. However, Pietri, in a state of collapse, received help over the line and was subsequently disqualified. It was the first time the now standard marathon distance of 26 miles 385 yards was used. The biggest winning margin was in the first-ever Olympic marathon in 1896 when Spiridon Louis of Greece beat his compatriot Charilaos Vasilakos by 7 minutes 13 seconds.

Daley Thompson, the greatest decathlete of all time, on his way to a second Olympic title and the world record at the 1984 Los Angeles Games.

THE 10 SMALLEST WINNING MARGINS IN THE MEN'S MARATHON AT THE OLYMPIC GAMES

	Year	Winner	Runner-up	Margin (sec)
1	1920	Hannes Kolehmainen (Fin)	Jüri Lossmann (Est)	12.8
2	1988	Gelindo Bordin (Ita)	Douglas Wakiihuri (Ken)	15.0
3	1948	Delfo Cabrera (Arg)	Tom Richards (GB)	16.0
4	1980	Waldemar Cierpinski (GDR)	Gerald Nijboer (Hol)	17.0
5	1932	Juan Carlos Zabala (Arg)	Sam Ferris (GB)	19.0
6	1992	Hwang Young-cho (SK)	Koichi Morishita (Jap)	22.0
7	1960	Abebe Bikila (Eth)	Rhadi Ben Abdesselem (Mor)	25.4
8	1928	Boughéra El Quafi (Fra)	Miguel Plaza Reyes (Chi)	26.0
9	1984	Carlos Lopes (Por)	John Treacy (Ire)	35.0
10	1908	John Hayes (USA)	Charles Hefferon (SA)	47.6

THE FIRST 10 ATHLETES TO RUN A MILE IN UNDER FOUR MINUTES

	Athlete/nationality	Location	Time min:sec	Date
1	Roger Bannister (GB)	Oxford	3:59.4	6 May 1954
2	John Landy (Aus)	Turku, Finland	3:57.9	21 Jun 1954
3	Laszlo Tabori (Hun)	London	3:59.0	28 May 1955
4=	Chris Chataway (GB)	London	3:59.8	28 May 1955
4=	Brian Hewson (GB)	London	3:59.8	28 May 1955
6	Jim Bailey (Aus)	Los Angeles	3:58.6	5 May 1956
7	Gunnar Nielsen (Den)	Compton, USA	3:59.1	1 Jun 1956
8	Ron Delany (Ire)	Compton, USA	3:59.4	1 Jun 1956
9	Derek Ibbotson (GB)	London	3:59.4	6 Aug 1956
10	István Rózsavölgyi (Hun)	Budapest	3:59.0	26 Aug 1956

Within a little over two years of Roger Bannister's capturing the imagination of the world by shattering the four-minute-mile barrier, the number of athletes to do so had risen to 10, although none had succeeded in lopping more than two seconds off the record.

The time has been progressively reduced in subsequent years, however, by athletes such as Sebastian Coe (representing Great Britain and Northern Ireland), who at Brussels on 28 August 1981 ran the mile in 3 minutes 47.33 seconds. The world record is currently held by Steve Cram (GB) who at Oslo, Norway, on 27 July 1985 brought the time down to 3 minutes 46.32 seconds – 13.08 seconds faster than Bannister.

Chris Chataway, equal 4th in this list, was runner-up to Bannister when he first broke the four-minute barrier. He was also in second place behind John Landy when he became the next man to run the distance in less than four minutes.

The only other occasion on which Bannister ran the mile in under four minutes was at the 1954 Vancouver Commonwealth Games when he beat Landy in what was heralded as the 'Race of the Century'. It certainly lived up to its billing, with Bannister winning in 3 minutes 58.8 seconds.

Roger Bannister takes the tape ahead of Australia's John Landy at the 1954 Commonwealth Games, the only other time he ran the mile in under four minutes.

THE PROGRESSION OF THE WORLD MILE RECORD SINCE BANNISTER'S FIRST SUB-FOUR MINUTE MILE

Athlete/nationality	Venue	Date	Time min:sec
Roger Bannister (GB)	Oxford, England	6 May 1954	3:59.4
John Landy (Aus)	Turku, Finland	21 Jun 1954	3:58.0
Derek Ibbotson (GB)	London, England	19 Jul 1957	3:57.2
Herb Elliott (Aus)	Dublin, Ireland	6 Aug 1958	3:54.5
Peter Snell (NZ)	Wanganui, New Zealand	27 Jan 1962	3:54.4
Peter Snell (NZ)	Auckland, New Zealand	17 Nov 1964	3:54.1
Michel Jazy (Fra)	Rennes, France	9 Jun 1965	3:53.6
Jim Ryun (USA)	Berkeley, USA	17 Jul 1966	3:51.3
Jim Ryun (USA)	Bakersfield, USA	23 Jun 1967	3:51.1
Filbert Bayi (Tan)	Kingston, Jamaica	17 May 1975	3:51.0
John Walker (NZ)	Gothenburg, Sweden	12 Aug 1975	3:49.4
Sebastian Coe (GB)	Oslo, Norway	17 Jul 1979	3:49.0
Steve Ovett (GB)	Oslo, Norway	1 Jul 1980	3:48.8
Sebastian Coe (GB)	Zurich, Switzerland	19 Aug 1981	3:48.53
Steve Ovett (GB)	Koblenz, Germany	26 Aug 1981	3:48.40
Sebastian Coe (GB)	Brussels, Belgium	28 Aug 1981	3:47.33
Steve Cram (GB)	Oslo, Norway	27 Jul 1985	3:46.32

THE 10 FASTEST MILES EVER RUN

The mile is the only imperial distance recognized by the IAAF for world record purposes. John Paul Jones of the United States was the first official world record-holder when he covered 1,760 yards in 4 minutes 14.4 seconds at Cambridge, Massachusetts, on 1 May 1913.

In recent years British runners have dominated the event but the first British world record-holder was Sydney Wooderson who knocked four-tenths of a second off the old record at Motspur Park on 28 August 1937, setting a new record at 4 minutes 6.4 seconds. Wooderson held the record for five years before losing it to the Swede Gunder Hägg who lost and regained the record twice.

Hägg held it for nine years from 1945 until May 1954 when, at Iffley Road, Oxford, Roger Bannister took the record under four minutes for the first time when he clocked 3 minutes 59.4 seconds.

Since then several 'mile milestones' have been reached: Herb Elliott at Dublin in 1958 was the first to take the record under 3 minutes 55 seconds, and John Walker in 1975 was the first to run the distance in under 3 minutes 50 seconds. Since then the record has fallen gradually until Britain's Steve Cram established the current world record of 3 minutes 46.32 seconds at Oslo on 27 July 1985. The 10 fastest miles have been:

The women's world record of 4 minutes 15.61 seconds was established by Paula Ivan of Romania at Nice on 10 July 1989.

	Athlete/nationality	Venue	Date	Time min:sec
1	Steve Cram (GB)	Oslo	27 Jul 1985	3:46.32
2	Saïd Aouita (Mor)	Helsinki	2 Jul 1987	3:46.76
3	Saïd Aouita (Mor)	Zurich	21 Aug 1985	3:46.92
4	Sebastian Coe (GB)	Brussels	28 Aug 1981	3:47.33
5	Steve Scott (USA)	Oslo	7 Jul 1982	3:47.69
6	José Luis Gonzalez (Spa)	Oslo	27 Jul 1985	3:47.79
7	Steve Cram (GB)	Oslo	5 Jul 1986	3:48.31
8	Steve Ovett (GB)	Koblenz	26 Aug 1981	3:48.40
9=	Sebastian Coe (GB)	Zurich	19 Aug 1981	3:48.53
9=	Steve Scott (USA)	Oslo	26 Jun 1982	3:48.53

THE 10 FASTEST WINNING TIMES IN THE BOSTON MARATHON

	Winner/nationality	Year	Time hr:min:sec
1	Rob de Castella (Aus)	1986	2:07:51
2	Ibrahim Hussein (Ken)	1992	2:08:14
3	Gelindo Bordin (Ita)	1990	2:08:19
4	Ibrahim Hussein (Ken)	1988	2:08:43
5	Alberto Salazar (USA)	1982	2:08:52
6	Greg Meyer (USA)	1983	2:09:00
7	Abebe Mekonnen (Eth)	1989	2:09:06
8	Toshihiko Seko (Jap)	1981	2:09:26
9	Bill Rodgers (USA)	1979	2:09:27
10	Bill Rodgers (USA)	1975	2:09:55

The Boston Marathon is the oldest regularly contested marathon in the United States. Run annually on Patriots' Day each April, it was first contested in 1897. Clarence De Mar of Massachusetts won the race a record seven times between 1911 and 1930.

THE 10 FASTEST WINNING TIMES IN THE NEW YORK CITY MARATHON

	Winner/nationality	Year	Time hr:min:sec
1	Juma Ikangaa (Tan)	1989	2:08:01
2	Alberto Salazar (USA)	1981	2:08:13
3	Steve Jones (GB)	1988	2:08:20
4	Rod Dixon (NZ)	1983	2:08:59
5	Salvador Garcia (Mex)	1991	2:09:28
6	Alberto Salazar (USA)	1982	2:09:29
7	Alberto Salazar (USA)	1980	2:09:41
8	Bill Rodgers (USA)	1976	2:10:09
9	Ibrahim Hussein (Ken)	1987	2:11:01
10	Gianni Poli (Ita)	1986	2:11:06

First held in 1970, the New York Marathon takes in the city's five boroughs and finishes in Central Park. Bill Rodgers has won the men's race a record four times while Norway's Grete Waitz has won the women's race nine times. The fastest time by a woman is 2 hours 25 minutes 29 seconds by Allison Roe (NZ) in 1981.

THE 10 FASTEST MEN'S TIMES IN THE LONDON MARATHON

	Runner/nationality	Year	Time hr:min:sec
1	Steve Jones (GB)	1985	2:08:16
2	Charlie Spedding (GB)	1985	2:08:33
3	Douglas Wakiihuri (Ken)	1989	2:09:03
4	Steve Moneghetti (Aus)	1989	2:09:06
5	Ahmed Salah (Dji)	1989	2:09:09
6	Alister Hutton (GB)	1985	2:09:16
7	Iakov Tolstikov (USSR)	1991	2:09:17
8	Christoph Herle (FRG)	1985	2:09:23
9	Hugh Jones (GB)	1982	2:09:24
10=	Mike Gratton (GB)	1983	2:09:43
10=	Henrik Jorgensen (Den)	1985	2:09:43
10=	Manuel Mattias (Por)	1989	2:09:43

THE 10 FASTEST WOMEN'S TIMES IN THE LONDON MARATHON

	Runner/nationality	Year	Time hr:min:sec
1	Ingrid Kristiansen (Nor)	1985	2:21:06
2	Ingrid Kristiansen (Nor)	1987	2:22:48
3	Ingrid Kristiansen (Nor)	1984	2:24:26
4	Grete Waitz (Nor)	1986	2:24:54
5	Grete Waitz (Nor)	1983	2:25:29
6	Ingrid Kristiansen (Nor)	1988	2:25:41
7	Veronique Marot (GB)	1989	2:25:56
8	Rosa Mota (Por)	1991	2:26:14
9	Wanda Panfil (Pol)	1990	2:26:31
10	Priscilla Welch (GB)	1987	2:26:51

The marathon is one of international athletics' most prestigious events. Its history dates to 490BC when the Greeks enjoyed their first victory over the Persians. The battle was won at Marathon and a young messenger named Pheidippides was sent the 24 or so miles to Athens to pass on the good news to the Athenians. Having arrived, staggering and nearly breathless, he passed on the words, 'Rejoice, we conquer'. With that the unfortunate messenger collapsed and died. Thankfully all marathons don't end *that* way.

In view of its history, it was thought fitting to include the race as one of the events at the first modern Olympics, held in 1896, its inclusion being largely as a result of the efforts of a French scholar, Michel Bréal. Appropriately, the first Olympic marathon was run between Marathon and Athens and measured 40 kilometres.

There was no standard distance for the marathon in the early days of the Olympics and the first time the present distance of 26 miles 385 yards was used was in 1908 when the race was from Windsor Castle to the White City. To enable the royal children to watch the start of the race, the starting line was moved beneath their bedroom window and when measured the race distance was found to be 26 miles 385 yards. Since 1924 this has been the distance for all Olympic marathons and is the recognized distance for all major races worldwide.

THE 10 FASTEST MEN'S MARATHONS OF ALL TIME

	Athlete/nationality	Venue	Date	Time* hr:min:sec
1	Belayneh Dinsamo (Eth)	Rotterdam	17 Apr 1988	2:06:50
2	Ahmed Salah (Dji)	Rotterdam	17 Apr 1988	2:07:07
3	Carlos Lopes (Por)	Rotterdam	20 Apr 1985	2:07:12
4	Steve Jones (GB)	Chicago	20 Oct 1985	2:07:13
5=	Taisuke Kodama (Jap)	Beijing	19 Oct 1986	2:07:35
5=	Abebe Mekonnen (Eth)	Beijing	16 Oct 1988	2:07:35
7	Hiromi Taniguchi (Jap)	Beijing	16 Oct 1988	2:07:40
8	Rob de Castella (Aus)	Boston	21 Apr 1986	2:07:51
9	Kunimitsu Itoh (Jap)	Beijing	19 Oct 1986	2:07:57
10	Juma Ikangaa (Tan)	New York	5 Nov 1989	2:08:01

Because courses vary so much, world records for the marathon are not recognized by the IAAF, which registers only world 'best' times.

THE TOP 10 COUNTRIES AT THE WORLD CROSS-COUNTRY CHAMPIONSHIPS*

	Country	Men individual	team	Women individual	team	Total
1	Kenya	5	7	0	1†	13
2	USA	2	0	4	6	12
3	Ethiopia	2	5	0	2†	9
4=	England	0	3	2	3	8
4=	USSR	0	0	0	8	8
6	Norway	0	0	6	0	6
7	Belgium	2	3	0	0	5
8=	France	0	1	2	0	3
8=	Portugal	3	0	0	0	3
8=	Romania	0	0	2	1	3

Based on wins in the men's, women's and team events.
†*Kenya and Ethiopia shared the women's team title in 1991.*

The championships were inaugurated in 1903 but only runners from the four home countries competed in the eight-mile event at Hamilton Park racecourse in Scotland. It became more of an international event in the 1920s. The first women's race did not take place until 1967 and in 1973 the championships gained official recognition when the IAAF took them under their control. This Top 10 is therefore based only on performances since 1973 since it would otherwise favour the four home countries, and in particular England, which provided 34 winners of the men's race between 1903 and 1972. In fact there has not been an English winner of the men's race since David Bedford triumphed in 1971. Zola Budd, however, won the women's race for England in 1985 and 1986.

THE 10 LONGEST LONG JUMPS

Since Bob Beamon increased the world record by a staggering 55.25cm/1ft 9¾in during the 1968 Mexico Olympics, many men have been trying to get within sight of the world record they said 'would never be beaten in the twentieth century'. But during the 1991 World Championships at Tokyo the 'unbeatable' world record was eventually broken when American Mike Powell jumped a remarkable 8.95m/29ft 4½in. (It was widely expected that his compatriot Carl Lewis would, if anybody, be the man to erase Beamon's mark, and just a few minutes before Powell's record-breaking leap, Lewis did exceed the old distance by one centimetre – but his effort was ruled invalid because of wind assistance.) Beamon's record remained for nearly 23 years but that is not the longest period for which the long jump record has stood: Jesse Owens was the record-holder for 25 years and 104 days between 1935 and 1960.

The women's world record of 7.52m/24ft 8¾in was established by Galina Chistyakova (USSR) at Leningrad on 11 June 1988.

	Athlete/nationality	Location	Date	Distance (m)
1	Mike Powell (USA)	Tokyo	30 Aug 1991	8.95
2	Bob Beamon (USA)	Mexico City	18 Oct 1968	8.90
3	Robert Emmiyan (USSR)	Tsakhadzor	22 May 1987	8.86
4=	Carl Lewis (USA)	Indianapolis	19 Jun 1983	8.79
4=	Carl Lewis (USA)	New York*	27 Jan 1984	8.79
6=	Carl Lewis (USA)	Indianapolis	24 Jul 1982	8.76
6=	Carl Lewis (USA)	Indianapolis	18 Jul 1988	8.76
8	Carl Lewis (USA)	Indianapolis	16 Aug 1987	8.75
9	Larry Myricks (USA)	Indianapolis	18 Jul 1988	8.74
10	Carl Lewis (USA)	Seoul	26 Sep 1988	8.72

*Indoors.

Bob Beamon's record-breaking leap of 8.90m in the 1968 Mexico Olympics.

The women's world record of 2.09m/6ft 10in was established by Stefka Kostadinova of Bulgaria at Rome on 30 August 1987.

THE 10 HIGHEST HIGH JUMPS

	Athlete/nationality	Location	Date	Height (m)
1	Javier Sotomayor (Cub)	San Juan	29 Jul 1989	2.44
2=	Javier Sotomayor (Cub)	Salamanca	8 Sep 1988	2.43
2=	Javier Sotomayor (Cub)	Budapest*	4 Mar 1989	2.43
4=	Patrick Sjöberg (Swe)	Stockholm	30 Jun 1987	2.42
4=	Carlo Thränhardt (FRG)	Berlin*	26 Feb 1988	2.42
6=	Igor Paklin (USSR)	Kobe	4 Sep 1985	2.41
6=	Patrick Sjöberg (Swe)	Piraeus*	1 Feb 1987	2.41
8=	Rudolf Povarnitsyn (USSR)	Donetsk	11 Aug 1985	2.40
8=	Carlo Thränhardt (FRG)	Simmerath*	16 Jan 1987	2.40
8=	Patrick Sjöberg (Swe)	Berlin*	27 Feb 1987	2.40
8=	Javier Sotomayor (Cub)	Havana	12 Mar 1989	2.40
8=	Patrick Sjöberg (Swe)	Brussels	5 Aug 1989	2.40
8=	Javier Sotomayor (Cub)	Bogota	13 Aug 1989	2.40
8=	Sorin Matei (Rom)	Bratislava	20 Jun 1990	2.40
8=	Hollis Conway (USA)	Seville*	10 Mar 1991	2.40
8=	Javier Sotomayor (Cub)	St Denis	19 Jul 1991	2.40
8=	Charles Austin (USA)	Zurich	7 Aug 1991	2.40

*Indoors.

This event has been dominated by Sergey Bubka who has broken 29 world outdoor and indoor records since January 1984 and was the first man to take the world record beyond the magical 20-foot (6.096-metre) mark. The Top 10 highest vaults is, almost uniquely in athletic history, synonymous with his personal best chart.

THE 10 HIGHEST POLE VAULTS

	Athlete/nationality	Venue	Date	Height (m)
1	Sergey Bubka (CIS)	Berlin*	21 Feb 1992	6.13
2	Sergey Bubka (USSR)	Grenoble*	23 Mar 1991	6.12
3=	Sergey Bubka (USSR)	Donetsk*	19 Mar 1991	6.11
3=	Sergey Bubka (CIS)	Dijon	13 Jun 1992	6.11
5=	Sergey Bubka (USSR)	San Sebastian*	15 Mar 1991	6.10
5=	Sergey Bubka (USSR)	Malmo	5 Aug 1991	6.10
7	Sergey Bubka (USSR)	Formia	8 Jul 1991	6.09
8=	Sergey Bubka (USSR)	Volgograd*	9 Feb 1991	6.08
8=	Sergey Bubka (USSR)	Moscow	9 Jun 1991	6.08
10	Sergey Bubka (USSR)	Shizuoka	6 May 1991	6.07

* Indoors.

THE 10 FASTEST MEN ON EARTH

In clocking 9.86 seconds in the final of the 100 metres at the 3rd IAAF World Championships at Tokyo in 1991, Carl Lewis of the United States rightly claimed to be the fastest man on earth, by knocking four-hundreths of a second off the old record. The race was the fastest-ever 100 metres because four of the eight finalists appear in the first five places of this Top 10. The 10 fastest men of all time have been:

	Athlete/nationality	Venue	Date	Time (sec)
1	Carl Lewis (USA)	Tokyo	25 Aug 1991	9.86
2	Leroy Burrell (USA)	Tokyo	25 Aug 1991	9.88
3=	Dennis Mitchell (USA)	Tokyo	25 Aug 1991	9.91
3=	Davidson Ezinwa (Nig)	Azusa	11 Apr 1992	9.91
5	Linford Christie (GB)	Tokyo	25 Aug 1991	9.92
6=	Calvin Smith (USA)	Colorado Springs	3 Jul 1983	9.93
6=	Mike Marsh (USA)	Walnut	18 Apr 1992	9.93
8=	Jim Hines (USA)	Mexico City	14 Oct 1968	9.95
8=	Frankie Fredericks (Nam)	Tokyo	25 Aug 1991	9.95
10=	Mel Lattany (USA)	Athens, GA	5 May 1984	9.96
10=	Ray Stewart (Jam)	Tokyo	25 Aug 1991	9.96

Ben Johnson clocked 9.79 seconds during the 1988 Seoul Olympic Games, but his record was not allowed to stand as a result of his disqualification for drug abuse.

The fastest-ever 100 metres, with wind assistance, was at Indianapolis on 16 July 1988, when Carl Lewis was timed at 9.78 seconds but he had the benefit of wind assistance measuring 5.2m/17ft per second.

THE 10 FASTEST WOMEN ON EARTH*

	Athlete/nationality	Venue	Date	Time (sec)
1	Florence Griffith-Joyner (USA)	Indianapolis	16 Jul 1988	10.49
2	Evelyn Ashford (USA)	Zurich	22 Aug 1984	10.76
3=	Dawn Sowell (USA)	Provo	3 Jun 1989	10.78
3=	Merlene Ottey (Jam)	Seville	30 May 1990	10.78
5=	Marlies Göhr (GDR)	Berlin	8 Jun 1983	10.81
5=	Irina Privalova (CIS)	Moscow	22 Jun 1992	10.81
7	Gail Devers (USA)	Barcelona	1 Aug 1992	10.82
8=	Marita Koch (GDR)	Berlin	8 Jun 1983	10.83
8=	Sheila Echols (USA)	Indianapolis	16 Jul 1988	10.83
8=	Juliet Cuthbert (Jam)	Barcelona	1 Aug 1992	10.83

*Over 100 metres.

Florence Griffith-Joyner has actually recorded the four fastest-ever times for the 100 metres. In addition to the figure in this list, she has recorded times of 10.61, 10.62 and 10.70 seconds, all in 1988.

THE 10 LONGEST-STANDING OUTDOOR WORLD RECORDS

	Event	Record-holder/ nationality	Time/distance	Date set
1	Men's 4 x 1500 metres relay	West Germany	14min 38.8sec	17 Aug 1977
2	Men's 50km walk	Raul Gonzalez (Mex)	3hr 41min 38.4sec	25 May 1979
3	Men's 200 metres	Pietro Mennea (Ita)	19.72sec	12 Sep 1979
4	Women's 4 x 200 metres relay	East Germany	1min 28.15sec	9 Aug 1980
5	Women's 1500 metres	Tatyana Kazankina (USSR)	3min 52.47sec	13 Aug 1980
6	Men's 25 kilometres	Toshihiko Seko (Jap)	1hr 13min 55.8sec	22 Mar 1981*
7	Men's 30 kilometres	Toshihiko Seko (Jap)	1hr 29min 18.7sec	22 Mar 1981*
8	Women's one hour	Silvan Cruciata (Ita)	18,084m	4 May 1981
9	Men's 800 metres	Sebastian Coe (GB)	1min 41.73sec	10 Jun 1981
10	Men's 1000 metres	Sebastian Coe (GB)	2min 12.18sec	11 Jul 1981

* Records set in the same race.

AUSTRALIAN RULES FOOTBALL

THE 10 MOST SUCCESSFUL AUSTRALIAN FOOTBALL LEAGUE TEAMS

The Australian Football League, known as the Victoria Football League (VFL) until 1990, was formed in 1896 when six clubs broke away from the Victoria Football Association. Since 1897 a championship game has been staged to decide the VFL champions and Grand Final day is one of Australia's great sporting occasions. As a result of teams from Queensland and New South Wales being admitted into the VFL, it changed its name to the Australian Football League. Apart from the teams listed here, the only other winners have been Footscray and St Kilda.

	Team	Wins
1	Carlton	15
2=	Collingwood	14
2=	Essendon	14
4	Melbourne	12
5	Richmond	10
6	Hawthorn	9
7	Fitzroy	8
8	Geelong	6
9	South Melbourne	3
10	North Melbourne	2

Carlton, the most successful Australian Football League team, take on North Melbourne, 10th on the list.

AWARDS

THE TOP 10 SPORTS REPRESENTED IN THE BBC SPORTS PERSONALITY OF THE YEAR AWARD

	Sport	No. of winners
1	Athletics	13
2=	Boxing	3
2=	Cricket	3
2=	Ice skating	3
2=	Motor racing	3
6=	Equestrianism	2
6=	Golf	2
6=	Lawn tennis	2
6=	Soccer	2
6=	Swimming	2

THE TOP 10 SPORTS REPRESENTED IN THE JAMES E. SULLIVAN AWARD

	Sport	No. of winners
1	Athletics	36
2	Swimming and diving	12
3=	Basketball	2
3=	Golf	2
3=	Ice skating	2
3=	Rowing	2
7=	All-rounders	1
7=	American football	1
7=	Baseball	1
7=	Gymnastics	1
7=	Lawn tennis	1

Made annually each December, the winner of this award is decided by a poll among BBC television viewers. The first award, made in 1954, was won by athlete Chris Chataway. The only person to win the award twice is boxer Henry Cooper (1967 and 1970). The 1971 winner was HRH Princess Anne, following her achievement of winning the European Three Day Event championship at Burghley.

Cycling, motorcycling and snooker have each provided one winner.

The award is made annually to the American sportsman or woman who has contributed most to good sportsmanship. The trophy is in memory of James E. Sullivan, the president of the American Athletic Union (AAU) from 1906 to 1914. The first award, in 1930, was won by amateur golfer Robert Tyre 'Bobby' Jones who captured the Amateur and Open titles of both the United States and Great Britain to achieve one of sport's greatest Grand Slams.

Recent winners include track and field champions Florence Griffith-Joyner, Ed Moses, Mary Decker and Carl Lewis. Only one man, Jim Ryun in 1966, has won the *Sports Illustrated* and Sullivan awards in the same year.

QUIZ

AWARD WINNERS

1 What is the award given to the top League goalscorer in European football each year?
2 Which sport presents the Con Smythe Trophy each year?
3 Who in 1962 became the first woman to win the BBC Sports Personality of the Year Award?
4 Paul Gascoigne in 1990 was only the second footballer to win the BBC Sports Personality Award. Who was the first?
5 Which Briton was the first recipient of the European Player of the Year Award in 1955?
6 To whom is the Ritz Trophy awarded annually?

7 Name the current British-based jockey who was *Sports Illustrated*'s Sportsman of the Year in 1977.
8 The British Sportswriters have been making annual sportsmen and women awards since 1975. The first time both winners were from the same sport was in 1984 when Seb Coe won the men's award. Who won the women's award that year?
9 Who is the only British footballer to win the Football Writers' Player of the Year Award, PFA Player of the Year Award, and European Player of the Year Award?
10 In cricket, to whom is the Lawrence Trophy awarded annually?

THE TOP 10 SPORTS REPRESENTED IN THE *SPORTS ILLUSTRATED* SPORTSMAN OF THE YEAR AWARD

	Sport	No. of winners
1=	Athletics	7
1=	Baseball	7
3	Basketball	5
4=	American football	4
4=	Golf	4
6=	Boxing	3
6=	Ice hockey	3
8	Lawn tennis	2
9=	'Athletes Who Care'	1
9=	Cycling	1
9=	Gymnastics	1
9=	Horse racing	1
9=	Motor racing	1

The first winner of this award, which was launched in 1954, was British athlete Roger Bannister. He is one of just two British winners, the other being racing driver Jackie Stewart in 1973. The 1987 award was won by 'Athletes Who Care'. The award has been shared on three occasions, in 1972, 1979 and 1984.

BADMINTON

THE 10 MEN WITH THE MOST ALL-ENGLAND CHAMPIONSHIP SINGLES WINS

The All-England Championships were for many years regarded as badminton's foremost event and are today still held in high esteem. The event (doubles only) was first staged in 1899, and the singles championship was launched the following year.

Between 1903 and 1928 George Thomas won a record 21 titles at singles and doubles. The Thomas Cup, the sport's premier international team event, is named after the trophy which he presented.

	Player/nationality	Years	Titles
1	Rudy Hartono (Ina)	1968–76	8
2	Erland Kops (Den)	1958–67	7
3	Frank Devlin (Ire)	1925–31	6
4	Ralph Nichols (Eng)	1932–38	5
5=	George Thomas (Eng)	1920–23	4
5=	Wong Peng Soon (Mal)	1950–55	4
5=	Eddie Choong (Mal)	1953–57	4
5=	Morten Frost (Den)	1982–87	4
9=	Henry Marrett (Eng)	1904–08	3
9=	Liem Swie King (Ina)	1978–81	3

THE 10 WOMEN WITH THE MOST ALL-ENGLAND CHAMPIONSHIP SINGLES WINS

	Player/nationality	Years	Titles
1	Judy Hashman (*née* Devlin) (USA)	1954–67	10
2	Meriel Lucas (Eng)	1902–10	6
3=	Ethel Thomson (Eng)	1900–06	5
3=	Marjorie Barrett (Eng)	1926–31	5
5	Kitty McKane (Eng)	1920–24	4
6=	Margaret Tragett (*née* Larminie) (Eng)	1911–28	3
6=	Lavinia Radeglia (Eng)	1913–23	3
6=	Hiroe Yuki (Jap)	1974–77	3
9=	Leonie Kingsbury (Eng)	1932–34	2
9=	Thelma Kingsbury (Eng)	1936–37	2
9=	Marie Ussing (Den)	1947–53	2
9=	Aase Jacobsen (Den)	1949–51	2
9=	Tonny Olsen-Ahm (Den)	1950–52	2
9=	Margaret Varner (USA)	1955–56	2
9=	Eva Twedberg (Swe)	1968–71	2
9=	Gillian Gilks (Eng)	1976–78	2
9=	Lene Köppen (Den)	1979–80	2
9=	Zang Ailing (Chn)	1982–83	2
9=	Li Lingwei (Chn)	1984–89	2
9=	Susi Susanti (Ina)	1990–91	2

Meriel Lucas and Judy Hashman (*née* Devlin) each won a record 17 women's titles at singles and doubles. Kitty McKane, winner of four titles between 1920 and 1924, was also the women's singles champion at Wimbledon on two occasions and was the holder of both titles in 1924.

The World Championship was launched as recently as 1977. Originally it was held every three years but since 1985 has been a biennial event. China, Indonesia and South Korea have dominated the seven championships held so far.

Park Joo-bong of South Korea, holder of the most badminton world titles.

THE 10 PLAYERS WITH THE MOST WORLD TITLES

	Player/nationality	Male/female	Titles
1	Park Joo-bong (SK)	M	5
2=	Han Aiping (Chn)	F	3
2=	Li Lingwei (Chn)	F	3
2=	Guan Weizhan (Chn)	F	3
2=	Lin Ying (Chn)	F	3
6=	Tian Bingyi (Chn)	M	2
6=	Hadinata Christian (Ina)	M	2
6=	Lene Köppen (Den)	F	2
6=	Kim Moon-soo (SK)	M	2
6=	Chung Myung-hee (SK)	F	2
6=	Nora Perry (Eng)	F	2
6=	Yang Yang (Chn)	M	2
6=	Li Yongbo (Chn)	M	2

BASEBALL

THE 10 TEAMS WITH THE MOST WORLD SERIES WINS

	Team*	Wins
1	New York Yankees	22
2=	Philadelphia/Kansas City/Oakland Athletics	9
2=	St Louis Cardinals	9
4	Brooklyn/Los Angeles Dodgers	6
5=	Boston Red Sox	5
5=	Cincinnati Reds	5
5=	New York/San Francisco Giants	5
5=	Pittsburgh Pirates	5
9	Detroit Tigers	4
10	St Louis/Baltimore Orioles	3

*Teams separated by / indicate changes of franchise and are regarded as the same team for Major League record purposes.

Major League baseball in the United States started with the forming of the National League in 1876. The rival American League was started in 1901, and two years later Pittsburgh, champions of the National League, invited American League champions Boston to take part in a best-of-nine games series to establish the 'real' champions. Boston won 5–3. The following year the National League champions, New York, refused to play Boston and there was no World Series. However, it was resumed in 1905 and has been held every year since. It has been a best-of-seven games series since 1905, with the exception of 1919–21 when it reverted to a nine-game series.

THE TOP 10 AVERAGE ATTENDANCES IN MAJOR LEAGUE BASEBALL IN 1990

	Club	AL/NL	Average attendance
1	Toronto Blue Jays	AL	47,966
2	Los Angeles Dodgers	NL	37,067
3	Oakland Athletics	AL	36,253
4	New York Mets	NL	35,490
5	St Louis Cardinals	NL	31,772
6	Boston Red Sox	AL	31,612
7	California Angels	AL	31,552
8	Cincinnati Reds	NL	30,781
9	Baltimore Orioles	AL	30,572
10	Chicago Cubs	NL	29,140

The combined average for the American League (AL) and National League (NL) was 26,637. A total of 54,871,718 people were said to have watched the 2,060 games, but this is impossible to confirm since the AL and NL use different methods of enumerating attendances, the AL, for example, reckoning 'attendance' by tickets sold (whether or not seats are occupied) while the NL counts actual spectators.

THE FIRST 10 PLAYERS TO HIT FOUR HOME RUNS IN ONE GAME

	Player	Club	Date
1	Bobby Lowe	Boston	30 May 1884
2	Ed Delahanty	Philadelphia	13 Jul 1896
3	Lou Gehrig	New York	3 Jun 1932
4	Chuck Klein	Philadelphia	10 Jul 1936
5	Pat Seerey	Chicago	18 Jul 1948
6	Gil Hodges	Brooklyn	31 Aug 1950
7	Joe Adcock	Milwaukee	31 Jul 1954
8	Rocky Colavito	Cleveland	10 Jun 1959
9	Willie Mays	San Francisco	30 Apr 1961
10	Mike Schmidt	Philadelphia	17 Apr 1976

The only other player to score four homers in one game is Bob Horner, who did so for Atlanta on 6 July 1986.

THE FIRST 10 PITCHERS TO THROW PERFECT GAMES

	Player	Match	Date
1	Lee Richmond	Worcester v Cleveland	12 Jun 1880
2	Monte Ward	Provident v Boston	17 Jun 1880
3	Cy Young	Boston v Philadelphia	5 May 1904
4	Adrian Joss	Cleveland v Chicago	2 Oct 1908
5	Ernie Shore*	Boston v Washington	23 Jun 1917
6	Charlie Robertson	Chicago v Detroit	30 Apr 1922
7	Don Larson†	New York v Brooklyn	8 Oct 1956
8	Harvey Haddix‡	Pittsburgh v Milwaukee	26 May 1959
9	Jim Bunning	Philadelphia v New York	21 Jun 1964
10	Sandy Koufax	Los Angeles v Chicago	9 Sep 1965

Shore came in as Boston's pitcher only after Babe Ruth was thrown out of the game for punching umpire Brick Owens. Washington's opening bat, Ray Morgan, who had walked to first base, was then out, caught walking, and Shore dismissed the remaining 26 batters. He is still credited with a perfect game.
†*Larson's perfect game was, uniquely, in the World Series.*
‡*Haddix actually pitched 12 perfect innings before losing in the 13th. Milwaukee won the game 1–0.*

Fifteen pitchers have thrown perfect games; that is, they have pitched in all nine innings, dismissing 27 opposing batters, and without conceding a run.

The last player to pitch a perfect innings was Denis Martinez for the Montreal Expos against the Los Angeles Dodgers on 28 July 1991.

THE 10 LARGEST MAJOR LEAGUE BALLPARKS*

	Stadium	Home team	Capacity
1	Cleveland Stadium	Cleveland Indians	77,797
2	Yankee Stadium	New York Yankees	67,224
3	Anaheim Stadium	California Angels	65,158
4	Olympic Stadium	Montreal Expos	60,011
5	The Kingdome	Seattle Mariners	59,438
6	San Diego/Jack Murphy Stadium	San Diego Padres	59,192
7	Candlestick Park	San Francisco Giants	59,083
8	Veterans Stadium	Philadelphia Phillies	56,581
9	Dodger Stadium	Los Angeles Dodgers	56,000
10	Three Rivers Stadium	Pittsburgh Pirates	50,235

By capacity.

Stadium capacities vary constantly, some being adjusted according to the event: Veterans Stadium, for example, holds 56,581 for baseball games and 66,592 for football matches. Baseball's newest ballpark, the New Comiskey Park, home of the Chicago White Sox, was opened on 18 April 1991 and has a capacity of 43,000.

THE 10 BIGGEST BALLPARKS IN MAJOR LEAGUE BASEBALL*

	Stadium	Home team	Distance (ft)
1	Tiger Stadium	Detroit Tigers	440
2	Candlestick Park	San Francisco Giants	420
3	Yankee Stadium	New York Yankees	417
4	Busch Stadium	St Louis Cardinals	414
5=	The Kingdome	Seattle Mariners	410
5=	Royals Stadium	Kansas City Royals	410
5=	San Diego/Jack Murphy Stadium	San Diego Padres	410
5=	Shea Stadium	New York Mets	410
9=	Hubert H. Humphrey Metrodome	Minnesota Twins	408
9=	Veterans Stadium	Philadelphia Phillies	408

Measured from the plate to the centre field outfield fence.

The smallest stadium in Major League baseball is one of the sport's most famous ballparks, Fenway Park, home of the Boston Red Sox. The distance from the plate to the centre field outfield is 390 feet, but extends to 420 feet in deep centre. It is also the smallest stadium in terms of capacity, with an upper limit of 34,182. An alternative method of measuring ballparks by calculating the total distance to centre right and left fields gives somewhat different results.

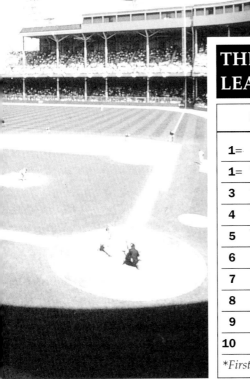

Tiger Stadium, home of the Detroit Tigers, is the biggest and joint oldest ballpark in Major League baseball.

THE 10 OLDEST STADIUMS IN MAJOR LEAGUE BASEBALL

	Stadium	Home club	Year built
1=	Fenway Park	Boston Red Sox	1912
1=	Tiger Stadium	Detroit Tigers	1912
3	Wrigley Field	Chicago Cubs	1914
4	Yankee Stadium	New York Yankees	1923
5	Cleveland Stadium	Cleveland Indians	1931*
6	County Stadium	Milwaukee Brewers	1953
7	Candlestick Park	San Francisco Giants	1960
8	Dodger Stadium	Los Angeles Dodgers	1962
9	Shea Stadium	New York Mets	1964
10	The Astrodome	Houston Astros	1965

First used for baseball 1933.

THE TOP 10 SALARIES IN MAJOR LEAGUE BASEBALL IN 1991

	Player	Team	Salary ($)*
1	Darryl Strawberry	Los Angeles Dodgers	3,800,000
2	Will Clark	San Francisco Giants	3,750,000
3	Mark Davis	Kansas City Royals	3,625,000
4	Eric Davis	Cincinnati Reds	3,600,000
5	Willie McGee	San Francisco Giants	3,562,500
6	Mark Langston	California Angels	3,550,000
7=	Jose Canseco	Oakland Athletics	3,500,000
7=	Tim Raines	Chicago White Sox	3,500,000
7=	Dave Stewart	Oakland Athletics	3,500,000
10	Bob Welch	Oakland Athletics	3,450,000

Figures include base salary and pro-rated signing bonuses for the term of guaranteed contracts for players who had signed contracts by 5 April 1991, but exclude other performance bonuses and shares in play-off and World Series games.

THE 10 PLAYERS WITH THE MOST RUNS IN A CAREER*

	Player	Runs
1	Ty Cobb	2,245
2=	Hank Aaron	2,174
2=	Babe Ruth	2,174
4	Pete Rose	2,165
5	Willie Mays	2,062
6	Stan Musial	1,949
7	Lou Gehrig	1,888
8	Tris Speaker	1,881
9	Mel Ott	1,859
10	Frank Robinson	1,829

Regular season only, excluding World Series.

THE 10 PLAYERS WITH THE MOST CONSECUTIVE GAMES IN A CAREER

	Player	Consecutive games
1	Lou Gehrig	2,130
2	Cal Ripken	1,411
3	Everett Scot	1,307
4	Steve Garvey	1,209
5	Billy Williams	1,117
6	Joe Sewell	1,103
7	Stan Musial	895
8	Eddie Yost	829
9	Gus Suhr	822
10	Nellie Fox	798

THE 10 PLAYERS WITH THE MOST GAMES IN A CAREER

	Player	Games
1	Pete Rose	3,562
2	Carl Yastrzemski	3,308
3	Hank Aaron	3,298
4	Ty Cobb	3,034
5	Stan Musial	3,026
6	Willie Mays	2,992
7	Rusty Staub	2,951
8	Brooks Robinson	2,896
9	Al Kaline	2,834
10	Eddie Collins	2,826

THE 10 PLAYERS WITH THE MOST HOME RUNS IN A CAREER

	Player	Home runs
1	Hank Aaron	755
2	Babe Ruth	714
3	Willie Mays	660
4	Frank Robinson	586
5	Harmon Killebrew	573
6	Reggie Jackson	563
7	Mike Schmidt	548
8	Mickey Mantle	536
9	Jimmie Foxx	534
10=	Willie McCovey	521
10=	Ted Williams	521

Ruth's total of 714 came from 8,399 'at bats' which represents an average of 8.5 per cent – considerably better than the next man in the averages, Harmon Killebrew, who averages at 7.0 per cent.

Right *Darryl Strawberry, who received a salary of $3,800,000 from the Los Angeles Dodgers in 1991.*

THE 10 TEAMS WITH THE BIGGEST PAYROLLS IN MAJOR LEAGUE BASEBALL IN 1991

	Team	Payroll ($)
1	Oakland Athletics	36,332,500
2	Los Angeles Dodgers	33,316,664
3	Boston Red Sox	32,767,500
4	New York Mets	32,590,002
5	California Angels	31,782,501
6	San Francisco Giants	30,839,333
7	Kansas City Royals	28,131,662
8	Detroit Tigers	27,756,001
9	New York Yankees	27,615,835
10	Toronto Blue Jays	27,538,751

BABE RUTH

Babe Ruth is unquestionably the best-known name in baseball. Born George Herman Ruth in 1895, he started his career as a pitcher with the Boston Red Sox in 1914. He acquired the nickname 'Babe' when, as a youngster, he was taken under the wing of Baltimore Orioles' owner Jack Dunn and became known as 'Jack's Babe'. He switched to batting after the First World War and soon started hitting the headlines, and runs, with the Yankees. His approach to the game did much to further its popularity in the 1920s, and such were the crowds that flocked to the Polo Grounds to see Ruth that soon a new, larger, stadium had to be built for the Yankees. When the Yankee Stadium was opened in 1923, it became known as 'The House Babe Built' because the revenue he brought in to the club was sufficient to finance its construction. Ruth retired in 1935 and his record of 714 home runs stood for nearly 40 years. When Babe Ruth died in 1948, the whole nation mourned.

Babe Ruth, whose record of 714 home runs stood for nearly 40 years.

THE 10 PLAYERS WITH THE HIGHEST CAREER BATTING AVERAGES

	Player	At bat	Hits	Average*
1	Ty Cobb	11,429	4,191	.367
2	Rogers Hornsby	8,137	2,930	.360
3	Joe Jackson	4,981	1,774	.356
4=	Wade Boggs	5,699	1,965	.345
4=	Ed Delahanty	7,502	2,591	.345
6=	Billy Hamilton	6,284	2,163	.344
6=	Tris Speaker	10,208	3,515	.344
6=	Ted Williams	7,706	2,654	.344
9	Willie Keeler	8,585	2,947	.343
10=	Dan Brouthers	6,711	2,296	.342
10=	Harry Heilmann	7,787	2,660	.342
10=	Babe Ruth	8,399	2,873	.342

Calculated by dividing the number of hits by the number of times a batter was 'at bat'.

THE 10 PLAYERS WITH THE MOST STRIKEOUTS IN A CAREER

	Player	Strikeouts
1	Nolan Ryan	5,511
2	Steve Carlton	4,136
3	Tom Seaver	3,640
4	Bert Byleven	3,631
5	Don Sutton	3,574
6	Gaylord Perry	3,534
7	Walter Johnson	3,508
8	Phil Niekro	3,342
9	Ferguson Jenkins	3,192
10	Bob Gibson	3,117

THE 10 PITCHERS WITH THE MOST WINS IN A CAREER

	Player	Wins
1	Cy Young	511
2	Walter Johnson	416
3=	Grover Alexander	373
3=	Christy Mathewson	373
5	Warren Spahn	363
6=	Pud Galvin	361
6=	Kid Nichols	361
8	Tim Keefe	342
9	Steve Carlton	329
10	Eddie Plank	327

THE 10 PITCHERS WITH THE LOWEST EARNED RUN AVERAGES IN A CAREER

	Player	ERA*
1	Ed Walsh	1.82
2	Addie Joss	1.88
3	Three Finger Brown	2.06
4	Monte Ward	2.10
5	Christy Mathewson	2.13
6	Rube Waddell	2.16
7	Walter Johnson	2.17
8	Orval Overall	2.24
9	Tommy Bond	2.25
10=	Ed Reulbach	2.28
10=	Will White	2.28

Earned Run Average is the average number of runs scored off a pitcher as a ratio of the number of innings in which he has pitched.

THE ORIGIN OF BASEBALL

There are many sports of uncertain origin, and baseball is one of them. Today most students of baseball acknowledge that it was derived from the English game of rounders, while a few diehard Americans continue to insist that Abner Doubleday, a West Point cadet, invented the game spontaneously, laying out the first baseball 'diamond' in 1839 – even though there is little evidence and he himself never made such a claim.

It seems likely that a game from which cricket, rounders and baseball are all ultimately derived dates back to ancient times, for in a manuscript miniature in the Bodleian Library, Oxford, dated to 1344, a woman is depicted in the act of bowling a ball to a man with a bat, while fielders stand behind. The first record of a game actually called 'Base-Ball' appears in a woodcut published in John Newbery's popular children's book, *A Little Pretty Pocket-Book*, published in London in 1744. 'Baseball' was also featured in Jane Austen's novel *Northanger Abbey*, which she began writing in 1798 (it was published posthumously in 1818). The rules of this game are unknown, but many early games involved the use of bats and balls and running between various sorts of bases. The first such game to become formalized with established rules was rounders, first described in detail in William Clarke's *The Boy's Own Book* (1828). It may well be that this game, or similar games, were familiar to British settlers in North America, and that baseball was thus a development of rounders.

What is certain is that Alexander Joy Cartwright jr drew up baseball's first rules on 23 September 1845. He also founded the first organized team, the Knickerbocker Base Ball Club of New York. The first game of baseball played according to the Cartwright Rules took place at the Elysian Fields, Hoboken, New Jersey, on 19 June 1846 between the New York Nine and the Knickerbocker Club, when Cartwright's team was defeated by the newly-formed New York Base Ball Club by 23 runs to 1.

From these early beginnings, and despite its uncertain origin, the game of baseball has become America's national sport. Pack Yankee Stadium with thousands of fervent fans on a Saturday night and they won't care who invented the game – just so long as the Yankees win.

BASKETBALL

THE 10 MOST SUCCESSFUL DIVISION 1 NCAA TEAMS

	College	Division 1 wins
1	North Carolina	1,508
2	Kentucky	1,501
3	Kansas	1,486
4	St John's	1,444
5	Duke	1,411
6	Oregon State	1,373
7	Temple	1,353
8	Pennsylvania	1,324
9	Notre Dame	1,323
10	Syracuse	1,318

The first National Collegiate Athletic Association (NCAA) basketball championship was held in 1939. Between then and 1951 the winners of the Eastern and Western titles met for the championship but since 1952 it has been a 'Final Four' play-off series.

THE 10 TEAMS WITH THE MOST NCAA CHAMPIONSHIP WINS

	College	Wins
1	UCLA	10
2=	Indiana	5
2=	Kentucky	5
4=	Cincinnati	2
4=	Duke	2
4=	Kansas	2
4=	Louisville	2
4=	North Carolina	2
4=	North Carolina State	2
4=	Oklahoma A & M*	2
4=	San Francisco	2

Now known as Oklahoma State.

THE 10 PLAYERS TO HAVE PLAYED THE MOST GAMES IN THE NBA AND ABA

	Player	Games played
1	Kareem Abdul-Jabbar	1,560
2	Moses Malone	1,372
3	Artis Gilmore	1,329
4	Elvin Hayes	1,303
5	Caldwell Jones	1,299
6	John Havlicek	1,270
7	Robert Parish	1,260
8	Paul Silas	1,254
9	Julius Irvin	1,243
10	Dan Issel	1,218

The ABA (American Basketball Association) was established as a rival to the NBA in 1968 and survived until 1976. Because many of the sport's top players 'defected', their figures are still included in this list.

With 16 titles, the Boston Celtics are the most successful team in the NBA.

THE 10 HIGHEST SCORES IN THE NBA

	Team	Opponents	Date	Score*
1	Detroit	Denver	13 Dec 1983	186 (3)
2	Denver	Detroit	13 Dec 1983	184 (3)
3=	Boston	Minneapolis	27 Feb 1959	173
3=	Phoenix	Denver	10 Nov 1990	173 (3)
5	San Antonio	Milwaukee	6 Mar 1982	171 (3)
6	Philadelphia†	New York	2 Mar 1962	169
7	Milwaukee	San Antonio	6 Mar 1982	166 (3)
8	Cincinnati	San Diego	12 Mar 1970	165
9=	Philadelphia	San Francisco	10 Mar 1963	163
9=	San Antonio	San Diego	8 Nov 1978	163
9=	Denver	San Antonio	11 Jan 1984	163

Figures in brackets indicate periods of overtime played.
†*Game played at Hershey, Pennsylvania.*

The Denver–Detroit match on 13 December 1983 is the highest-scoring game in aggregate with a total of 370 points scored. The score stood at 145-all at the end of normal play, Detroit eventually winning after three extra periods of play.

THE 10 TEAMS WITH THE MOST NBA TITLES

	Team*	Titles
1	Boston Celtics	16
2	Minnesota/ Los Angeles Lakers	11
3=	Philadelphia/ Golden State Warriors	3
3=	Syracuse Nationals/ Philadelphia 76ers	3
5=	Chicago Bulls	2
5=	Detroit Pistons	2
5=	New York Knicks	2
8=	Baltimore Bullets	1
8=	Milwaukee Bucks	1
8=	Portland Trail Blazers	1
8=	Rochester Royals†	1
8=	St Louis Hawks‡	1
8=	Seattle Supersonics	1
8=	Washington Bullets	1

Teams separated by / indicate changes of franchise and mean they have won the championship under both names.
†*Now the Sacramento Kings.*
‡*Now the Atlanta Hawks.*

Basketball is one of the few sports that can trace its exact origins. It was invented by Dr James Naismith at Springfield, Massachusetts, in 1891. Professional basketball in the United States dates to 1898 but the National Basketball Association (NBA) was not formed until 1949 when the National Basketball League and Basketball Association of America merged. The NBA consists of 27 teams split into Eastern and Western Conferences. At the end of an 82-game regular season, the top eight teams in each Conference play off and the two Conference champions meet in a best-of-seven final for the NBA Championship.

THE TOP 10 POINTS AVERAGES IN AN NBA SEASON

	Player	Club	Season	Average
1	Wilt Chamberlain	Philadelphia	1961–62	50.4
2	Wilt Chamberlain	San Francisco	1962–63	44.8
3	Wilt Chamberlain	Philadelphia	1960–61	38.4
4	Elgin Baylor	Los Angeles	1961–62	38.3
5	Wilt Chamberlain	Philadelphia	1959–60	37.6
6	Michael Jordan	Chicago	1986–87	37.1
7	Wilt Chamberlain	San Francisco	1963–64	36.9
8	Rick Barry	San Francisco	1966–67	35.6
9	Michael Jordan	Chicago	1987–88	35.0
10=	Elgin Baylor	Los Angeles	1960–61	34.8
10=	Kareem Abdul-Jabbar	Milwaukee	1971–72	34.8

THE 10 MOST SUCCESSFUL FREE THROW EXPERTS IN THE NBA

	Player	Free throws made
1	Moses Malone	8,395
2	Oscar Robertson	7,694
3	Jerry West	7,160
4	Dolph Schayes	6,979
5	Adrian Dantley	6,832
6	Kareem Abdul-Jabbar	6,712
7	Bob Pettit	6,182
8	Wilt Chamberlain	6,057
9	Elgin Baylor	5,763
10	Lenny Wilkins	5,394

Dolph Schayes has the best percentage record, having made 6,979 out of 8,273 attempts for a record high percentage of 0.844. If records from the shortlived ABA are considered, then Moses Malone would be even further ahead with 8,862 free throws made.

THE 10 MOST SUCCESSFUL NBA COACHES

	Coach	Games won*
1	Red Auerbach	938
2	Dick Motta	878
3	Jack Ramsay	864
4	Bill Fitch	845
5	Lenny Wilkens	815
6	Cotton Fitzsimmons	805
7	Gene Shue	784
8	Don Nelson	719
9	John MacLeod	707
10	Red Holzman	696

Regular season games only.

Pat Riley, who coached LA Lakers between 1981 and 1990, has the best percentage record with 533 wins from 727 games in nine seasons, representing a 0.733 per cent success rate.

THE TOP 10 POINTS-SCORERS IN AN NBA CAREER*

	Player	Total points
1	Kareem Abdul-Jabbar	38,387
2	Wilt Chamberlain	31,419
3	Elvin Hayes	27,313
4	Moses Malone	27,016
5	Oscar Robertson	26,710
6	John Havlicek	26,395
7	Alex English	25,466
8	Jerry West	25,192
9	Adrian Dantley	23,177
10	Elgin Baylor	23,149

*Regular season games only.

If points from the ABA were also considered then Abdul-Jabbar would still be No. 1, with the same total. The greatest points-scorer in NBA history, he was born Lew Alcindor but adopted a new name when he converted to the Islamic faith in 1969. The following year he turned professional, playing for Milwaukee. His career spanned 20 seasons before he retired at the end of the 1989 season. Despite scoring an NBA record 38,387 points he could not emulate the great Wilt Chamberlain by scoring 100 points in a game, which Chamberlain achieved for Philadelphia against New York at Hershey, Pennsylvania on 2 March 1962. Chamberlain also scored 70 points in a game six times, a feat Abdul-Jabbar never succeeded in rivalling.

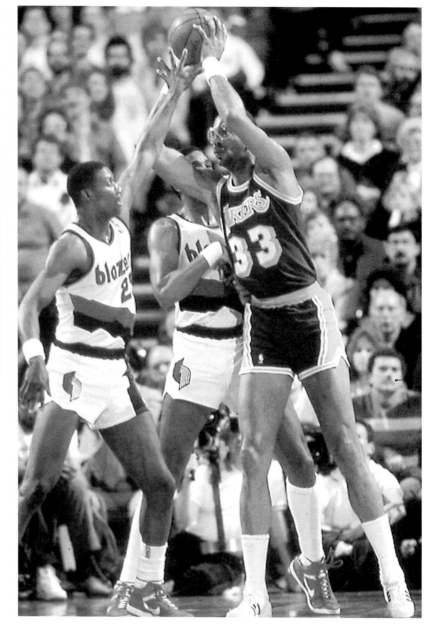

Above right Kareem Abdul-Jabbar, top points-scorer in an NBA career with 38,387.

THE 10 HIGHEST-EARNING PLAYERS IN THE NBA, 1991–92

	Player	Team	Earnings ($)
1	Larry Bird	Boston Celtics	7,070,000
2	John Williams	Cleveland Cavaliers	3,780,000
3	Kevin McHale	Boston Celtics	3,500,000
4	Reggie Lewis	Boston Celtics	3,340,000
5	Michael Jordan	Chicago Bulls	3,250,000
6	Reggie Miller	Indiana Pacers	3,210,000
7	Charles Barkley	Philadelphia 76ers	3,200,000
8	Hakeem Olajuwon	Houston Rockets	3,160,000
9	Patrick Ewing	New Yorks Knicks	3,130,000
10	Dominique Wilkins	Atlanta Hawks	3,100,000

The smallest arena is Salt Palace, home of Utah Jazz, with a capacity of 12,616. The largest-ever NBA stadium was the Louisiana Superdrome (also used by Utah Jazz from 1975 to 1979) which was capable of holding crowds of 47,284.

THE 10 BIGGEST ARENAS IN THE NBA

	Arena/location	Home team	Capacity
1	Charlotte Coliseum, Charlotte, N. Carolina	Charlotte Hornets	23,388
2	The Palace, Auburn Hills, Michigan	Detroit Pistons	21,454
3	The Coliseum, Richfield, Ohio	Cleveland Cavaliers	20,273
4	Meadowlands Arena, East Rutherford, New Jersey	New Jersey Nets	20,089
5	Madison Square Garden, New York	New York Knicks	19,081
6	Capital Centre, Landover, Maryland	Washington Bullets	18,756
7	Bradley Center, Milwaukee	Milwaukee Bucks	18,633
8	Target Centre, Minnesota	Minnesota Timberwolves	18,500
9	The Spectrum, Philadelphia	Philadelphia 76ers	18,168
10	The Forum, Inglewood, Los Angeles	Los Angeles Lakers	17,505

BILLIARDS

THE 10 PLAYERS WITH THE MOST ENGLISH AMATEUR TITLES

	Player	Years	Titles
1	Norman Dagley	1965–84	15
2=	S. H. Fry	1893–1925	8
2=	Leslie Driffield	1952–67	8
4=	A. P. Gaskell	1888–91	6
4=	Harry Virr	1907–14	6
6	Frank Edwards	1949–56	5
7=	Arthur Wisdom	1892–1903	4
7=	A. W. T. Good	1902–15	4
7=	Sydney Lee	1931–34	4
7=	Kingsley Kennerley	1937–40	4

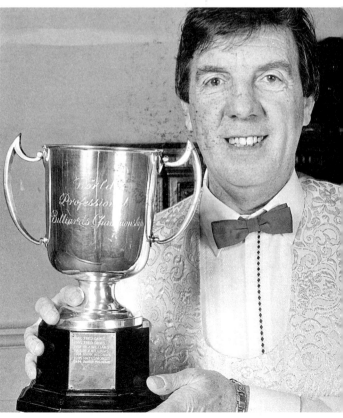

Norman Dagley, winner of a record 15 English amateur titles and twice world professional champion.

The English Amateur Championship was first contested in 1888 on a challenge basis but is now a knockout competition and is regarded as the most prestigious event for non-professionals in Britain.

Sydney Lee was perhaps better known as the regular referee on BBC Television's *Pot Black* programme, which was largely responsible for the phenomenal growth in snooker's popularity in the 1970s.

THE 10 PLAYERS WITH THE MOST WORLD PROFESSIONAL TITLES

	Player	Titles*
1	Tom Newman†	6
2=	Melbourne Inman	5
2=	H. W. Stevenson	5
4=	Joe Davis	4
4=	John Roberts jr	4
4=	Rex Williams	4
7	Charles Dawson	3
8=	Joseph Bennett	2
8=	William Cook	2
8=	Norman Dagley	2
8=	Fred Davis	2
8=	Walter Lindrum‡	2
8=	Willie Smith	2

First held in 1870, this competition was contested on a challenge basis only until 1909 when it became a knockout-style event. It was discontinued in 1934 but was revived on a challenge basis once again in 1951, and in 1980 became a knockout-type event (won on this occasion by the veteran player, 66-year-old Fred Davis).

*The number of titles indicates the number of times the title was won, and not the number of successful challenges.
†Newman's six titles, won between 1921 and 1927, were all under knockout conditions.
‡All the players were English except Lindrum (Australian).

BOBSLEIGHING

THE 10 MOST SUCCESSFUL OLYMPIC COUNTRIES

	Country	gold	Medals silver	bronze	Total
1	Switzerland	8	6	8	22
2	USA	5	4	5	14
3=	East Germany	5	5	3	13
3=	Germany/West Germany	3	5	5	13
5	Italy	3	4	2	9
6=	Austria	1	2	0	3
6=	Great Britain	1	1	1	3
6=	USSR	1	0	2	3
9	Belgium	0	1	1	2
10=	Canada	1	0	0	1
10=	Romania	0	0	1	1

third). Nash and Dixon noticed that an axle bolt on their sled was broken shortly before their second run. Monti immediately removed a bolt from his own sled and gave it to the British pair.

Bobsleighing was introduced into the Olympics at the first Winter celebration at Chamonix, France, in 1924 when teams of four or five men could compete in what is now known as the four-man bob event. The two-man event was introduced in 1932. British success at the Winter Olympics is rare but in 1964 Tony Nash and Robin Dixon outraced the Italians to capture the gold medal in the two-man event. But success was largely due to the generosity of one of their Italian rivals, the great Eugenio Monti (who finished

Britain's Tony Nash and Robin Dixon, gold medallists in the two-man bob at the 1964 Winter Olympics in Innsbruck, Austria.

BOWLING (TENPIN)

THE TOP 10 GOLD MEDAL WINNING COUNTRIES AT THE WORLD CHAMPIONSHIPS

	Country	Titles
1	USA	27
2	Sweden	21
3	Finland	10
4=	Germany/West Germany	5
4=	Great Britain	5
4=	Mexico	5
4=	Philippines	5
8=	Australia	3
8=	Japan	3
10	Puerto Rico	2

Introduced in 1923, the World Championships are now held every four years and since 1954 have been under the control of the Fédération Internationale des Quilleurs (FIQ). There are men's and women's singles titles as well as various team events with varying numbers of team members.

Wayne Webb, scorer of the most perfect games in PBA-approved tournaments and 6th on the list of top money winners of all time.

THE TOP 10 MONEY WINNERS OF ALL TIME IN PROFESSIONAL BOWLERS ASSOCIATION (PBA) TOURNAMENTS

	Bowler	Winnings ($)
1	Marshall Holman	1,555,851
2	Mark Roth	1,400,881
3	Earl Anthony	1,361,931
4	Pete Weber	1,319,142
5	Mike Aulby	1,194,905
6	Wayne Webb	984,691
7	Brian Voss	971,353
8	Amleto Monacelli	964,866
9	Dave Husted	964,441
10	Walter Ray Williams jr	854,449

THE 10 BOWLERS WITH THE MOST PERFECT GAMES IN PBA-APPROVED TOURNAMENTS

	Bowler	Perfect games
1	Wayne Webb	32
2	Steve Cook	29
3=	Pete Couture	27
3=	Marshall Holman	27
3=	Gubby Troup	27
6	Steve Wunderlich	26
7=	Tommy Baker	23
7=	Gary Dickinson	23
9=	Mark Roth	22
9=	Jim Stefanich	22

A perfect game is a score of 300 obtained by rolling 12 consecutive strikes in one game.

BOWLS

THE 10 MOST SUCCESSFUL COUNTRIES IN THE WORLD OUTDOOR CHAMPIONSHIPS

The World Outdoor Championships were launched in 1966 after being excluded from the Commonwealth Games in Kingston, Jamaica. The first women's championship was held the following year and men's and women's competitions are now held every four years, with titles for singles, pairs, triples, fours and team. Britain's David Bryant has won a record five individual titles. In 1976 South Africa swept the board by winning all five men's titles. The 1984 men's pairs was won by Skippy Arculli of the United States and George Adrain of Scotland who stood in for Arculli's team-mate Jim Candelet.

	Country	Titles men	women	Total
1	Australia	4	9	13
2	England	8	4	12
3=	New Zealand	4	5	9
3=	South Africa	5	4	9
5=	Hong Kong	2	2	4
5=	Ireland	2	2	4
7	Scotland	2½	1	3½
8	Wales	1	2	3
9	USA	1½	0	1½
10	Papua New Guinea	0	1	1

David Bryant, winner of a record five individual world titles.

BOXING

THE 10 HEAVIEST WORLD HEAVYWEIGHT CHAMPIONS

	Boxer*	Heaviest weight kg	lb
1	Primo Carnera (Ita)	122.5	270
2	James 'Buster' Douglas	111.6	246
3	John Tate	108.9	240
4	Greg Page	108.6	239¼
5	Tony Tubbs	108.0	238
6	Tim Witherspoon	106.6	235
7	Mike Weaver	105.2	232
8=	Muhammad Ali	104.3	230
8=	Jess Willard	104.3	230
10	Francesco Damiani (Ita)	104.0	229¼

American unless otherwise stated.

A fighter's weight can, of course, change dramatically, and the figures given are the heaviest at which a champion fought.

Bob Fitzsimmons of Great Britain took the heavyweight crown in 1897 and remains the lightest champion of all time.

THE 10 LIGHTEST WORLD HEAVYWEIGHT CHAMPIONS

	Boxer*	Opponent	Date	Weight† kg	lb
1	Bob Fitzsimmons (GB)	James J. Corbett	17 Mar 1897	75.8	167
2	James J. Corbett	John L. Sullivan	7 Sep 1892	80.7	178
3	Tommy Burns (Can)	Marvin Hart	23 Feb 1906	81.6	180
4	Ezzard Charles	Jersey Joe Walcott	22 Jun 1949	82.4	181¾
5	Floyd Patterson	Archie Moore	30 Nov 1956	82.7	182¼
6	Rocky Marciano	Jersey Joe Walcott	23 Sep 1952	83.5	184
7	Jack Dempsey	Jess Willard	4 Jul 1919	84.8	187
8	Max Schmeling (Ger)	Jack Sharkey	12 Jun 1930	85.3	188
9	Gene Tunney	Jack Dempsey	23 Sep 1926	86.0	189¼
10	Marvin Hart	Jack Root	3 Jul 1905	86.2	190

American unless otherwise stated.
†At time of winning title.

THE 10 OLDEST WORLD HEAVYWEIGHT CHAMPIONS

Rocky Marciano, at 32 years 238 days, is in 11th place.

	Boxer*	Title lost	Age† yrs	Age† days
1	Jersey Joe Walcott	23 Sep 1952	38	235
2	Jess Willard	4 Jul 1919	37	186
3	Muhammad Ali	22 Jun 1979	37	155
4	Jack Johnson	5 Apr 1915	37	4
5	Bob Fitzsimmons (GB)	9 Jun 1899	36	13
6	Larry Holmes	21 Sep 1985	35	321
7	Ken Norton	9 Jun 1978	34	303
8	Joe Louis	1 Mar 1949	34	291
9	Trevor Berbick (Jam)	22 Nov 1986	34	112
10	James 'Bonecrusher' Smith	7 Mar 1987	32	337

*American unless otherwise stated.
†At time of losing or relinquishing title.

THE 10 TALLEST HEAVYWEIGHT CHAMPIONS

	Boxer*	Height m	ft	in
1	Ernie Terrell	1.98	6	6
2	Primo Carnera (Ita)	1.97	6	5½
3	Jess Willard	1.96	6	5½
4	Tony Tucker	1.96	6	5
5=	Francesco Damiani (Ita)	1.93	6	4
5=	James 'Buster' Douglas	1.93	6	4
5=	James 'Bonecrusher' Smith	1.93	6	4
5=	John Tate	1.93	6	4
9	Larry Holmes	1.92	6	3½
10=	Muhammad Ali	1.91	6	3
10=	James J. Braddock	1.91	6	3
10=	Gerrie Coetzee (SA)	1.91	6	3
10=	Mike Dokes	1.91	6	3
10=	George Foreman	1.91	6	3
10=	Ken Norton	1.91	6	3
10=	Tim Witherspoon	1.91	6	3

*American unless otherwise stated.

THE 10 SHORTEST WORLD HEAVYWEIGHT CHAMPIONS

	Boxer*	Height m	ft	in
1	Tommy Burns (Can)	1.70	5	7
2	Rocky Marciano	1.78	5	10¼
3=	Joe Frazier	1.80	5	11
3=	Marvin Hart	1.80	5	11
3=	Floyd Patterson	1.80	5	11
6	Mike Tyson	1.82	5	11½
7=	Ezzard Charles	1.83	6	0
7=	Jack Dempsey	1.83	6	0
7=	Bob Fitzsimmons (GB)	1.83	6	0
7=	Ingemar Johansson (Swe)	1.83	6	0
7=	Jack Sharkey	1.83	6	0
7=	Gene Tunney	1.83	6	0

*American unless otherwise stated.

The true height for Primo Carnera was never accurately measured and some sources believe he was anything up to 2.05m/6ft 8½in. Jess Willard is often incorrectly stated as being 1.99m/6ft 6½in tall.

THE FIRST 10 WHITE HEAVYWEIGHT CHAMPIONS OF THE WORLD

	Boxer/nationality	Year title won
1	James J. Corbett (USA)	1892
2	Bob Fitzsimmons (GB)	1897
3	James J. Jeffries (USA)	1899
4	Marvin Hart (USA)	1905
5	Tommy Burns (Can)	1906
6	Jess Willard (USA)	1915
7	Jack Dempsey (USA)	1919
8	Gene Tunney (USA)	1926
9	Max Schmeling (Ger)	1930
10	Jack Sharkey (USA)	1932

Although Fitzsimmons was British born, he was boxing out of the United States at the time of winning the title.

JACK JOHNSON

The only black boxer among the first 10 world heavyweight champions is Jack Johnson, who took the crown from Tommy Burns in Sydney, Australia, on Boxing Day 1908. But then his troubles started. Sadly, he reached the peak of his career at a time when black boxers were accepted in the United States only if they were defeated! Despite having become champion, he was one of the most hated men in America, and his out-of-the ring arrogance and exploits did nothing to help his cause. The American boxing authorities desperately wanted a white champion but, despite a succession of 'Great White Hopes', they could not find one to beat Johnson. In 1913 he was charged with importing a woman into America for illegal purposes and was forced to flee to Europe in order to avoid a prison sentence. Two years later the boxing authorities found their next 'Great White Hope' in the giant Jess Willard. Johnson agreed to return to America on condition the charges against him were dropped but, fearing race riots, the fight was staged in Havana, Cuba. Willard, with age, weight and size advantage, eventually won in 26 rounds although Johnson later maintained he was forced to throw the fight. Nevertheless, the authorities were pleased because they had a white champion again, and it was not until Joe Louis' success in 1937 that there was another black heavyweight champion of the world. However, a look down the list of subsequent champions clearly shows that Jack Johnson paved the way for future generations of Negro heavyweights.

THE 10 REFEREES MOST FREQUENTLY EMPLOYED IN WORLD HEAVYWEIGHT TITLE FIGHTS

	Referee	No. of title fights refereed
1	Arthur Donovan	14
2	Mills Lane	11
3	Arthur Mercante	8
4=	Ruby Goldstein	7
4=	Carlos Padilla	7
6	Richard Steele	6
7	Tony Perez	5
8=	Frank Sikora	4
8=	George Siler	4
10=	Zack Clayton	3
10=	Ed Graney	3
10=	Richard Greene	3
10=	James J. Jeffries	3
10=	Eddie Joseph	3
10=	Harvey Kesler	3
10=	David Pearl	3

James J. Jeffries was the first ex-world heavyweight champion to officiate in a heavyweight contest when he refereed the fight between Marvin Hart and Jack Root at Reno, Nevada, on 3 July 1905 to decide which man should succeed him as world champion. Hart won when Jeffries stopped the bout in the 12th round. The only other ex-heavyweight champion to referee a heavyweight contest is Jersey Joe Walcott who was in charge of the Floyd Patterson–Tom McNeeley bout in 1956 and also the Muhammad Ali–Sonny Liston contest in 1965.

THE LONGEST-REIGNING WORLD HEAVYWEIGHT CHAMPIONS

Boxer	Years	Duration yrs	days
Joe Louis	1937–49	11	252
Jack Dempsey	1919–26	7	81
Jack Johnson	1908–15	6	110
James J. Jeffries	1899–1903	5	338
James J. Corbett	1892–97	4	191

THE TOP 10 ATTENDANCES FOR WORLD HEAVYWEIGHT TITLE FIGHTS

	Fight	Venue	Date	Attendance
1	Jack Dempsey v Gene Tunney	Philadelphia	23 Sep 1926	120,757
2	Jack Dempsey v Gene Tunney	Chicago	22 Sep 1927	104,943
3	Jack Dempsey v Luis Angel Firpo	New York	14 Sep 1923	82,000
4	Georges Carpentier v Jack Dempsey	Jersey City	2 Jul 1921	80,183
5	Max Schmeling v Jack Sharkey	New York	12 Jun 1930	79,222
6	Joe Louis v Max Schmeling	New York	22 Jun 1938	70,043
7	Muhammad Ali v George Foreman	Kinshasa, Zaïre	30 Oct 1974	65,000
8	Muhammad Ali v Leon Spinks	New Orleans	15 Sep 1978	63,350
9	Primo Carnera v Joe Louis	New York	25 Jun 1935	62,000
10	Max Schmeling v Jack Sharkey	Long Island	21 Jun 1932	61,863

The Ali–Spinks fight was staged indoors and the crowd is a record for an indoor contest. The non-title fight between Max Baer and Joe Louis at New York's Yankee Stadium on 24 September 1935 drew a crowd of 88,150, a record for a non-title heavyweight contest. The smallest attendance for a world heavyweight title fight is 2,434 for the Muhammad Ali v Sonny Liston contest at Lewiston, Maine, on 25 May 1965.

THE 10 CITIES THAT HAVE STAGED THE MOST WORLD HEAVYWEIGHT TITLE FIGHTS

	City	Fights staged
1	New York	49
2	Las Vegas	33
3	Chicago	9
4	Los Angeles	8
5=	Atlantic City	7
5=	Philadelphia	7
5=	San Francisco	7
8	Detroit	6
9=	Houston	5
9=	London	5

Las Vegas, Nevada, now the venue for many world title fights, did not stage its first heavyweight title bout until 25 September 1962 when Sonny Liston beat Floyd Patterson to capture the title.

❏ **The five world heavyweight title fights in London were:**

2 Dec 1907
  Tommy Burns *v* Gunner Moir (NSC)
10 Feb 1908
  Tommy Burns *v* Jack Palmer (Wonderland Centre)
21 May 1966
  Muhammad Ali *v* Henry Cooper (Highbury)
6 Aug 1966
  Muhammad Ali *v* Brian London (Earl's Court)
20 Jul 1986
  Tim Witherspoon *v* Frank Bruno (Wembley)

THE 10 OLDEST WORLD CHAMPIONS

	Boxer/nationality	Weight	Age* yrs	Age* days
1	Archie Moore (USA)	Light-heavyweight	39	4
2	Jersey Joe Walcott (USA)	Heavyweight	37	168
3	Fulgencio Obelmejias (Ven)	Super-middleweight	35	144
4	Johnny Thompson (USA)	Middleweight	34	236
5	Toufik Belbouli (Fra)	Cruiserweight	34	105
6	Luis Estaba (Ven)	Junior-flyweight	34	31
7	Dado Marino (Haw)	Flyweight	33	340
8	Trevor Berbick (Jam)	Heavyweight	33	233
9	Joey Giardello (USA)	Middleweight	33	144
10	Johnny Buff (USA)	Bantamweight	33	103

At time of first winning a world title.

There is some uncertainty about the age of Archie Moore. He was never sure in what year he was born: it was either 1913 or 1916. The above figure assumes he was born in 1913. If he was born in 1916 then he would be ranked No. 2 behind Jersey Joe Walcott. However, there is no disputing the fact that he is the oldest person to hold a world title because he was either 45 years 49 days or 48 years 49 days when he relinquished his world light-heavyweight title in 1952.

The Dempsey–Tunney fight of 1926 attracted a record crowd of 120,757, the highest-ever attendance for a world heavyweight title contest.

THE 10 YOUNGEST WORLD CHAMPIONS

	Boxer/nationality	Weight	Age* yrs	Age* days
1	Wilfred Benitez (USA)	Junior-welterweight	17	176
2	Pipino Cuevas (Mex)	Welterweight	18	203
3	Hiroki Ioka (Jap)	Straw-weight	18	284
4	Tony Canzoneri (USA)	Featherweight	18	352
5	Netrnoi Vorasingh (Tha)	Junior-flyweight	19	15
6	Cesar Polanco (Dom)	Junior-bantamweight	19	79
7	Jimmy Walsh (USA)	Bantamweight	19	95
8=	Al McCoy (USA)	Middleweight	19	167
8=	Ben Villaflor (Phi)	Junior-lightweight	19	167
10	Terry McGovern (USA)	Bantamweight	19	188

At time of first winning a world title.

THE 10 BOXERS WITH THE MOST WINS IN WORLD TITLE FIGHTS

	Boxer/nationality	Wins
1	Joe Louis (USA)	26
2=	Muhammad Ali (USA)	22
2=	Henry Armstrong (USA)	22
4=	Julio Cesar Chavez (Mex)	21
4=	Larry Holmes (USA)	21
4=	Manuel Ortiz (USA)	21
7=	Kaosai Galaxy (Tha)	20
7=	Wilfredo Gomez (PR)	20
9=	Alexis Arguello (Nic)	19
9=	Eusebio Pedroza (Pan)	19

	Boxer/nationality/titles held	No. of titles
1	Thomas Hearns (USA) WBA Light-heavyweight, Welterweight; WBC Light-heavyweight, Middleweight, Junior-middleweight; WBO Super-middleweight	6
2	Sugar Ray Leonard (USA) WBC Light-heavyweight, Super-middleweight, Middleweight, Welterweight; WBA Junior-middleweight	5
3	Roberto Duran (Pan) WBC Middleweight, Welterweight; WBA Junior-middleweight, Lightweight	4
4=	Alexis Arguello (Nic) WBC Lightweight, WBC Junior-lightweight; WBA Featherweight	3
4=	Henry Armstrong (USA) Welterweight, Lightweight, Featherweight	3
4=	Tony Canzoneri (USA) Junior-welterweight, Lightweight, NY Featherweight	3
4=	Julio Cesar Chavez (Mex) WBC Junior-welterweight; WBC/WBA Lightweight; WBC Junior-lightweight	3
4=	Jeff Fenech (Aus) WBC Featherweight; WBC Junior-featherweight; IBF Bantamweight	3
4=	Bob Fitzsimmons (GB) Heavyweight, Light-heavyweight, Middleweight	3
4=	Wilfredo Gomez (PR) WBC Junior-lightweight, Featherweight; WBA Junior-featherweight	3
4=	Barney Ross (USA) Welterweight, Junior-welterweight, Lightweight	3

THE 10 BOXERS HOLDING THE MOST WORLD TITLES IN A CAREER

With the proliferation of world titles available to present-day boxers, the winning of two or three titles is no longer the rarity it used to be. However, the records of Tommy Hearns and Sugar Ray Leonard should not be taken lightly; both have been outstanding champions. But compare their feats with those of the likes of Henry Armstrong, who held three titles simultaneously in the 1930s, and whose achievement must be regarded as outstanding in the pugilistic world.

Right Sugar Ray Leonard (right) defeats Marvin Hagler to become WBC middleweight champion in 1987. He has won a total of five world boxing titles in his career.

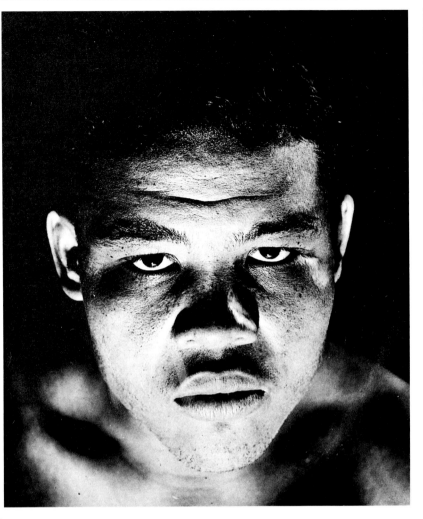

THE 10 BOXERS WITH THE MOST WORLD TITLE FIGHTS

	Boxer/ nationality	Title fights
1	Joe Louis (USA)	27
2	Henry Armstrong (USA)	26
3	Muhammad Ali (USA)	25
4	Larry Holmes (USA)	24
5=	Wilfredo Gomez (PR)	23
5=	Manuel Ortiz (USA)	23
5=	Hilario Zapata (Pan)	23
8=	Alexis Arguello (Nic)	22
8=	Tony Canzoneri (USA)	22
8=	George Dixon (Can)	22
8=	Emile Griffith (USA)	22
8=	Eusebio Pedroza (Pan)	22
8=	Sugar Ray Robinson (USA)	22

Joe Louis, who remained undefeated heavyweight champion of the world for nearly 12 years

JOE LOUIS

Joe Louis captured the world heavyweight title with an eighth-round knockout of James J. Braddock at Comiskey Park, Chicago, on 13 June 1937. He remained the undefeated heavyweight champion of the world for a record 11 years and 252 days until announcing his retirement. During that time he made 25 successful defences of his title, stopping all but three of his opponents. The three to take him the full 15 rounds were Britain's Tommy Farr, Arturo Godoy, and future champion Jersey Joe Walcott. Tax demands forced Joe to make a comeback in September 1950 when he challenged Ezzard Charles in the hope of becoming the first man to regain the heavyweight title. He failed, losing on points over 15 rounds. Louis carried on boxing for another year until being put through the ropes by another future champion, Rocky Marciano, on 26 October 1951. It was Louis' last fight. He died on 12 April 1981 at the age of 66.

WHO WAS THE FIRST WORLD HEAVYWEIGHT CHAMPION?

Boxing records have long regarded James J. Corbett as being the first world heavyweight champion under the Marquess of Queensberry Rules, following his 21st-round knockout of John L. Sullivan at New Orleans in 1892. But in recent years evidence has come to light to suggest this was *not* the first heavyweight contest under the Queensberry Rules.

At Chester Driving Park, Cincinnati, on Saturday, 29 August 1885, John L. Sullivan and Dominick McCaffrey engaged in a fight for 'the world heavyweight title'. It was a scheduled six-round contest, and since prizefighting was illegal in Cincinnati at the time, the fight was scheduled to take place just outside the city boundary. When he arrived in town, Sullivan was arrested for his part in organizing the contest. He insisted it was only a sparring bout and not a title fight and was duly released on payment of a bond.

The fight went ahead and, at 5.13 p.m., Sullivan entered the ring at 93.0kg/205lb with McCaffrey a mere 72.6kg/160lb. The fight was under Marquess of Queensberry Rules in a 7.31-metre/24-foot ring and with both fighters wearing 3oz 'hard gloves'. The duration of the fight was to be 'six rounds *or* to a finish', thus contradicting what Sullivan had told the authorities on his arrest.

A local man, Billy Tait of Toledo, was called upon to referee and he was asked before the contest if he understood the terms of the contest. He said he 'thought' he did and the fight got under way. It lasted the six rounds with neither man being knocked out. It was then that the confusion started: McCaffrey was under the impression that if neither man was knocked out then *he* was the winner. Sullivan's camp, however, believed the referee should declare the winner 'on points' and he duly awarded it to Sullivan. McCaffrey's camp then pointed out that if the rules were 'six rounds *or* to a finish', then the contest should continue to the finish. The fighters and authorities left the ring without resolving the matter satisfactorily and a couple of days later the referee tried to clear matters up. He said that he understood his role was to decide the contest on points since there would be no slugging or knockouts because of the court's decision a few days earlier that released Sullivan from custody only on the condition that it was *not* a prizefight.

The question therefore has to be asked: was this the first world heavyweight title fight under Queensberry Rules, or, as seems more likely, merely a sparring contest?

THE FIRST 10 DIFFERENT WORLD CHAMPIONS UNDER QUEENSBERRY RULES

	Boxer/nationality	Weight	Year
1	Jack Dempsey (Ire)	Middleweight	1884
2	Jack McAuliffe (Ire)	Lightweight	1888
3	Paddy Duffy (USA)	Welterweight	1888
4	Ike Weir (GB)	Featherweight	1889
5	Billy Murphy (NZ)	Featherweight	1890
6	George Dixon (Can)	Bantamweight	1890
7	Young Griffo (Aus)	Featherweight	1890
8	Bob Fitzsimmons (GB)	Middleweight	1891
9	James J. Corbett (USA)	Heavyweight	1892
10	'Mysterious' Billy Smith (Can)	Welterweight	1892

QUIZ

WORLD HEAVYWEIGHT BOXING CHAMPIONS

1 Who was the last non-American-born heavyweight champion of the world as recognized by the three main world governing bodies?

2 Who captured the world heavyweight title in the first ever world championship bout to be held in Cuba?

3 In how many world title fights did Muhammad Ali box under the name of Cassius Clay?

4 The Jack Dempsey versus Georges Carpentier fight at Jersey City on 2 July 1921 was the first world heavyweight contest to attract what?

5 Which two men once engaged in three successive world heavyweight title contests?

6 Of all the men to have held world titles at three or more weights, who is the only one to have included the heavyweight crown in his successes?

7 Who was the first man to take Mike Tyson the distance in a world title fight?

8 Who reigned as world champion for just 64 days between May and August 1987?

9 Who won the only world heavyweight title fight to be staged on Boxing Day?

10 Three world heavyweight champions were born in Louisville. Muhammad Ali was one, name the other two.

THE FIRST 10 AMERICAN-BORN WORLD CHAMPIONS

	Boxer	Birthplace	Weight	First title won
1	Paddy Duffy	Boston, Massachusetts	Welterweight	30 Oct 1888
2	James J. Corbett	San Francisco	Heavyweight	7 Sep 1892
3	Tommy Ryan	Redwood, New York	Welterweight	26 Jul 1894
4	Charles 'Kid' McCoy	Rush County, Indiana	Welterweight	2 Mar 1896
5	George 'Kid' Lavigne	Bay City, Michigan	Lightweight	1 Jun 1896
6	Solly Smith	Los Angeles	Featherweight	4 Oct 1897
7	Jimmy Barry	Chicago	Bantamweight	6 Dec 1897
8	James J. Jeffries	Carroll, Ohio	Heavyweight	9 Jun 1899
9	Terry McGovern	Johnstown, Pennsylvania	Bantamweight	12 Sep 1899
10	Rube Ferns	Pittsburgh, Kansas	Welterweight	15 Jan 1900

The first recognized world champion under Queensberry Rules was middleweight Jack 'Nonpareil' Dempsey who captured the title in 1884. However, although he represented America, Dempsey was in fact born in County Kildare in the Republic of Ireland.

THE 10 LONGEST WORLD CHAMPIONSHIP FIGHTS

	Boxers (winners first)	Weight	Date	Rounds
1	Ike Weir v Frank Murphy	Featherweight	31 Mar 1889	80
2	Jack McAuliffe v Jem Carney	Lightweight	16 Nov 1887	74
3	Paddy Duffy v Tom Meadows	Welterweight	29 Mar 1889	45
4	Joe Gans v Battling Nelson	Lightweight	3 Sep 1906	42
5=	George Dixon v Johnny Murphy	Bantamweight	23 Oct 1890	40
5=	Ad Wolgast v Battling Nelson	Lightweight	22 Feb 1910	40
7=	George LaBlanche v Jack Dempsey	Middleweight	27 Aug 1889	32
7=	Stanley Ketchel v Joe Thomas	Middleweight	2 Sep 1907	32
9	Jack Dempsey v Billy McCarthy	Middleweight	18 Feb 1890	28
10	Jack Dempsey v Jack Fogarty	Middleweight	3 Feb 1886	27

All these were world championship contests under the Marquess of Queensberry Rules (first published in 1866) which stipulate the length of a round at three minutes. Prior to the Rules, a round ended when a fighter was knocked down, and consequently a great number of fights in the bare-knuckle days consisted of many rounds, the longest being the 276-round contest between Jack Jones and Patsy Tunney in Cheshire in 1825. The fight lasted 4 hours 30 minutes. The longest heavyweight contest under Queensberry Rules was the Jess Willard v Jack Johnson contest on 5 April 1915, which lasted 26 rounds.

Because dates of many fights in the last century are not recorded it is impossible to establish the exact length of some careers. The longest career of any professional boxer is believed to be that of Bobby Dobbs who fought for 39 years between 1875 and 1914. His last fight is alleged to have been when he was 56. The former world heavyweight champion George Foreman was still fighting in 1991, more than 22 years after his first professional fight on 23 June 1969.

THE 10 WORLD CHAMPIONS WITH THE LONGEST PROFESSIONAL CAREERS

	Boxer*	Fought professionally	Career (yrs)
1=	Bob Fitzsimmons (GB)	1883–1914	31
1=	Jack Johnson	1897–1928	31
3	Archie Moore	1935–63	28†
4	Joe Brown	1943–70	27
5=	Billy Murphy (NZ)	1881–1907	26
5=	Willie Pep	1940–66	26
7=	Young Griffo (Aus)	1886–1911	25
7=	Charles 'Kid' McCoy	1891–1916	25
7=	Jack Britton	1905–30	25
7=	Sugar Ray Robinson	1940–65	25
7=	Harold Johnson	1946–71	25

*American unless otherwise stated.
†Archie Moore engaged in an exhibition bout in 1965 which, if counted, increases his career to 30 years.

THE FIRST 10 BRITISH-BORN WORLD CHAMPIONS

	Boxer	Birthplace	Weight at which first title won	First title won
1	Ike Weir	Belfast	Featherweight	1889
2	Bob Fitzsimmons	Helston, Cornwall	Middleweight	1891
3	Joe Bowker	Salford	Bantamweight	1904
4	Freddie Welsh	Pontypridd	Lightweight	1914
5	Ted 'Kid' Lewis	London	Welterweight	1915
6	Jimmy Wilde	Tylorstown, Wales	Flyweight	1916
7	Jack 'Kid' Berg	London	Light-welterweight	1930
8	Jackie Brown	Manchester	Flyweight	1932
9	Benny Lynch	Clydesdale	Flyweight	1935
10	Peter Kane	Golborne, nr Warrington	Flyweight	1938

Bob Fitzsimmons went on to win world titles at three weights including heavyweight; he is the only British-born boxer to win the sport's premier title. Some sources regard Weir's assertion to be the first world featherweight champion as dubious because he claimed the title following an 80-round draw with Frank Murphy (England) at Kouts, Indiana, on 31 March 1889.

THE 10 MOST KNOCKDOWNS IN WORLD TITLE FIGHTS

	Boxers*	Weight	Date	Total knockdowns
1	Vic Toweel (0) v Danny O'Sullivan (14)	Bantamweight	2 Dec 1950	14
2=	Mike O'Dowd (2) v Al McCoy (9)	Middleweight	14 Nov 1917	11
2=	Jack Dempsey (2) v Luis Angel Firpo (9)	Heavyweight	14 Sep 1923	11
2=	Max Baer (0) v Primo Carnera (11)	Heavyweight	14 Jun 1934	11
5=	Benny Lynch (0) v Jackie Brown (10)	Flyweight	9 Sep 1935	10
5=	Jimmy Carter (0) v Tony Collins (10)	Lightweight	24 Apr 1953	10
7=	Terry McGovern (1) v George Dixon (8)	Featherweight	9 Jan 1900	9
7=	Virgil Akins (0) v Vince Martinez (9)	Welterweight	6 Jun 1958	9
9=	Archie Moore (4) v Yvon Durelle (4)	Light-heavyweight	10 Dec 1958	8
9=	Floyd Patterson (0) v Tom McNeeley (8)	Heavyweight	4 Dec 1961	8

Figures in brackets indicate how many times each fighter was on the canvas. The winner of each bout is the first named.

The first round of the Dempsey–Firpo contest saw Dempsey on the floor twice and Firpo down seven times. It is the most knockdowns in any single round of a world title fight. In 1913 Bill Ladbury floored Bill Smith 16 times in a flyweight title fight but it is not universally acknowledged as being for the world title.

THE 10 FASTEST KNOCKOUTS OR STOPPAGES IN WORLD TITLE FIGHTS

	Boxers (winners first)	Weight	Date	Duration (sec)
1	James Warring v James Pritchard	Cruiserweight	6 Sep 1991	24
2=	Al McCoy v George Chip	Middleweight	7 Apr 1914	45
2=	Lloyd Honeyghan v Gene Hatcher	Welterweight	30 Aug 1987	45
4	Mark Breland v Lee Seung-soon	Welterweight	4 Feb 1989	54
5	Emile Pladner v Frankie Genaro	Flyweight	2 Mar 1929	58
6=	Jackie Paterson v Peter Kane	Flyweight	19 Jun 1943	61
6=	Bobby Czyz v David Sears	Light-heavyweight	26 Dec 1986	61
8	Michael Dokes v Mike Weaver	Heavyweight	10 Dec 1982	63
9	Tony Canzoneri v Al Singer	Lightweight	14 Nov 1930	66
10	Marvin Hagler v Caveman Lee	Middleweight	7 Mar 1982	67

Lightweight world champion Al Singer engaged in only two world title bouts in his career. The first was when he beat Sammy Mandell for the title on 1 July 1930. The fight lasted one minute 46 seconds. He lost the title four months later to Tony Canzoneri in a bout lasting one minute six seconds. Altogether, his world title career lasted less than three minutes!

THE 10 MOST SUCCESSFUL COUNTRIES AT THE WORLD AMATEUR CHAMPIONSHIPS

Inaugurated at Havana, Cuba, in 1974, the World Amateur Championships have been held approximately every four years since, with a special challenge series in 1983. Teofilio Stevenson, Adolfo Horta and Pablo Romero (all Cuba) have won a record three titles. The top nations have been:

	Country	Medals gold	silver	bronze	Total
1	Cuba	30	14	9	53
2	USSR	16	10	18	44
3=	East Germany	1	8	15	24
3=	USA	8	7	9	24
5=	Yugoslavia	1	6	10	17
5=	Bulgaria	3	4	10	17
7	Germany/West Germany	2	1	7	10
8=	Poland	1	1	7	9
8=	Romania	1	2	6	9
10	Venezuela	0	4	4	8

No boxer from Great Britain and Northern Ireland has won a medal at the championships. Two Republic of Ireland fighters have, however, won bronze medals: Tommy Corr (light-middleweight) in 1982, and Michael Carruth (light-welterweight) in 1989.

THE FIRST 10 OLYMPIC CHAMPIONS TO WIN PROFESSIONAL WORLD TITLES

	Boxer/nationality	Olympic title	First professional title
1	Fidel la Barba (USA)	1924	1925
2	Frankie Genaro (USA)	1920	1928
3	Jackie Fields (USA)	1924	1929
4	Pascual Perez (Arg)	1948	1954
5	Floyd Patterson (USA)	1952	1956
6	Cassius Clay (USA)	1960	1964
7	Nino Benvenuti (Ita)	1960	1965
8	Joe Frazier (USA)	1964	1968
9	George Foreman (USA)	1968	1973
10	Mate Parlov (Yug)	1972	1978

Willie Smith (USA) took the Olympic bantamweight title in 1924 and three years later won the British version of the world title. However, he is not universally acknowledged as the world champion.

George Foreman, Joe Frazier and Ray Mercer are the only Olympic heavyweight champions to go on to win the professional world heavyweight title.

Boxing was included in the Olympic programme for the first time in 1904. Sweden did not allow boxing so the sport did not appear at the 1912 Stockholm Games but it has been included ever since 1920. Two men have won a record three gold medals. The first was Hungary's Laszlo Papp who won the middleweight title in 1948 and the light-middleweight division in 1952 and 1956. The other, Teofilio Stevenson of Cuba, has uniquely won three gold medals in one weight division, heavyweight, at the 1972, 1976 and 1980 Games. Former world heavyweight champion Ingemar Johansson (Sweden) was disqualified from the 1952 Olympic heavyweight final for 'not trying'. However, 30 years later he was presented with his medal. The two Britons who contested the 1908 middleweight final were a pair of sporting all-rounders. Gold medallist Johnny Douglas was to become the captain of the England cricket team, and runner-up Reginald Baker competed in the springboard diving competition at the 1908 London Olympics.

THE 10 MOST SUCCESSFUL OLYMPIC COUNTRIES

	Country	Medals gold	silver	bronze	Total
1	USA	47	20	29	96
2	USSR/CIS	14	20	18	52
3=	Great Britain	12	10	21	43
3=	Poland	8	9	26	43
5	Italy	14	12	13	39
6	Cuba	19	10	5	34
7	Germany/West Germany	6	11	10	27
8	Argentina	7	7	9	23
9	Romania	1	8	11	20
10	South Africa	6	4	9	19

Cuba's Teofilio Stevenson, seen here in action at the 1980 Moscow Games, holds a unique record: three Olympic gold medals in one weight division. He won the heavyweight title in 1972, 1976 and 1980.

WEIGHT DIVISIONS

Weight divisions were introduced in the mid-nineteenth century and were categorized as follows:

Heavyweight – over 156lb

Middleweight – up to 156lb

Lightweight – up to 133lb

Today there are 17 weight divisions ranging from Heavyweight to Straw-weight (also known as Mini-flyweight). With four major bodies recognizing world champions it means there are potentially 68 world champions at any one time.

THE 10 HEAVIEST WEIGHT DIVISIONS

	Weight	Limit kg	lb
1	Heavyweight	over 86	over 190
2	Cruiserweight	86	190
3	Light-heavyweight	79	175
4	Super-middleweight	76	168
5	Middleweight	73	160
6	Junior-middleweight/Super-welterweight	70	154
7	Welterweight	67	147
8	Junior-welterweight/Super-lightweight	65	140
9	Lightweight	61	135
10	Junior-lightweight/Super-featherweight	59	130

THE 10 LIGHTEST WEIGHT DIVISIONS

	Weight	Limit kg	lb
1	Straw-weight/Mini-flyweight	48	105
2	Junior flyweight/Light-flyweight	49	108
3	Flyweight	51	112
4	Junior-bantamweight/Super-flyweight	52	115
5	Bantamweight	54	118
6	Junior-featherweight/Super-bantamweight	55	122
7	Featherweight	57	126
8	Junior-lightweight/Super-featherweight	59	130
9	Lightweight	61	135
10	Junior-welterweight/Super-lightweight	65	140

THE 10 BOXERS WITH THE MOST KNOCKOUTS IN A CAREER

	Boxer	Career	Knockouts
1	Archie Moore	1936–63	129
2	Young Stribling	1921–63	126
3	Billy Bird	1920–48	125
4	Sam Langford	1902–26	116
5	George Odwell	1930–45	114
6	Sugar Ray Robinson	1940–65	110
7	Sandy Saddler	1944–65	103
8	Henry Armstrong	1931–45	100
9	Jimmy Wilde	1911–23	99
10	Len Wickwar	1928–47	93

Although this is the most generally accepted Top 10, boxing historians disagree considerably on this subject. Some historians, for example, include exhibition matches as well as professional bouts.

All 10 boxers were from the USA except Jimmy Wilde (1892–1969), who was Welsh.

THE 10 BOXERS WITH THE MOST ABA TITLES

The Amateur Boxing Association (ABA) was formed in 1880 and the following year at the first championships heavyweight, middleweight, lightweight and featherweight divisions were organized. The inaugural heavyweight champion was R. Frost-Smith, one of the men responsible for the formation of the ABA.

	Boxer	Years	Titles
1	John Lyon	1981–89	8
2	Joseph Steers	1890–1903	6
3=	Frederick Parks	1899–1906	5
3=	Ruben Warnes	1899–1910	5
3=	G. Baker	1912–21	5
3=	Harry Mallin	1919–23	5
3=	Fred Mallin	1928–32	5
3=	Thomas Pardoe	1929–33	5
3=	Dick McTaggart	1956–65	5
3=	Terence Waller	1967–74	5
3=	George Gilbody	1974–81	5

The 1954 ABA heavyweight champion was Brian Harper who went on to earn fame as a professional as Brian London. Frank Bruno was the 1980 heavyweight champion.

THE FIRST 10 MEN TO WIN LONSDALE BELTS OUTRIGHT

	Boxer	Weight	Date won
1	Jim Driscoll	Featherweight	30 Jan 1911
2	Freddie Welsh	Lightweight	11 Nov 1912
3	Digger Stanley	Bantamweight	27 Oct 1913
4	Johnny Basham	Welterweight	1 May 1916
5	Bombardier Billy Wells	Heavyweight	18 Dec 1916
6	Jimmy Wilde	Flyweight	11 Mar 1917
7	Joe Fox	Bantamweight	25 Jun 1917
8	Pat O'Keefe	Middleweight	28 Jan 1918
9	Dick Smith	Light-heavyweight	25 Feb 1918
10	Tancy Lee	Featherweight	24 Feb 1919

To keep permanent possession of a Lonsdale Belt, the most cherished prize in British professional boxing, a fighter has to win three fights in one weight division. The first Lonsdale Belts were given to the National Sporting Club by the 5th Earl of Lonsdale in 1909. The belts were redesigned by the British Boxing Board of Control in 1936 but still retained the name of Lonsdale Belt.

In 1945 Nel Tarleton (featherweight) became the first man to win two Belts outright. Henry Cooper is the only man to win three Belts outright (1961, 1964 and 1967).

Super Bowl XXVI: Gerald Riggs of the Washington Redskins runs in to touch down in his team's 37–24 victory over the Buffalo Bills. The Redskins are one of the most successful Super Bowl teams of all time. (Allsport)

Pete Rose, who scored 2,165 runs in his career, the 4th highest total ever. He is also the player with most games in a career and on retiring he went on to coach his old team, the Cincinnati Reds. (Allsport)

Ian Wright of Arsenal (on ground), top League goalscorer in 1991–92 with 29, slides a valuable equaliser past the sprawling Chelsea defence. (Colorsport)

Peter Shilton, seen here in action for Derby County, has made more Football League appearances than any other player. He also holds the record for most international caps in the world with 125. (Empics)

Paul Gascoigne comes in for some rough treatment from Germany's Andreas Brehme during the 1990 World Cup semi-final which England lost on penalties. 'Gazza' was the 2nd most fouled player in the competition and went on to become one of the most expensive players in the world when the Italian side Lazio bought him from Spurs for £5,500,000. (Bob Thomas)

Right Mike Powell's world record-breaking jump of 8.95m at the 1991 Tokyo World Championships. The previous record for the long jump of 8.90m, set by Bob Beamon at the 1968 Mexico Olympics, had stood for nearly 23 years. (Associated Sports Photography)

Above *The men's 100m final at the World Championships in Tokyo in 1991 produced four of the fastest times ever recorded in the event. Left to right: Dennis Mitchell (9.91sec), Carl Lewis (9.86 – a new world record), Linford Christie (9.92), Leroy Burrell (9.88). (Colorsport)*

Below *James 'Buster' Douglas knocks out Mike Tyson to take the world heavyweight crown in 1990.* Boxing Illustrated *rate Tyson's shock defeat as the biggest upset in boxing history. (Colorsport)*

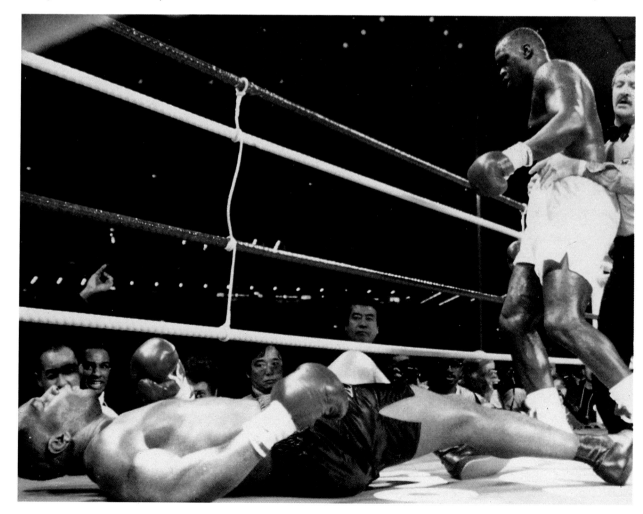

Heavyweight boxer Evander Holyfield, the highest-earning sportsman in the world. (Colorsport)

Boxing referee Mills Lane, 2nd on the list of referees most frequently employed in world heavyweight title fights. (Allsport)

Mike Gatting, who scored 2,044 runs for Middlesex in the 1991 County Championship, the 2nd highest total of the season. (Patrick Eagar)

Waqar Younis of Surrey and Pakistan, top wicket-taker in the 1991 County Championship with 113. (Patrick Eagar)

Seve Ballesteros on his way to winning the 1991 Volvo PGA Championship at Wentworth and claiming the £83,330 prizemoney. In 1991 Seve overtook Ian Woosnam as the top career money-winner on the European Tour. (Colorsport)

Ballesteros's compatriot and Ryder Cup partner José Maria Olazabal is one of the youngest and most successful golfers on the European Tour. (Colorsport)

Lester Piggott wins the 1992 2,000 Guineas on Rodrigo de Triano to take his tally of English Classic victories to 30, some 38 years after his first Classic success on Never Say Die in the 1954 Derby. (Trevor Jones)

Red Rum in the lead in the 1974 Grand National, on his way to his second successive victory in the race. He won a record third time in 1977 to become the National's most successful horse. (Gerry Cranham)

GREAT PUGILISTS OF THE PAST

In 1776 Harry Sellers beat Peter Corcoran over 38 rounds at the Crown Inn, Staines for a prize of 100 guineas. This was indeed a princely sum in those days, but how far removed was it from the multi-million dollar purses and showbusiness razzamatazz that is associated with championship boxing these days?

Man has always had the ability, desire and, in many cases, good cause, to hit his fellow man, but bare-knuckle fighting as a sport developed only in the eighteenth century when James Figg (or Fig as he was also known) opened a school of arms at his Amphitheatre on the corner of Tottenham Court Road and Oxford Road (now Oxford Street) in 1719. There he taught fighting skills, both with bare knuckles and with cudgels, and in 1720 Figg fought and beat Ned Sutton from Gravesend to claim the title 'champion of England' and thus became the sport's first such champion.

Many great pugilists learned their skills at Figg's Amphitheatre and it was he who helped to develop George Taylor and Jack Broughton, who both succeeded Figg as champion. Broughton, who became known as 'The Father of British Boxing', was responsible for drawing up the sport's first rules in 1743. They governed the sport until 1838 when the London Prize Fighting Rules were introduced. Broughton, whose rules stipulated no gouging or hitting a fallen opponent, lived until he was 85 and was buried in Westminster Abbey – an honour unlikely to befall any of our modern-day champions.

Eighteenth-century prizefighting was popular among all ranks of society, and impoverished aristocrats often attended fights in the hope of winning extra cash as a result of betting. The Duke of Cumberland was one such punter but he lost heavily when Jack Broughton was defeated by Norwich butcher Jack Slack in 1750. The Duke then became the principal backer of Slack but lost again when Bill 'The Nailer' Stevens beat Slack in 1760 (the fight was allegedly rigged, with Stevens engaging in a double-cross).

For more than 20 years the British title had little meaning because fighters were often paid to lose and the sport gained little respect with the fans. It was only after Tom Johnson took the crown in 1783 that pugilism regained its lost ground. Johnson, born Thomas Jackling, reigned until 1791 when he was surprisingly beaten by Benjamin Brain ('Big Ben') who was sponsored by the Duke of Hamilton, another member of the nobility who enjoyed boxing – or, more accurately, betting on boxing.

A new era of heavyweight boxing came when Daniel Mendoza captured the title by beating Bill Warr in November 1794. Mendoza, the first Jewish champion, was more intelligent than the former champions and whereas strength alone had previously determined each new champion, Mendoza introduced a scientific approach to the sport never seen before.

Another fighter who followed Mendoza's lead was John Gully, who became champion in 1807. Gully was one of the most interesting champions in the bare-knuckle days of boxing. The son of a merchant, he went into business on his own account, failed miserably, and ended up in a debtors' prison, where he could have remained for the rest of his life. It was thanks only to another pugilist of the day, Henry Pearce ('The Game Chicken'), a friend of Gully's, who paid to have him released. All his debts were eventually cleared in full as a result of Gully's meeting Pearce for the title. Pearce won the 600 guineas first prize over 64 rounds at Hailsham, Sussex, on 8 October 1805. Gully collected 400 guineas and was financially solvent again. Gully succeeded Pearce as champion in 1807, but announced his retirement after one successful defence of the title. He became a wealthy landowner and successful racehorse owner, winning the Derby with Pyrrhus the First (1846) and Andover (1854), and also became a Member of Parliament.

Three 'Toms' succeeded Gully as champion. Firstly there was Tom Cribb, then Tom Spring, and finally Tom Cannon, nicknamed 'The Great Gun of Windsor', who, ironically, committed suicide in 1858 – by shooting himself. By the time Cannon had taken the English title in 1824, the sport had gained in popularity across the Atlantic and the United States produced its first champion, Jacob Hyer, in 1816. However, the first international fight, for a purse of $1,000, did not take place until 17 April 1860 at Farnborough, Hampshire, England. The contest, between Britain's Tom Sayers and America's John C. Heenan, is regarded as the first-ever world title fight. After 37 rounds the contest was declared a draw. The police tried to stop the fight but such was the interest expressed by high-ranking army officials, Members of Parliament and clergymen (even the writers Charles Dickens and William Thackeray were in the crowd), they dared not halt proceedings.

'Gypsy' Jem Mace first became champion of England in 1861 and brought new-found interest to the sport after Sayers' retirement. The man who succeeded Sayers, Sam Hurst, lacked appeal and the sport in Britain was in danger of dying. However, Mace, a one-time itinerant fiddler, was a popular champion and he would have fought Heenan for the world crown in 1863 had he not lost to Tom King the previous year. King went on to beat Heenan and thus became boxing's first world champion. Mace regained the English title in 1863 and in 1870 beat Tom Allen for the world title. Mace retired the following year after fighting a draw with Joe Coburn and his retirement brought to an end the era of the great bare-knuckle pugilists.

There were others still around, such as the Americans Paddy Ryan and John L. Sullivan, but they were to be the last link between the bare-knuckle days and the new era of fighting with gloves after the introduction of the Queensberry Rules in 1867. The sport came a long way in the 148 years from Figg to Queensberry, and has come still further since the first gloved world champion, Jack Dempsey, in 1884.

THE 10 BIGGEST UPSETS IN BOXING HISTORY ACCORDING TO *BOXING ILLUSTRATED*

	Boxers (winners first)*	Weight	Year
1	James 'Buster' Douglas *v* Mike Tyson	Heavyweight	1990
2	Max Schmeling *v* Joe Louis	Heavyweight	1936
3	James J. Braddock *v* Max Baer	Heavyweight	1935
4	Cassius Clay *v* Sonny Liston	Heavyweight	1964
5	James J. Corbett *v* John L. Sullivan	Heavyweight	1892
6	Fritzie Zivic *v* Henry Armstrong	Welterweight	1940
7	Billy Papke *v* Stanley Ketchel	Middleweight	1908
8	Randolph Turpin *v* Sugar Ray Robinson	Middleweight	1951
9	Jess Willard *v* Jack Johnson	Heavyweight	1915
10	Battling Siki *v* Georges Carpentier	Light-heavyweight	1922

All were world title bouts except the Schmeling–Louis contest.

This list was drawn up by *Boxing Illustrated* after Mike Tyson's shock defeat by James 'Buster' Douglas. Since then James Toomey has emerged as another candidate for this list, when he beat Michael Nunn in 11 rounds to win the IBF middleweight title on 10 May 1991.

THE TOP 10 MONEY-WINNERS IN 1990

	Boxer*	Earnings ($)
1	James 'Buster' Douglas	25,400,000
2	Mike Tyson	18,500,000
3	Evander Holyfield	9,500,000
4	George Foreman	3,000,000
5	Nigel Benn (GB)	2,760,000
6	Gerry Cooney	2,500,000
7=	Julio Cesar Chavez (Mex)	1,500,000
7=	Hector Camacho (PR)	1,500,000
7=	Michael Nunn	1,500,000
7=	Tommy Hearns	1,500,000

American unless otherwise stated.

CANOEING

THE 10 MOST SUCCESSFUL OLYMPIC COUNTRIES

	Country	Medals gold	silver	bronze	Total
1	USSR/CIS	30	14	9	53
2	Hungary	8	22	18	48
3	Germany/West Germany	15	18	12	45
4	East Germany	14	7	9	30
5	Romania	9	9	11	29
6	Sweden	13	10	3	26
7	France	1	6	13	20
8	Bulgaria	5	3	7	15
9=	Austria	3	6	5	14
9=	USA	5	3	6	14

Canoeing has been an official Olympic sport since 1936, although it was first seen as a demonstration sport 12 years earlier. Great Britain won its first-ever Olympic canoeing medal (silver) at the 1992 Games.

COMMONWEALTH GAMES

THE TOP 10 GOLD MEDAL WINNING COUNTRIES

Held every four years (except 1942 and 1946) since their inception at Hamilton, Canada, in 1930, the Commonwealth Games are a sporting contest among Commonwealth countries held in between Olympic celebrations. Badminton and bowls are two Commonwealth Games sports not contested at the Olympics.

	Country	Gold medals
1	England	420
2	Australia	397
3	Canada	287
4	New Zealand	94
5	South Africa	60
6	Scotland	56
7	India	37
8	Kenya	35
9	Wales	32
10=	Jamaica	20
10=	Pakistan	20

A total of 36 nations have won gold medals while 42 have won a medal of some sort. England, Australia and Canada retain 1st, 2nd and 3rd in the overall medal list (gold, silver and bronze) with 1,156, 1,093 and 887 medals respectively.

Marcus Stephen was Nauru's first and only competitor in the Commonwealth Games. He won three medals – a gold in the weightlifting snatch category, and silvers in the clean and jerk and combined competitions. Nauru is an island in the south-west Pacific with a population of 8,042.

At the 1990 Commonwealth Games in Auckland the victorious 4 x 100m relay squad (Linford Christie, Marcus Adam, John Regis and Clarence Callender) provided England with yet another gold medal.

THE TOP 10 COUNTRIES AT THE 1990 COMMONWEALTH GAMES*

	Country	Medals won	Population per medal
1	Nauru	3	2,681
2	Jersey	2	40,106
3	Guernsey	1	54,380
4	Bermuda	1	57,145
5	Western Samoa	2	79,470
6	Australia	162	98,604
7	Wales	25	112,840
8	Bahamas	2	117,500
9	Northern Ireland	9	174,089
10	Scotland	22	232,773
14	*England*	*129*	*366,314*

*Based on ratio of medals won to population.

The first Games, then known as the Empire Games, were held in 1930 at Hamilton, Canada, when athletics, bowls, boxing, rowing, swimming, and wrestling were included in the programme. The only other sports to have been featured are archery, gymnastics and judo, the last-named making its debut in 1990. The only time bowls was not included in the programme was at Kingston, Jamaica, in 1966. To compensate, the first world bowls championships were held that year.

THE 10 SPORTS CONTESTED AT THE MOST CELEBRATIONS

	Sport	Year first included	No. of times included
1=	Athletics	1930	14
1=	Boxing	1930	14
1=	Swimming	1930	14
4=	Bowls	1930	13
4=	Cycling	1934	13
4=	Wrestling (freestyle)	1930	13
7	Weightlifting	1950	11
8=	Badminton	1966	7
8=	Rowing	1930	7
10=	Fencing	1950	6
10=	Shooting	1966	6

CRICKET

THE 10 HIGHEST INDIVIDUAL TEST INNINGS

	Batsman	Match/venue	Year	Runs
1	Gary Sobers	West Indies v Pakistan (Kingston)	1957–58	365 *
2	Len Hutton	England v Australia (The Oval)	1938	364
3	Hanif Mohammad	Pakistan v West Indies (Bridgetown)	1957–58	337
4	Walter Hammond	England v New Zealand (Auckland)	1932–33	336 *
5	Don Bradman	Australia v England (Leeds)	1930	334
6	Graham Gooch	England v India (Lord's)	1990	333
7	Andrew Sandham	England v West Indies (Kingston)	1929–30	325
8	Bobby Simpson	Australia v England (Manchester)	1964	311
9	John Edrich	England v New Zealand (Leeds)	1965	310 *
10	Bob Cowper	Australia v England (Melbourne)	1965–66	307

* Not out.

Perhaps surprisingly, Gary Sobers' next best score was 226 against England at Bridgetown in 1959–60. Apart from his 365 not out, it was his only other Test double century. Sobers' record-breaking score came in his 17th Test, which was the 3rd Test of the series against Pakistan.

Prior to his 365, his highest Test innings had been 80 in the previous Test at Port-of-Spain just three weeks earlier. Before scoring his 365 his Test average stood at 34.24. After his record-breaking score it rose to 48.84.

THE PROGRESSION OF THE HIGHEST INDIVIDUAL TEST INNINGS

Batsman/match	Venue	Year	Runs
Charles Bannerman (Australia v England)	Melbourne	1876–77	165*
Billy Murdoch (Australia v England)	The Oval	1884	211
Reginald Foster (England v Australia)	Sydney	1903–04	287
Andrew Sandham (England v West Indies)	Kingston	1929–30	325
Don Bradman (Australia v England)	Leeds	1930	334
Walter Hammond (England v New Zealand)	Auckland	1932–33	336*
Len Hutton (England v Australia)	The Oval	1938	364
Gary Sobers (West Indies v Pakistan)	Kingston	1957–58	365*

* Not out.

THE 10 BEST BOWLING HAULS IN A TEST INNINGS

	Bowler	Match/venue	Year	Figures
1	Jim Laker	England v Australia (Manchester)	1956	10–53
2	George Lohmann	England v South Africa (Johannesburg)	1895–96	9–28
3	Jim Laker	England v Australia (Manchester)	1956	9–37
4	Richard Hadlee	New Zealand v Australia (Brisbane)	1985–86	9–52
5	Abdul Qadir	Pakistan v England (Lahore)	1987–88	9–56
6	Jasubhai Patel	India v Australia (Kanpur)	1959–60	9–69
7	Kapil Dev	India v West Indies (Ahmedabad)	1983–84	9–83
8	Sarfraz Nawaz	Pakistan v Australia (Melbourne)	1978–79	9–86
9	Jack Noreiga	West Indies v India (Port-of-Spain)	1970–71	9–95
10	Subhash Gupte	India v West Indies (Kanpur)	1958–59	9–102

Less than three months before taking all 10 Australian wickets in an innings in the 4th Test at Old Trafford, Jim Laker performed the feat for his county, Surrey – also against the Australians. He took 10–88 in the first innings but only 2–42 in the second. England colleague Tony Lock did the damage in the second innings with 7–49. Surrey won by 10 wickets and the only man to be dismissed by Laker four times in the two matches was Ken Mackay.

Jim Laker claims the wicket of Australian batsman Leonard Maddocks in the 4th Test at Old Trafford in 1956. The England bowler took a record 10 wickets in an innings, and 19 in the match.

THE TOP 10 WICKET-TAKERS IN A TEST MATCH

	Bowler	Match/venue	Year	Wickets
1	Jim Laker	England v Australia (Manchester)	1956	19
2	Sydney Barnes	England v South Africa (Johannesburg)	1913–14	17
3=	Bob Massie	Australia v England (Lord's)	1972	16
3=	Narenda Hirwani	India v West Indies (Madras)	1987–88	16
5=	Johnny Briggs	England v South Africa (Cape Town)	1888–89	15
5=	George Lohmann	England v South Africa (Port Elizabeth)	1895–96	15
5=	Wilf Rhodes	England v Australia (Melbourne)	1903–04	15
5=	Colin Blythe	England v South Africa (Leeds)	1907	15
5=	Hedley Verity	England v Australia (Lord's)	1934	15
5=	Richard Hadlee	New Zealand v Australia (Brisbane)	1985–86	15

THE 10 MOST CATCHES IN A TEST CAREER BY AN OUTFIELDER*

	Fielder/country	Years	Catches
1	Allan Border (Australia)	1978–92	135
2=	Greg Chappell (Australia)	1970–84	122
2=	Viv Richards (West Indies)	1974–91	122
4	Colin Cowdrey (England)	1954–75	120
5	Ian Botham (England)	1977–92	118
6=	Walter Hammond (England)	1927–47	110
6=	Bobby Simpson (Australia)	1957–78	110
8	Gary Sobers (West Indies)	1954–74	109
9	Sunil Gavaskar (India)	1971–87	108
10	Ian Chappell (Australia)	1964–80	105

*To end 1991–92.

THE TOP 10 RUN-MAKERS IN A TEST CAREER*

	Batsman/country	Years	Runs
1	Sunil Gavaskar (India)	1971–87	10,122
2	Allan Border (Australia)	1978–92	9,532
3	Viv Richards (West Indies)	1974–91	8,540
4	Geoff Boycott (England)	1964–82	8,114
5	Javed Miandad (Pakistan)	1976–92	8,101
6	David Gower (England)	1978–91	8,081
7	Gary Sobers (West Indies)	1954–74	8,032
8	Colin Cowdrey (England)	1954–75	7,624
9	Gordon Greenidge (West Indies)	1974–91	7,558
10	Clive Lloyd (West Indies)	1966–85	7,515

*To end 1991–92.

HOW JIM LAKER CLAIMED HIS 19 VICTIMS IN THE ENGLAND v AUSTRALIA 4th TEST, 26–31 July 1956

Australia	1st innings		2nd innings	
C. C. McDonald	c Lock b Laker	32	c Oakman b Laker	89
J. W. Burke	c Cowdrey b Lock	22	c Lock b Laker	33
R. N. Harvey	b Laker	0	c Cowdrey b Laker	0
I. D. Craig	lbw Laker	8	lbw Laker	38
K. R. Miller	c Oakman b Laker	6	b Laker	0
L. V. Maddocks	b Laker	4	lbw Laker	2
I. W. Johnson	b Laker	0	not out	1
K. D. Mackay	c Oakman b Laker	0	c Oakman b Laker	0
R. G. Archer	st Evans b Laker	6	c Oakman b Laker	0
R. Benaud	c Statham b Laker	0	b Laker	18
R. R. Lindwall	not out	6	c Lock b Laker	8
Extras		0		16
Total		**84**		**205**

Laker's figures:	Overs	Maidens	Runs	Wickets
1st innings	16.4	4	37	9
2nd innings	51.2	23	53	10

Hadlee's record against each country:

Opponents	Tests	Wkts	Wickets per match
Sri Lanka	6	37	6.17
Australia	23	130	5.65
West Indies	10	51	5.10
India	14	65	4.64
England	21	97	4.62
Pakistan	12	51	4.25

His best single match haul was 9–52 against Australia at Brisbane in 1985–86, and his best haul in a series was 33, also against Australia in 1985–86.

THE 10 MOST DISMISSALS BY A WICKETKEEPER IN TEST CRICKET*

	Wicketkeeper/country	Years	Dismissals
1	Rodney Marsh (Australia)	1970–84	355
2	Jeffrey Dujon (West Indies)	1981–91	272
3	Alan Knott (England)	1967–81	269
4	Wasim Bari (Pakistan)	1967–84	228
5	Godfrey Evans (England)	1946–59	219
6	Syed Kirmani (India)	1976–86	198
7	Derryck Murray (West Indies)	1963–80	189
8	Wally Grout (Australia)	1957–66	187
9	Ian Smith (New Zealand)	1980–92	176
10	Bob Taylor (England)	1971–84	174

To end 1991–92.

THE TOP 10 WICKET-TAKERS IN A TEST CAREER*

	Bowler/country	Years	Wickets
1	Richard Hadlee (New Zealand)	1973–90	431
2	Kapil Dev (India)	1978–92	401
3	Ian Botham (England)	1977–92	383
4	Malcolm Marshall (West Indies)	1978–91	376
5	Imran Khan (Pakistan)	1971–92	362
6	Dennis Lillee (Australia)	1971–84	355
7	Bob Willis (England)	1971–84	325
8	Lance Gibbs (West Indies)	1958–76	309
9	Fred Trueman (England)	1952–65	307
10	Derek Underwood (England)	1966–82	297

To end 1991–92.

THE TOP 10 WICKET-TAKERS IN A TEST SERIES

	Bowler	Series*	Year	Wickets
1	Sydney Barnes	England v South Africa (4)	1913–14	49
2	Jim Laker	England v Australia (5)	1956	46
3	Clarrie Grimmett	Australia v South Africa (5)	1935–36	44
4	Terry Alderman	Australia v England (6)	1981	42
5=	Rodney Hogg	Australia v England (6)	1978–79	41
5=	Terry Alderman	Australia v England (6)	1989	41
7	Imran Khan	Pakistan v India (6)	1982–83	40
8=	Alec Bedser	England v Australia (5)	1953	39
8=	Dennis Lillee	Australia v England (6)	1981	39
10	Maurice Tate	England v Australia (5)	1924–25	38

Figures in brackets indicate number of Tests.

How Sydney Barnes's total was made up:

	1st innings	2nd innings
1st Test	5–57	5–48
2nd Test	8–56	9–103
3rd Test	3–26	5–102
4th Test	7–56	7–88
5th Test	Did not play†	

†Barnes refused to play in the 5th and final Test because he was in dispute at the time.

THE TOP 10 RUN-MAKERS IN A TEST SERIES

	Batsman	Series*	Year	Runs
1	Don Bradman	Australia v England (5)	1930	974
2	Walter Hammond	England v Australia (5)	1928–29	905
3	Mark Taylor	Australia v England (6)	1989	839
4	Neil Harvey	Australia v South Africa (5)	1952–53	834
5	Viv Richards	West Indies v England (4)	1976	829
6	Clyde Walcott	West Indies v Australia (5)	1954–55	827
7	Gary Sobers	West Indies v Pakistan (5)	1957-58	824
8	Don Bradman	Australia v England (5)	1936–37	810
9	Don Bradman	Australia v South Africa (5)	1931–32	806
10	Everton Weekes	West Indies v India (5)	1948–49	779

Figures in brackets indicate number of Tests.

How Bradman's figure of 974 was made up:

	1st innings		2nd innings	
1st Test	b Tate	8	b Robins	131
2nd Test	c Chapman b White	254	c Chapman b Tate	1
3rd Test	c Duckworth b Tate	334		
4th Test	c Duleepsinjhi b Peebles	14		
5th Test	c Duckworth b Larwood	232		

THE 10 PLAYERS TO MAKE THE MOST TEST RUNS IN A CALENDAR YEAR

	Batsman/country	Year*	Runs
1	Viv Richards (West Indies)	1976 (11)	1,710
2	Sunil Gavaskar (India)	1979 (18)	1,555
3	Gundappa Viswanath (India)	1979 (17)	1,388
4	Bobby Simpson (Australia)	1964 (14)	1,381
5	Dennis Amiss (England)	1974 (13)	1,379
6	Sunil Gavaskar (India)	1983 (18)	1,310
7	Graham Gooch (England)	1990 (9)	1,264
8	Mark Taylor (Australia)	1989 (11)	1,219
9	Gary Sobers (West Indies)	1958 (7)	1,193
10	Dilip Vengsarkar (India)	1979 (18)	1,174

Figures in brackets indicate number of Tests played.

Taylor was playing in his first year in Test cricket.

THE TOP 10 TEST PARTNERSHIPS

	Batsmen	Match	Venue	Year	Wicket	Stand
1	Andrew Jones/Martin Crowe	New Zealand v Sri Lanka	Wellington	1990–91	3rd	467
2=	Bill Ponsford/Don Bradman	Australia v England	The Oval	1934	2nd	451
2=	Mudassar Nazar/Javed Miandad	Pakistan v India	Hyderabad	1982–83	3rd	451
4	Conrad Hunte/Gary Sobers	West Indies v Pakistan	Kingston	1957–58	2nd	446
5	Vinoo Mankad/Pankaj Roy	India v New Zealand	Madras	1955–56	1st	413
6	Peter May/Colin Cowdrey	England v West Indies	Birmingham	1957	4th	411
7	Sidney Barnes/Don Bradman	Australia v England	Sydney	1946–47	5th	405
8	Gary Sobers/Frank Worrell	West Indies v England	Bridgetown	1959–60	4th	399
9	Qasim Omar/Javed Miandad	Pakistan v Sri Lanka	Faisalabad	1985–86	3rd	397
10	Bill Ponsford/Don Bradman	Australia v England	Leeds	1934	4th	388

India's 3rd wicket stand against England at Madras in 1981–82 was for 415 runs but involved three batsmen: Gundappa Viswanath, Yashpal Sharma and Dilip Vengsarkar. The last-named retired hurt when the stand was on 99.

THE 10 HIGHEST TEAM TOTALS IN TEST CRICKET

	Match	Venue	Year	Score
1	England v Australia	The Oval	1938	903–7dec
2	England v West Indies	Kingston	1929–30	849
3	West Indies v Pakistan	Kingston	1957–58	790–3dec
4	Australia v West Indies	Kingston	1954–55	758–8dec
5	Australia v England	Lord's	1930	729–6dec
6	Pakistan v England	The Oval	1987	708
7	Australia v England	The Oval	1934	701
8	Pakistan v India	Lahore	1989–90	699–5dec
9	Australia v England	The Oval	1930	695
10	West Indies v England	The Oval	1976	687–8dec

THE 10 LOWEST COMPLETED INNINGS IN TEST CRICKET

	Match	Venue	Year	Total
1	New Zealand v England	Auckland	1954–55	26
2=	South Africa v England	Port Elizabeth	1895–96	30
2=	South Africa v England	Birmingham	1924	30
4	South Africa v England	Cape Town	1898–99	35
5=	Australia v England	Birmingham	1902	36
5=	South Africa v Australia	Melbourne	1931–32	36
7=	Australia v England	Sydney	1887–88	42
7=	New Zealand v Australia	Wellington	1945–46	42
7=	India* v England	Lord's	1974	42
10	South Africa v England	Cape Town	1888–89	43

India batted one man short.

Engand's lowest total is 45, when dismissed by Australia at Sydney in 1886–87.

ENGLAND'S RECORD-BREAKING SCORECARD

L. Hutton	c Hassett b O'Reilly	364
W. J. Edrich	lbw O'Reilly	12
M. Leyland	run out	187
W. R. Hammond	lbw Fleetwood-Smith	59
E. Paynter	lbw O'Reilly	0
D. C. S. Compton	b Waite	1
J. Hardstaff jr	not out	169
A. Wood	c & b Barnes	53
H. Verity	not out	8
Extras	(b22, lb19, w1, nb8)	50
Total	**(7 wickets dec)**	**903**
Did not bat:	K. Farnes, W. E. Bowes	

Australian bowler 'Chuck' Fleetwood-Smith returned figures of 87 overs, 11 maidens, one wicket for 298 runs, the greatest number of runs conceded by a bowler in Test cricket.

England No. 5 Eddie Paynter was padded up for a day and a half while Len Hutton piled on the runs. He was eventually dismissed for a duck!

NEW ZEALAND'S RECORD LOW SCORECARD

2nd innings

B. Sutcliffe	b Wardle	11
J. G. Leggat	c Hutton b Tyson	1
M. B. Poore	b Tyson	0
J. R. Reid	b Statham	1
S. N. McGregor	c May b Appleyard	1
G. O. Rabone	lbw Statham	7
H. B. Cave	c Graveney b Appleyard	5
A. R. MacGibbon	lbw Appleyard	0
I. A. Colquhoun	c Graveney b Appleyard	0
A. M. Moir	not out	0
J. A. Hayes	b Statham	0
Extras		0
Total		**26**

Fall of wickets: 1–6, 2–8, 3–9, 4–14, 5–14, 6–22, 7–22, 8–22, 9–26

Bowling: Tyson 7–2–10–2; Statham 9–3–9–3; Appleyard 6–3–7–4; Wardle 5–5–0–1

England won by an innings and 20 runs

THE 10 FASTEST TEST CENTURIES

	Batsman	Match	Venue	Year	Time (min)
1	Jack Gregory	Australia *v* South Africa	Johannesburg	1921–22	70
2	Gilbert Jessop	England *v* Australia	The Oval	1902	75
3	Richie Benaud	Australia *v* West Indies	Kingston	1954–55	78
4	Jimmy Sinclair	South Africa *v* Australia	Cape Town	1902–03	80
5	Viv Richards	West Indies *v* England	St John's	1985–86	81*
6	Bruce Taylor	New Zealand *v* West Indies	Auckland	1968–69	86
7=	Joe Darling	Australia *v* England	Sydney	1897–98	91
7=	Stan McCabe	Australia *v* South Africa	Johannesburg	1935–36	91
9	Victor Trumper	Australia *v* England	Sydney	1903–04	94
10=	Jack Brown	England *v* Australia	Melbourne	1894–95	95
10=	Percy Sherwell	South Africa *v* England	Lord's	1907	95

The fastest in terms of fewest balls received (56).

THE 10 MOST TEST APPEARANCES*

	Player/country	Years	Tests
1	Allan Border (Australia)	1978–92	130
2	Sunil Gavaskar (India)	1971–87	125
3	Viv Richards (West Indies)	1974–91	121
4	Dilip Vengsarkar (India)	1976–92	116
5	Kapil Dev (India)	1978–92	115
6=	Colin Cowdrey (England)	1954–75	114
6=	David Gower (England)	1978–91	114
8	Javed Miandad (Pakistan)	1976–92	112
9	Clive Lloyd (West Indies)	1966–85	110
10=	Geoff Boycott (England)	1964–82	108
10=	Gordon Greenidge (West Indies)	1974–91	108

To end 1991–92.

Colin Cowdrey made a total of 114 Test appearances for England.

THE 10 MOST TEST CENTURIES*

	Batsman/country	Centuries
1	Sunil Gavaskar (India)	34
2	Don Bradman (Australia)	29
3	Gary Sobers (West Indies)	26
4=	Greg Chappell (Australia)	24
4=	Viv Richards (West Indies)	24
6	Allan Border (Australia)	23
7=	Geoff Boycott (England)	22
7=	Colin Cowdrey (England)	22
7=	Walter Hammond (England)	22
7=	Javed Miandad (Pakistan)	22

*To end 1991–92.

THE 10 MOST TEST APPEARANCES AS CAPTAIN*

	Captain/country	Appearances as captain
1	Clive Lloyd (West Indies)	74
2	Allan Border (Australia)	67
3=	Greg Chappell (Australia)	48
3=	Imran Khan (Pakistan)	48
3=	Viv Richards (West Indies)	48
6	Sunil Gavaskar (India)	47
7	Peter May (England)	41
8	Nawab of Pataudi jr (India)	40
9=	Bobby Simpson (Australia)	39
9=	Gary Sobers (West Indies)	39

*To end 1991–92.

Viv Richards never lost a Test series as captain.

Gavaskar scored 13 centuries in 48 innings against the West Indies, representing a century every 3.69 innings. His tally against other countries and innings played was:

Opponents	Centuries	Innings	Incidence
Australia	8	31	3.88
Sri Lanka	2	11	5.50
New Zealand	2	16	8.00
Pakistan	5	41	8.20
England	4	67	16.75

THE FIRST 10 TEST CENTURIES SCORED BY ENGLAND BATSMEN

	Batsman	Venue	Score	Date
1	W. G. Grace	The Oval	152	6–8 Sep 1880
2	George Ulyett	Melbourne	149	10–14 Mar 1882
3	Allan Steel	Sydney	135*	17–21 Feb 1883
4	Allan Steel	Lord's	148	21–23 Jul 1884
5	Walter Read	The Oval	117	11–13 Aug 1884
6	William Barnes	Adelaide	134	12–16 Dec 1884
7	John Briggs	Melbourne	121	1–5 Jan 1885
8	Arthur Shrewsbury	Melbourne	105*	21–25 Mar 1885
9	Arthur Shrewsbury	Lord's	164	19–21 Jul 1886
10	W. G. Grace	The Oval	170	12–14 Aug 1886

*Not out.

All 10 centuries were scored against Australia. W. G. Grace's two centuries were the only ones he scored in Test cricket.

THE 10 HIGHEST SCORES BY CAPTAINS IN TEST CRICKET

	Player	Match	Venue	Year	Runs
1	Graham Gooch	England v India	Lord's	1990	333
2	Bobby Simpson	Australia v England	Manchester	1964	311
3	Martin Crowe	New Zealand v Sri Lanka	Wellington	1990–91	299
4	Peter May	England v West Indies	Birmingham	1957	285*
5	Don Bradman	Australia v England	Melbourne	1936–37	270
6	Clive Lloyd	West Indies v India	Bombay	1974–75	242*
7	Walter Hammond	England v Australia	Lord's	1938	240
8	Graham Dowling	New Zealand v India	Christchurch	1967–68	239
9	Greg Chappell	Australia v Pakistan	Faisalabad	1979–80	235
10	Don Bradman	Australia v England	Sydney	1946–47	234

*Not out.

THE 10 MOST APPEARANCES AS ENGLAND TEST CAPTAIN*

	Player	Matches as captain
1	Peter May	41
2	David Gower	32
3=	Mike Brearley	31
3=	Ray Illingworth	31
5	Ted Dexter	30
6	Colin Cowdrey	27
7	Mike Smith	25
8=	Mike Gatting	23
8=	Graham Gooch	23
8=	Len Hutton	23

*To end 1991–92.

THE 10 COUNTIES TO HAVE SUPPLIED THE MOST ENGLAND CAPTAINS

	County	No. of England captains
1	Middlesex	11
2=	Sussex	7
2=	Yorkshire	7
4=	Kent	6
4=	Surrey	6
6	Lancashire	5
7=	Essex	4
7=	Nottinghamshire	4
7=	Warwickshire	4
10	Worcestershire	3

THE 10 BEST BOWLING AVERAGES IN A TEST CAREER*

	Bowler/country	Tests	Wickets	Average
1	George Lohmann (England)	18	112	10.75
2	Sydney Barnes (England)	27	189	16.43
3	Charlie Turner (Australia)	17	101	16.53
4	Robert Peel (England)	20	102	16.81
5	Johnny Briggs (England)	33	118	17.74
6	Colin Blythe (England)	19	100	18.63
7	Johnny Wardle (England)	28	102	20.39
8	Alan Davidson (Australia)	44	186	20.53
9	Malcolm Marshall (West Indies)	81	376	20.94
10	Joel Garner (West Indies)	58	259	20.97

*Minimum qualification: 100 wickets.

Every one of the 17 counties has supplied at least one skipper. Derbyshire and Glamorgan have supplied the fewest – just one each. Derbyshire's only England captain was Donald Carr and Glamorgan's the broadcaster Tony Lewis. Durham became the 18th first-class county in 1992.

Two of England's best-known bowlers, Jim Laker and Freddie Trueman, are in 11th and 12th places with averages of 21.24 and 21.57 respectively.

Left *Clive Lloyd, seen here with England's Ian Botham, captained the West Indies a record 74 times in Test matches.*

THE 10 BEST BATTING AVERAGES IN A TEST CAREER*

	Batsman/country	Years	Innings	Not out	Runs	Average
1	Don Bradman (Australia)	1928–48	80	10	6,996	99.94
2	Graeme Pollock (South Africa)	1963–70	41	4	2,256	60.97
3	George Headley (West Indies)	1930–54	40	4	2,190	60.83
4	Herbert Sutcliffe (England)	1924–35	84	9	4,555	60.73
5	Eddie Paynter (England)	1931–39	31	5	1,540	59.23
6	Ken Barrington (England)	1955–68	131	15	6,806	58.67
7	Everton Weekes (West Indies)	1948–58	81	5	4,455	58.61
8	Walter Hammond (England)	1927–47	140	16	7,249	58.45
9	Gary Sobers (West Indies)	1954–74	160	21	8,032	57.78
10	Jack Hobbs (England)	1908–30	102	7	5,410	56.94

Minimum qualification: 20 innings.

Don Bradman took to the field for his last Test innings to a standing ovation at The Oval in August 1948. His career total stood at 6,996 runs in Test cricket and four runs would have given him a career average of 100 but England bowler Eric Hollies spoiled the celebration, much to the dismay of Bradman, and the England fans, by bowling the great man second ball.

The great Don Bradman of Australia, whose record Test batting average of 99.94 has stood since 1948.

THE 10 BIGGEST WINS BY ENGLAND IN TEST CRICKET

	Opponents	Venue	Year	Winning margin
1	Australia	The Oval	1938	Inns & 579 runs
2	Australia	Brisbane	1928–29	675 runs
3	India	Lord's	1974	Inns & 285 runs
4	West Indies	The Oval	1957	Inns & 237 runs
5	Australia	Adelaide	1891–92	Inns & 230 runs
6	Australia	Melbourne	1911–12	Inns & 225 runs
7	Australia	The Oval	1886	Inns & 217 runs
8	New Zealand	Auckland	1962–63	Inns & 215 runs
9	India	Manchester	1952	Inns & 207 runs
10	South Africa	Cape Town	1888–89	Inns & 202 runs

THE 10 OLDEST TEST CRICKETERS

	Player/country	Last day of last Test	Age yrs	days
1	Wilf Rhodes (England)	12 Apr 1930	52	165
2	Herbert Ironmonger (Australia)	28 Feb 1933	50	327
3	W. G. Grace (England)	3 Jun 1899	50	320
4	George Gunn (England)	12 Apr 1930	50	303
5	James Southerton (England)	4 Apr 1877	49	139
6	Miran Bux (Pakistan)	16 Feb 1955	47	302
7	Jack Hobbs (England)	22 Aug 1930	47	249
8	Frank Woolley (England)	22 Aug 1934	47	87
9	Donald Blackie (Australia)	8 Feb 1929	46	309
10	Dave Nourse (South Africa)	19 Aug 1924	46	206

THE 10 YOUNGEST TEST CRICKETERS

	Player/country	Date of debut	Age yrs	days
1	Mushtaq Mohammad (Pakistan)	26 Mar 1959	15	124
2	Aqib Javed (Pakistan)	10 Feb 1989	16	189
3	Sachin Tendulkar (India)	15 Nov 1989	16	205
4	Aftab Baloch (Pakistan)	8 Nov 1969	16	221
5	Nasim-ul-Ghani (Pakistan)	17 Jan 1958	16	248
6	Khalid Hassan (Pakistan)	1 Jul 1954	16	352
7	Laxman Sivaramakrishnan (India)	28 Apr 1983	17	118
8	Derek Sealy (West Indies)	11 Jan 1930	17	122
9	Sanjeeva Weerasinghe (Sri Lanka)	6 Sep 1985	17	189
10	Maninder Singh (India)	23 Dec 1982	17	193

Because some wins are achieved by a runs margin and some by an innings margin it is impossible to assess which is the better performance. However, merging the two into one chart and assuming an innings to be worth 200 runs (the follow-on figure in Test cricket), these are England's 10 biggest wins in the Test arena.

When England established their record-winning margin against Australia, this is how the potted scorecards read:

England: 903–7 dec (L. Hutton 364, M. Leyland 187, J. Hardstaff jr 169*)
Australia: 201 (W. E. Bowes 5–49) & 123 (K. Barnes 4–63)

Not out.

Southerton played in only two Tests, the first at Melbourne on 15–19 March 1877 and the second, also at Melbourne, two weeks later. At 49 years 119 days he is the oldest Test match debutant. Gunn and Rhodes both played their last match in the 4th Test against West Indies at Sabina Park, Kingston, Jamaica in 1930. Wilf Rhodes, who went on to become the oldest Test player, made his debut in W. G. Grace's last Test match.

England's youngest Test player is Brian Close who was 18 years 149 days when he made his debut against New Zealand at Old Trafford in 1949.

George Gunn was recalled to the England team for the 1st Test against West Indies at Bridgetown on 11 January 1930 on the same day that Derek Sealy (No. 8 above) became the then youngest-ever Test cricketer. Gunn's previous Test appearance was 17 years 316 days earlier when Sealy's mother was two-and-a-half months pregnant with her future Test-playing offspring! When Sealy made his debut he became the youngest Test cricketer since Tom Garrett, who played in the first-ever Test match at the age of 18 years 232 days in 1877.

THE 10 HIGHEST TEST INNINGS BY SUNIL GAVASKAR

Sunil Gavaskar of India is the top run-maker in Test cricket. His 10 highest innings were:

	Opponents/venue	Year	Runs
1	West Indies (Madras)	1983–84	236*
2	England (The Oval)	1979	221
3	West Indies (Port-of-Spain)	1970–71	220
4	West Indies (Bombay)	1978–79	205
5	West Indies (Calcutta)	1978–79	182*
6	Sri Lanka (Kanpur)	1986–87	176
7=	England (Bangalore)	1981–82	172
7=	Australia (Sydney)	1985–86	172
9=	Pakistan (Madras)	1979–80	166
9=	Australia (Adelaide)	1985–86	166*

*Not out.

Gavaskar's highest score against New Zealand was 119 at Bombay in 1976–77.

Sunil Gavaskar hit 221 runs against England at The Oval in 1979, his second highest total in a Test innings.

Bramall Lane at the turn of the century. The ground is now better known as the home of Sheffield United FC.

THE FIRST 10 GROUNDS TO BE USED FOR TEST CRICKET

	Ground	Date first used
1	Melbourne Cricket Ground	15 Mar 1877
2	Kennington Oval, London	6 Sep 1880
3	Sydney Cricket Ground	17 Feb 1882
4	Old Trafford, Manchester	11 Jul 1884
5	Lord's, London	21 Jul 1884
6	Adelaide Oval	12 Dec 1884
7	St George's Park, Port Elizabeth	12 Mar 1889
8	Newlands, Cape Town	25 Mar 1889
9	Old Wanderers Ground, Johannesburg	2 Mar 1896
10	Trent Bridge, Nottingham	1 Jun 1899

The other three English Test grounds were first used as follows: Headingley, Leeds 29 June 1899; Edgbaston, Birmingham 29 May 1902; Bramall Lane, Sheffield 3 July 1902.

QUIZ

TEST CRICKET

1 The winning margin in the very first Test match in 1877 was identical to that in the Centenary Match in 1977. What was it?

2 On which English ground have three of the 12 Test triple centuries been scored?

3 How long did the 'never ending' Test match between South Africa and England last in 1939?

4 What was unique about the hat-trick Peter Petherick took for New Zealand against Pakistan in 1976–77?

5 Ian Botham has scored a century and taken five wickets in an innings in the same Test match on five occasions. Only one other England all-rounder has ever achieved this match double. Who is he?

6 Who established a wicketkeeping Test record at Bombay in 1979–80 by dismissing 10 batsmen in one match?

7 Who was the last Englishman before Graham Gooch to score a Test triple century?

8 Which country has been dismissed for less than 40 in a Test match on no fewer than four occasions?

9 Which pair of brothers played together in 10 Test matches for New Zealand between 1973–78?

10 What did Reginald Stanley Brooks give to Test cricket in August 1882?

THE 10 HIGHEST INDIVIDUAL FIRST-CLASS INNINGS

	Batsman	Match/venue	Year	Runs
1	Hanif Mohammad	Karachi v Bahawalpur (Karachi)	1958–59	499
2	Don Bradman	New South Wales v Queensland (Sydney)	1929–30	452*
3	Bhausahib Nimbalkar	Maharashtra v Kathiawar (Poona)	1948–49	443*
4	Bill Ponsford	Victoria v Queensland (Melbourne)	1927–28	437
5	Bill Ponsford	Victoria v Tasmania (Melbourne)	1922–23	429
6	Aftab Baloch	Sind v Baluchistan (Karachi)	1973–74	428
7	Archie MacLaren	Lancashire v Somerset (Taunton)	1895	424
8	Graeme Hick	Worcestershire v Somerset (Taunton)	1988	405*
9	Bert Sutcliffe	Otago v Canterbury (Christchurch)	1952–53	385
10	Charles Gregory	New South Wales v Queensland (Brisbane)	1906–07	383

Not out.

Twenty-four-year-old Hanif Mohammad came agonizingly close to becoming the first man to score 500 runs in a first-class innings. Playing for Karachi in the semi-final of the Quaid-e-Azam trophy on 8–12 January 1959, he amassed 499 runs in Karachi's first innings total of 772–7 declared. However, having reached 499 he faced the last ball of the day on the third day's play and, keen to take his total to 500, he went for a run but was run out. Altogether he batted for 10 hours 35 minutes and hit 64 fours.

THE 10 BEST BOWLING HAULS IN A FIRST-CLASS INNINGS

	Bowler	Match/venue	Year	Figures
1	Hedley Verity	Yorkshire v Nottinghamshire (Leeds)	1932	10–10
2	George Geary	Leicestershire v Glamorgan (Pontypridd)	1929	10–18
3	Premanshu Chatterjee	Bengal v Assam (Jorhat)	1956–57	10–20
4	Bert Vogler	E. Province v Griqualand West (Johannesburg)	1906–07	10–26
5=	A. E. Moss*	Canterbury v Wellington (Christchurch)	1889–90	10–28
5=	Bill Howell	Australians v Surrey (The Oval)	1899	10–28
7	Colin Blythe	Kent v Northamptonshire (Northampton)	1907	10–30
8	Henry Pickett	Essex v Leicestershire (Leyton)	1895	10–32
9	Alonzo Drake	Yorkshire v Somerset (Weston-super-Mare)	1914	10–35
10=	F. Hinds	A. B. St. Hills XI v Trinidad (Port-of-Spain)	1900–01	10–36
10=	Hedley Verity	Yorkshire v Warwickshire (Leeds)	1931	10–36
10=	Tim Wall	South Australia v New South Wales (Sydney)	1932–33	10–36

Moss's feat occurred on his first-class debut.

THE TOP 10 WICKET-TAKERS IN A FIRST-CLASS CAREER

	Bowler	Career	Wickets
1	Wilf Rhodes	1898–1930	4,187
2	Alfred 'Tich' Freeman	1914–36	3,776
3	Charlie Parker	1903–35	3,278
4	Jack Hearne	1888–1923	3,061
5	Tom Goddard	1922–52	2,979
6	W. G. Grace	1865–1908	2,876
7	Alex Kennedy	1907–36	2,874
8	Derek Shackleton	1948–69	2,857
9	Tony Lock	1946–71	2,844
10	Fred Titmus	1949–82	2,830

Some sources give Rhodes's total as 4,204 and Grace's as 2,808. This is because of the confusion over what constituted a first-class match towards the end of the last century and in the early twentieth century. However, even if these second totals were considered Rhodes would still be No. 1 and Grace would still be in the Top 10 at No. 10.

Wilf Rhodes, the most prolific wicket-taker of all time in first-class cricket.

WILFRED RHODES

Not only is Wilf Rhodes the most prolific bowler in cricketing history but he was also useful with the bat and, uniquely, was involved in the highest opening stand for England against Australia and the highest 10th wicket stand. He achieved the double of 1,000 runs and 100 wickets in a season no fewer than 16 times. Born in Yorkshire, it is hardly surprising that his native county reigned supreme during Rhodes's 33-year career, winning the County Championship 11 times. Rhodes was capped for England 58 times between 1899 and 1930, and when he played his last game against West Indies at Kingston he was 52 years and 165 days old, making him the oldest Test cricketer of all time.

THE 10 WICKETKEEPERS WITH THE MOST DISMISSALS IN A FIRST-CLASS CAREER

	Wicketkeeper	Years	Total
1	Bob Taylor	1960–88	1,649
2	John Murray	1952–75	1,527
3	Herbert Strudwick	1902–27	1,497
4	Alan Knott	1964–85	1,344
5	Fred Huish	1895–1914	1,310
6	Brian Taylor	1949–73	1,294
7	David Hunter	1889–1909	1,253
8	Harold Butt	1890–1912	1,228
9	Jack Board	1891–1915	1,207
10	Harold Elliott	1920–47	1,206

THE TOP 10 RUN-MAKERS IN A FIRST-CLASS CAREER

	Batsman	Years	Runs*
1	Jack Hobbs	1905–34	61,237
2	Frank Woolley	1906–38	58,969
3	Patsy Hendren	1907–38	57,611
4	Phillip Mead	1905–36	55,061
5	W. G. Grace	1865–1908	54,896
6	Walter Hammond	1920–51	50,551
7	Herbert Sutcliffe	1919–45	50,138
8	Geoff Boycott	1962–86	48,426
9	Tom Graveney	1948–72	47,793
10	Tom Hayward	1893–1914	43,551

Some sources quote the following figures: Hobbs 61,670; Woolley 58,959; Grace 54,211; Sutcliffe 50,670.

THE 10 MOST CENTURIES IN A FIRST-CLASS CAREER

	Batsman	Centuries
1	Jack Hobbs	197
2	Patsy Hendren	170
3	Walter Hammond	167
4	Phillip Mead	153
5	Geoff Boycott	151
6	Herbert Sutcliffe	149
7	Frank Woolley	145
8	Len Hutton	129
9	W. G. Grace	126
10	Denis Compton	123

Jack Hobbs of Surrey passes W. G. Grace's record of 54,896 runs in a first-class career against Middlesex at The Oval in August 1930.

SIR JOHN BERRY HOBBS

Known simply as Jack, or more appropriately 'The Master', Jack Hobbs was the most prolific batsman the cricketing world has seen. He was born in Cambridge in 1882 and spent his entire first-class career with Surrey after a few games for his native county. Remarkably, Hobbs first offered his services to Essex and they turned the youngster down! His revenge came when, in his County Championship debut for Surrey against Essex in 1905, he scored 155. His highest score of 316 not out was made against Middlesex at Lord's in 1926 and it remained the record for the highest individual innings at the home of cricket until it was surpassed by Graham Gooch in 1990. Hobbs played for England 61 times between 1908 and 1930, when he left the Test scene with a then record 5,410 runs. In all first-class matches he scored 197 centuries, 98 of them coming after his 40th birthday.

THE 10 MOST DOUBLE CENTURIES IN A FIRST-CLASS CAREER

	Batsman	Double centuries
1	Don Bradman	37
2	Walter Hammond	36
3	Patsy Hendren	22
4	Herbert Sutcliffe	17
5=	C. B. Fry	16
5=	Jack Hobbs	16
7	K. S. Ranjitsinhji	14
8=	W. G. Grace	13
8=	Phillip Mead	13
8=	Bill Ponsford	13
8=	Johnny Tyldesley	13

THE 10 MOST CATCHES IN A FIRST-CLASS SEASON

	Player	Season	Catches
1	Walter Hammond	1928	78
2	Micky Stewart	1957	77
3	Peter Walker	1961	73
4	Phil Sharp	1962	71
5	John Tunnicliffe	1901	70
6=	John Langridge	1955	69
6=	Peter Walker	1960	69
8	John Tunnicliffe	1895	66
9=	Walter Hammond	1925	65
9=	Peter Walker	1959	65
9=	Dick Richardson	1961	65

THE 10 MOST CATCHES IN A FIRST-CLASS CAREER

	Player	Catches
1	Frank Woolley	1,018
2	W. G. Grace	887
3	Tony Lock	830
4	Walter Hammond	819
5	Brian Close	813
6	John Langridge	784
7	Wilf Rhodes	764
8	Colin Milton	758
9	Patsy Hendren	754
10	Peter Walker	697

THE 10 BEST BATTING AVERAGES IN A FIRST-CLASS CAREER*

	Batsman	Runs	Average
1	Don Bradman	28,067	95.14
2	Vijay Merchant	13,248	71.22
3	Bill Ponsford	13,819	65.18
4	Bill Woodfull	13,388	64.99
5	Graeme Hick	17,665	59.48
6	Lindsay Hassett	16,890	58.24
7	Vijay Hazare	18,621	58.19
8	Alan Kippax	12,762	57.22
9	Martin Crowe	16,602	57.05
10	Geoff Boycott	48,426	56.83

Minimum qualification: 10,000 runs to end 1991–92.

The sport's most prolific run-maker, Jack Hobbs, has a career average of 50.65.

THE 10 BEST BOWLING AVERAGES IN A FIRST-CLASS CAREER*

	Bowler	Wickets	Average
1	Alfred Shaw	2,027	12.12
2	Tom Emmett	1,571	13.56
3	George Lohmann	1,841	13.73
4	James Southerton	1,681	14.44
5	Hedley Verity	1,956	14.90
6	William Attewell	1,950	15.33
7	Arthur Mold	1,673	15.54
8	Schofield Haigh	2,012	15.94
9	Johnny Briggs	2,221	15.95
10	Robert Peel	1,753	16.22

Minimum qualification: 1,500 wickets to end 1991–92.

Wilf Rhodes, cricket's leading wicket-taker with 4,187 victims, is in 12th place with an average of 16.71.

THE TOP 10 PARTNERSHIPS IN FIRST-CLASS CRICKET

	Batsmen	Match/venue	Year	Wicket	Stand
1	Vijay Hazare/Gul Mahomed	Baroda v Holkar (Baroda)	1946–47	4th	577
2	Frank Worrell/Clyde Walcott	Barbados v Trinidad (Port-of-Spain)	1945–46	4th	574*
3	Waheed Mirza/Mansoor Akhtar	Karachi Whites v Quetta (Karachi)	1976–77	1st	561
4	Percy Holmes/Herbert Sutcliffe	Yorkshire v Essex (Leyton)	1932	1st	555
5	John Brown/John Tunnicliffe	Yorkshire v Derbyshire (Chesterfield)	1898	1st	554
6	Frank Worrell/John Goddard	Barbados v Trinidad (Bridgetown)	1943–44	4th	502*
7	Edward Bowley/John Langridge	Sussex v Middlesex (Hove)	1933	1st	490
8	George Headley/Clarence Passailaigue	Jamaica v Lord Tennyson's XI (Kingston)	1931–32	6th	487*
9	Alvin Kallicharran/Geoff Humpage	Warwickshire v Lancashire (Southport)	1982	4th	470
10	Andrew Jones/Martin Crowe	New Zealand v Sri Lanka (Wellington)	1990–91	3rd	467

Unbroken.

THE 10 HIGHEST TEAM TOTALS IN FIRST-CLASS CRICKET

	Match	Venue	Year	Score
1	Victoria v New South Wales	Melbourne	1926–27	1,107
2	Victoria v Tasmania	Melbourne	1922–23	1,059
3	Sind v Baluchistan	Karachi	1973–74	951–7dec
4	New South Wales v South Australia	Sydney	1900–01	918
5=	Holkar v Mysore	Indore	1945–46	912–8dec
5=	Tamil Nadu v Goa	Panjim	1988–89	912–6dec
7	Railways v Dera Ismail Khan	Lahore	1964–65	910–6dec
8	England v Australia	The Oval	1938	903–7dec
9	Yorkshire v Warwickshire	Birmingham	1896	887
10	Lancashire v Surrey	The Oval	1990	863

Tamil's total included 52 penalty runs because Goa failed to meet the required bowling rate. Without the penalties this entry would have moved down to No. 10.

THE 10 LOWEST COMPLETED INNINGS IN FIRST-CLASS CRICKET

	Match	Venue	Year	Total
1=	Oxford University *v* MCC and Ground	Oxford	1877	12
1=	Northamptonshire *v* Gloucestershire	Gloucester	1907	12
3=	Auckland *v* Canterbury	Auckland	1877–78	13
3=	Nottinghamshire *v* Yorkshire	Nottingham	1901	13
5	Surrey *v* Essex	Chelmsford	1983	14
6=	MCC *v* Surrey	Lord's	1839	15
6=	Victoria *v* MCC	Melbourne	1903–04	15
6=	Northamptonshire *v* Yorkshire	Northampton	1908	15
6=	Hampshire *v* Warwickshire	Birmingham	1922	15
10=	MCC and Ground *v* Surrey	Lord's	1872	16
10=	Derbyshire *v* Nottinghamshire	Nottingham	1879	16
10=	Surrey *v* Nottinghamshire	The Oval	1880	16
10=	Warwickshire *v* Kent	Tonbridge	1913	16
10=	Trinidad *v* Barbados	Bridgetown	1942–43	16
10=	Border *v* Natal*	East London	1959–60	16

Border were dismissed for 18 runs in their second innings.

THE 10 MOST RUNS SCORED OFF ONE OVER IN FIRST-CLASS CRICKET

	Batsman	Match	Year	Bowler	Runs
1=	Gary Sobers	Nottinghamshire *v* Glamorgan	1968	Malcolm Nash	36
1=	Ravi Shastri	Bombay *v* Baroda	1984–85	Tilak Raj	36
3=	Edwin Alletson	Nottinghamshire *v* Sussex	1911	Ernest Killick	34
3=	Frank Hayes	Lancashire *v* Glamorgan	1977	Malcolm Nash	34
5=	Cyril Smart	Glamorgan *v* Hampshire	1935	Gerald Hill	32
5=	Clive Inman	Leicestershire *v* Nottinghamshire	1965	Norman Hill	32
5=	Ian Redpath	Australians *v* Orange Free State	1969–70	Neil Rosendorff	32
5=	Paul Parker	Sussex *v* Warwickshire	1982	Alvin Kallicharran	32
5=	Ian Botham	England XI *v* Central Districts	1983–84	I. R. Snook	32
5=	Trevor Jesty	Hampshire *v* Northamptonshire	1984	Robin Boyd-Moss	32

During the Canterbury *v* Wellington Shell Trophy match at Christchurch during the 1989–90 season, a staggering 77 runs were scored off one over when Wellington bowler Robert Vance deliberately bowled 17 no balls in an effort to produce a positive result from the match. Canterbury's wicketkeeper Lee Gernon hit eight sixes and five fours during the amazing over, in his total of 69. In the confusion, the umpires miscalculated and only five official balls were delivered. Because of the nature of the 'record', however, it cannot be treated as legitimate.

THE 10 MEN WHO CLEAN-BOWLED W. G. GRACE MOST OFTEN IN FIRST-CLASS CRICKET

	Bowler	Times clean-bowled Grace
1	Alfred Shaw	20
2	Thomas Richardson	14
3	Richard Barlow	13
4	Fred Morley	11
5=	Johnny Briggs	10
5=	Thomas Emmett	10
5=	Allen Hill	10
8=	Edmund Peate	9
8=	James Shaw	9
10=	Wilfred Flowers	8
10=	James Southerton	8

The bowler who dismissed Grace most often in Test cricket was Australia's Charles Turner: he bowled the Doctor once, and had him caught five times.

THE 10 PLAYERS WITH THE MOST FIRST-CLASS APPEARANCES

	Player	Appearances
1	Wilf Rhodes	1,106
2	Frank Woolley	978
3	W. G. Grace	872
4	Patsy Hendren	831
5	Jack Hobbs	825
6	George Hirst	824
7	Phillip Mead	814
8	Fred Titmus	792
9	Ray Illingworth	787
10	Brian Close	786

Rhodes's total includes a record 763 games in the County Championship.

THE 10 LONGEST FIRST-CLASS CAREERS IN ENGLISH CRICKET

	Player	Years	No. of seasons
1	W. G. Grace	1865–1908	44
2	Lord Harris	1870–1911	42
3	Ernest Smith	1888–1928	41
4	Alfred Hornby	1867–1906	40
5=	Rev Reginald Moss	1887–1925	39
5=	George Hirst	1891–1929	39
5=	Henry Leveson Gower	1893–1931	39
8	Brian Close	1949–86	38
9=	Charles De Trafford	1884–1920	37
9=	Sydney Barnes	1894–1930	37
9=	John Gunn	1896–1932	37

THE FIRST 10 KNOWN SETS OF TWINS TO PLAY FIRST-CLASS CRICKET IN ENGLAND

	Players	Year of debut	
		1st twin	**2nd twin**
1	Alfred and Arthur Payne	1852	1854
2	Edwin and George Ede	1861	1864
3	Gilbert and Orlando Spencer-Smith	1864	1866
4	Herbert and Walter Phipps	1865	1867
5	Herbert and Charles Pigg	1877	1878
6	Frank and George Stephens	1907	1907
7	Jack and Billy Denton	1909	1909
8	Albert and Arthur Rippon	1914	1914
9	Peter and Clive Garthwaite	1929	1930
10	Alec and Eric Bedser	1939	1939

Alec and Eric Bedser pictured in 1938, the year before their first-class debuts.

The only other post-war twins to appear are: Derek and Michael Taylor, Roger and Stuart Westley, David and Jonathan Varey, and Mark and Stephen Waugh. The Waughs are uniquely the only twins to play international cricket, making their debut for the Australians in the West Indies in December 1988. Eight months later, again uniquely in cricketing history, they became the first twins to score a century for different sides in the same match when Mark did so for Essex against the touring Australians while brother Stephen hit a century for the visitors.

The Northamptonshire–Somerset match in 1914 was unique because the Northamptonshire batting was opened by the Denton twins, while the Somerset opening pair was the Rippon twins.

George Ede (No. 2 in the list) was a versatile sportsman, not only playing first-class cricket for Hampshire but, in 1868, riding The Lamb to victory in the Grand National.

THE 10 MOST SUCCESSFUL FIRST-CLASS COUNTIES 1969–91

Since the re-organization of the County Championship in 1969 the most successful counties, based on average finishing positions in the table, have been:

	County	Average finishing position*
1	Essex	5.50 (4)
2	Middlesex	6.41 (6)
3	Surrey	6.59 (1)
4	Leicestershire	7.13 (1)
5	Hampshire	7.45 (1)
6	Kent	7.77 (3)
7	Worcestershire	8.41 (2)
8	Northamptonshire	9.14 (–)
9=	Gloucestershire	9.18 (–)
9=	Nottinghamshire	9.18 (2)

Figures in brackets indicate titles won during the same period; Kent and Middlesex shared the title in 1977.

Derbyshire have the worst record, with an average finishing position of 12.36.

THE 10 TEAMS WITH THE MOST COUNTY CHAMPIONSHIP WINS

County teams have been playing each other since the early part of the eighteenth century and in 1864 the first county championship, involving eight teams, was inaugurated and won by Surrey. However, the championship as we know it today, with a points structure, was launched in 1890 and is recognized as the first official County Championship. The list is based on wins from that date only.

	County	Wins*
1	Yorkshire	30
2	Surrey	16
3	Middlesex	11
4	Lancashire	8
5	Kent	7
6	Worcestershire	5
7=	Essex	4
7=	Nottinghamshire	4
9	Warwickshire	3
10=	Glamorgan	2
10=	Hampshire	2

Including shared wins.

Gloucestershire, Northamptonshire, Somerset and Sussex have never won the title.

THE 1991 COUNTY CHAMPIONSHIP

THE TOP 10 RUN-MAKERS

	Player	County	Runs
1	Jimmy Cook	Somerset	2,370
2	Mike Gatting	Middlesex	2,044
3	Salim Malik	Essex	1,891
4	Alan Wells	Sussex	1,777
5	Mohammad Azharuddin	Derbyshire	1,773
6	Tom Moody	Worcestershire	1,770
7	Matthew Maynard	Glamorgan	1,766
8	Darren Bicknell	Surrey	1,762
9	Chris Broad	Nottinghamshire	1,739
10	Alan Fordham	Northamptonshire	1,725

THE TOP 10 WICKET-TAKERS

	Player	County	Wickets
1	Waqar Younis	Surrey	113
2	Neil Foster	Essex	91
3	Allan Donald	Warwickshire	83
4	Franklin Stephenson	Nottinghamshire	78
5	Tim Munton	Warwickshire	71
6	Philip Tufnell	Middlesex	70
7	John Maguire	Leicestershire	69
8	Steve Watkin	Glamorgan	66
9	Andy Pick	Nottinghamshire	65
10	John Emburey	Middlesex	64

THE 10 MOST UNSUCCESSFUL COUNTIES*

	County	CC	NW	BH	RL	Total
1=	Glamorgan	2	0	0	0	2
1=	Gloucestershire	0	1	1	0	2
1=	Northamptonshire	0	1	1	0	2
4	Derbyshire	1	1	0	1	3
5=	Somerset	0	2	2	1	5
5=	Sussex	0	4	0	1	5
7	Leicestershire	1	0	3	2	6
8=	Hampshire	2	1	1	3	7
8=	Nottinghamshire	4	1	1	1	7
8=	Warwickshire	3	3	0	1	7

Based on success in the four major domestic competitions to end 1991– County Championship (CC), NatWest Trophy (NW), Benson & Hedges Cup (BH) and Refuge Assurance League (RL). Successes in the NatWest and Refuge League's predecessors (Gillette Cup and John Player League) are included.

THE TOP 10 WICKETKEEPERS

	Player	County	Dismissals
1	Colin Metson	Glamorgan	69
2	Steven Marsh	Kent	65
3	Bruce French	Nottinghamshire	62
4=	Mike Garnham	Essex	58
4=	Karl Krikken	Derbyshire	58
4=	Peter Moores	Sussex	58
7	Steven Rhodes	Worcestershire	55
8	Paul Farbrace	Middlesex	52
9=	Keith Piper	Warwickshire	48
9=	Neil Sargeant	Surrey	48

THE TOP 10 FIELDERS

	Player	County	Catches
1	Nasser Hussain	Essex	34
2	Keith Brown	Middlesex	33
3=	Raj Maru	Hampshire	29
3=	Tom Moody	Worcestershire	29
5=	Mohammad Azharuddin	Derbyshire	23
5=	Kim Barnett	Derbyshire	23
5=	Paul Terry	Hampshire	23
8=	Richard Davis	Kent	22
8=	Salim Malik	Essex	22
10=	Damian D'Oliveira	Worcestershire	21
10=	John Emburey	Middlesex	21
10=	Jeremy Lloyds	Gloucestershire	21
10=	Tim O'Gorman	Derbyshire	21
10=	Paul Pollard	Nottinghamshire	21

Essex, Middlesex and Nottinghamshire have players appearing in all four lists while Lancashire and Yorkshire are not represented in any.

SURREY – 1st innings

G. S. Clinton	c Patterson b DeFreitas	8
R. I. Alikhan	st Hegg b Fitton	55
A. J. Stewart	c Fowler b Patterson	70
M. A. Lynch	c & b Watkinson	95
G. P. Thorpe	c Atherton b Fitton	27
D. M. Ward	c Hughes b Fitton	36
I. A. Greig	c Jesty b Hughes	291
K. T. Medlycott	c Fairbrother b Patterson	33
M. P. Bicknell	c Hegg b Hughes	42
N. M. Kendrick	not out	18
Extras (b6, lb16, nb10)		32
Total (9 wkts dec)		**707**

Fall of wickets: 1–10, 2–118, 3–187, 4–261, 5–275, 6–316, 7–401, 8–606, 9–707
Did not bat: A. J. Murphy
Bowling: Patterson 27–4–108–2; DeFreitas 26–4–99–1; Watkinson 23–2–113–1; Fitton 45–6–185–3; Atherton 22–5–75–0; Hughes 22.1–0–105–2

LANCASHIRE – 1st innings

G. D. Mendis	run out	102
G. Fowler	run out	20
M. A. Atherton	c Greig b Kendrick	191
N. H. Fairbrother	c Kendrick b Greig	366
T. E. Jesty	rtd hurt	18
M. Watkinson	b Greig	46
W. K. Hegg	c Ward b Bicknell	45
P. A. J. DeFreitas	b Murphy	31
D. P. Hughes	not out	8
J. D. Fitton	c Stewart b Murphy	3
B. P. Patterson	c Greig b Medlycott	0
Extras (b8, lb15, w1, nb9)		33
Total		**863**

Fall of wickets: 1–45, 2–184, 3–548, 4–745, 5–774, 6–844, 7–848, 8–862, 9–863
Bowling: Murphy 44–6–160–2; Bicknell 43–2–175–1; Kendrick 56–10–192–1; Medlycott 50.5–4–177–1; Lynch 5–2–17–0; Greig 19–3–73–2; Thorpe 7–1–46–0

SURREY – 2nd innings

G. S. Clinton	c Watkinson b Atherton	15
A. J. Stewart	not out	54
M. A. Lynch	not out	6
Extras (b2, lb1, nb2)		5
Total (1 wkt)		**80**

Fall of wicket: 1–57
Bowling: DeFreitas 4–0–10–0; Fitton 16–4–42–0; Atherton 13–5–25–1

Match drawn: Surrey (4pts) Lancashire (6pts)

THE 10 HIGHEST TEAM TOTALS IN THE COUNTY CHAMPIONSHIP

	Match	Venue	Year	Score
1	Yorkshire v Warwickshire	Birmingham	1896	887
2	Lancashire v Surrey	The Oval	1990	863
3	Surrey v Somerset	The Oval	1899	811
4	Kent v Essex	Brentwood	1934	803–4dec
5	Lancashire v Somerset	Taunton	1895	801
6	Essex v Leicestershire	Chelmsford	1990	761–6dec
7	Surrey v Hampshire	The Oval	1909	742
8	Nottinghamshire v Leicestershire	Nottingham	1903	739–7dec
9	Nottinghamshire v Sussex	Nottingham	1895	726
10	Surrey v Lancashire	The Oval	1990	707–9dec

The Surrey v Lancashire game at The Oval on 3–7 May 1990 was a remarkable match and produced no fewer than 1,650 runs for the loss of 20 wickets. The first innings totals of both teams figure in the above Top 10. The full scorecard from that memorable encounter is given on the previous page.

THE 10 OLDEST* FIRST-CLASS COUNTIES

	County	Year formed
1	Northamptonshire	1820
2	Sussex	Mar 1839
3	Nottinghamshire	Mar–Apr 1841
4	Surrey	Aug 1845
5	Kent	Mar 1859
6	Yorkshire	Jan 1863
7	Hampshire	Aug 1863
8	Lancashire	Jan 1864
9	Middlesex	Feb 1864
10	Worcestershire	Mar 1865

*Based on date of formation of present club.

Although the present Essex club was not formed until 1876, an Essex county team existed in 1790 and can rightly claim to be the oldest county cricket side.

THE 10 HIGHEST INDIVIDUAL FIRST-CLASS INNINGS IN 1991

	Batsman	Match	Runs
1	Graham Gooch	Essex v Middlesex	259
2	Mark Benson	Kent v Hampshire	257
3	Alan Wells	Sussex v Yorkshire	253*
4	Tim Curtis	Worcestershire v Somerset	248
5	Matthew Maynard	Glamorgan v Hampshire	243
6	Damian D'Oliveira	Worcestershire v Oxford University	237
7	Trevor Ward	Kent v Middlesex	235*
8	Kim Barnett	Derbyshire v Nottinghamshire	217
9=	Mike Gatting	Middlesex v Derbyshire	215*
9=	Salim Malik	Essex v Leicestershire	215

*Not out.

The highest innings of the season, Graham Gooch's 259 against Middlesex, came in the last County Championship match of the season in which Essex captured the title from Warwickshire.

THE 10 MOST NORTHERLY VENUES USED FOR FIRST-CLASS MATCHES IN ENGLAND IN 1991

1	Middlesbrough
2	Scarborough
3	Harrogate
4	Leeds
5	Blackpool
6	Lytham
7	Manchester
8	Liverpool
9	Sheffield
10	Worksop

THE 10 GROUNDS MOST USED FOR 1991 COUNTY CHAMPIONSHIP MATCHES

Ground	Occasions used
1= Edgbaston, Birmingham	10
1= Grace Road, Leicester	10
1= New Road, Worcester	10
1= Trent Bridge, Nottingham	10
5= County Ground, Derby	9
5= County Ground, Northampton	9
5= The Oval, London	9
8= Lord's, London	8
8= Old Trafford, Manchester	8
10= County Ground, Hove	7
10= County Ground, Taunton	7

A total of 52 grounds were used in 1991.

THE 10 HIGHEST INDIVIDUAL FIRST-CLASS INNINGS IN ENGLAND

	Batsman	Match/venue	Year	Score
1	Archie MacLaren	Lancashire v Somerset (Taunton)	1895	424
2	Graeme Hick	Worcestershire v Somerset (Taunton)	1988	405*
3	Neil Fairbrother	Lancashire v Surrey (The Oval)	1990	366
4	Len Hutton	England v Australia (The Oval)	1938	364
5	Bobby Abel	Surrey v Somerset (The Oval)	1899	357*
6	Charlie Macartney	Australians v Nottinghamshire (Nottingham)	1921	345
7	W. G. Grace	MCC v Kent (Canterbury)	1876	344
8	Percy Perrin	Essex v Derbyshire (Chesterfield)	1904	343*
9	George Hirst	Yorkshire v Leicestershire (Leicester)	1905	341
10	Walter Read	Surrey v Oxford University (The Oval)	1888	338

Not out.

THE TOP 10 RUN-MAKERS IN AN ENGLISH FIRST-CLASS SEASON

	Batsman	Season	Runs
1	Denis Compton	1947	3,816
2	Bill Edrich	1947	3,539
3	Tom Hayward	1906	3,518
4	Len Hutton	1949	3,429
5	Frank Woolley	1928	3,352
6	Herbert Sutcliffe	1932	3,336
7	Walter Hammond	1933	3,323
8	Patsy Hendren	1928	3,311
9	Bobby Abel	1901	3,309
10	Walter Hammond	1937	3,252

Since the reduction in the number of County Championship matches in 1969 the best total has been 2,755 by Jimmy Cook in 1991.

THE 10 LOWEST COMPLETED FIRST-CLASS INNINGS IN ENGLAND

Match/venue	Venue	Year	Total
1= Oxford University v MCC and Ground	Oxford	1877	12
1= Northamptonshire v Gloucestershire	Gloucester	1907	12
3 Nottinghamshire v Yorkshire	Nottingham	1901	13
4 Surrey v Essex	Chelmsford	1983	14
5= MCC v Surrey	Lord's	1839	15
5= Northamptonshire v Yorkshire	Northampton	1908	15
5= Hampshire v Warwickshire	Birmingham	1922	15
8= MCC and Ground v Surrey	Lord's	1872	16
8= Derbyshire v Nottinghamshire	Nottingham	1879	16
8= Surrey v Nottinghamshire	The Oval	1880	16
8= Warwickshire v Kent	Tonbridge	1913	16

Oxford University and Northamptonshire (1908) both batted one man short.

Despite being dismissed by Warwickshire for 15 in 1922 Hampshire went on to win the match by 155 runs:

HAMPSHIRE'S TWO CONTRASTING SCORECARDS

Kennedy	c Smith b Calthorpe	0	b Calthorpe	7
Bowell	b Howell	0	c Howell b W. Quaife	45
H. V. L. Day	b Calthorpe	0	c Bates b W. Quaife	15
Mead	not out	6	b Howell	24
Hon L. H. Tennyson	c Calthorpe b Howell	4	c C. Smart b Calthorpe	45
Brown	b Howell	0	b C. Smart	172
Newman	c C. Smart b Howell	0	c & b W. Quaife	12
W. R. Shirley	c J. Smart b Calthorpe	1	lbw Fox	30
A. S. McIntyre	lbw Calthorpe	0	lbw Howell	5
Livsey	b Howell	0	not out	110
Boyes	lbw Howell	0	b Howell	29
Extras		4		27
Total		**15**		**521**

Fall of wickets:
1–0, 2–0, 3–0, 4–5, 5–5, 6–9, 7–10, 8–10, 9–15

Fall of wickets:
1–15, 2–63, 3–81, 4–127, 5–152, 6–177, 7–262, 8–274, 9–451

Bowling:
Howell 4.5–2–7–6; Calthorpe 4–3–4–4

Bowling:
Howell 53–10–156–3; Calthorpe 33–7–97–2; W. Quaife 49–8–154–3; Fox 7–0–30–1; J. Smart 13–2–37–0; Santall 5–0–15–0; C. Smart 1–0–5–1

Following-on in their second innings, Hampshire, with six wickets down, still trailed by 31 runs, and with two wickets remaining held a slender lead of 66. But then came that remarkable 9th-wicket stand of 177 between Brown and Livsey which set them on their way to an extraordinary victory. Warwickshire made 223 and 158 in their two innings.

THE TOP 10 WICKET-TAKERS IN AN ENGLISH FIRST-CLASS SEASON

	Bowler	Year	Wickets
1	Alfred Freeman	1928	304
2	Alfred Freeman	1933	298
3	Tom Richardson	1895	290
4	Charlie Turner	1888	283
5	Alfred Freeman	1931	276
6	Alfred Freeman	1930	275
7	Tom Richardson	1897	273
8	Alfred Freeman	1929	267
9	Wilf Rhodes	1900	261
10	Jack Hearne	1896	257

Although Kent and England bowler Alfred Freeman, better known as 'Tich', took 200 wickets in a season no fewer than eight times, the sport's most prolific wicket-taker, Wilf Rhodes, performed the feat on just three occasions. The first man to claim more than 200 victims in one season was James Southerton who took 210 wickets in 1870. Since the reduction in the number of County Championship matches in 1969, the best haul has been 134 by Malcolm Marshall in 1982.

THE 10 WINNERS OF THE MOST MAJOR ONE-DAY TITLES* IN ENGLISH CRICKET

	County	NW	BH	RL	Total
1	Lancashire	5	2	3	10
2	Kent	2	3	3	8
3	Middlesex	4	2	0	6
4=	Essex	1	1	3	5
4=	Hampshire	1	1	3	5
4=	Leicestershire	0	3	2	5
4=	Somerset	2	2	1	5
4=	Sussex	4	0	1	5
9=	Warwickshire	3	0	1	4
9=	Worcestershire	0	1	3	4
9=	Yorkshire	2	1	1	4

NatWest (formerly Gillette) Trophy, Benson & Hedges Cup and Refuge Assurance (formerly John Player) League to end 1991.

Glamorgan is the only county not to have won a major one-day title.

THE 10 HIGHEST INDIVIDUAL INNINGS IN THE WORLD CUP

The World Cup was launched in 1975 with all matches played in Britain. The first winners were West Indies, who also won the second competition, also in Britain, four years later. It is now established as a quadrennial event and in 1987 was played outside Britain for the first time when Pakistan and India co-hosted the competition, with the final being played at Calcutta. In 1991–92 Australia and New Zealand were the hosts and Pakistan the winners.

	Batsman	Match/venue	Year	Runs
1	Viv Richards	West Indies v Sri Lanka (Karachi)	1987	181
2	Kapil Dev	India v Zimbabwe (Tunbridge Wells)	1983	175*
3	Glenn Turner	New Zealand v East Africa (Birmingham)	1975	171*
4	David Houghton	Zimbabwe v England (Hyderabad)	1987	141
5	Viv Richards	West Indies v England (Lord's)	1979	138*
6	Dennis Amiss	England v India (Lord's)	1975	137
7	Keith Fletcher	England v New Zealand (Nottingham)	1975	131
8	David Gower	England v Sri Lanka (Taunton)	1983	130
9	Geoff Marsh	Australia v New Zealand (Chandigarh)	1987	126*
10=	Ramiz Raja	Pakistan v New Zealand (Christchurch)	1992	119*
10=	Viv Richards	West Indies v India (The Oval)	1983	119

*Not out.

THE 10 HIGHEST INDIVIDUAL INNINGS IN THE THREE MAJOR ONE-DAY COMPETITIONS IN ENGLAND

	Batsman	Match/venue	Competition	Year	Runs
1	Alvin Kallicharran	Warwickshire v Oxfordshire (Birmingham)	NatWest	1984	206
2	Graham Gooch	Essex v Sussex (Hove)	Benson & Hedges	1982	198*
3=	Gordon Greenidge	Hampshire v Glamorgan (Southampton)	Gillette	1975	177
3=	Jimmy Cook	Somerset v Sussex (Hove)	Benson & Hedges	1990	177
5	Graham Gooch	Essex v Glamorgan (Southend)	John Player	1983	176
6	Ian Botham	Somerset v Northamptonshire (Wellingborough)	John Player	1986	175*
7	Gordon Greenidge	Hampshire v Minor Counties (S) (Amersham)	Benson & Hedges	1973	173*
8=	Graeme Hick	Worcestershire v Devon (Worcester)	NatWest	1987	172*
8=	Wayne Larkins	Northamptonshire v Warwickshire (Luton)	John Player	1983	172*
8=	Gordon Greenidge	Hampshire v Surrey (Southampton)	Refuge Assurance	1987	172

Not out.

LORD'S – THE HOME OF CRICKET

Lord's Cricket Ground is the most famous ground in the world. Contrary to the often mistaken belief its name has nothing to do with the aristocracy. In fact, the cricketing world is indebted to the son of a Yorkshire farmer for the sport's best-known venue.

Thomas Lord (1755–1832) moved from Thirsk to London as a youngster and was employed as a bowler and general assistant at the White Conduit Club. In 1786 he was asked by the Earl of Winchelsea and Charles Lennox (later the Duke of Richmond) to establish a new ground in London in readiness for the formation of the Marylebone Cricket Club (MCC) which evolved from the White Conduit Club.

Lord opened his new ground in 1787 at Dorset Fields (now Dorset Square), near Marylebone Station, and on 31 May the first match was played between Middlesex and Essex. However, the lease expired in 1810 and Lord had to develop another ground, less than a mile away, at North Bank, Regent's Park.

London was rapidly expanding northwards at this time and within three years of moving to his second ground, Thomas Lord was told he had to move on again because the course of the new Regent's Canal was to pass through the ground. Off he went again, but this time the move was even shorter, just a few hundred yards to the north-west to the present home in St John's Wood. The first match at the third and final Lord's ground was on 22 June 1814 when the MCC played Hertfordshire.

Lord retired in 1825 and, being the leaseholder on the ground, sought planning permission to build houses on part of it in order to increase its value. MCC member William Ward saw what Lord had in mind and, to prevent any further building and possible loss of the ground, he bought out Lord for £5,000; no doubt the fact that he was a director of the Bank of England and MP for the City of London helped his cause considerably.

Ward passed over his interest to J. H. Dark who was keen for the MCC to buy the freehold but, for some unknown and shortsighted reason, saw no need to do so. They could have acquired it for £7,000 in 1860 but declined. However, they eventually bought the freehold in 1866 for £18,000 thanks to a loan from a member, William Nicholson, later President of the MCC.

In 1887 another £18,000 acquired Henderson's four-acre flower and fruit nursery, noted for its tulips and pineapples, to help with ground expansion. The MCC's plans were nearly shattered when, in 1888, the Great Central Railway wanted to acquire the land and to run its track through the ground. However, a compromise was reached and a tunnel was built under the nursery ground.

The present pavilion and the magnificent Long Room were built in 1890 and eight years later the Mound Stand was built. The ground underwent major extensions in the 1920s when the Grand Stand, upon which Father Time is situated, was erected and an extra tier was added to the Nursery End stands. A members' stand was added in 1934 and in 1957 the Warner Stand, in honour of Pelham Warner, was built. Lord's has undergone more changes and facelifts in recent times but it has not lost any of its character and it remains the one cricket ground where cricketers worldwide always dream of playing.

Viv Richards of West Indies in blistering form in the 1984 Texaco Trophy against England at Old Trafford. He scored 189 not out, the highest individual score in a one-day international.

THE TOP 10 RUN-MAKERS IN ONE-DAY INTERNATIONALS*

	Batsman/country	Runs
1	Desmond Haynes (West Indies)	7,392
2	Viv Richards (West Indies)	6,721
3	Javed Miandad (Pakistan)	6,424
4	Allan Border (Australia)	5,900
5	Gordon Greenidge (West Indies)	5,134
6	Dean Jones (Australia)	5,048
7	Richie Richardson (West Indies)	4,882
8	Geoff Marsh (Australia)	4,357
9	Graham Gooch (England)	3,950
10	John Wright (New Zealand)	3,880

To end 1991–92.

THE TOP 10 WICKET-TAKERS IN ONE-DAY INTERNATIONALS*

	Bowler/country	Wickets
1	Kapil Dev (India)	206
2	Imran Khan (Pakistan)	182
3	Wasim Akram (Pakistan)	162
4	Richard Hadlee (New Zealand)	158
5	Joel Garner (West Indies)	146
6=	Michael Holding (West Indies)	142
6=	Malcolm Marshall (West Indies)	142
8=	Ian Botham (England)	140
8=	Ewan Chatfield (New Zealand)	140
10	Abdul Qadir (Pakistan)	131

To end 1991–92.

THE 10 HIGHEST INDIVIDUAL INNINGS IN THE NATWEST TROPHY/GILLETTE CUP†

	Batsman	Match/venue	Year	Runs
1	Alvin Kallicharran	Warwickshire v Oxfordshire (Birmingham)	1984	206
2	Gordon Greenidge	Hampshire v Glamorgan (Southampton)	1975	177
3	Graeme Hick	Worcestershire v Devon (Worcester)	1987	172*
4	Paul Terry	Hampshire v Berkshire (Southampton)	1985	165*
5	Chris Tavaré	Somerset v Devon (Torquay)	1990	162*
6	Chris Smith	Hampshire v Cheshire (Chester)	1989	159
7=	Zaheer Abbas	Gloucestershire v Leicestershire (Leicester)	1983	158
7=	Graham Barlow	Middlesex v Lancashire (Lord's)	1984	158
9	David Gower	Leicestershire v Derbyshire (Leicester)	1984	156
10	John Whitaker	Leicestershire v Wiltshire (Swindon)	1984	155

†1963–80 Gillette Cup; 1981–91 NatWest Trophy.
Not out.

QUIZ

SPORTING NICKNAMES

1 'Guy the Gorilla' and 'Beefy' are two of the nicknames of which well-known English sportsman?

2 How is 'Billy Williams' Cabbage Patch' better known?

3 Which well-known baseball player was known as 'The Georgia Peach'?

4 Greg Norman is the 'Great White Shark', but who is the 'Walrus'?

5 If you were watching the Chemics playing the Wire in a local derby, which two rugby league teams would be in action?

6 Muhammad Ali was known as the 'Louisville Lip', but which boxer was known as the 'Liverpool Lip'?

7 Which Grand Slam winning tennis player had the nickname 'The Rocket'?

8 What is the nickname of Chicago Bears player William Perry?

9 If the Valiants and the Potters were playing each other in an association football match, in which English city would you be?

10 Over the years many Finnish athletes have acquired the nickname 'The Flying Finn' but who, in 1912, was the first to be so named?

THE 10 HIGHEST FIRST-CLASS INNINGS BY W. G. GRACE

	Match	Venue	Year	Runs
1	MCC *v* Kent	Canterbury	1876	344
2	Gloucestershire *v* Yorkshire	Cheltenham	1876	318*
3	Gloucestershire *v* Sussex	Bristol	1896	301
4	Gloucestershire *v* Somerset	Bristol	1895	288
5	South *v* North	The Oval	1871	268
6	South *v* North	Prince's	1877	261
7	Gloucestershire *v* Kent	Gravesend	1895	257
8	Gloucestershire *v* Sussex	Brighton	1896	243*
9	England *v* Surrey	The Oval	1866	224*
10	Gloucestershire *v* Middlesex	Clifton	1885	221*

Not out.

Grace hit 126 first-class centuries, including 13 double centuries and three triple centuries. His 344 in 1876 was the first-ever individual score of 300 in the first-class game. His 344 and 318 not out in 1876 came within eight days between 11–18 August. His 288 against Somerset in 1895 was the 100th century of his career. The 100th run of his 100th century was off the bowling of Samuel Woods who played Test cricket for both Australia and England. Despite these achievements, Grace scored only two Test centuries.

During a match in 1893 Grace was on 93 and surely heading for yet another century. Suddenly, he called a halt to his team's innings by declaring. When asked why he had not delayed this course of action at least until he had reached treble figures, the Doctor replied that 93 was the only score between 0 and 100 he had never achieved and he thought it was time to put the records straight!

The three brothers Grace: G.F. (rear, holding ball), W. G. (front centre, with bat) and E. M. (front right, wearing cap).

THE FIRST 10 PRICE RISES OF *WISDEN CRICKETERS' ALMANACK*

Cricket's 'bible' was first published in 1864 by John Wisden & Co at a cost of one shilling (5p). It was a paperback edition and contained 116 pages. The 129th edition of the *Almanack*, published in 1992, contained 1,344 pages and the paperback edition cost £18.50 (£18 10s 0d). Here is a list of the first 10 price rises of the book as it headed towards today's price:

	Year	New price*
1	1915	1s 6d (7½p)
2	1918	2s 0d (10p)
3	1919	2s 6d (12½p)
4	1921	5s 0d (25p)
5	1943	6s 0d (30p)
6	1947	7s 6d (37½p)
7	1948	9s 6d (47½p)
8	1951	10s 6d (52½p)
9	1952	12s 6d (62½p)
10	1956	15s 0d (75p)

All prices are for the paperback edition.

The 100 per cent price rise in 1921 is perhaps explained by the fact that in that year the book increased in size from 327 to 727 pages. The first time it contained 1,000 pages was in 1924 and the first time the paperback edition reached £1 was in 1962.

THE 10 MOST POPULAR SURNAMES IN THE BIRTHS AND DEATHS OF CRICKETERS SECTION IN *WISDEN* (1991 EDITION)

	WITHOUT CONNOTATIONS Name	No. of entries		WITH CONNOTATIONS Name(s)	No. of entries
1	Smith	39	**1**	Smith	39
2	Taylor	22	**2**	Taylor	22
3	Jones	18	**3**	Jones	18
4	Brown	15	**4**	Davis/Davies	17
5	Robinson	12	**5**	Brown/Browne	16
6=	Grace	11	**6**	Johnson/Johnston	13
6=	Hill	11	**7=**	Robinson	12
6=	Johnson	11	**7=**	White/Wight	12
9=	Davis	10	**9=**	Clark/Clarke	11
9=	Scott	10	**9=**	Grace	11
9=	Ward	10	**9=**	Hill	11
9=	Wilson	10	**9=**	Parker/Parkar	11

Among the list of 11 Graces is the name of Mrs H. M. Grace, mother of W. G., E. M. and G. F. – the only woman to appear in the section. A surname that appears just once is that of Caesar, a nineteenth-century player with Surrey and All-England. His first name – Julius, of course!

THE 10 HIGHEST TEST INNINGS BY DON BRADMAN

	Opponents	Venue	Year	Runs
1	England	Leeds	1930	334
2	England	Leeds	1934	304
3	South Africa	Adelaide	1931–32	299*
4	England	Melbourne	1936–37	270
5	England	Lord's	1930	254
6	England	The Oval	1934	244
7	England	Sydney	1946–47	234
8	England	The Oval	1930	232
9	South Africa	Brisbane	1931–32	226
10	West Indies	Brisbane	1930–31	223

Not out.

A CRICKETING LEGEND – W. G. GRACE

There can be no bigger name in the world of cricket than W. G. Grace and, looking at the rotund frame of the West Country cricketing doctor, there can have been fewer bigger cricketers. The adjective 'legendary' is used all too often when describing sports people (somebody has probably even talked about 'the legendary Gazza' already) but, in the case of William Gilbert Grace, it can never be over-used.

Born at Downend, Bristol, on 18 July 1848, he was the fourth of five cricketing sons of Dr Henry and Martha Grace. Two of his brothers, E. M. and G. F., once appeared in the same England team as W. G., while their mother was so highly regarded that she is the only woman to appear in the obituaries of cricketers in *Wisden Cricketers' Almanack*. Like his father, W. G. was to become a doctor, joining the Royal College of Surgeons in 1879 and working as a surgeon at Bristol until 1899 when he moved to Kent. At the age of 16, W. G. was over six feet tall and weighed 14 stone 5 pounds. He made his Lord's debut that same year; the previous year the 15-year-old Grace had scored his first century, 170, against the Gentlemen of Sussex. A rare talent was certainly unfolding. His first season of first-class cricket was in 1865 when he was 17 years old. Altogether he spent 44 seasons in the first-class game and the stories and anecdotes about Grace have passed into cricketing legend – akin in modern times to those stories about

Liverpool soccer manager Bill Shankly.

Although he remained an amateur throughout his cricketing career, he made the modern-day equivalent of about £1,250,000 from a bat endorsement with the L. J. Nicholls company of Sussex.

Grace was not only an excellent cricketer but, as a teenager, was a very keen athlete and in 1866 won the 440 yards hurdles at Crystal Palace in the first National Olympic Association meeting. Extraordinarily, he was in the middle of a match at The Oval at the time. But, having made his contribution with an unbeaten innings of 224 not out, he left the match to compete at Crystal Palace.

W. G. was also a keen bowls player and in 1903 became the first President of the English Bowls Association and played for England until 1908. Shortly after his appointment as manager of cricket and other sports at the old Crystal Palace in 1899, he turned the tennis courts into bowling greens and pioneered indoor bowls.

Grace made his name in the County Championship with Gloucestershire but in 1899 he fell out with them and formed the short-lived London County team. He played senior cricket until he was 66 when he scored 69 not out for Eltham against Grove Park on 25 July 1914. A year later, on 23 October 1915, Dr William Gilbert Grace, cricketing legend, died at Eltham in Surrey.

THE TOP 10 BATTING AVERAGES IN THE 1947 SEASON

The 1947 season was memorable as a glorious year when runs flowed all summer. The Middlesex pair of Compton and Edrich stole the limelight with a staggering 7,355 runs and 30 centuries between them. But they weren't the only two men to pile on the runs as a look at that season's top 10 batting averages shows:

	Batsman/county	Innings	Not out	Runs	Highest score	Centuries	Average
1	Denis Compton (Middlesex)	50	8	3,816	246	18	90.85
2	Bill Edrich (Middlesex)	52	8	3,539	268*	12	80.43
3	Ted Lester (Yorkshire)	11	2	657	142	3	73.00
4	Cyril Washbrook (Lancashire)	47	8	2,662	251*	11	68.25
5	Les Ames (Kent)	42	7	2,272	212*	7	64.91
6	Joe Hardstaff (Nottinghamshire)	44	7	2,396	221*	7	64.75
7	Len Hutton (Yorkshire)	44	4	2,585	270*	11	64.62
8	Winston Place (Lancashire)	47	7	2,501	266*	10	62.52
9	Martin Donnelly (Oxford University)	30	6	1,488	162*	5	62.00
10	Michael Walford (Somerset)	18	2	971	264	2	60.68

*Not out.

CROQUET

THE 10 PLAYERS WITH THE MOST OPEN CHAMPIONSHIP TITLES

Croquet's oldest championship, the Open, was first held in 1867 when it was won by Walter Jones Whitmore. It has been won most frequently by:

	Player	Years	Wins
1	John Solomon	1953–68	10
2	Nigel Aspinall	1969–84	8
3	Humphrey Hicks	1932–52	7
4	Cyril Corbally	1902–13	5
5=	A. H. Spong	1878–82	4
5=	P. D. Matthews	1914–27	4
5=	Dorothy Steel	1925–36	4
8=	B. C. Evelegh	1877–99	3
8=	C. L. O'Callaghan	1910–21	3
8=	Ben Apps	1926–31	3
8=	Edmond Cotter	1955–62	3
8=	David Openshaw	1979–85	3

THE 10 PLAYERS WITH THE MOST PRESIDENT'S CUP WINS

The President's Cup is a competition for the season's best eight players. Entry is by invitation only and, occasionally, if overseas players are invited, the number of contestants is increased to 10, which was the number invited when the competition was first held in 1901 and known as the Champions Cup. In 1926 it became known as the Beddow Cup for one year only, then reverted to the Champions Cup the following year, but became the Beddow Cup again between 1931 and 1934. After Dorothy Steel won it outright in 1934 the competition became known as the President's Cup when the then president of the Croquet Association, Trevor Williams, donated the new trophy. The number of entrants was reduced to eight after the competition's revival in 1945.

	Player	Years	Wins
1	Nigel Aspinall	1969–85	11
2	John Solomon	1955–71	9
3=	Dorothy Steel	1923–37	6
3=	Edmond Cotter	1949–60	6
5	Humphrey Hicks	1930–54	5
6	Stephen Mulliner	1981–87	4
7=	G. H. Woolston	1902–08	3
7=	C. L. O'Callaghan	1909–20	3
9=	C. F. Barry	1919–21	2
9=	J. B. Morgan	1929–32	2

The President's Cup is a round-robin event with competitors playing each other twice. Nobody won all 18 matches in the days of 10 entrants, but since it has been reduced to eight players, Humphrey Hicks in 1954, John Solomon in 1962, and Nigel Aspinall in 1975 have won the trophy with a maximum 14 wins.

CYCLING

THE TOP 10 TOUR DE FRANCE WINS

Rider/nationality	Wins
1= Jacques Anquetil (Fra)	5
1= Eddy Merckx (Bel)	5
1= Bernard Hinault (Fra)	5
4= Philippe Thys (Bel)	3
4= Louison Bobet (Fra)	3
4= Greg LeMond (USA)	3
7= Lucien Petit-Breton (Fra)	2
7= Firmin Lambot (Bel)	2
7= Ottavio Bottecchia (Ita)	2
7= Nicholas Frantz (Lux)	2
7= André Leducq (Fra)	2
7= Antonin Magne (Fra)	2
7= Gino Bartali* (Ita)	2
7= Sylvere Maës (Bel)	2
7= Fausto Coppi (Ita)	2
7= Bernard Thevenet (Fra)	2
7= Laurent Fignon (Fra)	2
7= Miguel Indurain (Spa)	2

* Bartali won the race in 1938 and 1948 and is the only man to win both before and after World War II.

THE 10 FASTEST AVERAGE WINNING SPEEDS IN THE TOUR DE FRANCE

	Winner/nationality	Year	Average speed kph	mph
1	Miguel Indurain (Spa)	1992	39.494	24.541
2	Pedro Delgado (Spa)	1988	39.142	24.322
3	Miguel Indurain (Spa)	1991	39.021	24.247
4	Greg LeMond (USA)	1990	38.933	24.192
5	Bernard Hinault (Fra)	1981	37.844	23.515
6	Greg LeMond (USA)	1989	37.818	23.499
7	Bernard Hinault (Fra)	1982	37.458	23.275
8	Jacques Anquetil (Fra)	1962	37.306	23.181
9	Stephen Roche (Ire)	1987	37.294	23.173
10	Gastone Nencini (Ita)	1960	37.210	23.121

Greg LeMond of the USA (right), winner of the 1990 Tour de France in which he recorded an average speed of 38.933kph/24.192mph.

THE 10 LONGEST TOURS DE FRANCE

	Year	Winner/nationality	Stages	Distance km	miles
1	1926	Lucien Buysse (Bel)	17	5,745	3,570
2	1919	Firmin Lambot (Bel)	15	5,560	3,455
3	1911	Gustave Garrigou (Fra)	15	5,544	3,445
4	1920	Philippe Thys (Bel)	15	5,503	3,419
5	1921	Léon Scieur (Bel)	15	5,484	3,408
6	1925	Ottavio Bottecchia (Ita)	18	5,430	3,374
7	1924	Ottavio Bottecchia (Ita)	15	5,427	3,372
8	1914	Philippe Thys (Bel)	15	5,414	3,364
9	1913	Philippe Thys (Bel)	15	5,387	3,347
10	1923	Henri Pélissier (Fra)	15	5,386	3,347

The longest post-war race was in 1948 when Italy's Gino Bartali won the 4,922-km/3,058-mile race. The shortest-ever race was the second Tour in 1904, and measured just 2,388km/1,484 miles. The winner was Henri Cornet of France.

THE 10 COUNTRIES WITH MOST STAGE WINNERS IN THE TOUR DE FRANCE

	Country	Stage wins
1	France	629
2	Belgium	447
3	Italy	186
4	Holland	150
5	Spain	77
6	Luxembourg	63
7	Switzerland	41
8	Germany	29
9	Great Britain	17
10	Ireland	11

The last British rider to win a stage was Scotsman Robert Millar in 1989. In 1991 Brazil became the 19th nation to win a stage in the Tour.

THE 10 LONGEST STAGES IN THE 1992 TOUR DE FRANCE

	Between	Stage no.	Length km	miles
1	Dole – St Gervais	12	267.5	166
2	San Sebastián (Spain) – Pau	2	255	159
3	St Gervais – Sestrières (Italy)	13	254.5	158
4	Strasbourg – Mulhouse	11	249.5	155
5	Blois – Nanterre	20	222	138
6	Pau – Bordeaux	3	218	135
7	Luxembourg – Strasbourg	10	217	135
8	St Etienne – La Bourboule	16	212	132
9	Montluçon – Tours	18	212	132
10	Valkenburg (Holland) – Koblenz (Germany)	8	206.5	128

Excluding the Prologue Time Trial, the shortest stage was Stage 4, the Team Time Trial around Libourne. It totalled just 63.5km/39½ miles.

The longest-ever stage in the Tour was the 486-km/302-mile stage from Les Sables D'Olonne to Bayonne in 1919. The shortest-ever, again excluding Prologues, was the 19.6-km/12-mile stage from Luçon to Superbagnères in 1971.

THE 10 TOWNS AND CITIES MOST VISITED BY RIDERS DURING THE TOUR DE FRANCE

	Town/city	No. of times visited
1	Paris	79
2	Bordeaux	73
3	Pau	49
4	Luçon	47
5	Nice	34
6=	Bayonne	32
6=	Perpignan	32
8	Marseille	30
9	Briançon	29
10	Brest	28

Paris has been visited by the riders in all 79 Tours to date.

THE 10 TOURS DE FRANCE WITH THE MOST FINISHERS

	Year	Starters	Finishers
1	1991	198	158
2	1990	198	156
3	1988	198	151
4	1989	198	148
5	1985	180	144
6	1987	207	135
7	1986	210	132
8	1992	198	130
9	1982	169	125
10	1984	170	124

The first time 100 riders finished the Tour was in 1970, when exactly 100 of the 150 starters reached Paris at the end of 4,366 km/2,713 miles. The 100th placed rider, Hoogerhelde of Holland, finished 3 hours 52 minutes and 12 seconds behind the winner, Eddy Merckx of Belgium.

The 105 finishers from 130 starters in 1974 represents 80.76 per cent of riders to finish the race, the biggest-ever percentage.

The fewest number of finishers was in 1919 when only 11 of the 69 starters completed the 5,560-km/3,455-mile race.

THE 10 MOST SUCCESSFUL OLYMPIC COUNTRIES

	Country	gold	Medals silver	bronze	Total
1	France	27	16	21	64
2	Italy	28	15	6	49
3	Great Britain	9	21	14	44
4	Germany/ West Germany	10	14	13	37
5	Holland	9	13	6	28
6	USSR/CIS	11	4	9	24
7	Belgium	6	6	10	22
8=	Australia	6	10	4	20
8=	Denmark	6	6	8	20
10	East Germany	7	6	4	17

Although it is the most successful country, France has not won a gold medal since Daniel Morelon won the sprint title in 1972.

THE 10 FASTEST AVERAGE WINNING SPEEDS IN THE MILK RACE

	Winner/nationality	Year	Average speed kph	mph
1	Conor Henry (Ire)	1992	43.71	27.16
1	Joey McLoughlin (GB)	1986	42.20	26.22
2	Chris Walker (GB)	1991	41.33	25.68
3	Piet van Katwijk (Hol)	1973	40.83	25.37
4	Sergey Krivocheyev (USSR)	1981	40.75	25.32
5	Fedor den Hertog (Hol)	1971	40.56	25.20
6	Eric van Lancker (Bel)	1985	40.51	25.17
7	Roy Schuiten (Hol)	1974	40.36	25.08
8	Ivan Mitchtenko (USSR)	1980	40.35	25.07
9	Matt Eaton (USA)	1983	40.28	25.03

DARTS

THE 10 PLAYERS WITH THE MOST APPEARANCES IN THE EMBASSY WORLD PROFESSIONAL DARTS CHAMPIONSHIP FINAL

The 'Embassy' is the darts world's premier tournament and is held every January. First contested in 1977 and won by Leighton Rees, it has had three homes – Nottingham, Stoke-on-Trent, and currently the Lakeside Country Club, Frimley Green, Surrey.

	Player	Appearances*
1	Eric Bristow	10(5)
2	John Lowe	7(2)
3=	Phil Taylor	2(2)
3=	Jocky Wilson	2(2)
3=	Leighton Rees	2(1)
3=	Dave Whitcombe	2(0)
7=	Bob Anderson	1(1)
7=	Keith Deller	1(1)
7=	Dennis Priestley	1(1)
7=	Bobby George	1(0)
7=	Mike Gregory	1(0)

Figures in brackets indicate number of wins.

England's Eric Bristow, who has made more appearances in the final of the Embassy World Professional Darts Championship than any other player.

All players are from England except Wilson (Scotland) and Rees (Wales).

THE TOP 10 CHECKOUTS IN THE 1992 EMBASSY WORLD PROFESSIONAL DARTS CHAMPIONSHIP

	Player	Checkout
1	Keith Sullivan	170
2	Phil Taylor	167
3	Alan Warriner	164
4=	Bob Anderson	161
4=	Mike Gregory	161
4=	John Lowe	161
7	Kevin Kenny	160
8=	Bob Anderson	146
8=	Phil Taylor	146
10	John Lowe	145

A ll except Sullivan (Aus) are British players.

THE 10 HIGHEST POSSIBLE CHECKOUTS

The highest checkouts with three darts, assuming a double to finish, are:

	Suggested throws	Score
1	Treble 20, Treble 20, Bull	170
2	Treble 20, Treble 19, Bull	167
3	Treble 19, Treble 19, Bull	164
4	Treble 20, Treble 17, Bull	161
5	Treble 20, Treble 20, Double 20	160
6	Treble 20, Treble 20, Double 19	158
7	Treble 20, Treble 19, Double 20	157
8	Treble 20, Treble 20, Double 18	156
9	Treble 20, Treble 19, Double 19	155
10	Treble 20, Treble 18, Double 20	154

EQUESTRIANISM

These figures include the medal totals for the three disciplines: Show Jumping, Three-Day Event and Dressage.

THE 10 MOST SUCCESSFUL OLYMPIC COUNTRIES

	Country	gold	Medals silver	bronze	Total
1	Germany/West Germany	29	16	19	64
2	Sweden	17	8	14	39
3	USA	8	15	11	34
4	France	11	12	10	33
5	Italy	7	9	7	23
6	Great Britain	5	7	9	21
7	Switzerland	4	8	7	19
8	USSR/CIS	6	5	4	15
9	Holland	6	5	1	12
10	Belgium	4	2	5	11

GAELIC FOOTBALL

THE 10 COUNTIES WITH THE MOST WINS IN THE ALL-IRELAND FINAL

Gaelic football's premier event is the All-Ireland final played at Croke Park, Dublin, on the third Sunday in September each year. An inter-county event, it was first held in 1887 and won by Limerick. The winning team collects the coveted Sam Maguire Trophy.

	County	Wins
1	Kerry	30
2	Dublin	21
3	Galway	7
4	Cork	6
5=	Cavan	5
5=	Meath	5
5=	Wexford	5
8=	Down	4
8=	Kildare	4
8=	Tipperary	4

Down (dark shorts) win their fourth Sam Maguire Trophy by beating Meath 16–14 in the All-Ireland final of 1991.

GOLF

Renowned for his flamboyant dress style, Walter Hagen, seen here in the 1923 British Open at Troon, won a total of 11 Majors in his career.

The four Majors are the British Open, US Open, US Masters, and US PGA. The oldest is the British Open, first played at Prestwick in 1860 and won by Willie Park. The first US Open was at the Newport Club, Rhode Island, in 1895 and won by Horace Rawlins, playing over his home course. The US PGA Championship, probably the least prestigious of the four Majors, was first held at the Siwanoy Club, New York. Jim Barnes beat Jock Hutchison by one hole in the match-play final. It did not become a stroke-play event until 1958. The youngest of the four Majors is the Masters, played over the beautiful Augusta National course in Georgia. It is the only Major played over the same course each year. Entry is by invitation only and the first winner was Horton Smith. The Masters, and the Augusta course, were the idea of Robert Tyre 'Bobby' Jones, the greatest amateur player the world of golf has ever seen.

THE 10 PLAYERS TO WIN THE MOST PROFESSIONAL MAJORS IN A CAREER

	Player/ nationality	British Open	US Open	Masters	PGA	Total
1	Jack Nicklaus (USA)	3	4	6	5	18
2	Walter Hagen (USA)	4	2	0	5	11
3=	Ben Hogan (USA)	1	4	2	2	9
3=	Gary Player (SA)	3	1	3	2	9
5	Tom Watson (USA)	5	1	2	0	8
6=	Bobby Jones (USA)	3	4	0	0	7
6=	Arnold Palmer (USA)	2	1	4	0	7
6=	Gene Sarazen (USA)	1	2	1	3	7
6=	Sam Snead (USA)	1	0	3	3	7
6=	Harry Vardon (GB)	6	1	0	0	7

No man has won all four Majors in one year. Ben Hogan, in 1953, won three of the four, but did not compete in the PGA Championship. Bobby Jones achieved a unique Grand Slam in 1930 by winning the British Open and US Open, as well as winning the amateur titles in both countries.

THE 10 MOST FREQUENTLY USED COURSES FOR THE BRITISH OPEN

	Course	First used	Last used	Times used
1=	Prestwick	1860	1925	24
1=	St Andrews	1873	1990	24
3	Muirfield	1892	1992	14
4	Royal St George's, Sandwich	1894	1985	11
5	Hoylake	1897	1967	10
6	Royal Lytham	1926	1988	8
7	Royal Birkdale	1954	1991	7
8=	Musselburgh	1874	1889	6
8=	Royal Troon	1923	1989	6
10	Carnoustie	1931	1975	5

The first Open in 1860 was organized by the Prestwick Club, which was also solely responsible for the first 11 championships. After Tom Morris jr won the title for a third consecutive year in 1870 he was allowed to keep the winner's prize, a red Moroccan leather belt. With no trophy to play for, there was no championship in 1871. However, it was revived the following year when responsibility for its organization was shared jointly by the Prestwick Club, the Honourable Company of Edinburgh Golfers, and the Royal and Ancient. That same year, the now famous claret jug was first presented to the winner, Young Tom Morris, again.

The only other courses to have staged the Open are Deal (twice), Turnberry (twice), Prince's (once), Sandwich (once) and Royal Portrush (once), the only Irish course to play host to Britain's only Major. The Carnoustie course in 1968 was the longest ever used for the Open, measuring 7,252 yards.

THE 10 MOST SUCCESSFUL BRITONS IN MAJORS

	Player	Titles
1	Harry Vardon	7
2=	James Braid	5
2=	John Henry Taylor	5
2=	Nick Faldo	5
5=	Tom Morris sr	4
5=	Tom Morris jr	4
5=	Willie Park sr	4
8=	Willie Anderson	3
8=	Henry Cotton	3
8=	Robert Ferguson	3

All except Vardon (US Open 1900) and Faldo (US Masters 1989 and 1990) won their Majors on British soil.

THE 10 LOWEST FOUR-ROUND TOTALS IN THE BRITISH OPEN

The first time the Open Championship was played over four rounds of 18 holes was at Muirfield in 1892 when the amateur Harold H. Hilton won with scores of 78, 81, 72 and 74 for a total of 305. Since then the record has kept falling and at Turnberry in 1977 Tom Watson and Jack Nicklaus decimated British Open records with Watson winning by one stroke with a championship record 268. The lowest complete rounds in the Open have been:

	Player/nationality	Venue	Year	Total
1	Tom Watson (USA)	Turnberry	1977	268
2	Jack Nicklaus (USA)	Turnberry	1977	269
3	Nick Faldo (GB)	St Andrews	1990	270
4	Tom Watson (USA)	Muirfield	1980	271
5=	Ian Baker-Finch (Aus)	Royal Birkdale	1991	272
5=	Nick Faldo (GB)	Muirfield	1992	272
7=	Severiano Ballesteros (Spa)	Royal Lytham	1988	273
7=	John Cook (USA)	Muirfield	1992	273
9=	Mike Harwood (Aus)	Royal Birkdale	1991	274
9=	José Maria Olazabal (Spa)	Muirfield	1992	274

The lowest individual round is 63, which has been achieved by five golfers: Mark Hayes (USA), Turnberry 1977; Isao Aoki (Jap), Muirfield 1980; Greg Norman (Aus), Turnberry 1986; Paul Broadhurst (GB), St Andrews 1990; and Jodie Mudd (USA), Royal Birkdale 1991.

Craig Stadler (1983), Tom Watson (1980), Hubert Green (1980), Christy O'Connor jr (1985), Seve Ballesteros (1986), Rodger Davis (1987), Ian Baker-Finch (1990 and 1991), Fred Couples (1991), Nick Faldo (1992), Steve Pate (1992) and Ray Floyd (1992) have all recorded rounds of 64. A further 22 men have registered rounds of 65; the first to do so was Henry Cotton at Sandwich in 1934. His total was not surpassed until 1977.

THE PROGRESSION OF LOWEST FOUR-ROUND TOTALS IN THE BRITISH OPEN

Player	Venue	Year	Total
Harold Hilton	Muirfield	1892	305
Harry Vardon	Prestwick	1903	300
Jackie White	Sandwich	1904	296
James Braid	Prestwick	1908	291
Bobby Jones	St Andrews	1927	285
Gene Sarazen	Prince's	1932	283
Bobby Locke	Troon	1950	279
Peter Thomson	Royal Lytham	1958	278
Arnold Palmer	Troon	1962	276
Tom Watson	Turnberry	1977	268

Jack Nicklaus and Tom Watson (left) at Turnberry in 1977. The two American golfers decimated British Open records, with Watson eventually winning by a single stroke.

THE 10 OLDEST GOLF CLUBS IN BRITAIN

	Club	Year formed
1	Royal Burgess Golfing Society of Edinburgh	1735
2	Honourable Company of Edinburgh Golfers (Muirfield)	1744
3	Royal and Ancient (St Andrews)	1754
4	Bruntsfield Links Golfing Society	1761
5	Royal Blackheath	1766
6	Royal Musselburgh	1774
7	Royal Aberdeen	1780
8=	Glasgow Gailes	1787
8=	Glasgow Killermont	1787
10	Cruden Bay (Aberdeenshire)	1791

All these clubs are in Scotland with the exception of Royal Blackheath. The oldest in Northern Ireland is Royal Belfast (1881) and the Republic's oldest is Curragh, Co Kildare (1883). The oldest Welsh club is Pontnewydd, Cwmbran (1875).

The exact date of the formation of the Blackheath Club is uncertain and some sources record that golf was played there in the seventeenth century by James VI of Scotland. However, it is generally accepted that the club was formed in 1766.

THE 10 HIGHEST FOUR-ROUND TOTALS IN THE BRITISH OPEN

The first Open to consist of four 18-hole rounds was in 1892 when Fred Fitzjohn of Musselburgh finished last of the pack with a total of 372 (105–95–83–89). Yet surprisingly, his total does not figure in the all-time list of the 10 highest recorded completed rounds, which were all achieved in the three years between 1893 and 1895.

	Player/club	Venue	Year	1	2	3	4	Total
1	Tom Morris sr (St Andrews)	St Andrews	1895	107	92	96	97	392
2	C. Thom (West Herts)	Sandwich	1894	97	102	99	90	388
3	J. Boyd (unattached)	Sandwich	1894	103	96	95	90	384
4	Tom Morris sr (St Andrews)	Prestwick	1893	96	94	100	93	383
5=	E. Lehmann (Royal and Ancient)	Sandwich	1894	91	98	94	99	382
5=	R. Kirk (Wallasey)	Sandwich	1894	98	97	94	93	382
7	J. Douglas (Pollokshaws)	Prestwick	1893	96	92	95	95	378
8=	Tom Milne (Neasden)	Sandwich	1894	98	98	91	90	377
8=	Dr Bruce Goff (Royal and Ancient)	Sandwich	1894	98	92	88	99	377
10	L. G. Ross (Sutton Coldfield)	Sandwich	1894	92	98	90	96	376

In the early days of the championship, play was over three 12-hole rounds and at Prestwick in 1863 William Moffat (Musselburgh) registered rounds of 75–78–80 for a 36-hole total of 233, the highest recorded 36-hole total. It is the equivalent of 466 for 72 holes.

The highest 18-hole total on the scorecard of *any* champion is 91 by the 1873 winner Tom Kidd, whose two rounds consisted of scores of 91 and 88. The last champion with an 80 on his card was the 1920 winner George Duncan, who started his championship quest with two opening rounds of 80 and was 13 strokes behind the leader Abe Mitchell at that stage. One round later they were all square after Duncan shot a 71 to Mitchell's 84.

THE 10 HIGHEST INDIVIDUAL ROUNDS OF POST-WAR BRITISH OPEN CHAMPIONS

	Player/nationality	Venue	Year	Score
1	Fred Daly (GB)	Hoylake	1947	78
2	Bobby Locke (SA)	Sandwich	1949	76
3=	Sam Snead (USA)	St Andrews	1946	75
3=	Henry Cotton (GB)	Muirfield	1948	75
3=	Gary Player (SA)	Muirfield	1959	75
3=	Jack Nicklaus (USA)	Muirfield	1966	75
3=	Gary Player (SA)	Royal Lytham	1974	75
3=	Severiano Ballesteros (Spa)	Royal Lytham	1979	75
9=	Sam Snead (USA)	St Andrews	1946	74
9=	Max Faulkner (GB)	Portrush	1951	74
9=	Bobby Locke (SA)	Royal Lytham	1952	74
9=	Peter Thomson (Aus)	Hoylake	1956	74
9=	Peter Thomson (Aus)	Royal Birkdale	1965	74
9=	Gary Player (SA)	Carnoustie	1968	74
9=	Tom Watson (USA)	Royal Troon	1982	74
9=	Greg Norman (Aus)	Turnberry	1986	74*

Norman had two 74s in his winning total of 280.

THE 10 YOUNGEST WINNERS OF THE BRITISH OPEN

	Player*	yrs	Age months
1	Tom Morris jr	17	5
2	Willie Auchterlonie	21	1
3	Severiano Ballesteros (Spa)	22	3
4	John H. Taylor	23	3
5	Gary Player (SA)	23	8
6	Jack Simpson	24	0
7	Bobby Jones (USA)	24	3
8	Peter Thomson (Aus)	24	11
9=	Arthur Havers	25	0
9=	Tony Jacklin	25	0

British unless otherwise stated.

The exact date of birth of the 1884 champion Jack Simpson has not been established. He was born in 1860, the year of the very first Open, and was anything between 23 years 6 months and 24 years 6 months at the time of his triumph.

Young Tom Morris wearing the Championship belt. He is the youngest golfer ever to win the British Open.

THE 10 OLDEST WINNERS ON THE PGA EUROPEAN TOUR, 1991

	Player/nationality	yrs	Age days
1	Rodger Davis (Aus)	40	162
2	Jeff Hawkes (Aus)	38	5
3	Mark McNulty (Zim)	37	304
4	Sam Torrance (Sco)	37	233
5	Gavin Levenson (SA)	37	82
6	Eduardo Romero (Arg)	36	353
7	Tony Johnstone (Zim)	35	38
8	Payne Stewart (USA)	34	179
9	Severiano Ballesteros (Spa)	34	54
10	Bernhard Langer (Ger)	34	40

THE 10 YOUNGEST WINNERS ON THE PGA EUROPEAN TOUR, 1991

	Player/nationality	yrs	Age days
1	Per-Ulrik Johansson (Swe)	24	192
2	Steven Richardson (Eng)	24	215
3	José Maria Olazabal (Spa)	25	40
4	Craig Parry (Aus)	25	127
5	David Gilford (Eng)	25	338
6	Paul Broadhurst (Eng)	25	362
7	Mark Davis (Eng)	27	87
8	Colin Montgomerie (Sco)	28	42
9	Anders Forsbrand (Swe)	29	364
10	Andrew Sherbourne (Eng)	30	48

THE TOP 10 MONEY-WINNERS ON THE PGA EUROPEAN TOUR, 1991

	Player/nationality	Winnings (£)*
1	Severiano Ballesteros (Spa)	546,353
2	Steven Richardson (Eng)	393,155
3	Bernhard Langer (Ger)	372,703
4	Colin Montgomerie (Sco)	343,575
5	Craig Parry (Aus)	328,116
6	Rodger Davis (Aus)	317,441
7	José Maria Olazabal (Spa)	302,270
8	Ian Woosnam (Wal)	257,433
9	David Gilford (Eng)	249,240
10	Nick Faldo (Eng)	245,892

Official prizemoney, which includes special events, pro-am tournaments, etc.

THE TOP 10 CAREER MONEY-WINNERS ON THE PGA EUROPEAN TOUR

	Player/nationality	Winnings (£)*
1	Severiano Ballesteros (Spa)	2,691,090
2	Ian Woosnam (Wal)	2,482,983
3	Nick Faldo (Eng)	2,111,660
4	Bernhard Langer (Ger)	2,024,323
5	José Maria Olazabal (Spa)	1,751,702
6	Sandy Lyle (Sco)	1,671,962
7	Ronan Rafferty (NI)	1,597,939
8	Mark McNulty (Zim)	1,596,416
9	Sam Torrance (Sco)	1,515,669
10	Mark James (Eng)	1,426,037

To end 1991 Tour.

Seve Ballesteros took 17 seasons to reach the £2 million mark, which Ian Woosnam achieved in 13.

The PGA European Tour was started in 1977 after the Tournament Players' Division, who had split from the PGA in 1975, merged with the Continental Tournament Players' Association to become the European Players' Division. Prior to their merger and the subsequent birth of the PGA European Tour, there had been separate British and European Tours for several years.

THE 10 LOWEST FOUR-ROUND TOTALS ON THE PGA EUROPEAN TOUR

	Player	Competition	Year	Score
1=	David Llewellyn	AGF Biarritz Open	1988	258
1=	Ian Woosnam	Torras Monte Carlo Open	1990	258
3	Mark McNulty	German Open	1987	259
4=	Mike Clayton	Timex Open	1984	260
4=	Peter Senior	Johnnie Walker Monte Carlo Open	1987	260
4=	Ian Woosnam	Panasonic European Open	1988	260
7=	Jerry Anderson	Ebel European Masters-Swiss Open	1984	261
7=	Rodger Davis	Johnnie Walker Monte Carlo Open	1987	261
7=	José Rivero	Monte Carlo Open	1988	261
7=	Mark McNulty	Monte Carlo Open	1989	261
7=	Ian Woosnam	Monte Carlo Open	1991	261

All except Davis were the winners of the Tournament.

Prior to the inception of the PGA European Tour, these low totals were achieved and would figure in the main list:

Eric Brown	Portuguese Open	1953	260
Kel Nagle	Irish Hospitals Tournament	1961	260

THE TOP 10 WINS IN A EUROPEAN SEASON

	Player/nationality	Year	Wins
1=	Norman von Nida (Aus)	1947	7
1=	Flory van Donck (Bel)	1953	7
3	Severiano Ballesteros (Spa)	1986	6
4=	Norman von Nida (Aus)	1948	5
4=	Bobby Locke (SA)	1954	5
4=	Bernard Hunt (Eng)	1963	5
4=	Nick Faldo (Eng)	1983	5
4=	Ian Woosnam (Wal)	1987	5
4=	Severiano Ballesteros (Spa)	1988	5
4=	Ian Woosnam (Wal)	1990	5

THE TOP 10 MONEY-WINNERS ON THE US TOUR, 1991

	Player*	Winnings ($)
1	Corey Pavin	979,430
2	Craig Stadler	827,628
3	Fred Couples	791,749
4	Tom Purtzer	750,568
5	Andrew Magee	750,082
6	Steve Pate	727,997
7	Nick Price (Zim)	714,389
8	Davis Love III	686,361
9	Paul Azinger	685,603
10	Russ Cochran	684,851

*American unless otherwise stated.

THE TOP 10 MONEY-WINNERS ON THE US SENIORS TOUR, 1991

	Player*	Winnings ($)
1	Mike Hill	1,065,657
2	George Archer	963,455
3	Jim Colbert	880,749
4	Chi Chi Rodriguez	794,013
5	Lee Trevino	723,163
6	Bob Charles (NZ)	673,910
7	Dale Douglass	606,949
8	Charles Coody	543,326
9	Jim Dent	529,315
10	Al Geiberger	519,926

*American unless otherwise stated.

THE TOP 10 CAREER MONEY-WINNERS ON THE US TOUR

	Player	Winnings ($)*
1	Tom Kite	6,655,474
2	Tom Watson	5,729,108
3	Curtis Strange	5,626,225
4	Jack Nicklaus	5,294,261
5	Lanny Wadkins	5,265,876
6	Payne Stewart	5,059,959
7	Ben Crenshaw	4,690,831
8	Greg Norman	4,571,466
9	Hale Irwin	4,488,732
10	Paul Azinger	4,372,987

*To end 1991 Tour.

All are American with the exception of Greg Norman, who is Australian.

Arnold Palmer, on 21 July 1968, was the first man to take his career earnings past $1 million. Since then more than 100 men have won in excess of $1 million on the US Tour, and since 1988 the top money-winner each year has won a seven-figure sum.

Since Palmer's breakthrough, the other money-winning milestones have been:

First to $2 million:	Jack Nicklaus	1 December 1973
First to $3 million:	Jack Nicklaus	22 May 1977
First to $4 million:	Jack Nicklaus	6 February 1983
First to $5 million:	Jack Nicklaus	20 August 1988
First to $6 million:	Tom Kite	5 August 1990

THE 10 BIGGEST WINNING MARGINS ON THE PGA EUROPEAN TOUR

	Player	Tournament	Year	Winning margin
1	Bernhard Langer	Cacharel Under-25 Championship	1979	17
2=	Henry Cotton	French Open	1946	15
2=	Peter Thomson	Yorkshire Evening News Tournament	1957	15
4	Guy Wolstenholme	Jeyes Tournament	1963	12
5=	Tony Jacklin	Scandinavian Enterprise Open	1974	11
5=	Dale Hayes	French Open	1978	11
5=	Ken Brown	Glasgow Open	1984	11
5=	Colin Montgomerie	Portuguese Open	1989	11
9=	Greg Norman	French Open	1980	10
9=	Bernhard Langer	Carrolls Irish Open	1987	10

The first prize in the Scandinavian Masters was the biggest-ever payout to a winner on the European Tour. The Tour has come a long way since Christy O'Connor won the first four-figure cheque (£1,000) for his victory in the 1955 Swallow-Penfold Tournament at Southport and Ainsdale.

THE 10 BIGGEST FIRST PRIZES ON THE VOLVO TOUR, 1991*

	Tournament	Winner	Prizemoney (£)
1	Scandinavian Masters	Colin Montgomerie	100,000
2	British Open	Ian Baker-Finch	90,000
3=	Bell's Scottish Open	Craig Parry	83,330
3=	G. A. European Open	Mike Harwood	83,330
3=	Heineken Dutch Open	Payne Stewart	83,330
3=	Mercedes German Masters	Bernhard Langer	83,330
3=	Volvo PGA Championship	Severiano Ballesteros	83,330
8=	Dunhill British Masters	Severiano Ballesteros	75,000
8=	Epson Grand Prix of Europe	José Maria Olazabal	75,000
8=	Lancôme Trophy	Frank Nobilo	75,000
8=	NM English Open	David Gilford	75,000

*Including special approved events.

THE TOP 10 WINS IN A US SEASON

	Player	Year	Wins
1	Byron Nelson	1945	18
2	Ben Hogan	1946	13
3	Sam Snead	1950	11
4	Ben Hogan	1948	10
5	Paul Runyan	1933	9
6=	Horton Smith	1929	8
6=	Gene Sarazen	1930	8
6=	Harry Cooper	1937	8
6=	Sam Snead	1938	8
6=	Henry Picard	1939	8
6=	Byron Nelson	1944	8
6=	Lloyd Mangrum	1948	8
6=	Arnold Palmer	1960	8
6=	Johnny Miller	1974	8

Since Miller's eight in 1974, the best total has been six by Tom Watson in 1980.

BYRON NELSON'S REMARKABLE RECORD

Having won eight Tour events in 1944, Byron Nelson went on to shatter the US record the following year with a stunning 18 wins. His remarkable year started on 14 January when he won the Phoenix Open, and by the time he won the Miami Four Ball at Palm Springs on 11 March he had achieved his fourth success of the season. This victory at Miami sparked off a run of 11 consecutive tournament wins, which is also a US record. Included in his 11-tournament winning streak were the PGA Championship and the Canadian Open, often regarded as the 'Fifth Major'. His run ended with that victory in the Canadian Open on 4 August. He finished joint fourth in his next tournament, the Memphis Open, but the following week he was back to winning ways and before the season was out he added three more tournaments for a remarkable record total of 18 wins.

Byron Nelson, who holds the record for the most wins in a US season with a total of 18.

THE 10 LONGEST HOLES AT AUGUSTA

The Augusta National at Georgia was the brainchild of top US amateur golfer Bobby Jones and his close friend Clifford Roberts. The course was designed by the Scottish architect Alistair Mackenzie and it was completed in 1931. It has been the home of the US Masters since its inauguration in 1934 and it is the only venue to stage a Major championship every year. The course is currently 6,905 yards in length (3,465 yards outward, and 3,440 yards inward) and each of the 18 holes is named after the flower, bush, shrub or tree that can be found adjacent to it. The Top 10 longest holes are:

	Hole	No.	Length (yds)
1	Pink dogwood	2	555
2	Yellow jasmine	8	535
3	Fire thorn	15	500
4	Camellia	10	485
5	Azalea	13	465
6	White dogwood	11	455
7=	Carolina cherry	9	435
7=	Magnolia	5	435
9=	Chinese fir	14	405
9=	Holly	18	405

JACK NICKLAUS'S 10 BEST SEASONS ON THE REGULAR US TOUR

Between his first Tour win, the 1962 US Open, and his last, the 1986 Masters, Jack Nicklaus has won 70 events on the regular Tour. His total is second only to Sam Snead's all-time record tally. Nicklaus topped the money-winning charts eight times. His best seasons were:

	Year	Winnings ($)	Tournaments won
1=	1972	320,542	7
1=	1973	308,362	7
3=	1963	100,040	5
3=	1965	140,752	5
3=	1967	188,998	5
3=	1971	244,490	5
3=	1975	298,149	5
8	1964	113,285	4
9=	1962	61,869	3
9=	1969	140,167	3
9=	1977	284,509	3
9=	1978	256,672	3

Nicklaus's $320,542 prizemoney made 1972 his best year in terms of earnings. After winning the 1991 US Seniors title he took his Seniors Tour earnings for the season beyond his best-ever regular Tour season – and still had four months of the season remaining.

Souchak's record-breaking total of 257 was achieved at the Brackenridge Park Golf Course, San Antonio, Texas. A par 71, it measured 6,185 yards. His four-round totals were 60–68–64–65 for a US Tour record of 27 under par.

The lowest single round on the US Tour is 59 by Al Geiberger in the second round of the 1977 Memphis Classic at the Colonial Country Club, Memphis, Tennessee, and by Chip Beck in the second round of the 1991 Las Vegas International.

THE 10 LOWEST FOUR-ROUND TOTALS ON THE US TOUR

	Player	Tournament	Year	Total
1	Mike Souchak	Texas Open	1955	257
2	Donnie Hammond	Texas Open	1989	258
3=	Byron Nelson	Seattle Open	1945	259
3=	Chandler Harper	Texas Open	1954	259
3=	Tim Norris	Greater Hartford Open	1982	259
3=	Corey Pavin	Texas Open	1988	259
7=	Jack Burke	Texas Open	1952	260
7=	Johnny Miller	Phoenix Open	1975	260
7=	Peter Persons	Chattanooga Classic	1990	260
7=	Dillard Pruitt	Chattanooga Classic	1991	260

THE 10 PLAYERS WITH THE MOST WINS ON THE US TOUR IN A CAREER

	Player*	Tour wins
1	Sam Snead	81
2	Jack Nicklaus	70
3	Ben Hogan	63
4	Arnold Palmer	60
5	Byron Nelson	52
6	Billy Casper	51
7=	Walter Hagen	40
7=	Cary Middlecoff	40
9	Gene Sarazen	38
10	Lloyd Mangrum	36

All American.

For many years Sam Snead's total of wins was held to be 84 but the PGA Tour amended his figure in 1990 after discrepancies had been found in their previous lists. They deducted 11 wins from his total but added eight others, which should have been included, for a revised total of 81.

The highest-placed current member of the regular Tour is Tom Watson, in joint 11th place with 32 wins. The highest-placed overseas player is Gary Player (South Africa), in joint 23rd place with 22 wins.

Sam Snead, despite being the most successful golfer on the US Tour, never won the US Open. After more than 25 attempts his best finish was 2nd on four occasions. The nearest he came to winning the title was in 1947 when he lost the play-off to Lew Worsham. Having holed a six-yard putt at the 18th to force the play-off, Snead missed a putt from three feet at the same hole to lose by one stroke. The most successful woman on the US Women's Tour is Kathy Whitworth with 88 Tour wins – and, like Snead, she never won the US Open.

THE RYDER CUP

The Ryder Cup is a biennial match between professional golfers from the United States and Europe. Its forerunner was a match between the British and US professionals at Gleneagles in 1921. Five years later a second match took place and it was this that inspired Samuel Ryder, the Manchester-born son of a seed merchant, to donate a trophy to be contested every two years between the professional golfers of these two countries. The following year the first match for the Ryder Cup was played at Worcester, Massachusetts. The Americans won with ease but on home soil two years later the British levelled the series, and after the first four competitions it was 2–2. By the time they gathered at Lindrick, Sheffield, for the 12th Ryder Cup in 1957 the Americans led the series 9–2. The Great Britain side had a memorable win at Lindrick under skipper Dai Rees but that was to be the last victory for the British. Despite continued efforts they could not overcome the wealth of talent the Americans produced. In 1979 it was agreed that the British team should receive help from European golfers and, that year, Antonio Garrido and Seve Ballesteros became the first overseas players to represent the new team, 'Europe'. Within four years the Americans were, at last, being seriously challenged and at The Belfry, Sutton Coldfield, in 1985 their domination was eventually broken when the European team, skippered by Tony Jacklin, won by five points. But their greatest triumph was to come two years later at Muirfield Village, Ohio, when the Americans lost on home soil for the first time ever. Europe retained the trophy at The Belfry in 1989 thanks to a hard-fought draw, only the second in Ryder Cup history. In 1991 the trophy returned to American hands after a closely fought contest.

The jubilant European Ryder Cup team of 1989.

THE 10 AMERICAN PLAYERS WITH THE MOST APPEARANCES IN THE RYDER CUP

	Player	Years	Appearances
1	Billy Casper	1961–75	8
2=	Sam Snead	1937–59	7
2=	Gene Littler	1961–75	7
2=	Raymond Floyd	1969–91	7
2=	Lanny Wadkins	1977–91	7
6=	Gene Sarazen	1927–37	6
6=	Arnold Palmer	1961–73	6
6=	Jack Nicklaus	1969–81	6
6=	Lee Trevino	1969–81	6
6=	Tom Kite	1979–89	6

Sam Snead was selected for the 1939 and 1941 teams and would have been No. 1 had the competition not been cancelled due to the war.

THE 10 BRITISH/EUROPEAN PLAYERS WITH THE MOST APPEARANCES IN THE RYDER CUP

	Player	Years	Appearances
1	Christy O'Connor	1955–73	10
2	Dai Rees	1937–61	9
3=	Peter Alliss	1953–69	8
3=	Bernard Hunt	1953–69	8
3=	Neil Coles	1961–77	8
3=	Bernard Gallacher	1969–83	8
3=	Nick Faldo	1977–91	8
8=	Harry Weetman	1951–63	7
8=	Tony Jacklin	1967–79	7
10=	Charles Whitcombe	1927–37	6
10=	Brian Huggett	1963–75	6
10=	Brian Barnes	1969–70	6
10=	Peter Oosterhuis	1971–81	6
10=	Severiano Ballesteros	1979–91	6
10=	Bernhard Langer	1981–91	6
10=	Sam Torrance	1981–91	6

THE 10 BRITISH/EUROPEAN PLAYERS TO PLAY THE MOST INDIVIDUAL MATCHES IN THE RYDER CUP

	Player	Appearances
1	Neil Coles	40
2	Christy O'Connor	36
3	Tony Jacklin	35
4=	Nick Faldo	31
4=	Bernard Gallacher	31
6=	Peter Alliss	30
6=	Severiano Ballesteros	30
8=	Bernard Hunt	28
8=	Peter Oosterhuis	28
10	Brian Barnes	26

THE 10 AMERICAN PLAYERS TO PLAY THE MOST INDIVIDUAL MATCHES IN THE RYDER CUP

	Player	Appearances
1	Billy Casper	37
2	Arnold Palmer	32
3=	Lee Trevino	30
3=	Lanny Wadkins	30
5	Jack Nicklaus	28
6=	Raymond Floyd	27
6=	Gene Littler	27
8	Tom Kite	24
9	Hale Irwin	20
10	Curtis Strange	17

THE 10 BRITISH/EUROPEAN PLAYERS WITH THE MOST WINS IN THE RYDER CUP

	Player	Wins
1=	Severiano Ballesteros	17
1=	Nick Faldo	17
3	Peter Oosterhuis	14
4=	Bernard Gallacher	13
4=	Tony Jacklin	13
6	Neil Coles	12
7=	Brian Barnes	11
7=	Bernhard Langer	11
7=	Christy O'Connor	11
10=	Peter Alliss	10
10=	José Maria Olazabal	10

THE 10 AMERICAN PLAYERS WITH THE MOST WINS IN THE RYDER CUP

	Player	Wins
1	Arnold Palmer	22
2	Billy Casper	20
3	Lanny Wadkins	18
4=	Jack Nicklaus	17
4=	Lee Trevino	17
6	Gene Littler	14
7=	Hale Irwin	13
7=	Tom Kite	13
9=	Sam Snead	10
9=	Tom Watson	10

THE TOP 10 WINNERS OF WOMEN'S MAJORS

	Player*	Titles
1	Patty Berg	16
2=	Louise Suggs	13
2=	Mickey Wright	13
4	Babe Zaharias	12
5	Betsy Rawls	8
6	JoAnne Carner	7
7=	Pat Bradley	6
7=	Julie Inkster	6
7=	Glenna C. Vare	6
7=	Kathy Whitworth	6

All American.

The present-day Majors are: the US Open, Mazda LPGA Championship, du Maurier Classic, and Nabisco Dinah Shore Classic. Also taken into account in this Top 10 are wins in the former Majors: the Western Open, Titleholders Championship, and the amateur championships of both Britain and the United States.

American golfer Patty Berg, winner of 16 women's Majors.

QUIZ

BRITISH GOLFING CHAMPIONS

1 Who was the last British winner of the British Open before Tony Jacklin in 1969?
2 The only man to win the British Open both before and after World War II was a Briton. Name him.
3 The last British winner of the US Open before Tony Jacklin was in 1920. Who was he?
4 Who was the last English-born winner of the US Masters?
5 Who was the first British winner of the World Match-Play Championship at Wentworth?
6 Who is the only British woman to have won the US Women's Open?
7 The last winner of the British Open before the outbreak of World War II was a Briton. Name him.
8 Who is the only Briton ever to win two Majors in one year?
9 The only time a British pair won the World Cup was in 1987 when Ian Woosnam and his partner lifted the title for Wales. Who partnered 'Woosie'...?
10 ... and which Englishman won the individual title at the World Cup in 1985?

GREYHOUND RACING

THE 10 FASTEST WINNING TIMES OF THE DERBY

	Greyhound	Year	Time (sec)
1	Endless Gossip	1952	28.50
2	Faithful Hope	1966	28.52
3	Hit the Lid	1988	28.53
4	Patricia's Hope	1972	28.55
5	Ballylanigan Tanist	1951	28.62
6	Pigalle Wonder	1958	28.65
7	Patricia's Hope	1973	28.68
8	Slippy Blue	1990	28.70
9	Ballmac Ball	1950	28.72
10	Dolores Rocket	1971	28.74

The Derby is greyhound racing's most prestigious event. It was first run at White City in 1927 and the famous London track remained the race's home until its closure in 1984. Since then the Derby has been run at Wimbledon. The distance was originally 500 yards, but from 1928 to 1974 it was extended to 525 yards. It went metric in 1975 and was run over 500 metres and in 1986 it was reduced to its present-day length of 480 metres. The most famous greyhound of them all, Mick the Miller, won the race in 1929 and 1930 and, along with Patricia's Hope (see list), is one of only two dual winners.

The famous Mick the Miller, as seen today in the Natural History Museum in London.

THE 10 LONGEST-PRICED WINNERS OF THE DERBY

	Greyhound	Year	Starting price
1=	Duleek Dandy	1960	25–1
1=	Tartan Khan	1975	25–1
3=	Hack Up Chieftain	1964	20–1
3=	Jimsun	1974	20–1
5	G. R. Archduke	1940	100–7
6	Signal Spark	1987	14–1
7	Camira Flash*	1968	100–8
8	Daw's Dancer	1953	10–1
9	Pagan Swallow	1985	9–1
10=	Faithful Hope	1966	8–1
10=	Slippy Blue	1990	8–1

Owned by HRH the Duke of Edinburgh.

THE 10 SHORTEST-PRICED WINNERS OF THE DERBY

	Greyhound	Year	Starting price
1	Entry Badge	1927	1–4
2	Mick the Miller	1930	4–9
3	Priceless Border	1948	1–2
4	Paul's Fun	1954	8–15
5	Mick the Miller	1929	4–7
6=	Pigalle Wonder	1958	4–5
6=	Parkdown Jet	1981	4–5
8	Fine Jubilee	1936	10–11
9=	Ballyhennessy Seal	1945	Evens
9=	Endless Gossip	1952	Evens
9=	Ford Spartan	1957	Evens
9=	Mile Bush Pride	1959	Evens
9=	Lucky Boy Boy	1963	Evens
9=	Balliniska Band	1977	Evens
9=	Lartigue Note	1989	Evens

GYMNASTICS

THE 10 MOST SUCCESSFUL OLYMPIC COUNTRIES

	Country	gold	Medals silver	bronze	Total
1	USSR/CIS	80	73	46	199
2	Japan	27	27	31	85
3	USA	24	20	25	69
4	Switzerland	15	19	13	47
5	Romania	15	11	14	40
6	Hungary	13	11	14	38
7=	Czechoslovakia	12	13	10	35
7=	East Germany	6	13	16	35
9	Germany/ West Germany	12	9	13	34
10	Italy	12	8	9	29

Great Britain has won just three medals: one silver and two bronzes. The last was a bronze in the women's team competition in 1928.

Larissa Latynina, the Soviet gymnast who won a total of 18 Olympic medals – nine of them gold.

THE TOP 10 INDIVIDUAL OLYMPIC GOLD MEDAL WINNERS

Latynina is the most successful Olympian of all time, with a total of 18 medals.

	Gymnast/nationality	Years	Gold medals
1	Larissa Latynina (USSR)	1956–64	9
2	Sawao Kato (Jap)	1968–76	8
3=	Viktor Chukarin (USSR)	1952–56	7
3=	Boris Shakhlin (USSR)	1956–64	7
3=	Vera Cáslavská (Cze)	1964–68	7
3=	Nikolay Andrianov (USSR)	1972–80	7
7=	Akinori Nakayama (Jap)	1968–72	6
7=	Vitaly Chtcherbo (CIS)	1992	6
9=	Agnes Kaleti (Hun)	1952–56	5
9=	Polina Astakhova (USSR)	1956–64	5
9=	Takashi Ono (Jap)	1956–64	5
9=	Mitsuo Tsukahara (Jap)	1968–76	5
9=	Nadia Comaneci (Rom)	1976–80	5

HARNESS RACING

THE TOP 10 MONEY-WINNING HORSES IN A CAREER

Harness racing is very popular in the United States, Australia and New Zealand, and is gradually spreading to other corners of the globe. It has enjoyed a following in Britain since the opening of the trotting track at Prestatyn, North Wales, in the 1960s. Harness racing horses are specially bred and they have to pull a jockey on a two wheeled 'sulky' around an oval track. Unlike thoroughbred racehorses, standardbred harness racing horses are trained to trot and pace. They do not gallop. A trotter is a horse whose diagonally opposite legs move forward together, while a pacer's legs are extended laterally and with a 'swinging motion'. Pacers usually travel faster than trotters.

TROTTERS	
Horse	Winnings ($)*
1 Ourasi	4,408,857
2 Mack Lobell	3,907,452
3 Ideal du Gazeau	2,744,777
4 Grades Singing	2,607,552
5 Peace Corps	2,590,883
6 Napoletano	2,467,878
7 JEF's Spice	2,311,271
8 Reve d'Udon	2,178,516
9 Lutin d'Isigny	2,017,554
10 Jorky	1,970,432
*To end 1990 season.	

PACERS	
Horse	Winnings ($)*
1 Nihilator	3,225,653
2 Matt's Scooter	2,944,591
3 On The Road Again	2,819,102
4 Beach Towel	2,570,357
5 Jate Lobell	2,231,402
6 Camtastic	2,117,619
7 Cam Fella	2,041,367
8 Rambling Willie	2,038,219
9 Niatross	2,019,213
10 Goalie Jeff	2,003,439
*To end 1990 season.	

Cam Fella, seventh in the Top 10 pacers, was the sire of No. 6, Camtastic, and No. 10, Goalie Jeff.

THE TOP 10 DRIVERS OF ALL TIME

MOST RACE WINS	
Driver	Wins*
1 Herve Filion	12,667
2 Carmine Abbatiello	7,020
3 Michael Lachance	5,904
4 Buddy Gilmour	5,352
5 Walter Paisley	5,335
6 Joe Marsh jr	5,204
7 John Campbell	5,136
8 Ron Waples	5,084
9 Eddie Davis	5,066
10 Billy Haughton	4,910
*To end 1990 season.	

MOST MONEY WON	
Driver	Winnings ($)*
1 John Campbell	91,481,761
2 Bill O'Donnell	71,093,662
3 Herve Filion	71,005,819
4 Michael Lachance	53,730,189
5 Carmine Abbatiello	48,575,379
6 Ron Waples	43,797,245
7 Buddy Gilmour	43,474,617
8 Billy Haughton	40,160,336
9 Ben Webster	39,742,378
10 Doug Brown	32,931,160
*To end 1990 season.	

Bill O'Donnell is second in the all-time money-winning list but is only 16th in the list of top race wins with 4,435.

HOCKEY

THE 10 BIGGEST WINS IN THE PIZZA EXPRESS NATIONAL LEAGUE, 1991–92

	Match (winners first)	Score
1	Reading v Wakefield	13–1
2	Teddington v Indian Gymkhana*	9–0
3	Firebrands v Lyons	9–2
4=	Guildford v Wakefield*	8–0
4=	Slough v Indian Gymkhana	8–0
4=	Southgate v Bourneville	8–0
7=	Canterbury v Wakefield	7–0
7=	Cheltenham v Wakefield	7–0
7=	Havant v Lyons*	7–0
10	Harborne v Warrington*	7–1

Away win.

The British National League was launched in 1979 and was known as the Poundstretcher League from 1989 until the end of the 1990–91 season. In 1991–92 it became the Pizza Express League.

HORSE RACING

THE TOP 10 JOCKEYS IN ENGLISH CLASSICS*

	Jockey	Years	1,000 Guineas	2,000 Guineas	Derby	Oaks	St Leger	Wins
1	Lester Piggott	1954–92	2	5	9	6	8	30
2	Frank Buckle	1792–1827	6	5	5	9	2	27
3	Jem Robinson	1817–48	5	9	6	2	2	24
4	Fred Archer	1874–86	2	4	5	4	6	21
5=	Bill Scott	1821–46	0	3	4	3	9	19
5=	Jack Watts	1883–97	4	2	4	4	5	19
7=	John Day	1826–41	5	4	0	5	2	16
7=	George Fordham	1859–83	7	3	1	5	0	16
7=	Willie Carson	1972–91	1	5	3	4	3	16
10	Joe Childs	1912–33	2	2	3	4	4	15

At 6 June 1992.

The first of Piggott's record 30 winners was Never Say Die in the 1954 Derby. Piggott was only 19 years of age at the time. His 30th and last to date was Rodrigo de Triano in the 1992 2,000 Guineas.

THE TOP 10 TRAINERS OF ENGLISH CLASSIC WINNERS

	Trainer	Years	1,000 Guineas	2,000 Guineas	Derby	Oaks	St Leger	Total
1	John Scott	1827–63	4	7	5	8	16	40
2	Robert Robson	1793–1827	9	6	7	12	0	34
3	Mat Dawson	1853–95	6	5	6	5	6	28
4	John Porter	1868–1900	2	5	7	3	6	23
5	Alec Taylor jr	1905–27	1	4	3	8	5	21
6=	Fred Darling	1916–47	2	5	7	2	3	19
6=	Noel Murless	1948–73	6	2	3	5	3	19
8	Dixon Boyce	1805–29	3	5	5	4	0	17
9	Vincent O'Brien	1957–84	1	4	6	2	3	16
10=	Frank Butters	1927–48	1	1	2	6	5	15
10=	Dick Hern	1962–89	1	2	3	3	6	15

THE 10 LONGEST DISTANCES OVER WHICH ENGLISH CLASSICS HAVE BEEN RUN

	Race	Years	miles	Distance furlongs	yards
1	St Leger	1776–1812	2	0	0
2	St Leger	1940	1	7	0
3	St Leger	1813–25	1	6	193
4	St Leger	1942–44	1	6	150
5	St Leger	1826–1914, 1919–38, 1946–69	1	6	132
6	St Leger	1970–92	1	6	127
7	St Leger	1915–18, 1941, 1945	1	6	0
8=	Derby	1872–1914, 1919–20	1	4	29
8=	Oaks	1872–1914, 1919–20	1	4	29
10=	Derby	1934–37	1	4	5
10=	Oaks	1934–37	1	4	5

The current distances for the five Classics are:
Derby and Oaks: 1 mile 4 furlongs
1,000 and 2,000 Guineas: 1 mile
St Leger: 1 mile 6 furlongs 127 yards

THE TOP 10 OWNERS OF ENGLISH CLASSIC WINNERS

	Owner	Years	1,000 Guineas	2,000 Guineas	Derby	Oaks	St Leger	Total
1=	4th Duke of Grafton	1813–31	8	5	1	6	0	20
1=	17th Earl of Derby	1910–45	7	2	3	2	6	20
3	HH Aga Khan III	1924–57	1	3	5	2	6	17
4	6th Viscount Falmouth	1862–83	4	3	2	4	3	16
5=	5th Earl of Jersey	1824–37	2	5	3	1	0	11
5=	1st Duke of Westminster	1880–99	1	4	4	0	2	11
5=	5th Earl of Rosebery	1883–1924	3	3	3	1	1	11
5=	6th Duke of Portland	1888–1900	2	1	2	4	2	11
5=	Jack Joel	1903–21	2	1	2	4	2	11
5=	2nd Viscount Astor	1910–45	2	3	0	5	1	11

THE 10 LONGEST-PRICED WINNERS OF ENGLISH CLASSICS

	Horse	Race	Year	Starting price
1	Theodore	St Leger	1822	200–1
2=	Otterington	St Leger	1812	100–1
2=	Jeddah	Derby	1898	100–1
2=	Signorinetta	Derby	1908	100–1
2=	Aboyeur	Derby	1913	100–1
6=	Caller Ou	St Leger	1861	1,000–15
6=	Hermit	Derby	1867	1,000–15
8=	Psidium	Derby	1961	66–1
8=	Rockavon	2,000 Guineas	1961	66–1
10=	Azor	Derby	1817	50–1
10=	Lap–Dog	Derby	1826	50–1
10=	Spaniel	Derby	1831	50–1
10=	Vespa	Oaks	1833	50–1
10=	Touchstone	St Leger	1834	50–1
10=	Little Wonder	Derby	1840	50–1
10=	Throstle	St Leger	1894	50–1
10=	Night Hawk	St Leger	1913	50–1
10=	Ferry	1,000 Guineas	1918	50–1
10=	Polemarch	St Leger	1921	50–1
10=	Airborne	Derby	1946	50–1
10=	Gilles de Retz	2,000 Guineas	1956	50–1
10=	Mon Fils	2,000 Guineas	1973	50–1
10=	Snow Knight	Derby	1974	50–1
10=	Jet Ski Lady	Oaks	1991	50–1

Switzerland's Rolf Biland, winner of more sidecar Grand Prix races than any other rider. (Sporting Pictures (UK) Ltd)

Britain's Mike Hailwood, pictured here in action in 1979, is the most successful rider ever in the Isle of Man TT. (Allsport)

Dave Thorpe, winner of three individual moto cross world titles. (Sporting Pictures (UK) Ltd)

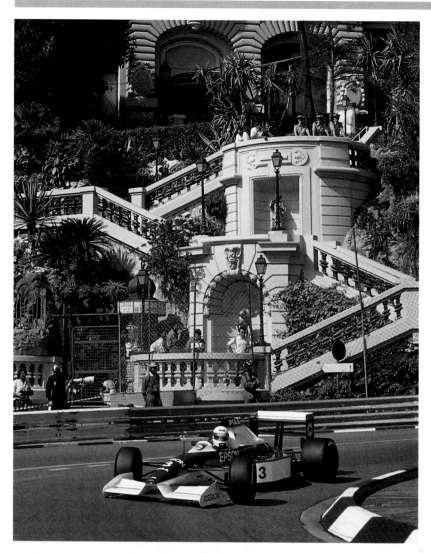

Monte Carlo, home of the Monaco Grand Prix and 2nd most frequently used Grand Prix circuit. (Bob Thomas)

Nigel Mansell is forced out of the 1986 Australian Grand Prix by an exploding tyre which not only robbed him of the race but deprived him of the world title. (Bob Thomas)

Above *The end of the 1991 British Grand Prix: a moment of sportsmanship and triumph as the victorious Mansell gives rival Ayrton Senna a lift after the Brazilian driver had run out of fuel on the last lap. (Sutton Photographic)*

Below *A Lancia has won the Monte Carlo rally more times than any other car. (Allsport)*

The 1992 Rugby League Challenge Cup final: Martin Offiah scores his second try in Wigan's 28–12 victory over Castleford. Offiah was awarded the Lance Todd Trophy after the match, the 10th time a Wigan player has received the honour. (Allsport)

Wigan's Shaun Edwards, top try-scorer of the 1991–92 season with 40. (Andrew Varley)

In the 1991–92 Five Nations Championship, England's Jonathan Webb set a new points-scoring record of 67. (Colorsport)

Above *Serge Blanco of France, the most-capped player in the world. He retired after the 1991 Rugby Union World Cup, having made a total of 93 appearances for his country.* (Colorsport)

Below *The 1984 Varsity Match: Rob Andrew of Cambridge is tackled by Oxford's Adrian Welsh. Cambridge went on to win 32–6, making it the 4th highest-scoring Match of all time.* (Colorsport)

Above *The Olympic Games remain the world's greatest sporting spectacle. Free from the boycotts which affected both the 1980 and 1984 Games, the 1988 Seoul Olympics attracted 9,101 competitors from 159 different countries. (Empics)*

Below *Austria's Annemarie Moser-Pröll, winner of a record 16 Alpine World Cup titles. (Colorsport)*

Jimmy White on his way to a maximum break of 147 in the 1992 World Professional Championship. He is only the 2nd player in the history of the tournament to achieve the feat. (Allsport)

Monica Seles, top money-winner in women's tennis in 1991. (Colorsport)

Seen here in action in the 1975 finals, Heather McKay of Australia holds more British Open squash titles than any other player, male or female. She was champion for 16 consecutive years (1962–77). (Colorsport)

Above *Steven Redgrave (left) and Andy Holmes added to Britain's Olympic rowing medal tally in 1988 by taking gold in the coxless pairs event and bronze in the coxed pairs. (Colorsport)*

Below *Sammy Duval of the USA, winner of six water skiing world titles. (Colorsport)*

THE 10 SHORTEST-PRICED WINNERS OF ENGLISH CLASSICS

The shortest-priced winner of a post-war Classic was Nijinsky, winner of the 1970 St Leger at 2–7.

	Horse	Race	Year	Starting price
1	Pretty Polly	Oaks	1904	8–100
2=	Crucifix	1,000 Guineas	1840	1–10
2=	Galtee More	St Leger	1897	1–10
4	St Frusquin	2,000 Guineas	1896	12–100
5=	Patron	2,000 Guineas	1829	1–8
5=	Achievement	1,000 Guineas	1867	1–8
7=	Ibrahim	2,000 Guineas	1835	1–7
7=	Ormonde	St Leger	1886	1–7
9=	Persimmon	St Leger	1896	2–11
9=	Gay Crusader	St Leger	1917	2–11

THE 10 LONGEST-PRICED ENGLISH CLASSIC WINNERS RIDDEN BY LESTER PIGGOTT

	Horse	Race	Year	Starting price
1	Never Say Die	Derby	1954	33–1
2	Carrozza	Oaks	1957	100–8
3	Juliette Marny	Oaks	1975	12–1
4	Empery	Derby	1976	10–1
5	St Paddy	Oaks	1960	7–1
6	Rodrigo de Triano	2,000 Gns	1992	6–1
7	Petite Etoile	Oaks	1959	11–2
8	The Minstrel	Derby	1977	5–1
9=	Aurelius	St Leger	1961	9–2
9=	Teenoso	Derby	1983	9–2

Piggott has ridden a record 30 Classic winners, the first being Never Say Die which remains his longest-priced winner at 33–1. He has ridden five winners at odds-on prices. His longest-priced winner of the 1,000 Guineas was Humble Duty (1971) at 3–1.

Lester Piggott is led in after his victory in the 1954 Derby on Never Say Die, his longest-priced English Classic winner at odds of 33–1.

THE TOP 10 JOCKEYS IN THE ST LEGER

	Jockey	Years	Wins
1	Bill Scott	1821–46	9
2=	John Jackson	1791–1822	8
2=	Lester Piggott	1960–84	8
4=	Ben Smith	1803–24	6
4=	Fred Archer	1877–86	6
6=	John Mangle	1780–92	5
6=	Tom Challoner	1861–75	5
6=	Jack Watts	1883–96	5
6=	Gordon Richards	1930–44	5
10=	Bob Johnson	1812–20	4
10=	Joe Childs	1918–26	4
10=	Charlie Smirke	1934–54	4
10=	Joe Mercer	1965–81	4

THE TOP 10 JOCKEYS IN THE OAKS

	Jockey	Years	Wins
1	Frank Buckle	1797–1823	9
2=	Frank Butler	1843–52	6
2=	Lester Piggott	1957–84	6
4=	Sam Chifney jr	1807–25	5
4=	John Day	1828–40	5
4=	George Fordham	1859–81	5
7=	Sam Chifney sr	1782–90	4
7=	Dennis Fitzpatrick	1787–1800	4
7=	Tom Cannon	1869–84	4
7=	Fred Archer	1875–85	4
7=	Jack Watts	1883–93	4
7=	Joe Childs	1912–21	4
7=	Harry Wragg	1938–46	4
7=	Willie Carson	1978–90	4

THE TOP 10 JOCKEYS IN THE 1,000 GUINEAS

	Jockey	Years	Wins
1	George Fordham	1859–83	7
2	Frank Buckle	1818–27	6
3=	Jem Robinson	1824–44	5
3=	John Day	1826–40	5
5=	Jack Watts	1886–97	4
5=	Fred Rickaby jr	1913–17	4
5=	Charlie Elliott	1924–44	4
8=	Bill Arnull	1817–32	3
8=	Nat Flatman	1835–57	3
8=	Tom Cannon	1866–84	3
8=	Charlie Wood	1880–87	3
8=	Dick Perryman	1926–41	3
8=	Harry Wragg	1934–45	3
8=	Rae Johnstone	1935–50	3
8=	Gordon Richards	1942–51	3

THE TOP 10 JOCKEYS IN THE EPSOM DERBY

	Jockey	Years	Wins
1	Lester Piggott	1954–83	9
2=	Jem Robinson	1817–36	6
2=	Steve Donoghue	1915–25	6
4=	John Arnull	1784–99	5
4=	Frank Buckle	1792–1823	5
4=	Bill Clift	1793–1819	5
4=	Fred Archer	1877–86	5
8=	Sam Arnull	1780–98	4
8=	Tom Goodison	1809–22	4
8=	Bill Scott	1832–43	4
8=	Jack Watts	1887–96	4
8=	Charlie Smirke	1934–58	4

Lester Piggott has been so dominant in the post-war era that his total of nine Derby winners is *six* more than the next highest post-war winning jockeys, Rae Johnstone, Willie Carson and Pat Eddery, who have each ridden three winners.

THE TOP 10 JOCKEYS IN THE 2,000 GUINEAS

	Jockey	Years	Wins
1	Jem Robinson	1825–48	9
2	John Osborne	1857–88	6
3=	Frank Buckle	1810–27	5
3=	Charlie Elliott	1923–49	5
3=	Lester Piggott	1957–92	5
3=	Willie Carson	1972–91	5
7=	John Day	1826–41	4
7=	Fred Archer	1874–85	4
7=	Tom Cannon	1878–89	4
7=	Herbert Jones	1900–09	4

THE TOP 10 TRAINERS OF EPSOM DERBY WINNERS

	Trainer	Years	Winners
1=	Robert Robson	1793–1823	7
1=	John Porter	1868–99	7
1=	Fred Darling	1922–41	7
4=	Frank Neale	1782–1804	6
4=	Mat Dawson	1860–95	6
4=	Vincent O'Brien	1962–82	6
7=	Richard Prince	1795–1819	5
7=	Dixon Boyce	1805–28	5
7=	James Edwards	1811–36	5
7=	John Scott	1835–53	5

THE TOP 10 OWNERS OF EPSOM DERBY WINNERS

	Owner	Years	Winners
1=	3rd Earl of Egremont	1782–1826	5
1=	HH Aga Khan III	1930–52	5
3=	John Bowes	1835–53	4
3=	Sir Joseph Hawley	1851–68	4
3=	1st Duke of Westminster	1880–99	4
3=	Sir Victor Sassoon	1953–60	4
7=	Sir Charles Bunbury	1780–1813	3
7=	5th Duke of Bedford	1789–97	3
7=	1st Earl of Grosvenor	1790–94	3
7=	Sir Frank Standish	1795–99	3
7=	3rd Duke of Grafton	1802–10	3
7=	5th Earl of Jersey	1825–36	3
7=	5th Earl of Rosebery	1894–1905	3
7=	HM King Edward VII*	1896–1909	3
7=	17th Earl of Derby	1924–42	3
7=	HH Aga Khan IV	1981–88	3

*First two winners as the Prince of Wales.

THE 10 FASTEST WINNING TIMES OF THE EPSOM DERBY

	Horse	Year	Time min	sec
1	Mahmoud	1936	2	33.80
2	Kahyasi	1988	2	33.84
3	Reference Point	1987	2	33.90
4=	Hyperion	1933	2	34.00
4=	Windsor Lad	1934	2	34.00
4=	Generous	1991	2	34.00
7	Golden Fleece	1982	2	34.27
8=	Call Boy	1927	2	34.40
8=	Felsted	1928	2	34.40
10	Captain Cuttle	1922	2	34.60

Electronic timing was first used in 1964.

Only races at Epsom are considered. Dante won the 1945 substitute race at Newmarket in 2 minutes 26.6 seconds.

The Derby is named after the 12th Earl of Derby, who owned the winner of the eighth race in 1787. But the race could well have been named after Sir Charles Bunbury, owner of three Derby winners. The two men were good friends and when the establishment of such a race was first discussed, they tossed a coin to decide which of them it should be named after. If Sir Charles had won the toss, we would have had the Epsom Bunbury each year – not to mention the Kentucky Bunbury, Soap Box Bunbury . . . and so on.

THE TOP 10 WINNING MARGINS IN THE EPSOM DERBY

	Horse	Year	Winning margin (lengths)
1	Shergar	1981	10
2	Manna	1925	8
3=	Troy	1979	7
3=	Slip Anchor	1985	7
5=	Sansovino	1924	6
5=	Arctic Prince	1951	6
5=	Relko	1963	6
8=	Kisber	1876	5
8=	Coronach	1926	5
8=	Hard Ridden	1958	5
8=	Nashwan	1989	5
8=	Generous	1991	5

The horse that trailed in 10 lengths behind Shergar in 1981 was Glint of Gold who, in 1982, surpassed Troy's record for most money won in a career by a British Isles-trained horse.

THE 10 LONGEST-PRICED EPSOM DERBY WINNERS

	Horse	Year	Starting price
1=	Jeddah	1898	100–1
1=	Signorinetta	1908	100–1
1=	Aboyeur	1913	100–1
4	Hermit	1867	1,000–15
5	Psidium	1961	66–1
6=	Azor	1817	50–1
6=	Lap-Dog	1826	50–1
6=	Spaniel	1831	50–1
6=	Little Wonder	1840	50–1
6=	Airborne	1946	50–1
6=	Snow Knight	1974	50–1

Terimon finished second to Nashwan in 1989 at odds of 500–1 – the longest-ever odds for a horse finishing in the first three. The only other horse to finish 'in the frame' at odds of more than 100–1 is Black Tommy, second in 1857, at odds of 200–1.

THE 10 SHORTEST-PRICED EPSOM DERBY WINNERS

	Horse	Year	Starting price
1	Ladas	1894	2–9
2	Galtee More	1897	1–4
3	Cicero	1905	4–11
4	Flying Fox	1899	2–5
5=	Ormonde	1886	4–9
5=	Isinglass	1893	4–9
7	Skyscraper	1789	4–7
8	Gainsborough	1918	8–13
9=	John Bull	1792	4–6
9=	Rock Sand	1903	4–6

The shortest-priced winner since the war was Sir Ivor at 4–5 in 1968. The only other post-war odds-on winner was Shergar (1981) at 10–11.

THE 10 DERBY WINNERS WITH THE LONGEST NAMES

	Horse	Year	No. of letters
1	The Flying Dutchman	1849	17
2	Cardinal Beaufort	1805	16
3=	Plenipotentiary	1834	15
3=	The Merry Monarch	1845	15
3=	Pyrrhus the First	1846	15
3=	George Frederick	1874	15
7=	Sir Peter Teazle	1787	14
7=	West Australian	1853	14
7=	Diamond Jubilee	1900	14
7=	Shirley Heights	1978	14
7=	Reference Point	1987	14

THE FIRST 10 IRISH-TRAINED EPSOM DERBY WINNERS

	Horse	Trainer	Year
1	Orby	Fred MacCabe	1907
2	Had Ridden	Mick Rogers	1958
3	Larkspur	Vincent O'Brien	1962
4	Santa Claus	Mick Rogers	1964
5	Sir Ivor	Vincent O'Brien	1968
6	Nijinsky	Vincent O'Brien	1970
7	Roberto	Vincent O'Brien	1972
8	The Minstrel	Vincent O'Brien	1977
9	Golden Fleece	Vincent O'Brien	1982
10	Secreto	David O'Brien	1984

WILLIE CARSON'S FIRST 10 RIDES IN THE EPSOM DERBY

	Horse	Starting price	Position	Year
1	Meaden	200–1	19th	1971
2	Meadow Mint	20–1	10th	1972
3	Ksar	5–1	4th	1973
4	Court Dancer	25–1	9th	1974
5	Royal Manacle	14–1	7th	1975
6	Tierra Fuego	25–1	11th	1976
7	Hot Grove	15–1	2nd	1977
8	Admirals Launch	10–1	12th	1978
9	Troy	6–1	1st	1979
10	Henbit	7–1	1st	1980

Carson has since ridden one other winner of the race, Nashwan, in 1989.

Left *Shergar, ridden by Walter Swinburn, wins the 1981 Derby with a record margin of 10 lengths over Glint of Gold.*

SIR GORDON RICHARDS' 10 BEST SEASONS

	Year	Winners*
1	1947	269(1)
2	1949	261(0)
3	1933	259(0)
4	1952	231(0)
5	1951	227(1)
6	1948	224(1)
7	1935	217(0)
8	1937	216(1)
9=	1934	212(0)
9=	1946	212(0)

Figures in brackets indicate number of Classic winners that year.

FRED ARCHER'S 10 BEST SEASONS

	Year	Winners*
1	1885	246(4)
2	1884	241(0)
3	1883	232(1)
4	1878	229(2)
5	1881	220(2)
6	1877	218(2)
7	1882	210(1)
8	1876	207(0)
9	1879	197(3)
10	1875	172(2)

Figures in brackets indicate number of Classic winners that year.

With such totals it is not surprising that Richards was champion jockey in each of those seasons. What is perhaps surprising, however, is that he only twice rode more than one Classic winner in a season: in 1930 when he rode two, and in 1942 when he rode four out of five Classic winners. The only one to elude him was the Derby which he did not win until 1953 – his first and only time. Richards rode his first winner, Gay Lord, at Leicester in 1921. His most remarkable riding feat was between 3 and 5 October 1933 when he rode the winner of the last race at Nottingham on the Tuesday, rode all six winners at Chepstow the next day and on the Thursday rode the first five winners, again at Chepstow – an amazing sequence of 12 consecutive winners.

Archer was champion jockey every year from 1874, when he was only 17, to 1886, the year he committed suicide. He was two months short of his 30th birthday at the time of his death. In his all-too-brief racing career he rode 2,748 winners which, to this day, places him 7th on the all-time list of most successful British jockeys. He rode his first winner at the age of 13 when he partnered Athol Daisy to victory at Chesterfield on 28 September 1870, his first race in public other than in pony races. At 15 he rode the winner of the Cesarewitch.

THE 10 FLAT RACE JOCKEYS WITH THE MOST WINS IN A CAREER IN BRITAIN*

	Jockey	Years	Wins
1	Gordon Richards	1921–54	4,870
2	Lester Piggott	1948–92	4,408
3	Willie Carson	1962–92	3,339
4	Pat Eddery	1969–92	3,116
5	Doug Smith	1931–67	3,111
6	Joe Mercer	1950–85	2,810
7	Fred Archer	1870–86	2,748
8	Edward Hide	1951–91	2,591
9	George Fordham	1850–84	2,587
10	Eph Smith	1930–65	2,313

At 28 May 1992.

THE TOP 10 JOCKEYS IN A FLAT RACING SEASON

	Jockey	Year	Wins
1	Gordon Richards	1947	269
2	Gordon Richards	1949	261
3	Gordon Richards	1933	259
4	Fred Archer	1885	246
5	Fred Archer	1884	241
6	Fred Archer	1883	232
7	Gordon Richards	1952	231
8	Fred Archer	1878	229
9	Gordon Richards	1951	227
10	Gordon Richards	1948	224

Richards rode 200 winners in a season 12 times while Archer did so on eight occasions. The only other men to reach double centuries are Tommy Loates (1893) and Pat Eddery (1990).

RICHARDS V ARCHER

Gordon Richards was the most successful British jockey of all time. He rode a total of 4,870 winners in Britain between 1920 and 1954, including 14 Classic winners, and was champion jockey a record 26 times. While Fred Archer's record appears to be inferior to that of Richards it must be remembered that his career spanned only 16 years, during which time he rode 2,748 winners from only 8,084 mounts for a ratio of one winner every three rides. He won 21 Classics, and was champion jockey for the 13 successive years prior to his untimely death at his own hands when, in a state of depression after his wife died in childbirth, he shot himself at the age of 29.

Fred Archer, whose tragic suicide cut short a marvellous career, and Gordon Richards riding his 100th winner of the 1945 season.

THE TOP 10 WINS BY CHAMPION NATIONAL HUNT JOCKEYS IN A SEASON*

	Jockey	Season	Wins
1	Peter Scudamore	1988–89	221
2	Peter Scudamore	1991–92	175
3	Peter Scudamore	1989–90	170
4	Jonjo O'Neill	1977–78	149
5	Peter Scudamore	1990–91	141
6	Peter Scudamore	1987–88	132
7	John Francome	1983–84	131
8	Ron Barry	1972–73	125
9	Peter Scudamore	1986–87	123
10	Josh Gifford	1966–67	122

*To end 1991–92 season.

THE 10 NATIONAL HUNT JOCKEYS WITH THE MOST WINS IN A CAREER*

	Jockey	Years	Wins
1	Peter Scudamore	1978–92	1,549
2	John Francome	1970–85	1,138
3	Stan Mellor	1954–72	1,035
4	Fred Winter	1947–64	923
5	Bob Davies	1966–82	911
6	Terry Biddlecombe	1958–74	908
7	Jonjo O'Neill	1972–86	885
8	Ron Barry	1964–83	823
9	Tim Molony	1946–58	726
10	Jeff King	1960–81	710

*To end 1991–92 season.

The only other time Scudamore won the title was in 1982 when he shared it with John Francome. The two men each rode 120 winners.

THE 10 LONGEST-PRICED WINNERS OF THE CHELTENHAM GOLD CUP

	Horse	Year	Starting price
1	Norton's Coin	1990	100–1
2=	Gay Donald	1955	33–1
2=	L'Escargot	1970	33–1
4	Cool Ground	1992	25–1
5	Four Ten	1954	100–6
6	Garrison Savannah	1991	16–1
7=	Royal Frolic	1976	14–1
7=	Davy Lad	1977	14–1
7=	Master Smudge	1980	14–1
10	Woodland Venture	1967	100–8

Although the Grand National is the world's most famous steeplechase, the Gold Cup is the most prestigious National Hunt race and attracts a quality field to Cheltenham every spring for the 3¼-mile race over 22 fences. The first Cheltenham Gold Cup was run in 1927 and its most famous winners were Golden Miller, five times winner in the 1930s, and Arkle, who won the race three times between 1964 and 1966. When he won in 1966 it was at odds of 1–10, the shortest-priced winner.

The year after L'Escargot won at 33–1 he won again, but this time at the much reduced odds of 7–2.

Arkle, ridden by Pat Taaffe, on his way to a third successive victory in the Cheltenham Gold Cup in 1966.

THE 10 HEAVIEST WEIGHTS CARRIED BY GRAND NATIONAL WINNERS THIS CENTURY

	Horse	Year	Weight st	lb
1=	Jerry M	1912	12	7
1=	Poethlyn	1919	12	7
3	Sprig	1927	12	4
4=	Golden Miller	1934	12	2
4=	Reynoldstown	1936	12	2
6	Red Rum	1974	12	0
7	Royal Mail	1937	11	13
8	Freebooter	1950	11	11
9	Vermouth	1916	11	10
10=	Troytown	1920	11	9
10=	Kellsboro' Jack	1933	11	9

The two horses that share 1st place were both ridden to victory by Ernie Piggott, Lester's grandfather.

THE TOP 10 JOCKEYS IN THE GRAND NATIONAL

	Jockey*	Years	Wins
1	George Stevens	1856–70	5
2	Tom Olliver	1838–53	4
3=	Mr Tommy Pickernell	1860–75	3
3=	Mr Tommy Beasley	1880–89	3
3=	Arthur Nightingall	1890–1901	3
3=	Mr Jack Anthony	1911–20	3
3=	Ernie Piggott	1912–19	3
3=	Brian Fletcher	1968–74	3
9=	Mr Alec Goodman	1852–66	2
9=	John Page	1867–72	2
9=	Mr Maunsell Richardson	1873–74	2
9=	Mr Ted Wilson	1884–85	2
9=	Percy Woodland	1903–13	2
9=	Arthur Thompson	1948–52	2
9=	Bryan Marshall	1953–54	2
9=	Fred Winter	1957–62	2

Amateur riders are traditionally indicated by the prefix 'Mr'.

Ernie Piggott, Lester Piggott's grandfather, is the only man to ride Grand National winners at two different courses. He rode Poethlyn to victory in the substitute race at Gatwick in 1918 and again at Aintree the following year.

THE 10 FASTEST WINNING TIMES OF THE GRAND NATIONAL

	Horse	Year	Time min	sec
1	Mr Frisk	1990	8	47.80
2	Red Rum	1973	9	01.90
3	Party Politics	1992	9	06.30
4	Grittar	1982	9	12.06
5	Maori Venture	1987	9	19.30
6	Reynoldstown	1935	9	20.00
7	Red Rum	1974	9	20.30
8	Golden Miller	1934	9	20.40
9	Bogskar	1940	9	20.60
10	Rag Trade	1976	9	20.90

The times of the substitute races at Gatwick (1916–18) are not included because the course bore little resemblance to Aintree.

THE 10 OLDEST GRAND NATIONAL WINNING HORSES

	Horse	Year	Age
1	Peter Simple	1853	15
2=	Why Not	1894	13
2=	Sergeant Murphy	1923	13
4=	Chandler	1848	12
4=	Kilmore	1962	12
4=	Team Spirit	1964	12
4=	Highland Wedding	1969	12
4=	L'Escargot	1975	12
4=	Red Rum	1977	12
4=	Ben Nevis	1980	12
4=	Little Polveir	1989	12

Alcibiade (1865), Regal (1876), Austerlitz (1877), Empress (1880) and Lutteur (1909) all won as five-year-olds and are the youngest-ever winners of the National.

THE 10 LARGEST GRAND NATIONAL FIELDS

	Year	No. of runners
1	1929	66
2	1947	57
3	1950	49
4=	1952	47
4=	1963	47
4=	1965	47
4=	1966	47
8	1968	45
9	1967	44
10=	1931	43
10=	1948	43
10=	1949	43

QUIZ

THE GRAND NATIONAL

1 Which horse gave Jenny Pitman Grand National success in 1983?
2 Brian Fletcher rode Red Rum to two of his three victories at Aintree. Who was aboard him on the other occasion?
3 What is the youngest age a horse must be before it can compete in the National?
4 The first Grand National at Aintree was in 1839. The three races prior to that, and the forerunner of the race, were held in which Liverpool suburb?
5 Which famous trainer was in the saddle when Reynoldstown won the National for the second time in 1936?
6 At the time of training Red Rum to his Grand National victories, what other occupation did Donald 'Ginger' McCain pursue?
7 Which was the first grey this century to win the race?
8 The Grand National had to wait 140 years for its first Scottish-trained winner. Which horse eventually gave them something to cheer north of the border?
9 Who sponsored the 1991 Grand National which was won by Seagram?
10 Red Rum is one of two horses to finish in the first three a record five times. Name the other.

THE 10 MOST NORTHERLY RACETRACKS IN BRITAIN

1	Perth
2	Hamilton Park
3	Edinburgh
4	Kelso
5	Ayr
6	Newcastle
7	Hexham
8	Carlisle
9	Sedgefield
10	Cartmel

THE TOP 10 JOCKEYS IN US TRIPLE CROWN RACES

The US Triple Crown consists of the Kentucky Derby, Preakness Stakes and Belmont Stakes. Since 1875 only 11 horses have won all three races in one season. The only jockey to complete the Triple Crown twice is Eddie Arcaro on Whirlaway in 1941 and on Citation in 1948. The most successful jockeys have been:

	Jockey	Kentucky Derby	Preakness Stakes	Belmont Stakes	Total
1	Eddie Arcaro	5	6	6	17
2	Bill Shoemaker	4	2	5	11
3=	Bill Hartack	5	3	1	9
3=	Earle Sande	3	1	5	9
5	Jimmy McLaughlin	1	1	6	8
6=	Angel Cordero jr	3	2	1	6
6=	Chas Kurtsinger	2	2	2	6
6=	Ron Turcotte	2	2	2	6
9=	Lloyd Hughes	0	3	2	5
9=	Johnny Loftus	2	2	1	5
9=	Willie Simms	2	1	2	5

THE TOP 10 JOCKEYS IN THE BREEDERS CUP

	Jockey*	Years	Wins
1=	Pat Day	1984–91	6
1=	Laffit Pincay jr	1985–90	6
3	José Santos	1987–90	5
4=	Angel Cordero	1985–89	4
4=	Pat Valenzuela	1986–91	4
6=	Craig Perrett	1984–90	3
6=	Eddie Delahoussaye	1984–91	3
6=	Chris McCarron	1985–89	3
6=	Randy Romero	1987–89	3
10=	Walter Guerra	1984–85	2
10=	Yves St Martin (Fra)	1984–86	2
10=	Jorge Velasquez	1985	2
10=	Pat Eddery (GB)	1985–91	2
10=	Freddy Head (Fra)	1987–88	2

* American unless otherwise stated.

The Breeders Cup is an end-of-season gathering with seven races on one day at a different venue each year. The season's best thoroughbreds gather to find the winners in each category. Held every October or November, there is $10 million prizemoney on offer with $3 million going to the winner of the day's senior race, the Classic. Pat Eddery (Pebbles, 1985 Turf and Sheikh Albadou, 1991 Sprint) and Lester Piggott (Royal Academy, 1990 Mile) are the only British winners of the main Breeders Cup races.

THE 10 FASTEST WINNING TIMES OF THE PRIX DE L'ARC DE TRIOMPHE

	Horse	Year	Time min	sec
1	Trempolino	1987	2	26.30
2	Tony Bin	1988	2	27.35
3	Dancing Brave	1986	2	27.70
4	Detroit	1980	2	28.00
5	All Along	1983	2	28.10
6=	Mill Reef	1971	2	28.30
6=	San San	1972	2	28.30
8	Three Troikas	1979	2	28.90
9	Levmoss	1969	2	29.00
10	Rainbow Quest	1985	2	29.50

The 1943 and 1944 races are not included because they were run at Le Tremblay over a reduced distance of 2,300 metres – 100 metres shorter than the 2,400 metres distance over which the race is usually run at Longchamp each October.

THE 10 FASTEST WINNING TIMES OF THE MELBOURNE CUP*

	Horse	Year	Time min	sec
1	Kingston Rule‡	1990	3	16.3
2	Tawrrific†	1989	3	17.1
3	Gold and Black	1977	3	18.4
4=	Black Knight	1984	3	18.9
4=	Kiwi†	1983	3	18.9
4=	Empire Rose†	1988	3	18.9
4=	Let's Elope†	1991	3	18.9
8	Piping Lane	1972	3	19.3
9	Gala Supreme	1973	3	19.5
10	Beldale Ball‡	1980	3	19.8

*Since 1972, when the distance was reduced from its original 2 miles (3,219 metres) to 3,200 metres.
Horses Australian, except:
†New Zealand.
‡United States.

THE 10 FASTEST WINNING TIMES OF THE KENTUCKY DERBY

	Horse	Year	Time min	sec
1	Secretariat*	1973	1	59.4
2	Northern Dancer	1964	2	00.0
3	Decidedly	1962	2	00.4
4	Proud Clarion	1967	2	00.6
5=	Lucky Debonair	1965	2	01.2
5=	Affirmed*	1978	2	01.2
7	Whirlaway*	1941	2	01.4
8=	Middleground	1950	2	01.6
8=	Hill Gail	1952	2	01.6
8=	Bold Forbes	1976	2	01.6

*Triple Crown winner.

America's best-known race, the Kentucky Derby, is run over 1¼ miles of the Churchill Downs track in Louisville, Kentucky, on the first Saturday each May. It was inaugurated in 1875 and between then and 1895 the race was run over 1½ miles. Eddie Arcaro and Bill Hartack, each with five wins, have been the most successful jockeys, and the top trainer, with six wins, is Ben A. Jones.

The slowest time for the current 1¼-mile distance was in 1908 when Stone Street won in 2 minutes 15.2 seconds.

Northern Dancer comes home ahead of Hill Rise in the 1964 Kentucky Derby in a time of two minutes dead.

HURLING

THE 10 COUNTIES WITH THE MOST WINS IN THE ALL-IRELAND FINAL

	County	Wins
1	Cork	27
2	Tipperary	24
3	Kilkenny	23
4	Limerick	7
5	Dublin	6
6	Wexford	5
7	Galway	4
8=	Offaly	2
8=	Waterford	2
10=	Clare	1
10=	Kerry	1
10=	Laois	1
10=	London Irish	1

Played on the first Sunday in September, the All-Ireland final, like its Gaelic football counterpart, is an inter-county event. First held in 1887, the final is also at Croke Park and the winning team collects the McCarthy Cup. Hurling is one of the world's fastest sports.

Fast and furious: Tipperary beat Kilkenny (vertical stripes) 16–15 in the All-Ireland hurling final of 1991.

ICE HOCKEY

THE 10 TEAMS WITH THE MOST STANLEY CUP WINS

	Team	Wins
1	Montreal Canadiens	23
2	Toronto Maple Leafs	11
3	Detroit Red Wings	7
4	Ottawa Senators	6
5=	Boston Bruins	5
5=	Edmonton Oilers	5
7=	Montreal Victorias	4
7=	Montreal Wanderers	4
7=	New York Islanders	4
10=	Chicago Black Hawks	3
10=	Montreal AAA	3
10=	New York Rangers	3
10=	Ottawa Silver Seven	3

D uring his time as Governor General of Canada from 1888 to 1893, Sir Frederick Arthur Stanley (Lord Stanley of Preston and 16th Earl of Derby) became interested in ice hockey – or just plain hockey as it is called in North America – and in 1893 presented a trophy to be contested by the best amateur teams in Canada. The first trophy went to the Montreal Amateur Athletic Association who won it without a challenge from any other team. In 1914 the Cup was contested by the champions of the National Hockey Association (formed 1910) and the Pacific Coast Hockey Association (formed 1912). Effectively it was a match between the champions of the East Coast and the West Coast. The NHA became the National Hockey League (NHL) in 1917 and their champions continued to play off against the PCHA champions. But in 1923 and 1924 it became a three-way challenge as a result of the formation of the Western Canadian Hockey League. The PCHA disbanded in 1926 and since then the NHL play-offs have decided the Stanley Cup finalists each spring.

THE TOP 10 POINTS-SCORERS IN STANLEY CUP PLAY-OFF MATCHES

	Player	Total points
1	Wayne Gretzky	299
2	Mark Messier	219
3	Jari Kurri	202
4	Glenn Anderson	183
5	Bryan Trottier	177
6	Jean Beliveau	176
7	Denis Potvin	164
8=	Mike Bossy	160
8=	Gordie Howe	160
10	Bobby Smith	155

THE TOP 10 GOALSCORERS IN AN NHL SEASON

	Player/team	Season	Goals
1	Wayne Gretzky (Edmonton Oilers)	1981–82	92
2	Wayne Gretzky (Edmonton Oilers)	1983–84	87
3	Brett Hull (St Louis Blues)	1990–91	86
4	Mario Lemieux (Pittsburgh Penguins)	1988–89	85
5	Phil Esposito (Boston Bruins)	1970–71	76
6	Wayne Gretzky (Edmonton Oilers)	1984–85	73
7	Brett Hull (St Louis Blues)	1989–90	72
8=	Wayne Gretzky (Edmonton Oilers)	1982–83	71
8=	Jari Kurri (Edmonton Oilers)	1984–85	71
10=	Mario Lemieux (Pittsburgh Penguins)	1987–88	70
10=	Bernie Nicholls (Los Angeles Kings)	1988–89	70
10=	Brett Hull (St Louis Blues)	1991–92	70

THE 10 BEST-PAID PLAYERS IN THE NATIONAL HOCKEY LEAGUE (NHL), 1991–92

	Player	Team	Salary ($)
1	Wayne Gretzky	Los Angeles Kings	3,000,000
2	Mario Lemieux	Pittsburgh Penguins	2,338,000
3	Brett Hull	St Louis Blues	1,500,000
4=	Pat Lafontaine	Buffalo Sabres	1,400,000
4=	Kevin Stevens	Pittsburgh Penguins	1,400,000
4=	Steve Yzerman	Detroit Red Wings	1,400,000
7	Luc Robitaille	Los Angeles Kings	1,300,000
8=	Ray Bourque	Boston Bruins	1,200,000
8=	John Cullen	Hartford Whalers	1,200,000
10	Scott Stevens	New Jersey Devils	1,155,000

Salaries take into account base salary and deferred payments. Signing bonuses are not included.

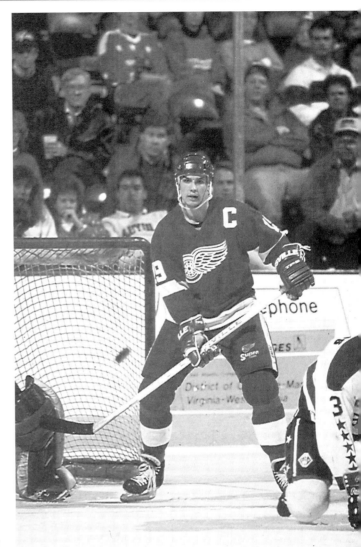

Steve Yzerman of the Detroit Red Wings, one of the best-paid players in the NHL.

THE TOP 10 ASSISTS IN AN NHL CAREER*

	Player	Seasons	Assists†
1	Wayne Gretzky	13	1,514
2	Gordie Howe	26	1,049
3	Marcel Dionne	18	1,040
4	Stan Mikita	22	926
5	Bryan Trottier	17	890
6	Phil Esposito	18	873
7	Bobby Clarke	15	852
8	Alex Delvecchio	24	825
9	Gilbert Perreault	17	814
10	John Bucyk	23	813

Regular season only.
†An assist is when a player is officially credited with assisting in the scoring of a goal by another player.

THE TOP 10 POINTS-SCORERS IN AN NHL CAREER*

	Player	Seasons	Goals	Assists	Total points
1	Wayne Gretzky	13	749	1,514	2,263
2	Gordie Howe	26	801	1,049	1,850
3	Marcel Dionne	18	731	1,040	1,771
4	Phil Esposito	18	717	873	1,590
5	Stan Mikita	22	541	926	1,467
6	Bryan Trottier	17	520	890	1,410
7	John Bucyk	23	556	813	1,369
8	Guy Lafleur	17	560	793	1,353
9	Gilbert Perreault	17	512	814	1,326
10	Alex Delvecchio	24	456	825	1,281

Regular season only.

THE TOP 10 GOALSCORERS IN AN NHL CAREER*

	Player	Seasons	Goals
1	Gordie Howe	26	801
2	Wayne Gretzky	13	749
3	Marcel Dionne	18	731
4	Phil Esposito	18	717
5	Bobby Hull	16	610
6	Mike Bossy	10	573
7	Guy Lafleur	16	560
8	John Bucyk	23	556
9	Maurice Richard	18	544
10	Stan Mikita	22	541

*Regular season only.

THE 10 NHL GAMES TO PRODUCE THE MOST GOALS

	Teams	Score	Date	Total goals
1=	Montreal Canadiens v Toronto St Patricks	14–7	10 Jan 1920	21
1=	Edmonton Oilers v Chicago Black Hawks	12–9	11 Dec 1985	21
3=	Edmonton Oilers v Minnesota North Stars	12–8	4 Jan 1984	20
3=	Toronto Maple Leafs v Edmonton Oilers	11–9	8 Jan 1986	20
5=	Montreal Wanderers v Toronto Arenas	10–9	19 Dec 1917	19
5=	Montreal Canadiens v Quebec Bulldogs	16–3	3 Mar 1920	19
5=	Montreal Canadiens v Hamilton Tigers	13–6	26 Feb 1921	19
5=	Boston Bruins v New York Rangers	10–9	4 Mar 1944	19
5=	Boston Bruins v Detroit Red Wings	10–9	16 Mar 1944	19
5=	Vancouver Canucks v Minnesota North Stars	10–9	7 Oct 1983	19

THE TOP 10 GOALTENDERS IN AN NHL CAREER*

	Goaltender	Seasons	Games won
1	Terry Sawchuk	21	435
2	Jacques Plante	18	434
3	Tony Esposito	16	423
4	Glenn Hall	18	407
5	Rogie Vachon	16	355
6	Gump Worsley	21	335
7	Harry Lumley	16	332
8	Turk Broda	12	302
9	Billy Smith	18	301
10	Mike Liut	13	293

*Regular season only.

THE 10 BIGGEST NHL ARENAS

	Stadium	Home team	Capacity
1	Olympic Saddledrome, Calgary	Calgary Flames	20,130
2	Joe Louis Sports Arena, Detroit	Detroit Red Wings	19,275
3	Byrne Meadowlands Arena, East Rutherford	New Jersey Devils	19,040
4	Capital Centre, Landover	Washington Capitals	18,130
5	Madison Square Garden, New York	New York Rangers	17,520
6	The Spectrum, Philadelphia	Philadelphia Flyers	17,425
7	Chicago Stadium	Chicago Black Hawks	17,317
8	Northlands Coliseum, Edmonton	Edmonton Oilers	17,313
9	St Louis Arena	St Louis Blues	17,188
10	Maple Leaf Gardens, Toronto	Toronto Maple Leafs	16,864

The smallest arena is Boston Garden, home of the Boston Bruins, which has a capacity of 14,637.

THE TOP 10 WINNERS OF THE HART TROPHY

	Player	Years	Wins
1	Wayne Gretzky	1980–89	9
2	Gordie Howe	1952–63	6
3	Eddie Shore	1933–38	4
4=	Howie Morenz	1928–32	3
4=	Bobby Orr	1970–72	3
4=	Bobby Clarke	1973–76	3
7=	Nels Stewart	1926–30	2
7=	Bill Cowley	1941–43	2
7=	Jean Beliveau	1956–64	2
7=	Bobby Hull	1965–66	2
7=	Stan Mikita	1967–68	2
7=	Phil Esposito	1969–74	2
7=	Guy Lafleur	1977–78	2
7=	Mark Messier	1990–92	2

The Hart Trophy has been awarded annually since 1924 and is presented to the player 'adjudged to be the most valuable to his team during the season'. The winner is selected by the Professional Hockey Writers' Association and the trophy is named after Cecil Hart, the former manager/coach of the Montreal Canadiens. The first winner of the trophy was Frank Nighbor of Ottawa, and the first man to win it three years in succession was Bobby Orr.

QUIZ

WINTER SPORTS

1 Which winter sport is a mixture of cross-country skiing and shooting?
2 Does ski jumping form part of the Alpine or Nordic skiing competition?
3 What well-known long-distance race has been won by Libby Riddles and Susan Butcher, among others?
4 What sport is governed by the FITB?
5 In which winter sport is the object to 'throw a stone into the house'?
6 The Art Ross Trophy is awarded annually in which sport?
7 The Flyers are a British ice hockey team. From which town or city do they come?
8 Who partnered Irina Rodnina to six of her 10 world ice skating pairs titles?
9 What was Eddie 'The Eagle's' occupation before his brief flirtation with ski jumping?
10 Name the brother and sister who won the respective men's and women's overall Alpine skiing World Cup titles in 1980.

ICE SKATING

Sonja Henie of Norway, winner of three Olympic gold medals (1928–36) and 10 world titles.

THE 10 MOST SUCCESSFUL OLYMPIC COUNTRIES

	Country	gold	Medals silver	bronze	Total
1	USA	11	11	15	37
2	USSR/CIS	14	10	6	30
3	Austria	7	9	4	20
4	Canada	2	6	7	15
5	Great Britain	5	3	6	14
6=	Sweden	5	3	2	10
6=	East Germany	3	3	4	10
8	Germany/West Germany	4	3	2	9
9	France	2	2	4	8
10=	Norway	3	2	1	6
10=	Hungary	0	2	4	6

Figure skating was introduced into the Olympic programme in 1908 when it formed part of the Summer Games. The first Olympic champion was Ulrich Salchow (Sweden) who lends his name to one of the sport's best-known jumps.

THE 10 SKATERS WITH THE MOST WORLD TITLES

	Skater/nationality	Event	Years	Titles
1=	Ulrich Salchow (Swe)	Men	1901–11	10
1=	Sonja Henie (Nor)	Women	1927–36	10
1=	Irina Rodnina (USSR)	Pairs	1969–78	10
4=	Herma Jaross-Szabo (*née* Planck) (Aut)	Women/Pairs	1922–27	7
4=	Karl Schäfer (Aut)	Men	1930–36	7
6=	Carol Heiss (USA)	Women	1956–61	6
6=	Alexandr Gorshkov (USSR)	Dance	1970–76	6
6=	Lyudmila Pakhomova (USSR)	Dance	1970–76	6
6=	Alexandr Zaitsev (USSR)	Pairs	1973–78	6
10	Richard Button (USA)	Men	1948–52	5

The British pair of Jean Westwood and Lawrence Demmy won five successive ice dance titles between 1951 and 1955, but the 1951 event is not regarded as an official championship.

JUDO

THE 10 MOST SUCCESSFUL OLYMPIC COUNTRIES

	Country	gold	Medals silver	bronze	Total
1	Japan	16	6	10	32
2	USSR/CIS	7	5	15	27
3	France	5	3	11	19
4	South Korea	5	5	7	17
5	Great Britain	0	6	10	16
6	Germany/West Germany	1	5	6	12
7	East Germany	1	2	6	9
8=	USA	0	3	4	7
8=	Holland	3	0	4	7
8=	Poland	2	2	3	7

Judo made its debut at the 1964 Tokyo Olympics but for men only. A women's competition was introduced as a demonstration sport at the 1988 Seoul Games.

LACROSSE

THE 10 TEAMS WITH THE MOST IROQUOIS CUP WINS

	Team	Years of first and last wins	Total wins
1	Stockport	1897–1989	17
2	South Manchester	1890–1980	11
3=	Old Hulmeians	1907–68	10
3=	Mellor	1935–88	10
5	Cheadle	1978–92	8
6	Old Waconians	1938–55	7
7	Heaton Mersey	1927–86	6
8=	Boardman and Eccles	1922–61	3
8=	Sheffield University	1977–83	3
10=	Lee	1921–70	2
10=	Old Mancunians	1930–57	2
10=	Urmston	1974–75	2

An early exponent of lacrosse, as depicted by American painter and explorer George Catlin c1835.

Contested annually by English club sides, the Iroquois Cup was first played for in 1890 and is named after the tribe of American Indians who were among the earliest exponents of lacrosse.

LAWN TENNIS

THE 10 MEN WITH THE MOST WIMBLEDON TITLES

	Player/nationality	Years	Singles	Doubles	Mixed	Total
1	William Renshaw (GB)	1880–89	7	7	0	14
2	Lawrence Doherty (GB)	1897–1905	5	8	0	13
3	Reginald Doherty (GB)	1897–1905	4	8	0	12
4	John Newcombe (Aus)	1965–74	3	6	0	9
5=	Ernest Renshaw (GB)	1880–89	1	7	0	8
5=	Tony Wilding (NZ)	1907–14	4	4	0	8
5=	John McEnroe (USA)	1979–92	3	5	0	8
8=	Wilfred Baddeley (GB)	1891–96	3	4	0	7
8=	Bob Hewitt (Aus/SA)	1962–79	0	5	2	7
8=	Rod Laver (Aus)	1959–69	4	1	2	7

Two of Renshaw's titles were in the doubles in 1880 and 1881, which were then known as the Oxford University Doubles Championship. However, they are now regarded as being of full Wimbledon championship status.

The Doherty and Renshaw brothers dominated the Wimbledon championship in its early days, winning 47 titles between them. The Renshaw twins, however, not only won 22 titles, but also revolutionized the game with their 'serve and volley' style of play which is now a major part of the modern game. William successfully won the singles title seven times while Ernest only once lifted the singles championship, although he was runner-up four times – three times to his brother. Both men died at an early age; William at 43 and Ernest five years earlier, when only 38.

Unlike the Renshaws, the Dohertys were not twins; Reginald was the older (born 1874) by two years. Their dominance of world tennis began with Reginald, known as 'Big Do', winning the 1897 Wimbledon singles title, and for the next eight years they reigned supreme, winning 25 titles between them. Lawrence, known as 'Little Do', was one of the game's finest volleyers and between them they were unquestionably one of the finest doubles teams ever seen. Such was their exemplary manner and good sportsmanship that they were known as ' The Princes Charming of Tennis'. At the 1900 Olympics they won the doubles title; in addition Lawrence won the singles, and Reginald the mixed doubles.

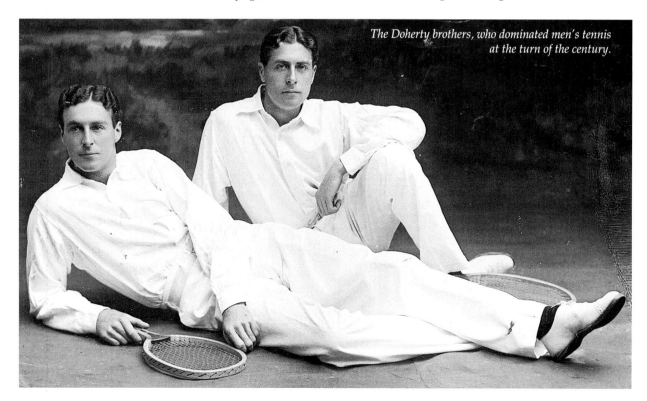

The Doherty brothers, who dominated men's tennis at the turn of the century.

THE 10 WOMEN WITH THE MOST WIMBLEDON TITLES

	Player/nationality	Years	Singles	Doubles	Mixed	Total
1	Billie Jean King (*née* Moffitt) (USA)	1961–79	6	10	4	20
2	Elizabeth Ryan (USA)	1914–34	0	12	7	19
3	Martina Navratilova (Cze/USA)	1976–90	9	7	1	17
4	Suzanne Lenglen (Fra)	1919–25	6	6	3	15
5	Louise Brough (USA)	1946–55	4	5	4	13
6	Helen Wills-Moody (USA)	1927–38	8	3	1	12
7=	Doris Hart (USA)	1947–55	1	4	5	10
7=	Margaret Court (*née* Smith) (Aus)	1953–75	3	2	5	10
9	Maria Bueno (Bra)	1958–66	3	5	0	8
10=	Dorothea Lambert Chambers (*née* Douglass)(GB)	1903–14	7	0	0	7
10=	Margaret du Pont (*née* Osborne) (USA)	1947–62	1	5	1	7
10=	Darlene Hard (USA)	1957–63	0	4	3	7
10=	Rosie Casals (USA)	1967–73	0	5	2	7

Billie Jean King's first and last Wimbledon titles were both in the ladies' doubles. The first, in 1961, as Billie Jean Moffitt, was with Karen Hantze when they beat Jan Lehane and Margaret Smith 6–3 6–4. When Billie Jean won her record-breaking 20th title in 1979 she partnered Martina Navratilova to victory over Betty Stove and Wendy Turnbull. Ironically, the day before she set the new record, the previous holder Elizabeth Ryan died. Billie Jean could have increased her total in 1983 but was beaten in the final of the mixed doubles by Wendy Turnbull and Britain's John Lloyd.

THE 10 SHORTEST MEN'S SINGLES FINALS AT WIMBLEDON

Match	Year	Set scores	Total games
1= William Renshaw *v* John Hartley	1881	6–0 6–1 6–1	20
1= Fred Perry *v* Gottfried von Cramm	1936	6–1 6–1 6–0	20
3= William Johnston *v* Frank Hunter	1923	6–0 6–3 6–1	22
3= Donald Budge *v* Bunny Austin	1938	6–1 6–0 6–3	22
3= John McEnroe *v* Jimmy Connors	1984	6–1 6–1 6–2	22
6= Lew Hoad *v* Ashley Cooper	1957	6–2 6–1 6–2	23
6= Rod Laver *v* Martin Mulligan	1962	6–2 6–2 6–1	23
6= John Newcombe *v* Wilhelm Bungert	1967	6–3 6–1 6–1	23
9= Ellsworth Vines *v* Bunny Austin	1932	6–4 6–2 6–0	24
9= Jack Kramer *v* Tom Brown	1947	6–1 6–3 6–2	24
9= Jimmy Connors *v* Ken Rosewall	1974	6–1 6–1 6–4	24
9= John McEnroe *v* Chris Lewis	1983	6–2 6–2 6–2	24

THE 10 LONGEST SETS IN A WIMBLEDON FINAL

	Match	Year	Score
1	John McEnroe & Michael Stich v Jim Grabb & Richey Reneberg*	1992	19–17
2	Rod Laver & Bob Mark v Roy Emerson & Neale Fraser	1959	16–14
3	Owen Davidson & Billie Jean King v Marty Riessen & Margaret Court	1971	15–13
4=	John Newcombe & Tony Roche v Ken Rosewall & Fred Stolle	1968	14–12
4=	Ken Fletcher & Margaret Court v Alex Metreveli & Olga Morozova	1968	14–12
4=	Margaret Court v Billie Jean King	1970	14–12
7=	Jacques Brugnon & Henri Cochet v John Hawkes & Gerald Patterson	1928	13–11
7=	Shirley Fry & Doris Hart v Louise Brough & Margaret du Pont	1951	13–11
7=	Jaroslav Drobny v Ken Rosewall	1954	13–11
7=	Ashley Cooper v Neale Fraser	1958	13–11
7=	Bob Howe & Lorraine Coghlan v Kurt Nielsen & Althea Gibson	1958	13–11
7=	Rod Laver & Darlene Hard v Bob Howe & Maria Bueno	1960	13–11
7=	Neale Fraser & Margaret du Pont v Dennis Ralston & Ann Haydon	1962	13–11

*Final set.

All first-named players/pairs except Laver & Mark went on to win the match.

The 1980 men's singles final at Wimbledon, which Bjorn Borg won after a gruelling 55-game match against John McEnroe. It was to be Borg's fifth and final Wimbledon singles title.

THE 10 SHORTEST WOMEN'S SINGLES FINALS AT WIMBLEDON

	Match	Year	Set scores	Total games
1	Dorothea Lambert Chambers v Dora Boothby	1911	6–0 6–0	12
2=	Doris Hart v Shirley Fry	1951	6–1 6–0	13
2=	Billie Jean King v Evonne Cawley	1975	6–0 6–1	13
4=	Lottie Dod v Blanche Bingley	1887	6–2 6–0	14
4=	Lottie Dod v Blanche Hillyard	1892	6–1 6–1	14
4=	Blanche Hillyard v Lucy Austin	1894	6–1 6–1	14
4=	Suzanne Lenglen v Elizabeth Ryan	1921	6–2 6–0	14
4=	Suzanne Lenglen v Molla Mallory	1922	6–2 6–0	14
4=	Suzanne Lenglen v Joan Fry	1925	6–2 6–0	14
4=	Alice Marble v Kay Stammers	1939	6–2 6–0	14

THE 10 LONGEST* MEN'S SINGLES FINALS AT WIMBLEDON

	Match	Year	Set scores	Total games
1	Jaroslav Drobny v Ken Rosewall	1954	13–11 4–6 6–2 9–7	58
2	Harold Mahoney v Wilfred Baddeley	1896	6–2 6–8 5–7 8–6 6–3	57
3=	Jack Crawford v Ellsworth Vines	1933	4–6 11–9 6–2 2–6 6–4	56
3=	Yvon Petra v Geoffrey Brown	1946	6–2 6–4 7–9 5–7 6–4	56
5	Bjorn Borg v John McEnroe	1980	1–6 7–5 6–3 6–7 8–6	55
6	Jimmy Connors v John McEnroe	1982	3–6 6–3 6–7 7–6 6–4	54
7	Ashley Cooper v Neale Fraser	1958	3–6 6–3 6–4 13–11	52
8=	Henri Cochet v Jean Borotra	1927	4–6 4–6 6–3 6–4 7–5	51
8=	Roy Emerson v Fred Stolle	1964	6–4 12–10 4–6 6–3	51
10=	Stan Smith v Ilie Nastase	1972	4–6 6–3 6–3 4–6 7–5	50
10=	Andre Agassi v Goran Ivanisevic	1992	6–7 6–4 6–4 1–6 6–4	50

Based on most games.

The longest-ever match was the first-round tie between Pancho Gonzales and Charlie Pasarell in 1969. It lasted a total of 112 games, and Gonzales won 22–24, 1–6, 16–14, 6–3, 11–9. It took place in the days before the tie-break, which was launched at Wimbledon in 1971.

THE 10 LONGEST* WOMEN'S SINGLES FINALS AT WIMBLEDON

	Match	Year	Set scores	Total games
1	Margaret Court v Billie Jean King	1970	14–12 11–9	46
2	Suzanne Lenglen v Dorothea Lambert Chambers	1919	10–8 4–6 9–7	44
3	Louise Brough v Margaret du Pont	1949	10–8 1–6 10–8	43
4	Maria Bueno v Margaret Smith	1964	6–4 7–9 6–3	35
5=	Helen Moody v Dorothy Round	1933	6–4 6–8 6–3	33
5=	Chris Evert v Evonne Cawley	1976	6–3 4–6 8–6	33
5=	Steffi Graf v Gabriela Sabatini	1991	6–4 3–6 8–6	33
8=	Blanche Hillyard v Charlotte Cooper	1897	5–7 7–5 6–2	32
8=	Angela Mortimer v Christine Truman	1961	4–6 6–4 7–5	32
10	Lottie Dod v Blanche Hillyard	1893	6–8 6–1 6–4	31

Based on most games.

THE TOP 10 WINNERS OF MEN'S GRAND SLAM SINGLES TITLES

	Player/nationality	A	F	W	US*	Total
1	Roy Emerson (Aus)	6	2	2	2	12
2=	Bjorn Borg (Swe)	0	6	5	0	11
2=	Rod Laver (Aus)	3	2	4	2	11
4=	Jimmy Connors (USA)	1	0	2	5	8
4=	Ivan Lendl (Cze)	2	3	0	3	8
4=	Fred Perry (GB)	1	1	3	3	8
4=	Ken Rosewall (Aus)	4	2	0	2	8
8=	René Lacoste (Fra)	0	3	2	2	7
8=	William Larned (USA)	0	0	0	7	7
8=	John McEnroe (USA)	0	0	3	4	7
8=	John Newcombe (Aus)	2	0	3	2	7
8=	William Renshaw (GB)	0	0	7	0	7
8=	Richard Sears (USA)	0	0	0	7	7
8=	Mats Wilander (Swe)	3	3	0	1	7

A = Australian Open; F = French Open; W = Wimbledon; US = US Open.

THE TOP 10 WINNERS OF WOMEN'S GRAND SLAM SINGLES TITLES

	Player/nationality	A	F	W	US*	Total
1	Margaret Court (*née* Smith) (Aus)	11	5	3	5	24
2	Helen Wills-Moody (USA)	0	4	8	7	19
3=	Chris Evert-Lloyd (USA)	2	7	3	6	18
3=	Martina Navratilova (Cze/USA)	3	2	9	4	18
5	Billie Jean King (*née* Moffitt) (USA)	1	1	6	4	12
6	Steffi Graf (Ger)	3	2	4	2	11
7	Maureen Connolly (USA)	1	2	3	3	9
8=	Suzanne Lenglen (Fra)	0	2	6	0	8
8=	Molla Mallory (*née* Bjurstedt) (USA)	0	0	0	8	8
10=	Maria Bueno (Bra)	0	0	3	4	7
10=	Evonne Cawley (*née* Goolagong) (Aus)	4	1	2	0	7

*A = Australian Open; F = French Open; W = Wimbledon; US = US Open.

THE 10 LONGEST* MEN'S GRAND SLAM SINGLES FINALS

	Match	Tournament	Year	Set scores	Total games
1	Gerald Patterson *v* John Hawkes	Australian	1927	3–6 6–4 3–6 18–16 6–3	71
2	Pancho Gonzales *v* Ted Schroeder	United States	1949	16–18 2–6 6–1 6–2 6–4	67
3=	John Doeg *v* Frank Sheilds	United States	1930	10–8 1–6 6–4 16–14	65
3=	Arthur Ashe *v* Tom Okker	United States	1968	14–12 5–7 6–3 3–6 6–3	65
5	René Lacoste *v* Bill Tilden	French	1927	6–4 4–6 5–7 6–3 11–9	61
6	Ashley Cooper *v* Malcolm Anderson	United States	1958	6–2 3–6 4–6 10–8 8–6	59
7=	Bill Tilden *v* William Johnston	United States	1925	4–6 11–9 6–3 4–6 6–3	58
7=	Jaroslav Drobny *v* Ken Rosewall	Wimbledon	1954	13–11 4–6 6–2 9–7	58
9=	Harold Mahoney *v* Wilfred Baddeley	Wimbledon	1896	6–2 6–8 5–7 8–6 6–3	57
9=	Rod Laver *v* Neale Fraser	Australian	1960	5–7 3–6 6–2 8–6 8–6	57

*Based on most games.

THE 10 LONGEST* WOMEN'S GRAND SLAM SINGLES FINALS

	Match	Tournament	Year	Set scores	Total games
1	Juliette Atkinson v Marion Jones	United States	1898	3–6 5–7 6–4 2–6 7–5	51
2	Mabel Cahill v Elizabeth Moore	United States	1892	5–7 6–3 6–4 4–6 6–2	49
3	Margaret du Pont v Louise Brough†	United States	1948	6–4 4–6 15–13	48
4	Elizabeth Moore v Myrtle McAteer	United States	1901	6–4 3–6 7–5 2–6 6–2	47
5=	Juliette Atkinson v Elizabeth Moore	United States	1897	6–3 6–3 4–6 3–6 6–3	46
5=	Margaret Court v Billie Jean King	Wimbledon	1970	14–12 11–9	46
7	Helen Hellwig v Aline Terry	United States	1894	7–5 3–6 6–0 3–6 6–3	45
8	Suzanne Lenglen v Dorothea Lambert Chambers	Wimbledon	1919	10–8 4–6 9–7	44
9	Louise Brough v Margaret du Pont	Wimbledon	1949	10–8 1–6 10–8	43
10	Darlene Hard v Maria Bueno	United States	1960	6–4 10–12 6–4	42

Based on most games.
†*The longest for a three-set match.*

The longest French and Australian finals were as follows:

Angela Mortimer v Dorothy Knode	French	1955	2–6 7–5 10–8	38
Daphne Akhurst v S. Harper	Australian	1930	10–8 2–6 7–5	38

THE TOP 10 MONEY-WINNERS IN 1991

	MEN Player/nationality	Winnings ($)
1	Pete Sampras (USA)	1,783,413
2	Jim Courier (USA)	1,748,171
3	Stefan Edberg (Swe)	1,713,575
4	Michael Stich (Ger)	1,217,636
5	Boris Becker (Ger)	1,216,568
6	Guy Forget (Fra)	1,072,252
7	Ivan Lendl (Cze)	1,038,983
8	Andre Agassi (USA)	705,611
9	Emilio Sanchez (Spa)	672,071
10	Karel Novacek (Cze)	647,540

	WOMEN Player/nationality	Winnings ($)
1	Monica Seles (Yug)	1,587,758
2	Steffi Graf (Ger)	1,092,336
3	Gabriela Sabatini (Arg)	939,971
4	Martina Navratilova (USA)	711,736
5	Arantxa Sanchez Vicario (Spa)	705,340
6	Jana Novotna (Cze)	616,869
7	Mary Joe Fernandez (USA)	564,385
8	Natalya Zvereva (USSR)	490,952
9	Jennifer Capriati (USA)	475,917
10	Gigi Fernandez (USA)	395,703

THE TOP 10 DAVIS CUP WINNING TEAMS

	Team	Years	Wins
1	USA	1900–90	29
2	Australia	1939–86	20
3	France	1927–91	7
4	Australasia	1907–19	6
5	British Isles	1903–12	5
6=	Great Britain	1933–36	4
6=	Sweden	1975–87	4
8	West Germany	1988–89	2
9=	South Africa	1974	1
9=	Italy	1976	1
9=	Czechoslovakia	1980	1

THE 10 MOST SUCCESSFUL OLYMPIC COUNTRIES

	Country	gold	Medals silver	bronze	Total
1	Great Britain	16	13	15	44
2	France	8	7	6	21
3	USA	11	5	3	19
4	Germany/West Germany	4	3	2	9
5=	Greece	1	5	2	8
5=	Bohemia/Czechoslovakia	1	1	6	8
7	Sweden	0	2	5	7
8	South Africa	3	2	0	5
9	Spain	0	3	1	4
10	CIS	0	0	3	3

The UK was represented by the British Isles from 1900 to 1921, England from 1922 to 1928, and Great Britain since 1929. The combined Australia/New Zealand team took part as Australasia between 1905 and 1922. Australia entered a separate team in 1923 and New Zealand in 1924.

South Africa's sole win was gained when, for political reasons, India refused to meet them in the 1974 final.

Tennis was first contested at the inaugural modern Olympics in 1896 but was discontinued after the 1924 Games. It was revived in 1988 when Miloslav Mecir (Cze) won the men's singles title and Steffi Graf (FRG) became the women's champion.

Norris Williams (right), who survived the sinking of the Titanic *to win Olympic and Wimbledon titles.*

QUIZ

GRAND SLAM TENNIS

1 Who did Martina Navratilova beat in the final when winning her record ninth Wimbledon title?

2 Which pair won all four Grand Slam doubles titles in 1951?

3 Who was the last person, male or female, to win all four Grand Slam singles titles in one year?

4 Which country provided both men's and women's singles champions at Wimbledon in 1934, the only time they had done so since 1922?

5 Who were the first brother and sister pairing for 70 years to win a Grand Slam mixed doubles title in 1980?

6 Martina Navratilova with 15 titles won the most Grand Slam events in the 1980s, but who was second to her with nine titles?

7 Who, in 1989, became the youngest-known winner of a men's singles Grand Slam title at 17 years 3 months?

8 Who had to retire from the final of the 1990 Australian Open and became only the second person to retire in the final of a Grand Slam event, and the first since 1911?

9 Who was the first man to win singles, doubles and mixed doubles titles at Wimbledon in one year?

10 What was unusual about the venue of the 1906 and 1912 Australian Championships?

THE TOP 10 WINNERS OF INDIVIDUAL OLYMPIC MEDALS

	Player/nationality	Years	Medals*
1	Max Decugis (Fra)	1900–20	6(4)
2	Kitty McKane (GB)	1920–24	5(1)
3=	Reginald Doherty (GB)	1900–08	4(3)
3=	Gunnar Setterwall (Swe)	1908–12	4(0)
5=	Harold Mahony (Ire)	1900	3(0)
5=	Josiah Ritchie (GB)	1908	3(1)
5=	Charles Dixon (GB)	1908–12	3(0)
5=	Charles Winslow (SA)	1912–20	3(2)
5=	Suzanne Lenglen (Fra)	1920	3(2)
5=	Vince Richards (USA)	1924	3(2)

Figures in brackets indicate gold medals.

Other well-known Olympic champions include Helen Wills-Moody, winner of eight Wimbledon singles titles; Hazel Wightman, who gave the Wightman Cup to tennis; and the 'Four Musketeers': Henri Cochet, Jacques Brugnon, Jean Borotra, and René Lacoste. Another Olympic tennis champion was the little-known Norris Williams. Swiss-born Williams became a naturalized US citizen and in 1920 won the men's doubles title at Wimbledon. Four years later he won the Olympic mixed doubles title. His feat is unique because he is the only survivor of the *Titanic* sinking to win an Olympic gold medal or, indeed, a Wimbledon title.

MISCELLANEOUS

THE 10 HIGHEST-EARNING SPORTSMEN IN THE WORLD

	Name	Sport	Salary/ winnings	Other income*	Total income, 1991 ($)
1	Evander Holyfield	Boxing	60,000,000	500,000	60,500,000
2	Mike Tyson	Boxing	30,000,000	1,500,000	31,500,000
3	Michael Jordan	Basketball	2,800,000	13,200,000	16,000,000
4	George Foreman	Boxing	14,000,000	500,000	14,500,000
5	Ayrton Senna	Motor racing	12,000,000	1,000,000	13,000,000
6	Alain Prost	Motor racing	10,000,000	1,000,000	11,000,000
7	Razor Ruddock	Boxing	10,000,000	200,000	10,200,000
8	Arnold Palmer	Golf	300,000	9,000,000	9,300,000
9	Nigel Mansell	Motor racing	8,000,000	1,000,000	9,000,000
10	Jack Nicklaus	Golf	500,000	8,000,000	8,500,000

From sponsorship and royalty income from endorsed sporting products.

In 1991 there were also several sports stars outside the Top 10 but with total incomes in excess of $5,000,000, among them American football players Joe Montana and Rocket Ismail; basketball players Larry Bird, Magic Johnson, David Robinson and Patrick Ewing; motor racing drivers Gerhard Berger and Jean Alesi; golfers Greg Norman and Nick Faldo; tennis players Monica Seles, Stefan Edberg, Steffi Graf, Andre Agassi, Boris Becker, Gabriela Sabatini and Jennifer Capriati; and ice hockey player Wayne Gretzky. In the $4,000,000 to $5,000,000 bracket were sportsmen in fields as diverse as baseball (Darryl Strawberry, Will Clark and Kevin Mitchell) and cycling (Greg LeMond).

Used by permission of Forbes Magazine.

THE 10 HIGHEST-EARNING SPORTSMEN IN BRITISH SPORT, 1990

	Name	Sport	Earnings (£)*
1	Nigel Mansell	Motor racing	5,364,864
2	Nick Faldo	Golf	3,490,200
3	Ian Woosnam	Golf	2,018,064
4	Pat Eddery	Horse racing	1,339,804
5	Stephen Hendry	Snooker	1,294,246
6	Willie Carson	Horse racing	1,147,518
7	Steve Cauthen†	Horse racing	903,258
8	Steve Davis	Snooker	855,851
9	Nigel Benn	Boxing	655,675
10	Gary Lineker	Soccer	644,000

Earnings include salary, prizemoney, endorsements, etc.
†Steve Cauthen is American but is now British-based.

THE TOP 10 CORPORATE SPORTS SPONSORS IN THE USA

	Sponsor	Budget ($)
1	Anheuser-Busch	175,000,000
2	General Motors	150,000,000
3	Philip Morris	128,000,000
4	Nabisco	115,000,000
5	Nike	86,000,000
6	Coca-Cola	71,000,000
7	McDonald's	66,000,000
8	Pepsi-Cola	64,000,000
9	Coors	53,000,000
10=	Eastman Kodak	49,000,000
10=	IBM	49,000,000

THE 10 MOST POPULAR PARTICIPATION SPORTS IN THE UK

WOMEN		
	Sport	%
1	Swimming, diving	13
2	Keep fit, yoga, aerobics, dance exercise	12
3	Cycling	7
4	Snooker, pool, billiards	5
5	Darts	4
6=	Jogging, running	3
6=	Badminton	3
8	Weight training, lifting	2
9=	Bowls	1
9=	Equestrian sports	1
9=	Golf	1
9=	Ice skating	1
9=	Netball	1
9=	Squash	1
9=	Table tennis	1
9=	Tennis	1
9=	Tenpin bowling	1
9=	Watersports	1

MEN		
	Sport	%
1	Snooker, pool, billiards	27
2	Darts	14
3	Swimming, diving	13
4=	Soccer	10
4=	Cycling	10
6	Jogging, running	8
7=	Golf	7
7=	Weight training, lifting	7
9	Keep fit, yoga, aerobics	5
10=	Fishing	4
10=	Badminton	4
10=	Squash	4
10=	Table tennis	4

The Office of Populations Censuses and Surveys conducted interviews of some 9,000 men and 10,000 women to assess the numbers participating in a wide range of sporting activities. The percentages listed refer to those interviewed who had participated in one or more of these sports during the four weeks prior to the interview, and cover all interviewees aged 16 to 60. As might be expected, in younger age groups certain sports predominate, the highest percentage participating being 62 for snooker, pool and billiards among 16 to 19-year-olds, followed by 40 per cent in the same age group playing soccer. Among women aged 16 to 19, keep fit, yoga, aerobics and dance exercise activities and swimming and diving both attracted 24 per cent, closely followed by snooker, pool and billiards (23 per cent).

THE 10 MOST SUCCESSFUL FILMS WITH SPORTING THEMES*

	Film	Star	Sport
1	*Rocky IV*	Sylvester Stallone	Boxing
2	*Rocky III*	Sylvester Stallone	Boxing
3	*Rocky*	Sylvester Stallone	Boxing
4	*Rocky II*	Sylvester Stallone	Boxing
5	*Days of Thunder*	Tom Cruise	Stock car racing
6	*Field of Dreams*	Kevin Costner	Baseball
7	*Chariots of Fire*	Ian Charleson	Athletics
8	*The Main Event*	Barbra Streisand	Boxing
9	*The Natural*	Robert Redford	Baseball
10	*The Color of Money*	Paul Newman	Pool

To 31 December 1990.

The boxing ring, a natural source of drama and thrills, dominates Hollywood's most successful sports-based epics, which are led by superstar Sylvester Stallone's *Rocky* series. This list is based on North American (US and Canadian) box office success, but an international list would not differ greatly.

Sylvester Stallone as Rocky. The Rocky *series dominates the list of most successful films with sporting themes.*

THE 10 BESTSELLING SPORTS VIDEOS OF ALL TIME IN THE UK*

	Video	Sport
1	Arsenal: Official Review of Division One Game by Game, 1988–89	Football
2	Liverpool FC: The Mighty Reds	Football
3	Botham's Ashes	Cricket
4	Italia '90: Gascoigne's Glory	Football
5	Genius: The George Best Story	Football
6	Gazza: The Real Me	Football
7	Liverpool: Team of the Decade	Football
8	Play Better Golf with Peter Alliss	Golf
9	Mike Tyson's Greatest Hits	Boxing
10	Wrestlemania 3	Wrestling

To 30 June 1991.

Football has for some years taken by far the largest slice of sporting video sales, with such normally TV-friendly sports as snooker faring surprisingly poorly on cassette. The early 1990s, however, has seen a sudden surge of public enthusiasm for showbiz-oriented professional wrestling tapes, of which *Wrestlemania 3* is the top seller so far.

LADBROKES' TOP 10 SPORTING EVENTS FOR BETS*, 1991

1 FA Cup
2 British Open Golf Championship
3 World Professional Snooker Championship
4 Rugby Union World Cup
5 Wimbledon Lawn Tennis Championships
6 US Masters Golf Championship
7 Ryder Cup
8 US Open Golf Championship
9 Rumbelows League Cup
10 British Masters Golf Championship

Excluding horse racing and non-regular sporting events such as individual boxing contests.

THE 10 MOST POPULAR* SPORTS USED BY SLIMMERS

1 Aerobics/keep fit
2 Swimming
3 Walking
4 Cycling
5 Weight training
6 Running/jogging
7 Exercise bike/multi-gym
8 Badminton
9 Dancing
10 Squash

Based on a survey conducted by Slimming Magazine.

THE 10 CATEGORIES OF SPORTSPEOPLE WITH THE LARGEST* HEARTS

1 Tour de France cyclists
2 Marathon runners
3 Rowers
4 Boxers
5 Sprint cyclists
6 Middle-distance runners
7 Weightlifters
8 Swimmers
9 Sprinters
10 Decathletes

Based on average medical measurements.

The size of the heart of a person who engages regularly in a demanding sport enlarges according to the strenuousness of the sport.

The race, which has been held annually since 1973, stretches from Anchorage to Nome in Alaska, the course following an old river mail route and covering 1,864km/1,158 miles. Iditarod is a deserted mining village along the route and the race commemorates an emergency operation in 1925 to get medical supplies to Nome following a diphtheria epidemic.

THE 10 FASTEST WINNING TIMES OF THE IDITAROD DOG SLED RACE

	Winner	Year	Time day	hr	min	sec
1	Susan Butcher	1990	11	01	53	28
2	Susan Butcher	1987	11	02	05	13
3	Joe Runyan	1989	11	05	24	34
4	Susan Butcher	1988	11	11	41	40
5	Susan Butcher	1986	11	15	06	00
6	Rick Swenson	1981	12	08	45	02
7	Rick Mackey	1983	12	14	10	44
8	Dean Osmar	1984	12	15	07	33
9	Rick Swenson	1991	12	16	34	39
10	Joe May	1980	14	07	11	51

Rick Swenson, five times winner of the Iditarod dog sled race, pictured here celebrating his victory in 1991.

Rick Swenson has won the race a record five times. Susan Butcher has won it four times (men and women compete together on equal terms). Swenson, who has competed in 16 of the 19 races and never finished out of the first 10, won a prize of $50,000 and a new truck in 1991.

THE TOP 10 SINGLES BY SPORTS TEAMS IN THE UK*

	Single	Team
1	Back Home	England 1970 World Cup Squad
2	World In Motion	England New Order (1990)
3	This Time We'll Get It Right	England 1982 World Cup Squad
4	Anfield Rap (Red Machine In Full Effect)	Liverpool FC (1988)
5	We Have A Dream	Scotland 1982 World Cup Squad
6	Ole Ola (Muhler Brasileira)	Rod Stewart with Scotland 1978 World Cup Squad
7	Ossie's Dream (Spurs Are On Their Way To Wembley)	Tottenham Hotspur FC (1981)
8	Blue Is The Colour	Chelsea FC (1972)
9	Snooker Loopy	Matchroom Mob with Chas & Dave (1986)
10	Leeds United	Leeds United FC (1972)

*To 30 June 1991.

All these singles made the UK Top 10, and the first two were chart-topping hits. Some of the sportsmen (none of the records feature women) received professional help from the likes of New Order and Rod Stewart, while Chas & Dave, who bolstered the only non-football entry (by the Matchroom Mob of snooker professionals), also had an uncredited appearance on the Spurs single at No. 7.

QUIZ

A LITTLE BIT OF THE UNUSUAL

1 In 1979 Ashley Doubtfire of the Isle of Wight set a world hang-gliding record for the highest descent. From where?

2 What world record did Australian cricketers Allan Porter and Joey Dyomm set in February 1977 with a new record of 219 feet?

3 Forty-four-year-old Alan Pearce succeeded Len Rush as the Queen's racing manager in 1984. In what sport?

4 Dewey Bartlett deposed David Hall as world champion in what sport at Beaver, Oklahoma, in 1972?

5 Which former television newsreader's father was responsible for giving cricket the 'googly'. . .?

6 . . . and which former newsreader was at one time the president of the All-England Bar Billiards Association?

7 For what did Baron de Coubertin, founder of the modern Olympics, win a gold medal at the 1912 Games?

8 When the World Cup was stolen in 1966 it was on display at an exhibition at Westminster's Central Hall. What replaced it after it went missing?

9 With what sport would you associate 'Hairy Dog', 'Cut Lips' and 'Twilight Beauty', among others?

10 What south-west of England junior title was won by the appropriately named 13-year-old Richard Flicker in 1991?

MODERN PENTATHLON

THE 10 MOST SUCCESSFUL OLYMPIC COUNTRIES

	Country	gold	Individual silver	bronze	gold	Team silver	bronze	Total
				Medals				
1	Sweden	9	6	4	0	1	1	21
2	Hungary	4	5	1	4	2	2	18
3	USSR/CIS	1	3	6	4	3	0	17
4	USA	0	2	2	0	3	1	8
5	Italy	1	1	2	1	1	1	7
6	Finland	0	1	1	0	0	3	5
7	Poland	2	0	0	1	0	0	3
8=	Germany	1	0	1	0	0	0	2
8=	Great Britain	0	0	0	1	0	1	2
8=	Czechoslovakia	0	0	1	0	1	0	2
8=	France	0	0	0	0	0	2	2

Britain's only gold came unexpectedly at Montreal in 1976, when Danny Nightingale, Jeremy Fox and Adrian Parker captured Britain's first-ever modern pentathlon medal. During his fencing bout against Fox, Soviet pentathlete Boris Onischenko was disqualified for cheating when he was discovered to have an electronic trigger wired to his sword which registered 'hits' whenever he pressed the button. Britain's only other medal was at Seoul in 1988 when Richard Phelps, Dominic Mahoney and Graham Brookhouse took the team bronze by a mere eight points. Perhaps the most famous competitor in the modern pentathlon was General (then Lieutenant) George Patton, when he competed at Stockholm in 1912. A member of the US team, he finished fifth in the individual competition and might even have won, had he not finished in 21st place (out of 32) in, of all events, the shooting competition! He maintained that he received no points for one shot because it passed cleanly through a hole he had previously made in the target, but his appeal was not upheld.

MOTORCYCLING

THE 10 RIDERS WITH THE MOST WORLD TITLES

Mike Hailwood also won the TT Formula One world title in 1978. Hailwood and Phil Read are the only men to win world titles in three different classes. Read won the 125, 250 and 500cc classes while Hailwood won titles at 250, 350 and 500cc.

	Rider/nationality	Years	Titles
1	Giacomo Agostini (Ita)	1966–75	15
2	Angel Nieto (Spa)	1969–84	13
3=	Carlo Ubbiali (Ita)	1951–60	9
3=	Mike Hailwood (GB)	1961–67	9
5=	John Surtees (GB)	1956–60	7
5=	Phil Read (GB)	1964–74	7
7=	Geoff Duke (GB)	1951–55	6
7=	Jim Redman (SR)	1962–65	6
7=	Klaus Enders (FRG)	1967–74	6
10	Anton Mang (FRG)	1980–87	5

Right Italy's Giacomo Agostini, holder of a record 15 world titles.

THE 10 RIDERS WITH THE MOST GRAND PRIX RACE WINS

	Rider/nationality	Years	Race wins
1	Giacomo Agostini (Ita)	1965–76	122
2	Angel Nieto (Spa)	1969–85	90
3	Mike Hailwood (GB)	1959–67	76
4	Rolf Biland (Swi)	1975–91	58
5	Phil Read (GB)	1961–75	52
6	Jim Redman (SR)	1961–66	45
7	Anton Mang (FRG)	1976–88	42
8	Carlo Ubbiali (Ita)	1950–60	39
9	John Surtees (GB)	1955–60	38
10	Jorge Martinez (Spa)	1984–90	35

All except Biland were solo machine riders. Britain's Barry Sheene won 23 races during his career and is the only man to win Grands Prix at 50 and 500cc.

Figures for both lists are to the end of the 1991 season.

THE 10 MANUFACTURERS WITH THE MOST GRAND PRIX WINS

	Manufacturer	Years	Race wins
1	Yamaha	1963–91	447*
2	Honda	1961–91	285†
3	MV Agusta	1952–76	273
4	Suzuki	1962–91	135
5	BMW	1954–74	110‡
6	Kawasaki	1969–83	85
7	Derbi	1968–89	70
8	Kreidler	1962–82	69
9	Norton	1949–69	60§
10	Garelli	1982–87	51

*Includes 90 sidecar wins.
†Includes 1 sidecar win.
‡ All sidecar wins.
§ Includes 19 sidecar wins.

Barry Sheene became world 500cc champion in 1977, the year in which he recorded the fastest championship race of all time at the Belgian Grand Prix in Spa-Francorchamps.

All races except No. 10 were during the 500cc class (unless stated) of the Belgian Grand Prix at the Spa-Francorchamps circuit. No. 10 was the German Grand Prix at Hockenheim.

The fastest-ever lap was by Barry Sheene during the 1977 Belgian Grand Prix when he lapped the Spa circuit at 220.72kph/137.15mph.

The first-ever 100-mph race was the 1950 Belgian Grand Prix at Spa on 2 July 1950. It was won by Umberto Masetti (Italy) on his Gilera at 162.69kph/101.09mph.

The fastest races in the other world championship categories are:

350cc 1973 Italian Grand Prix (Monza): 196.71kph/122.23mph Giacomo Agostini (Ita) MV Agusta.

125cc 1977 Belgian Grand Prix (Spa): 190.77kph/118.54mph Pier Paolo Bianchi (Ita) Morbidelli.

80cc 1986 British Grand Prix (Silverstone): 160.90kph/99.99mph Ian McConnachie (GB) Krauser.

50cc 1975 Belgian Grand Prix (Spa): 163.70kph/101.72mph Julien Van Zeebroeck (Bel) Kreidler.

Sidecar 1977 Belgian Grand Prix (Spa): 197.51kph/122.73mph Werner Schwärzel and Andreas Hüber (FRG) ARO-Fath.

THE 10 FASTEST WORLD CHAMPIONSHIP RACES OF ALL TIME

	Year	Rider/nationality	Bike	Average speed kph	mph
1	1977	Barry Sheene (GB)	Suzuki	217.37	135.07
2	1976	John Williams (GB)	Suzuki	214.83	133.49
3	1975	Phil Read (GB)	MV Agusta	214.40	133.22
4	1978	Wil Hartog (Hol)	Suzuki	213.88	132.90
5	1974	Phil Read (GB)	MV Agusta	212.41	131.98
6	1973	Giacomo Agostini (Ita)	MV Agusta	206.81	128.51
7	1977 (250cc)	Walter Villa (Ita)	Harley-Davidson	204.43	127.03
8	1976 (250cc)	Walter Villa (Ita)	Harley-Davidson	202.90	126.08
9	1969	Giacomo Agostini (Ita)	MV Agusta	202.53	125.85
10	1991	Kevin Schwantz (USA)	Suzuki	201.72	125.34

THE 10 MANUFACTURERS WITH THE MOST SOLO WORLD TITLES

	Manufacturer	Titles
1	MV Agusta	37
2	Honda	31
3	Yamaha	30
4	Suzuki	15
5	Kawasaki	9
6	Derbi	8
7	Kreidler	7
8	Moto-Guzzi	6
9=	Garelli	5
9=	Mondial	5
9=	Norton	5

Honda stands alone as the only manufacturer to win world titles in five solo classes: 500, 350, 250, 125, and 50cc. The only class in which they did not win a title was the short-lived 80cc class.

THE 10 RIDERS WITH THE MOST WORLD 500cc TITLES

	Rider/nationality	Titles
1	Giacomo Agostini (Ita)	8
2=	Geoff Duke (GB)	4
2=	Mike Hailwood (GB)	4
2=	Eddie Lawson (USA)	4*
2=	John Surtees (GB)	4
6	Kenny Roberts (USA)	3*
7=	Umberto Masetti (Ita)	2*
7=	Wayne Rainey (USA)	2*
7=	Phil Read (GB)	2
7=	Barry Sheene (GB)	2*
7=	Freddie Spencer (USA)	2

The rider's only world titles.

THE 10 RIDERS WITH THE MOST ISLE OF MAN TT WINS

	Rider*	Years	Race wins
1	Mike Hailwood	1961–69	14
2	Joey Dunlop	1977–88	13
3=	Stanley Woods	1923–39	10
3=	Giacomo Agostini (Ita)	1966–75	10
5=	Siegfried Schauzu (FRG)	1967–75	9
5=	Mick Boddice	1983–91	9
5=	Steve Hislop	1987–92	9
8=	Phil Read	1961–77	8
8=	Chas Mortimer	1970–78	8
8=	Charlie Williams	1973–80	8

From Great Britain and Northern Ireland unless otherwise stated.

Motorcycle racing on the Isle of Man started in 1905 when the island's authorities allowed sections of road to be closed off and used for the elimination races for the British team entering the International Cup – a decision made as a result of Westminster imposing a 20 mph speed limit on British roads. The International Cup was discontinued in 1906, but the Auto-Cycle Club (now Auto-Cycle Union) was keen to keep up competitive racing on the Isle of Man and on 28 May 1907 the first TT (Tourist Trophy) meeting was held. The Short Course gradually became too fast and in 1911 racing was transferred to the Mountain Course, over which present-day TT races are held. The 1911 races also saw the introduction of the Senior and Junior TTs, which remain the island's principal races during TT week. While many of the world's top grand prix stars shun the island because of its dangers, it remains popular with motorcycle enthusiasts and thousands make the ferry journey across the Irish Sea every June.

THE 10 FASTEST ISLE OF MAN SENIOR TTs

	Rider*	Year	Bike	Average speed kph	mph
1	Steve Hislop	1992	Norton	195.18	121.28
2	Steve Hislop	1991	Honda	194.87	121.09
3	Steve Hislop	1989	Honda	190.27	118.23
4	Joey Dunlop	1988	Honda	188.90	117.38
5	Rob McElnea	1984	Suzuki	186.14	115.66
6	Roger Burnett	1986	Honda	183.43	113.98
7	Joey Dunlop	1985	Honda	182.97	113.69
8	Mike Hailwood	1979	Suzuki	179.84	111.75
9	Tom Herron	1978	Suzuki	179.83	111.74
10	Norman Brown	1982	Suzuki	178.60	110.98

All from Great Britain and Northern Ireland.

The first 100-mph race took place in 1960 when John Surtees won at an average speed of 164.86kph/102.44mph. The first 100-mph lap had been achieved in 1957 by Bob McIntyre riding a Gilera.

THE 10 RIDERS WITH THE MOST ISLE OF MAN SENIOR TT WINS

	Rider*	Wins
1	Mike Hailwood	7
2	Giacomo Agostini (Ita)	5
3=	John Surtees	4
3=	Stanley Woods	4
5=	Alec Bennett	3
5=	Harold Daniell	3
5=	Geoff Duke	3
5=	Joey Dunlop	3
5=	Steve Hislop	3
10=	Ray Amm (SR)	2
10=	Howard Davies	2
10=	Charlie Dodson	2
10=	Mick Grant	2
10=	Jimmy Guthrie	2
10=	Tom Herron	2
10=	Rob McElnea	2

From Great Britain and Northern Ireland unless otherwise stated.

THE 10 RIDERS WITH THE MOST FIRST THREE PLACINGS IN THE ISLE OF MAN SENIOR TT

	Rider*	Total first three placings
1=	Mike Hailwood	8
1=	Stanley Woods	8
3=	Giacomo Agostini (Ita)	6
3=	Jimmy Guthrie	6
5=	Alec Bennett	5
5=	John Surtees	5
7=	Geoff Duke	4
7=	Joey Dunlop	4
7=	Freddie Frith	4
7=	Steve Hislop	4
7=	Harry Langman	4
7=	Jimmy Simpson	4
7=	Peter Williams†	4

From Great Britain and Northern Ireland unless otherwise stated.
†Williams' four top three placings were all as runner-up.

THE 10 RIDERS WITH THE MOST AMA SUPERCROSS TITLES

The AMA Supercross Championship was launched in 1974, two years after the start of the National Moto Cross Championships. Seventeen rounds currently constitute the championship which is for 125 and 250cc machines.

	Rider	Titles
1=	Bob Hannah	3
1=	Jeff Stanton	3
3=	Rick Johnson	2
3=	Jeff Ward	2
5=	David Bailey	1
5=	Mark Barnett	1
5=	Mike Bell	1
5=	Jim Ellis	1
5=	Donnie Hansen	1
5=	Pierre Karsmakers	1
5=	Johnny O'Mara	1
5=	Gary Semics	1
5=	Steve Stackable	1
5=	Jim Weinert	1

THE 10 FASTEST WINNING SPEEDS OF THE DAYTONA 200

	Rider*	Bike	Year	Average speed kph	mph
1	Kenny Roberts	Yamaha	1984	182.09	113.84
2	Kenny Roberts	Yamaha	1983	178.52	110.93
3	Scott Russell	Kawasaki	1992	178.10	110.67
4	Graeme Crosby (NZ)	Yamaha	1982	175.58	109.10
5	Steve Baker	Yamaha	1977	175.18	108.85
6	Johnny Cecotto (Ven)	Yamaha	1976	175.05	108.77
7	Dale Singleton	Yamaha	1981	174.65	108.52
8	Kenny Roberts	Yamaha	1978	174.41	108.37
9	Kevin Schwantz	Suzuki	1988	173.49	107.80
10	Dale Singleton	Yamaha	1979	173.31	107.69

From the USA unless otherwise stated.

The Daytona 200, which was first held in 1937, forms a round in the AMA (American Motorcyclist Association) Grand National Dirt Track series. It is raced over 57 laps of the 5.73-km/3.56-mile Daytona International Speedway. In addition to those riders named above the only other non-United States winners have been: Billy Matthews (Canada) 1941, 1950; Jaarno Saarinen (Finland) 1973; and Giacomo Agostini (Italy) 1974.

THE 10 RIDERS WITH THE MOST AMA GRAND NATIONAL SERIES RACE WINS

The AMA (American Motorcyclist Association) was founded in Chicago in 1924. For many years motorcycle sport in the United States evolved around dirt track racing and the AMA Grand National Series, which was launched in 1954, is the premier dirt track series in the world.

	Rider	Years	Race wins
1	Jay Springsteen	1975–85	40
2	Bubba Shobert	1982–88	38
3	Scott Parker	1979–90	37
4	Kenny Roberts	1974–84	33
5	Bart Markel	1960–71	28
6	Joe Leonard	1953–61	27
7=	Dick Mann	1958–72	24
7=	Ricky Graham	1980–86	24
9=	Carol Resweber	1957–62	19
9=	Gary Nixon	1963–74	19
9=	Gary Scott	1972–82	19

THE 10 RIDERS WITH THE MOST INDIVIDUAL MOTO CROSS WORLD TITLES

World Moto Cross Championships have been held since 1947 when the five-man Moto Cross des Nations team championship was launched. The first individual championship was in 1957 when the 500cc class was launched and since then 250cc (1962), 125cc (1975) and sidecar (1980) have been introduced.

	Rider/nationality	Titles
1	Joël Robert (Bel)	6
2=	Roger de Coster (Bel)	5
2=	Eric Geboers (Bel)	5
4=	Hans Bachtöld (Swi)	4
4=	Harry Everts (Bel)	4
4=	Torsten Hallman (Swe)	4
4=	Heikki Mikola (Fin)	4
8=	Georges Jobé (Bel)	3
8=	André Malherbe (Bel)	3
8=	Gennady Moisseyev (USSR)	3
8=	Gaston Rahier (Bel)	3
8=	Dave Thorpe (GB)	3

MOTOR RACING

	Driver/nationality	Year	Wins
1	Ayrton Senna (Bra)	1988	8
2=	Jim Clark (GB)	1963	7
2=	Alain Prost (Fra)	1984	7*
2=	Alain Prost (Fra)	1988	7*
2=	Ayrton Senna (Bra)	1991	7
6=	Alberto Ascari (Ita)	1952	6
6=	Juan Manuel Fangio (Arg)	1954	6
6=	Jim Clark (GB)	1965	6
6=	Jackie Stewart (GB)	1969	6
6=	Jackie Stewart (GB)	1971	6
6=	James Hunt (GB)	1976	6
6=	Mario Andretti (USA)	1978	6
6=	Nigel Mansell (GB)	1987	6*
6=	Ayrton Senna (Bra)	1990	6

Did not win world title that year.

THE 10 DRIVERS WITH THE MOST GRAND PRIX WINS IN A SEASON

In 1988 the Marlboro-McLaren pair of Ayrton Senna and Alain Prost completely dominated the Grand Prix scene by winning 15 of the 16 rounds between them. The only one they did not win was the Italian Grand Prix at Monza, which was won by the Austrian Gerhard Berger in a Ferrari.

THE 10 MANUFACTURERS WITH THE MOST GRAND PRIX WINS IN A SEASON

	Manufacturer	Year	Wins
1	McLaren-Honda	1988	15
2	McLaren-Porsche	1984	12
3	McLaren-Honda	1989	10
4=	Williams-Honda	1986	9
4=	Williams-Honda	1987	9
6=	Lotus-Ford	1978	8
6=	McLaren-Honda	1991	8
8=	Ferrari	1952	7
8=	Ferrari	1953	7
8=	Lotus-Climax	1963	7
8=	Tyrrell-Ford	1971	7
8=	Lotus-Ford	1973	7
8=	Williams-Renault	1991	7

Frenchman Alain Prost, who has amassed more points in a career than any other Formula One driver.

THE 10 DRIVERS WITH THE MOST GRAND PRIX POINTS IN A CAREER*

	Driver/nationality	Years	Points
1	Alain Prost (Fra)	1980–91	699$\frac{1}{2}$
2	Ayrton Senna (Bra)	1985–91	491
3	Nelson Piquet (Bra)	1978–91	485$\frac{1}{2}$
4	Niki Lauda (Aut)	1971–85	420$\frac{1}{2}$
5	Nigel Mansell (GB)	1985–91	361
6	Jackie Stewart (GB)	1965–73	360
7	Carlos Reutemann (Arg)	1972–82	310
8	Graham Hill (GB)	1958–75	289
9	Emerson Fittipaldi (Bra)	1970–80	281
10	Juan Manuel Fangio (Arg)	1950–58	277 $\frac{9}{14}$

To end 1991 season.

The World Drivers' Championship was launched in 1950 and over the years the format has changed allowing, in many cases, for only a certain number of successful drives to be taken into consideration. This Top 10, however, is a list of *all* points obtained, irrespective of whether they counted towards the championship or not. For example, in 1988 Alain Prost scored 105 points but only 87 were taken into account towards the championship.

THE 10 DRIVERS WITH THE MOST WORLD TITLES

	Driver/nationality	Titles
1	Juan Manuel Fangio (Arg)	5
2=	Jack Brabham (Aus)	3
2=	Niki Lauda (Aut)	3
2=	Nelson Piquet (Bra)	3
2=	Alain Prost (Fra)	3
2=	Ayrton Senna (Bra)	3
2=	Jackie Stewart (GB)	3
8=	Alberto Ascari (Ita)	2
8=	Jim Clark (GB)	2
8=	Emerson Fittipaldi (Bra)	2
8=	Graham Hill (GB)	2

THE 10 MANUFACTURERS WITH THE MOST WORLD TITLES

	Manufacturer	Titles
1	Ferrari	8
2=	Lotus	7
2=	McLaren	7
4	Williams	4
5=	Brabham	2
5=	Cooper	2
7=	BRM	1
7=	Matra	1
7=	Tyrrell	1
7=	Vanwall	1

THE 10 DRIVERS WITH THE MOST GRAND PRIX RACES*

	Driver/nationality	Races
1	Riccardo Patrese (Ita)	234
2	Nelson Piquet (Bra)	204
3	Alain Prost (Fra)	183
4=	Graham Hill (GB)	176
4=	Jacques Laffite (Fra)	176
6=	Andrea de Cesaris (Ita)	175
6=	Nigel Mansell (GB)	175
8	Niki Lauda (Aut)	171
9	Michele Alboreto (Ita)	163
10	John Watson (GB)	152

At 26 July 1992.

THE 10 MANUFACTURERS WITH THE MOST GRAND PRIX POINTS*

Based on points obtained in the Constructors' Championship which was launched in 1958.

	Manufacturer	Points†
1	Ferrari	1,730½
2	McLaren	1,690½
3	Lotus	1,343
4	Williams	1,062½
5	Brabham	864
6	Tyrrell	588
7	BRM	433
8	Cooper	342
9	Renault	312
10	Ligier	307

To end 1991 season.
†Half-points are awarded when a race is stopped early.

THE 10 DRIVERS WITH THE MOST GRAND PRIX WINS IN A CAREER *

	Driver/nationality	Years	Wins
1	Alain Prost (Fra)	1981–90	44
2	Ayrton Senna (Bra)	1985–92	33
3	Nigel Mansell (GB)	1985–92	29
4	Jackie Stewart (GB)	1965–73	27
5=	Jim Clark (GB)	1962–68	25
5=	Niki Lauda (Aut)	1974–85	25
7	Juan Manuel Fangio (Arg)	1950–57	24
8	Nelson Piquet (Bra)	1980–91	23
9	Stirling Moss (GB)	1955–61	16
10=	Jack Brabham (Aus)	1959–70	14
10=	Graham Hill (GB)	1962–69	14
10=	Emerson Fittipaldi (Bra)	1970–75	14

Up to and including the German Grand Prix, 26 July 1992.

Ligier's total includes 64 points obtained as Talbot Ligier.

THE 10 DRIVERS WITH THE MOST GRAND PRIX POLE POSITIONS*

	Driver/nationality	Years	Poles
1	Ayrton Senna (Bra)	1985–91	60
2	Jim Clark (GB)	1962–68	33
3	Juan Manuel Fangio (Arg)	1950–58	29
4	Nigel Mansell (GB)	1984–92	26
5=	Niki Lauda (Aut)	1974–78	24
5=	Nelson Piquet (Bra)	1980–87	24
7	Alain Prost (Fra)	1981–89	20
8=	Mario Andretti (USA)	1968–82	18
8=	René Arnoux (Fra)	1979–83	18
10=	Jackie Stewart (GB)	1969–73	17

*Up to and including the German Grand Prix, 26 July 1992.

THE 10 MANUFACTURERS WITH THE MOST GRAND PRIX* WINS

	Manufacturer	Years	Wins
1	Ferrari	1951–90	103
2	McLaren	1968–92	96
3	Lotus	1960–87	79
4	Williams	1979–92	59
5	Brabham	1964–85	35
6	Tyrrell	1971–83	23
7	BRM	1959–72	17
8	Cooper	1958–67	16
9	Renault	1979–83	15
10	Alfa Romeo	1950–51	10

*Up to and including the German Grand Prix, 26 July 1992.

FERRARI'S CENTURY

On 8 July 1990 Frenchman Alain Prost won his home Grand Prix at the Paul Ricard circuit at La Castellet, thereby creating motor racing history as Ferrari became the first manufacturer to win 100 Grands Prix. Ferrari's first win was at Silverstone in 1951 when the Argentinean José Froilan Gonzalez won the British Grand Prix. To date, a total of 30 different men have driven Ferraris to Grand Prix success including the Britons John Surtees (4 wins), Mike Hawthorn (3), Peter Collins (3), Nigel Mansell (3), and Tony Brooks (2).

THE 10 FASTEST FORMULA ONE GRAND PRIX RACES OF ALL TIME

	Grand Prix	Year	Circuit	Driver/car	Average speed kph	mph
1	Italian	1971	Monza	Peter Gethin (BRM)	246.62	150.75
2	Belgian	1970	Spa	Pedro Rodriguez (BRM)	241.31	149.94
3	Belgian	1968	Spa	Bruce McLaren (McLaren)	236.80	147.14
4	Italian	1991	Monza	Nigel Mansell (Williams)	236.75	147.11
5	Italian	1970	Monza	Clay Regazzoni (Ferrari)	236.70	147.08
6	Italian	1990	Monza	Ayrton Senna (McLaren)	236.57	147.00
7	Italian	1969	Monza	Jackie Stewart (Matra)	236.52	146.97
8=	British	1985	Silverstone	Alain Prost (McLaren)	235.42	146.28
8=	Austrian	1987	Österreichring	Nigel Mansell (Williams)	235.42	146.28
10	British	1987	Silverstone	Nigel Mansell (Williams)	235.30	146.21

Brazilian driver Ayrton Senna celebrates his 50th pole position at the 1990 Spanish Grand Prix in Jerez.

THE 10 GRAND PRIX CARS WITH THE MOST STARTS

	Manufacturer	Races
1	Ferrari	499
2	Lotus	453
3	Brabham	392
4	McLaren	372
5	Tyrrell	326
6	Williams	292
7	Ligier	255
8	Arrows/Footwork	217
9	BRM	197
10	March	194

*At 26 July 1992.

THE 10 LEAST SUCCESSFUL GRAND PRIX DRIVERS

	Driver/ nationality	Races without a win
1	Andrea de Cesaris (Ita)	175
2	Jean-Pierre Jarier (Fra)	136
3	Eddie Cheever (USA)	132
4	Derek Warwick (GB)	131
5	Chris Amon (NZ)	96
6	Philippe Alliot (Fra)	94
7	Martin Brundle (GB)	93
8=	Jonathan Palmer (GB)	82
8=	Marc Surer (Swi)	82
10	Stefan Johansson (Swe)	79

*At 26 July 1992.

THE 10 DRIVERS WITH THE MOST BRITISH GRAND PRIX WINS

The British Grand Prix at Silverstone on 13 May 1950 was the first race in the newly instituted World Drivers' Championship and it has remained a round in the championship every year since then. However, the race dates back to 1926 when it was run as the RAC Grand Prix over the famous banked track at Brooklands. It was held eight times prior to 1950 with Donington Park and Silverstone acting as its home. No man won the race twice in those pre-World Championship days. Since becoming a round of the championship it has been raced at three different venues: Silverstone, Brands Hatch and Aintree. Jim Clark and Jack Brabham both won the race at all three circuits, and Brabham's record is perhaps unique because he won the race only three times, with each victory on a different track.

	Driver/nationality	Years	Wins
1	Jim Clark (GB)	1962–65, 1967	5
2=	Alain Prost (Fra)	1983, 1985, 1989–90	4
2=	Nigel Mansell (GB)	1986, 1987, 1991–92	4
4=	Jack Brabham (Aus)	1959–60, 1966	3
4=	Niki Lauda (Aut)	1976, 1982, 1984	3
6=	José Froilan Gonzalez (Arg)	1951, 1954	2
6=	Alberto Ascari (Ita)	1952–53	2
6=	Stirling Moss (GB)	1955, 1957	2
6=	Jackie Stewart (GB)	1969, 1971	2
6=	Emerson Fittipaldi (Bra)	1972, 1975	2

THE 10 LEAST SUCCESSFUL GRAND PRIX CARS

	Manufacturer	Races without a win
1	Arrows/Footwork	217
2	Lola/Larousse Lola	152
3	Osella/Fondmetal	146
4=	Surtees	118
4=	Minardi	118
6	Fittipaldi	104
7=	ATS (Germany)	99
7=	Ensign	99
9	Dallara	72
10	Toleman	57

THE 10 MOST FREQUENTLY USED GRAND PRIX CIRCUITS*

	Circuit	Country	Years first and last used	No. of times used
1	Monza	Italy	1950–92	42
2	Monte Carlo	Monaco	1950–92	39
3	Zandvoort	Holland	1952–85	30
4	Spa-Francorchamps	Belgium	1950–92	27
5	Silverstone	Great Britain	1950–92	26
6	(Old) Nürburgring	Germany	1951–76	22
7	Watkins Glen	USA	1961–80	20
8	Österreichring	Austria	1970–87	18
9=	Buenos Aires	Argentina	1953–81	16
9=	Hockenheim	Germany	1970–92	16

Since the launch of the World Formula One Championship in 1950.

The only time that Monza was not used for the Italian Grand Prix was in 1980 when the race moved to Imola, and was won by Nelson Piquet of Brazil driving a Brabham.

Two other circuits have staged the British Grand Prix since 1950: Brands Hatch, used 15 times, and Aintree, used on five occasions.

THE 10 FASTEST GRANDS PRIX IN 1960 COMPARED WITH THE 10 FASTEST IN 1990*

	Grand Prix	Circuit	1960 Winner's speed kph	mph		Grand Prix	Circuit	1990 Winner's speed kph	mph
1	Indianapolis 500	Indianapolis	223.33	138.77	1	Italian	Monza	236.57	147.00
2	Belgian	Spa	215.06	133.63	2	British	Silverstone	233.76	145.25
3	Italian	Monza	212.53	132.06	3	West German	Hockenheim	227.34	141.26
4	French	Reims	211.13	131.19	4	Belgian	Spa	211.74	131.57
5	Portuguese	Oporto	175.85	109.27	5	San Marino	Imola	202.87	126.06
6	British	Silverstone	174.92	108.69	6	Mexican	Mexico City	198.82	123.54
7	United States	Riverside	159.33	99.00	7	Japanese	Suzuka	198.08	123.08
8	Dutch	Zandvoort	154.93	96.27	8	French	Paul Ricard	195.81	121.67
9	Argentine	Buenos Aires	133.21	82.77	9	Portuguese	Estoril	194.84	121.07
10	Monaco	Monte Carlo	108.60	67.48	10	Brazilian	São Paulo	189.19	117.56

There were only 10 races in 1960; there were 16 in 1990.

The Indianapolis 500 formed part of the World Championship between 1950 and 1960. In 1960 all supercharged cars were restricted to a 750cc engine capacity, while non-supercharged cars could have an upper limit of 2,500cc. In 1990, turbocharged cars had disappeared and all were restricted to normally aspirated engines, with an upper limit of 3,500cc.

THE 10 LONGEST CIRCUITS EVER USED FOR A FORMULA ONE GRAND PRIX

	Circuit	Country	Length* km	miles
1	Pescara	Italy	25.572	15.890
2	(Old) Nürburgring	Germany	22.835	14.189
3	Spa-Francorchamps	Belgium	14.120	8.774
4	Monza	Italy	10.000	6.214
5	Sebring	USA	8.369	5.200
6	Reims	France	8.348	5.187
7	Avus	Germany	8.230	5.157
8	Clermont-Ferrand	France	8.055	5.005
9	Interlagos	Brazil	7.960	4.946
10	Ain-Diab	Morocco	7.603	4.724

Where a circuit would appear twice because of changes, its greatest length only is included.

Pescara, Avus, Sebring and Ain-Diab were all used on one occasion only. The Avus circuit in Germany is perhaps the most unexciting ever used for a Grand Prix race, comprising two stretches of autobahn joined together at each end by banked curves.

THE 10 LONGEST CIRCUITS USED FOR GRANDS PRIX, 1991

	Circuit	Country	Length km	miles
1	Spa-Francorchamps	Belgium	6.939	4.312
2	Hockenheim	Germany	6.803	4.227
3	Suzuka	Japan	5.860	3.641
4	Monza	Italy	5.800	3.604
5	Silverstone	England	5.226	3.247
6	Imola	Italy*	5.041	3.132
7	Montreal	Canada	4.431	2.753
8	Mexico City	Mexico	4.421	2.747
9	Estoril	Portugal	4.350	2.703
10	Interlagos	Brazil	4.324	2.687

Venue for the San Marino Grand Prix.

The shortest circuit is Monaco at 3.328km/2.068 miles.

THE 10 OLDEST WORLD CHAMPIONS OF ALL TIME

	Driver/nationality	Year	Age* yrs	mths
1	Juan Manuel Fangio (Arg)	1957	46	2
2	Giuseppe Farina (Ita)	1950	43	11
3	Jack Brabham (Aus)	1966	40	6
4	Graham Hill (GB)	1968	39	9
5	Mario Andretti (USA)	1978	38	8
6	Niki Lauda (Aut)	1984	35	8
7	Nelson Piquet (Bra)	1987	35	3
8	Alberto Ascari (Ita)	1953	35	1
9	Alain Prost (Fra)	1989	34	8
10	Phil Hill (USA)	1961	34	5

If a driver would have appeared on the list twice, only his oldest age is considered.

THE 10 YOUNGEST WORLD CHAMPIONS OF ALL TIME

	Driver/nationality	Year	Age* yrs	mths
1	Emerson Fittipaldi (Bra)	1972	25	10
2	Niki Lauda (Aut)	1975	26	7
3	Jim Clark (GB)	1963	27	7
4	Jochen Rindt (Aut)	1970	28	6
5	Ayrton Senna (Bra)	1988	28	7
6=	James Hunt (GB)	1976	29	2
6=	Nelson Piquet (Bra)	1981	29	2
8	Mike Hawthorn (GB)	1958	29	6
9	Jody Scheckter (SA)	1979	29	8
10=	John Surtees (GB)	1964	30	8
10=	Alain Prost (Fra)	1985	30	8

If a driver would have appeared on the list twice, only his youngest age is considered.

Whilst Jochen Rindt clinched the world title in October 1970, 28 years and 6 months after his birth, he had, in fact, lost his life a month earlier while practising for the Italian Grand Prix at Monza, and is the only man to win the World Championship posthumously.

THE 10 DRIVERS WITH THE LONGEST FORMULA ONE CAREERS

	Driver/nationality	Career from	to	Length yrs	months
1	Graham Hill (GB)	May 1958	Jan 1975	16	8
2	Jack Brabham (Aus)	Jul 1955	Oct 1970	15	3
3	Riccardo Patrese (Ita)	May 1977	July 1992	15	2
4	Joe Bonnier (Swe)	Jan 1957	Oct 1971	14	9
5	Maurice Trintignant (Fra)	May 1950	Sep 1964	14	4
6	Niki Lauda (Aut)	Aug 1971	Nov 1985	14	3
7	Mario Andretti (USA)	Oct 1968	Sep 1982	13	11
8	Nelson Piquet (Bra)	Jul 1978	Nov 1991	13	4
9	Jacky Ickx (Bel)	Aug 1966	Oct 1979	13	2*
10	Chris Amon (NZ)	Jun 1963	Aug 1976	13	2*

Ickx's career was eight days longer than Amon's.

The Top 10 takes into account the gap between a driver's first and last Grand Prix (to July 1992). Periods of 'retirement' and inactivity are included.

Jack Brabham's Grand Prix career lasted 15 years and three months. The Australian driver retired from Formula One racing in 1970 to concentrate on manufacturing his own cars and was knighted in 1979.

QUIZ

FORMULA ONE GRAND PRIX RACING

1 Nigel Mansell's first Grand Prix was in 1980, but for which manufacturer?

2 When Mansell had the 15th win of his career in 1991 who did he succeed as the most successful English driver of all time?

3 Which ex-world champion was once on the verge of selection for the British Olympic shooting team?

4 Which team had all 11 points deducted from their 1990 Constructors' Championship total because of a false declaration made on their entry form?

5 Who, in 1953, was the first Briton to win a World Championship race?

6 Which Grand Prix was held at Brands Hatch in 1983 and 1985?

7 Which current driver's first Grand Prix win was in the 1981 French Grand Prix driving a Renault?

8 Who was the highest-placed Briton in the World Championship in both 1984 and 1988?

9 Who was the Welshman who lost his life in the 1977 South African Grand Prix?

10 Giuseppe Farina in the 1950 British Grand Prix and Giancarlo Baghetti in the 1961 French Grand Prix are the only men to do what?

THE 10 FASTEST WINNING SPEEDS OF THE INDIANAPOLIS 500

	Driver*	Car	Year	Average speed kph	mph
1	Arie Luyendyk (Hol)	Lola-Chevrolet	1990	299.307	185.981
2	Rick Mears	Chevrolet-Lumina	1991	283.980	176.457
3	Bobby Rahal	March-Cosworth	1986	274.750	170.722
4	Emerson Fittipaldi (Bra)	Penske-Chevrolet	1989	269.695	167.581
5	Rick Mears	March-Cosworth	1984	263.308	163.612
6	Mark Donohue	McLaren-Offenhauser	1972	262.619	162.962
7	Al Unser jr	March-Cosworth	1987	260.995	162.175
8	Tom Sneva	March-Coworth	1983	260.902	162.117
9	Gordon Johncock	Wildcat-Cosworth	1982	260.760	162.029
10	Al Unser	Lola-Cosworth	1978	259.689	161.363

From the United States unless otherwise stated.

The track record, set in the 1990 qualifying competition, is 362.587kph/225.301mph by Emerson Fittipaldi.

THE TOP 10 MONEY-WINNERS AT THE INDIANAPOLIS 500, 1992

	Driver	Car	Prizemoney ($)
1	Al Unser jr	Galmer-Chevrolet	1,244,184
2	Scott Goodyear (Can)	Lola-Chevrolet	609,333
3	Al Unser	Lola-Buick	368,533
4	Eddie Cheever	Lola-Cosworth	271,103
5	Bobby Rahal	Lola-Chevrolet	237,703
6	Danny Sullivan	Galmer-Chevrolet	211,803
7	Paul Boesel (Bra)	Lola-Chevrolet	191,503
8	A.J. Foyt	Lola-Chevrolet	189,883
9	John Andretti	Lola-Chevrolet	186,203
10	John Paul jr	Lola-Buick	171,403

The first Indianapolis 500, known affectionately as the Indy, was held on 30 May 1911 and won by Ray Harroun driving a Marmon Wasp. Then, like today, the race, over 200 laps of the 2½-mile Indianapolis Raceway, formed part of the Memorial Day celebrations.

THE 10 DRIVERS WITH THE MOST WINSTON CUP TITLES

	Driver*	Years	Titles
1	Richard Petty	1964–79	7
2	Dale Earnhardt	1980–90	4
3=	Lee Petty	1954–59	3
3=	David Pearson	1966–69	3
3=	Cale Yarborough	1976–78	3
3=	Darrell Waltrip	1981–85	3
7=	Herb Thomas	1951–53	2
7=	Tim Flock	1952–55	2
7=	Buck Baker	1956–57	2
7=	Ned Jarrett	1961–65	2
7=	Joe Weatherly	1962–63	2

All from the United States.

Yarborough is the only driver to win three successive titles.

THE 10 WINNERS OF THE INDIANAPOLIS 500 WITH THE HIGHEST STARTING POSITIONS

Of the 76 winners of the Indianapolis 500, 44 have started from a position between 1 and 5 on the starting grid. The winners from furthest back in the starting line-up have been:

	Driver*	Year	Starting position
1=	Ray Harroun	1911	28
1=	Louis Meyer	1936	28
3	Fred Frame	1932	27
4	Johnny Rutherford	1974	25
5=	George Souders	1927	22
5=	Kelly Petillo	1935	22
7	L. L. Corum and Joe Boyer	1924	21
8=	Tommy Milton	1921	20
8=	Frank Lockhart	1926	20
8=	Al Unser jr	1987	20

All from the United States.

THE 10 DRIVERS WITH THE MOST WINSTON CUP RACE WINS

	Driver*	Career wins
1	Richard Petty	200
2	David Pearson	105
3	Bobby Allison	84
4	Cale Yarborough	83
5	Darrell Waltrip	81
6	Lee Petty	54
7	Dale Earnhardt	52
8=	Ned Jarrett	50
8=	Junior Johnson	50
10	Herb Thomas	49

All from the United States. To end 1991 season.

The Winston Cup is a season-long series of races organized by the National Association of Stock Car Auto Racing, Inc (NASCAR). Winston Cup races, which take place over enclosed circuits such as Daytona Speedway, are among the most popular motor races in the United States. The series started in 1949 as the Grand National series, but changed its style to the Winston Cup in 1970 when sponsored by the R. J. Reynolds tobacco company, manufacturers of Winston cigarettes.

THE 10 FASTEST WINNING SPEEDS OF THE DAYTONA 500

	Driver*	Car	Year	Average speed kph	mph
1	Davey Allison	Ford	1992	306.211	190.271
2	Buddy Baker	Oldsmobile	1980	285.823	177.602
3	Bill Elliott	Ford	1987	283.668	176.263
4	Bill Elliott	Ford	1985	277.234	172.265
5	Richard Petty	Buick	1981	273.027	169.651
6	Derrike Cope	Chevrolet	1990	266.766	165.761
7	A. J. Foyt	Mercury	1972	259.990	161.550
8	Richard Petty	Plymouth	1966	258.504	160.627†
9	Bobby Allison	Ford	1978	257.060	159.730
10	LeeRoy Yarborough	Ford	1967	254.196	157.950

All from the United States.
†Race reduced to 797km/495 miles.

First held in 1959, the Daytona 500 is raced every February at the Daytona International Speedway, Daytona Beach, Florida. One of the most prestigious races of the NASCAR season, it covers 200 laps of the 2½-mile high-banked oval circuit.

THE TOP 10 DRIVERS IN THE LE MANS 24-HOUR RACE

	Driver/nationality	Years	Wins
1	Jacky Ickx (Bel)	1969–82	6
2	Derek Bell (GB)	1975–87	5
3=	Olivier Gendebien (Bel)	1972–84	4
3=	Henri Pescarolo (Fra)	1972–84	4
5=	Woolf Barnato (GB)	1928–30	3
5=	Luigi Chinetti (Ita/USA)	1932–49	3
5=	Phil Hill (USA)	1958–62	3
5=	Klaus Ludwig (FRG)	1979–85	3
5=	Al Holbert (USA)	1983–87	3
10=	André Rossignol (Fra)	1925–26	2
10=	Sir Henry Birkin (GB)	1929–31	2
10=	Raymond Sommer (Fra)	1932–33	2
10=	Jean-Pierre Wimille (Fra)	1937–39	2
10=	Ivor Bueb (GB)	1955–57	2
10=	Ron Flockhart (GB)	1956–57	2
10=	Jean-Pierre Jaussaud (Fra)	1978–80	2
10=	Hans Stuck (FRG)	1986–87	2

The 1955 Le Mans disaster in which 83 people died.

The Le Mans 24-Hour Race is one of the most demanding in motorsport. The first race, held on 26–27 May 1923, was won by André Lagache and René Leonard in a Chenard and Walcker. Sadly, it was at Le Mans in 1955 that motor racing's worst disaster occurred when Pierre Levagh's Mercedes left the track on the 42nd lap and somersaulted into the crowd. A total of 83 people, including Levagh, were killed, with another 100 injured. It was the one black spot in Le Mans' glorious history.

THE TOP 10 CARS AT LE MANS

	Car	Wins
1	Porsche	12
2	Ferrari	9
3	Jaguar	7
4	Bentley	5
5=	Alfa Romeo	4
5=	Ford	4
7	Matra-Simca	3
8=	Bugatti	2
8=	La Lorraine	2
8=	Mercedes-Benz	2

THE TOP 10 MONTE CARLO RALLY WINNING CARS*

	Car	Wins
1	Lancia	12
2=	Hotchkiss	6
2=	Renault	6
4=	Ford	4
4=	Porsche	4
6	Mini-Cooper	3
7=	Citroën	2
7=	Delahaye	2
7=	Fiat	2
7=	Opel	2
7=	Saab	2

Up to and including 1992.

The Monte Carlo Rally has been run since 1911 (with breaks in 1913–23, 1940–48, 1957 and 1974). The appearance of Hotchkiss in 2nd place is perhaps surprising, but it won the rally six times between 1932 and 1950.

The RAC International Rally of Great Britain was first held in 1927, but it has been recognized as an international event by the FIA only since 1951, and the Top 10 includes only winners since that year.

THE TOP 10 RAC RALLY WINNING CARS

	Car	Years	Wins
1	Ford*	1959–79	10
2	Lancia	1969–91	6
3	Saab	1960–71	5
4	Audi	1981–83	3
5=	Jaguar	1951–53	2
5=	Volvo	1963–64	2
5=	Peugeot	1984–86	2
8=	Allard Cadillac	1952	1
8=	Triumph	1954	1
8=	Standard	1955	1
8=	Aston Martin	1956	1
8=	Sunbeam	1958	1
8=	Mini-Cooper	1965	1
8=	Talbot	1980	1
8=	Mitsubishi	1989	1
8=	Toyota	1990	1

The Escort RS provided Ford with 8 of its 10 wins, with the Zephyr and Cortina-Lotus supplying the others.

THE TURBOCHARGER

In 1977 Renault introduced the first turbocharged car, the RS01. Its many critics felt such a power-boosting aid was not necessary, and they must have been feeling smug when the car ground to a halt on lap 17 of the British Grand Prix at Silverstone as a result of turbocharger failure. But Renault persevered and two years later, after further developments, they enjoyed their first success when Jean-Pierre Jabouille took the chequered flag at the French Grand Prix with fellow Frenchman, Alain Prost, in another of Renault's turbocharged cars in third place.

The motor racing world took notice and soon other manufacturers were following suit; notably Ferrari who, in 1982, were the first manufacturer to win the Constructors' Cup with a turbocharged car. Within a few years all manufacturers were powering their cars with turbocharged units including the last bastion of normally aspirated engines, Tyrrell. Within 10 seasons of the introduction of the RS01 every manufacturer in Formula One was following Renault's lead.

What was the magical turbocharger that caused such a transformation in the world of Grand Prix racing? It was a small turbine compressor located between the engine and gearbox, powered by the exhaust gases. The original RS01's engine was a twin overhead cam V6, 1,492cc engine which could produce 510bhp at 11,000rpm. But such was the technical advancement that it was soon capable of producing up to 1,300bhp.

Because of the improved performance and resulting faster speeds, the sport's governing body saw a need to clamp down, and in 1986 they announced plans for the phasing out of turbocharged engines, stating that the 1988 season was to be the last for these high-performance cars. From then on it was a return to normally aspirated 3,500cc engines and the end of the turbocharger.

Although the turbocharger had been criticized right from the start, Renault knew they had a winner and pressed ahead their advantage. Following their lead, all but 11 of the 111 Grand Prix races between 1982 and 1988 were won by turbocharged cars. The last non-turbocharged winner prior to its demise in 1988 was Michele Alboreto's Tyrrell-Ford in the 1983 Detroit Grand Prix.

OLYMPIC GAMES

James Connolly of the United States became the first Olympic champion in 1896 when he took the hop, step and jump (now triple jump) first prize which, in those days, was a silver medal. Runners-up used to receive bronze medals and 3rd-placed athletes were not rewarded for their efforts. However, all Olympic records consider the 1st, 2nd and 3rd athletes in 1896 to have received gold, silver and bronze medals.

THE TOP 10 GOLD MEDAL WINNING COUNTRIES AT THE SUMMER OLYMPICS

	Country	Years	Gold medals
1	USA	1896–1992	783
2	USSR/CIS	1952–92	440
3	Germany/West Germany	1896–1992	190
4	Great Britain	1896–1992	179
5	France	1896–1992	161
6=	East Germany	1968–88	153
6=	Italy	1900–92	153
8	Hungary	1900–92	135
9	Sweden	1900–92	132
10	Finland	1906–92	98

THE TOP 10 GOLD MEDAL WINNING COUNTRIES AT THE WINTER OLYMPICS

	Country	Years	Gold medals
1	USSR/CIS	1956–92	88
2	Norway	1924–92	63
3	USA	1924–92	47
4	East Germany	1968–88	39
5	Sweden	1924–92	37
6=	Finland	1924–92	36
6=	Germany/West Germany	1936–92	36
8	Austria	1924–92	34
9	Switzerland	1924–92	24
10	Italy	1948–92	18
15	*Great Britain*	*1936–84*	*6*

John Curry of Great Britain on his way to gold at the 1976 Winter Olympics in Innsbruck.

The first Winter Olympics were held at Chamonix in 1924 and have been held in the same years as the Summer Games. However, the next Winter Olympics will be in 1994 and quadrennially thereafter, between each Summer Olympiad.

Great Britain's six Winter Olympics gold medallists have been:
1936 Ice hockey team
1952 Jeanette Altwegg (figure skating)
1964 Tony Nash and Robin Dixon (two-man bobsleigh)
1976 John Curry (figure skating)
1980 Robin Cousins (figure skating)
1984 Jayne Torvill and Christopher Dean (ice dance)
Madge Syers also won a figure skating gold medal in 1908, but the event formed part of the Summer programme at the time.

THE 10 MOST SUCCESSFUL COUNTRIES AT THE SUMMER OLYMPICS

	Country	Years	gold	Medals silver	bronze	Total
1	USA	1896–1992	783	594	512	1,889
2	USSR/CIS	1952–92	440	361	328	1,129
3	Germany/West Germany	1896–1992	190	228	234	652
4	Great Britain	1896–1992	179	226	219	624
5	France	1896–1992	161	172	193	526
6	Sweden	1900–92	132	146	173	451
7	Italy	1900–92	153	126	132	411
8	East Germany	1968–88	153	129	127	409
9	Hungary	1896–1992	135	124	143	402
10	Finland	1906–92	98	77	112	287

THE 10 SPORTS TO APPEAR AT THE MOST SUMMER OLYMPICS*

	Sport†	Appearances
1=	Athletics	22
1=	Fencing	22
1=	Gymnastics	22
1=	Swimming	22
5=	Cycling (1904)	21
5=	Rowing (1896)	21
5=	Wrestling (1900)	21
8=	Association football (1896, 1932)	20
8=	Shooting (1904, 1928)	20
8=	Yachting (1896, 1904)	20

*The 1906 Intercalated Games are excluded.
†Figures in brackets indicate the year(s) the sport was not included.

American athlete Ray Ewry, whose Olympic career spanned three Games and brought him a record 10 gold medals.

A total of 25 sports have appeared at the Olympic Games, the last new ones being baseball and badminton, introduced in 1992. There have been 11 discontinued sports, including golf, cricket, polo, and rugby union. The discontinued sport that appeared most often was tug-of-war, which formed part of the track and field programme six times. Polo appeared five times. Rugby was last played in 1924 and the 'reigning' champions are, perhaps surprisingly, the United States.

THE TOP 10 INDIVIDUAL GOLD MEDAL WINNERS AT THE SUMMER OLYMPICS

Spitz's seven gold medals in 1972 is a record number for medals won at one celebration.

All Ewry's golds were in the standing jumps – long jump, high jump and triple jump – that once formed part of the track and field competition. Born in 1873, Ewry contracted polio as a boy and seemed destined to be confined to a wheelchair for life but, through a determined effort to overcome his handicap, he exercised and developed his legs to such a remarkable degree that he went on to become an outstanding athlete.

	Medallist/nationality	Sport	Years	Gold medals
1	Ray Ewry (USA)	Athletics	1900–08	10
2=	Paavo Nurmi (Fin)	Athletics	1920–28	9
2=	Larissa Latynina (USSR)	Gymnastics	1956–64	9
2=	Mark Spitz (USA)	Swimming	1968–72	9
5=	Sawao Kato (Jap)	Gymnastics	1968–76	8
5=	Carl Lewis (USA)	Athletics	1984–92	8
7=	Aladár Gerevich (Hun)	Fencing	1932–60	7
7=	Viktor Chukarin (USSR)	Gymnastics	1952–56	7
7=	Boris Shakhlin (USSR)	Gymnastics	1956–64	7
7=	Vera Čáslavská (Cze)	Gymnastics	1964–68	7
7=	Nikolay Andrianov (USSR)	Gymnastics	1972–80	7

THE 10 MOST SUCCESSFUL COUNTRIES AT THE WINTER OLYMPICS

	Country	Years	gold	Medals silver	bronze	Total
1	USSR/CIS	1956–92	88	63	67	218
2	Norway	1924–92	63	66	59	188
3	USA	1924–92	47	51	36	134
4	Austria	1924–92	34	45	40	119
5	Finland	1924–92	36	44	37	117
6	East Germany	1968–88	39	36	35	110
7	Germany/West Germany	1938–92	36	36	29	101
8	Sweden	1924–92	37	25	34	96
9	Switzerland	1924–92	24	25	27	76
10	Canada	1924–92	16	16	19	51
16	Great Britain	1924–84	6	4	10	20

THE TOP 10 INDIVIDUAL GOLD MEDAL WINNERS AT THE WINTER OLYMPICS

Heiden's five medals in 1980 is a record for one Games. He was the United States' *only* individual gold medallist in 1980 because the Americans boycotted the Summer Games in Moscow. Skoblikova, in 1964, was the first person to win four gold medals at one Winter Olympics.

	Medallist/nationality	Event	Years	Gold medals
1	Lydia Skoblikova (USSR)	Speed skating	1960–64	6
2=	Clas Thunberg (Nor)	Speed skating	1924–28	5
2=	Eric Heiden (USA)	Speed skating	1980	5
2=	Matti Nykänen (Fin)	Nordic skiing	1984–88	5
5=	Ivar Ballangrud (Nor)	Speed skating	1928–36	4
5=	Yevgeny Grischin (USSR)	Speed skating	1956–60	4
5=	Sixten Jernberg (Swe)	Nordic skiing	1956–64	4
5=	Galina Kulakova (USSR)	Nordic skiing	1972–76	4
5=	Thomas Wassberg (Swe)	Nordic skiing	1980–88	4
5=	Gunde Svan (Swe)	Nordic skiing	1984–88	4

THE TOP 10 MEDAL WINNERS IN A SUMMER OLYMPICS CAREER

	Medallist/nationality	Sport	Years	gold	Medals silver	bronze	Total
1	Larissa Latynina (USSR)	Gymnastics	1956–64	9	5	4	18
2	Nikolay Andrianov (USSR)	Gymnastics	1972–80	7	5	3	15
3=	Edoardo Mangiarotti (Ita)	Fencing	1936–60	6	5	2	13
3=	Takashi Ono (Jap)	Gymnastics	1952–64	5	4	4	13
3=	Boris Shakhlin (USSR)	Gymnastics	1956–64	7	4	2	13
6=	Paavo Nurmi (Fin)	Athletics	1920–28	9	3	0	12
6=	Sawao Kato (Jap)	Gymnastics	1968–76	8	3	1	12
8=	Carl Osborn (USA)	Shooting	1912–24	5	4	2	11
8=	Viktor Chukarin (USSR)	Gymnastics	1952–56	7	3	1	11
8=	Vera Čáslavská (Cze)	Gymnastics	1964–68	7	4	0	11
8=	Mark Spitz (USA)	Swimming	1968–72	9	1	1	11

LARISSA LATYNINA'S 18 MEDALS

	Medal	Event
1956	Gold	All-round
	Gold	Vault
	Gold	Team
	Gold	Floor
	Silver	Asymmetric bars
	Bronze	Team exercise with portable apparatus
1960	Gold	All-round
	Gold	Floor
	Gold	Team
	Silver	Asymmetric bars
	Silver	Beam
	Bronze	Vault
1964	Gold	Floor
	Gold	Team
	Silver	All-round
	Silver	Vault
	Bronze	Asymmetric bars
	Bronze	Beam

The only discipline at which Latynina did *not* win a medal between 1956 and 1964 was on the beam in 1956, when she came 4th.

THE 10 MOST GOLD MEDALS WON BY ONE COUNTRY AT ONE SUMMER OLYMPICS

	Country	Venue	Year	Golds
1	USA	Los Angeles	1984	83
2=	USA	St Louis	1904	80
2=	USSR	Moscow	1980	80
4	Great Britain	London	1908	56
5	USSR	Seoul	1988	55
6	USSR	Munich	1972	50
7	USSR	Montreal	1976	49
8	East Germany	Moscow	1980	47
9=	USA	Paris	1924	45
9=	USA	Mexico City	1968	45
9=	CIS	Barcelona	1992	45

East Germany's total in 1980 is the highest by a nation *not* topping the medal table.

THE 10 MOST SUCCESSFUL COUNTRIES AT ONE SUMMER OLYMPICS

	Country	Venue	Year	gold	Medals silver	bronze	Total
1	USA	St Louis	1904	80	86	72	238
2	USSR	Moscow	1980	80	69	46	195
3	USA	Los Angeles	1984	83	61	30	174
4	Great Britain	London	1908	56	50	39	145
5	USSR	Seoul	1988	55	31	46	132
6	East Germany	Moscow	1980	47	37	42	126
7	USSR	Montreal	1976	49	41	35	125
8	CIS	Barcelona	1992	45	38	29	112
9	USA	Barcelona	1992	37	34	37	108
10	USA	Mexico City	1968	45	28	34	107

The Soviet Union's total at Seoul in 1988 is the highest by a country *not* competing on home soil. East Germany's 126 in 1980 is the highest total of a country *not* heading the medal list. The only other nations with 100 medals at one Games are France (1900 Paris) and East Germany (1988 Seoul), both of whom had 102, USSR (1960 Rome) with 103 and USA (1932 Los Angeles) with 104.

THE TOP 10 INDIVIDUAL MEDAL WINNERS AT THE WINTER OLYMPICS

	Medallist/nationality	Sport	Years	gold	Medals silver	bronze	Total
1=	Sixten Jernberg (Swe)	Nordic skiing	1956–64	4	3	2	9
1=	Raisa Smetanina (USSR)	Nordic skiing	1976–88	3	5	1	9
3=	Galina Kulakova (USSR)	Nordic skiing	1968–80	4	2	2	8
3=	Karin Kania (*née* Enke) (GDR)	Speed skating	1980–88	3	4	1	8
5=	Clas Thunberg (Nor)	Speed skating	1924–28	5	1	1	7
5=	Ivar Ballangrud (Nor)	Speed skating	1928–36	4	2	1	7
5=	Veikko Hakulinen (Fin)	Nordic skiing	1952–60	3	3	1	7
5=	Eero Mantyranta (Fin)	Nordic skiing	1960–68	3	2	2	7
9=	Johan Gröttumsbråten (Nor)	Nordic skiing	1924–32	3	1	2	6
9=	Eugenio Monti (Ita)	Bobsleighing	1956–68	2	2	2	6
9=	Lydia Skoblikova (USSR)	Speed skating	1960–64	6	0	0	6
9=	Andrea Ehrig (*née* Mitsherlich; formerly Schöne) (GDR)	Speed skating	1976–88	1	4	1	6
9=	Gunde Svan (Swe)	Nordic skiing	1984–88	4	1	1	6

The only person to win gold medals at both the Summer and Winter Games is Eddie Eagan of the United States. After winning the 1920 light-heavyweight boxing title he then went on to win a gold medal as a member of the American four-man bob team in 1932. A fellow team-member on that day was Clifford 'Tippy' Gray who gained fame as the songwriter responsible for such hits as *If You Were the Only Girl in the World*.

THE TOP 10 OLYMPIC MEDAL WINNING COUNTRIES THAT HAVE NEVER WON A GOLD MEDAL

	Country	gold	Medals silver	bronze	Total
1	Mongolia	0	5	8	13
2=	Chile	0	6	2	8
2=	Philippines	0	1	7	8
4	Nigeria	0	3	4	7
5=	Colombia	0	2	4	6
5=	Latvia	0	4	2	6
7	Puerto Rico	0	1	4	5
8=	Lebanon	0	2	2	4
8=	Ghana	0	1	3	4
8=	Taipei	0	2	2	4
8=	Thailand	0	1	3	4

Eight of Mongolia's 13 medals have been won at wrestling.

THE TOP 10 SUMMER OLYMPICS FOR DISTRIBUTION OF GOLD MEDALS AMONG THE MOST COUNTRIES

	Venue	Year	Countries winning gold medals
1	Barcelona	1992	37
2	Seoul	1988	31
3	Mexico City	1968	30
4	Amsterdam	1928	28
5	Helsinki	1952	27
6=	Tokyo	1964	26
6=	Montreal	1976	26
8=	Melbourne	1956	25
8=	Munich	1972	25
8=	Moscow	1980	25
8=	Los Angeles	1984	25

The inaugural Games in 1896 saw 10 of the 13 competing countries win gold medals, equivalent to 76.9 per cent, the best of all Summer Olympics.

THE TOP 10 COUNTRIES AT THE SUMMER OLYMPICS*

	Country	Gold medals	Population per gold medal
1	Finland	98	51,010
2	Sweden	132	64,848
3	Estonia	7	69,143
4	Hungary	135	78,148
5	Norway	44	96,364
6	East Germany	153	108,985
7	New Zealand	27	125,556
8	Denmark	34	151,176
9	Switzerland	41	163,659
10	Australia	78	219,103
15	*Great Britain*	*179*	*311,179*

*Based on ratio of gold medals won to population.

Liechtenstein has won two Winter Olympic gold medals, which represents one medal per 13,699 people living in the country.

THE 10 SUMMER OLYMPICS TO ATTRACT THE MOST COMPETING COUNTRIES

	Venue	Year	Competing countries
1	Barcelona	1992	172
2	Seoul	1988	159
3	Los Angeles	1984	141
4	Munich	1972	122
5	Mexico City	1968	112
6	Tokyo	1964	93
7	Montreal	1976	92
8	Rome	1960	83
9	Moscow	1980	81
10	Helsinki	1952	69

Had there not been boycotts of the 1980 and 1984 Games, both would have figured higher in the Top 10. The first modern Games in 1896 attracted competitors from just 13 nations.

OLYMPIC GAMES

THE 10 SUMMER OLYMPICS ATTENDED BY THE MOST COMPETITORS

	Venue	Year	Countries represented	Competitors
1	Barcelona	1992	172	13,222
2	Seoul	1988	159	9,101
3	Munich	1972	122	7,156
4	Los Angeles	1984	141	7,058
5	Montreal	1976	92	6,085
6	Mexico City	1968	112	5,530
7	Rome	1960	83	5,346
8	Moscow	1980	81	5,326
9	Tokyo	1964	93	5,140
10	Helsinki	1952	69	4,925

The first Games in 1896 were attended by just 311 competitors, all of them men. Women took part for the first time four years later at the Paris Games.

THE 10 SPORTS TO WIN MOST OLYMPIC MEDALS FOR GREAT BRITAIN

	Sport	Medals
1	Athletics	179
2	Swimming/diving	65
3	Shooting	46
4=	Lawn tennis	44
4=	Cycling	44
6	Boxing	43
7	Rowing	39
8	Yachting	32
9	Equestrianism	21
10	Wrestling	17

THE 10 SPORTS TO WIN MOST OLYMPIC GOLD MEDALS FOR GREAT BRITAIN

	Sport	Gold medals
1	Athletics	48
2	Rowing	18
3	Lawn tennis	16
4	Yachting	15
5	Swimming/diving	14
6	Shooting	13
7	Boxing	12
8	Cycling	9
9	Equestrianism	5
10	Water polo	4

QUIZ

OLYMPIC GREATS

1 Which winner of nine Olympic gold medals planned a comeback in 1990 at the age of 40?

2 Which gymnast's floor routine to the *Mexican Hat Dance* at the 1968 Mexico Olympics was one of the all-time memorable moments in Olympic history?

3 The sister of which 1980 Olympic champion was the women's world road race cycling champion that same year?

4 Which post-war winner of several Olympic gold medals has the forenames Frederick Carlton?

5 Gina Hemphill was one of the torchbearers in the Coliseum at the start of the 1984 Olympics. Her grandfather was an all-time Olympic great. Name him.

6 Who is the only swimmer to win the same event at three consecutive Olympics?

7 One of 22 children, she suffered from polio, scarlet fever, and double pneumonia as a child and at the age of six lost the use of her left leg and had to wear a brace. Fourteen years later she won the sprint double at the Olympics. Who was she?

8 He won a record-equalling three Olympic rowing gold medals in the 1920s and was the father of one of Hollywood's most graceful ladies. Who is he?

9 At what weight did Floyd Patterson win his Olympic gold medal in 1952?

10 Who won two Olympic marathon titles, one barefooted and one in shoes?

THE 10 MOST SUCCESSFUL COUNTRIES AT THE 1988 SEOUL PARALYMPICS

	Country	gold	Medals silver	bronze	Total
1	USA	92	91	85	268
2	West Germany	77	64	48	189
3	Great Britain	62	66	51	179
4	Canada	54	42	57	153
5	France	45	48	49	142
6	Sweden	42	38	22	102
7=	Korea	40	35	19	94
7=	Austria	23	34	37	94
9	Holland	30	23	29	82
10	Poland	22	25	34	81

The 8th Paralympics took place in Seoul after the 1988 Summer Olympic Games. In the six-day event (15–20 October) a total of 48 countries won 2,185 medals (729 gold, 729 silver and 727 bronze).

The women's 800 metres wheelchair event at the Seoul Paralympics.

THE 10 SPORTS TO WIN MOST MEDALS AT THE 1988 SEOUL PARALYMPICS

	Sport	Medals
1	Athletics	1,029
2	Swimming	768
3	Table tennis	111
4	Shooting	69
5	Weightlifting	43
6	Fencing	42
7	Archery	27
8	Judo	24
9	Cycling	21
10	Lawn bowling	18

The sports at which fewest medals were awarded were soccer and snooker, with three each.

POLO

	Team	Wins
1=	Stowell Park	5
1=	Tramontana	5
3=	Cowdray Park	3
3=	Pimms	3
5=	Casarejo	2
5=	Falcons	2
5=	Jersey Lillies	2
5=	Southfield	2
5=	Windsor Park	2
5=	Woolmer's Park	2

The Open, which was first held in 1956, is played at Cowdray Park, Sussex.

The 1989 British Open at Cowdray Park, Sussex.

RACKETS

	Champion/nationality	Years title held	Total years
1	Geoffrey Atkins (GB)	1954–71	17
2=	Peter Latham (GB)	1887–1902	15
2=	Jock Souter (USA)	1913–28	15
4	L. C. Mitchell (GB)	1846–60	14
5	David Milford (GB)	1937–47	10
6=	Thomas Pitman (GB)	1825–34	9
6=	William Gray (GB)	1866–75	9
6=	Joseph Gray (GB)	1878–87	9
9	J. Jamsetji (Ind)	1903–11	8
10	James Dear (GB)	1947–54	7

The World Championship was inaugurated in 1820 and has been held on a challenge basis ever since.

REAL TENNIS

	Champion/nationality	Years title held	Total years
1	Edmond Barré (Fra)	1829–62	33
2	Joseph Barcellon (Fra)	1785–1816	31
3	Pierre Etchebaster (Fra)	1928–54	26
4	Raymond Masson (Fra)	1765–85	20
5	George Lambert (GB)	1871–85	14
6	Fred Covey (GB)	1916–28	12
7=	Clergé (Fra)	c1740–50	10
7=	Philip Cox (GB)	1819–29	10
7=	Peter Latham GB)	1895–1905	10
7=	Northrup Knox (USA)	1959–69	10

This is the oldest continuous world championship, dating back to c1740 when the first champion was the Frenchman Clergé (first name never established).

ROWING

THE 10 FASTEST WINNING TIMES FOR THE OXFORD AND CAMBRIDGE BOAT RACE

	Crew	Year	Winning distance (lengths)	Time min	sec
1	Oxford	1984	3¾	16	45
2	Oxford	1976	6½	16	58
3	Oxford	1991	4¼	16	59
4	Oxford	1985	4¾	17	11
5	Oxford	1990	2¼	17	15
6=	Oxford	1974	5½	17	35
6=	Oxford	1988	5½	17	35
8	Cambridge	1948	5	17	50
9=	Cambridge	1971	10	17	58
9=	Cambridge	1986	7	17	58

The Oxford and Cambridge Boat Race was first rowed at Henley in 1829, but the course from Putney to Mortlake (6.78 km/4 miles 374 yards) has been used since 1843 (Mortlake to Putney in 1846, 1856 and 1863). The course time has steadily improved from the 25 minutes or more of the early years to the record-breaking times of the post-war period. Cambridge has won 69 times, Oxford 68 and there has been one dead-heat (1877). The largest margin was the 20 lengths by which Cambridge won in 1900. Cambridge sank in 1859 and 1978 and Oxford in 1925; both crews sank in 1912 and Oxford won when the race was re-rowed a week later; Oxford sank near the start in 1951 and the race took place two days later, with Cambridge the winner.

The 1990 Boat Race, which Oxford won in the 5th fastest time ever and with the heaviest crew of all time.

THE 10 MOST SUCCESSFUL OLYMPIC COUNTRIES

A member of the winning United States eights team at the 1924 Paris Olympics was Benjamin Spock who later became famous as the 'baby expert' and whose book *The Common Sense Book of Baby and Child Care* has sold more than 39,200,000 copies worldwide.

	Country	gold	Medals silver	bronze	Total
1	USA	30	22	16	68
2	West Germany	21	15	15	51
3	East Germany	33	7	8	48
4	USSR/CIS	12	20	12	44
5	Great Britain	18	15	6	39
6	Italy	12	11	9	32
7	Romania	10	10	7	27
8	France	4	13	9	26
9	Canada	7	8	9	24
10	Switzerland	4	7	9	20

THE 10 HEAVIEST OXFORD AND CAMBRIDGE BOAT RACE CREWS

	Crew	Year	Average weight kg	lb
1	Oxford	1990	94.3	208
2	Oxford	1988	94.1	207½
3	Cambridge	1989	93.6	206⅛
4	Oxford	1983	92.9	204¾
5	Oxford	1987	91.7	202¼
6	Cambridge	1983	89.6	197½
7	Oxford	1986	89.3	196⅞
8	Oxford	1976	89.2	196⅝
9	Oxford	1982	88.8	195⅞
10	Oxford	1989	88.6	195½

THE 10 LIGHTEST OXFORD AND CAMBRIDGE BOAT RACE CREWS

	Crew	Year	Average weight kg	lb
1	Cambridge	1854	68.3	150½
2	Cambridge	1862	69.5	153⅛
3	Oxford	1854	69.9	154
4=	Oxford	1849*	70.1	154⅝
4=	Oxford	1856	70.1	154⅝
6	Cambridge	1839	70.2	154¾
7	Cambridge	1829	70.5	155½
8	Cambridge	1849*	70.8	156
9	Cambridge	1845	71.0	156⅝
10	Cambridge	1842	71.1	156¾

The first of the two races held that year.

THE 10 HEAVIEST COXSWAINS IN THE OXFORD AND CAMBRIDGE BOAT RACE

	Coxswain	Crew	Year	Result	kg	lb
1	F. J. Richards	Oxford	1845	Lost	68.0	150
2=	J. M. Croker	Cambridge	1841	Won	67.1	148
2=	C. J. Soanes	Oxford	1849*	Lost	67.1	148
2=	G. Booth	Cambridge	1849†	Lost	67.1	148
5	G. Booth	Cambridge	1849*	Won	66.7	147
6	A. T. W. Shadwell	Oxford	1842	Won	65.3	144
7=	E. W. L. Davies	Oxford	1836	Lost	64.9	143
7=	T. H. Marshall	Oxford	1854	Won	64.9	143
9	W. W. Ffooks	Oxford	1839	Lost	64.4	142
10	J. P. M. Denny	Cambridge	1956	Won	63.5	140

The first of the two races held that year.
†Second race.*

THE 10 LIGHTEST COXSWAINS IN THE OXFORD AND CAMBRIDGE BOAT RACE

	Coxswain	Crew	Year	Result	kg	lb
1=	Francis H. Archer	Cambridge	1862	Lost	32.7	72
1=	Hart P. V. Massey	Oxford	1939	Lost	32.7	72
3	Francis H. Archer	Cambridge	1863	Lost	36.1	79
4	Henrietta Shaw	Cambridge	1985	Lost	39.0	86
5=	Francis H. Archer	Cambridge	1864	Lost	40.8	90½
5=	F. T. H. Eyre	Oxford	1903	Lost	40.8	90
5=	C. H. Roberts	Cambridge	1972	Won	40.8	90
8	F. M. Beaumont	Oxford	1877	Dead heat	41.1	90½
9	Sue Brown	Oxford	1981	Won	41.7	92
10=	G. H. Baker	Cambridge	1886	Won	42.2	93
10=	Carol Burton	Cambridge	1986	Won	42.2	93

THE 10 COLLEGES THAT HAVE PROVIDED THE MOST OXFORD AND CAMBRIDGE BOAT RACE OARSMEN

	College	Univ	Oarsmen
1	First and Third Trinity	Cambridge	378
2	Magdalen	Oxford	156
3	Jesus	Cambridge	152
4	Christ Church	Oxford	144
5	Lady Margaret	Cambridge	136
6	Trinity Hall (St John's)	Cambridge	134
7	New	Oxford	124
8	Brasenose	Oxford	102
9	Balliol	Oxford	97
10	University	Oxford	82

QUIZ

WATER SPORTS

1 At which water sport have Englishmen Tom Pickering, Dave Thomas, Dave Roper and Kevin Ashurst all been world champions?

2 Which races, held every two years, take place in the Channel, at Cowes, in the Solent, and around Fastnet Rock?

3 Which ex-Formula One racing driver lost his life powerboat racing in the 1980s?

4 Which event is regarded as the Blue Riband of amateur sculling?

5 In what sport was a new world record of three buoys on a 10.25-metre line established in 1989?

6 What is the longest distance contested by swimmers at the Olympic Games?

7 Name the Englishman who won four Commonwealth Games diving gold medals in 1978 and 1982.

8 In a water polo match, how many per side are allowed in the water at any one time?

9 Who was the first men's 50 metres freestyle Olympic swimming champion?

10 Why did Marjorie Gestring enter the Olympic record books when winning the springboard diving gold medal in 1936?

RUGBY LEAGUE

THE TOP 10 RUGBY LEAGUE TEAMS

This list is based on the number of wins in the major competitions: Challenge Cup, Regal/John Player Trophy, Division 1 and 2 Premierships, Championship play-off (1906–73), Divisions 1 and 2 (since 1973), and the Lancashire/Yorkshire Cup.

	Club	Titles
1	Wigan	53
2	Leeds	34
3	St Helens	27
4=	Huddersfield	26
4=	Widnes	26
6	Bradford Northern	23
7	Warrington	22
8	Oldham	21
9=	Hull	17
9=	Hull Kingston Rovers	17
9=	Wakefield Trinity	17

QUIZ

RUGBY LEAGUE RECORD-BREAKERS

1 The record attendance for a league game was set on 27 March 1959 when 47,747 packed into which ground?
2 Who played in eight Challenge Cup finals between 1941 and 1952 with Leeds, Bradford and Featherstone?
3 The 1989 Charity Shield between Widnes and Wigan was played in front of a record 17,263 fans. At which soccer ground was the match played?
4 Before Martin Offiah on 10 May 1992, only two men had scored 10 or more tries in a senior match. Name either.
5 The BBC2 Floodlit Trophy was held between 1965 and 1980. Who won it a record four times?
6 Who was the last man to appear and score in all of his club's matches in a season?
7 Name the ex-Welsh rugby union international who kicked a rugby league record 221 goals in the 1972–73 season.
8 Who did Australia beat 70–8 in 1988 to register the biggest score in an international?
9 Who made a record 239 consecutive appearances for Widnes between May 1977 and September 1982?
10 Name the two teams involved in the highest-scoring Challenge Cup final, which produced 52 points.

THE 10 HIGHEST WINNING SCORES IN BRITISH RUGBY LEAGUE HISTORY

	Match (winners first)	Date	Competition	Score
1	Huddersfield v Swinton Park Rangers	28 Feb 1914	Challenge Cup	119–2
2	Wigan v Flimby and Fothergill	15 Feb 1925	Challenge Cup	116–0
3	St Helens v Carlisle	14 Sep 1986	Lancashire Cup	112–0
4	St Helens v Trafford Borough	15 Sep 1991	Lancashire Cup	104–12
5	Leeds v Coventry	12 Apr 1913	League	102–0
6	Hull Kingston Rovers v Nottingham City	19 Aug 1990	Yorkshire Cup	100–6
7	Castleford v Huddersfield	18 Sep 1988	Yorkshire Cup	94–12
8=	Rochdale Hornets v Runcorn Highfield	5 Nov 1989	Division 2	92–0
8=	Leigh v Keighley	30 Apr 1986	Division 2	92–2
8=	Wigan v Runcorn Highfield	13 Nov 1988	John Player Trophy	92–2
8=	Australians v Bramley	9 Nov 1921	Tour Match	92–7
8=	Hull Kingston Rovers v Whitehaven	18 Mar 1990	Division 2	92–10

The highest score in the First Division is Leeds' 90–0 victory over Barrow on 11 February 1990.

THE TOP 10 POINTS-SCORERS IN A MATCH

	Player	Match	Date	Points
1	George West	Hull Kingston Rovers *v* Brookland Rovers	4 Mar 1905	53
2	Jim Sullivan	Wigan *v* Flimby and Fothergill	14 Feb 1925	44
3	Sammy Lloyd	Castleford *v* Millom	16 Sep 1973	43
4=	Paul Loughlin	St Helens *v* Carlisle	14 Sep 1986	40
4=	Martin Offiah	Wigan *v* Leeds	10 May 1992	40
6=	James Lomas	Salford *v* Liverpool City	2 Feb 1907	39
6=	Major Holland	Huddersfield *v* Swinton Park Rangers	28 Feb 1914	39
8=	John Woods	Leigh *v* Blackpool Borough	11 Sep 1977	38
8=	Bob Beardmore	Castleford *v* Barrow	22 Mar 1987	38
8=	John Woods	Leigh *v* Ryedale-York	12 Jan 1992	38

THE TOP 10 POINTS-SCORERS IN A CAREER

	Player	Club(s)	Years	Points
1	Neil Fox	Wakefield, Bradford, Hull Kingston Rovers, York, Bramley, Huddersfield	1956–79	6,220
2	Jim Sullivan	Wigan	1921–46	6,022
3	Gus Risman	Salford, Workington, Batley	1929–54	4,050
4	John Woods	Leigh, Bradford, Warrington, Rochdale	1976–92	3,943
5	Cyril Kellett	Hull Kingston Rovers, Featherstone	1956–74	3,686
6	Kel Coslett	St Helens, Rochdale	1962–79	3,545
7	Steve Quinn	York, Featherstone	1962–88	3,447
8	Lewis Jones	Leeds	1952–64	3,445
9	Jimmy Ledgard	Leeds, Dewsbury, Leigh	1944–61	3,274
10	David Watkins	Salford, Swinton, Cardiff	1967–82	3,120

THE TOP 10 GOALKICKERS IN A CAREER

	Player	Club(s)	Years	Goals
1	Jim Sullivan	Wigan	1921–46	2,867
2	Neil Fox	Wakefield, Bradford, Hull Kingston Rovers, York, Bramley, Huddersfield	1956–79	2,575
3	Cyril Kellett	Hull Kingston Rovers, Featherstone	1956–74	1,768
4	Kel Coslett	St Helens, Rochdale	1962–79	1,698
5	Gus Risman	Salford, Workington, Batley	1929–54	1,678
6	Steve Quinn	York, Featherstone	1962–88	1,577
7	John Woods	Leigh, Bradford, Warrington, Rochdale	1976–92	1,572
8	Jimmy Ledgard	Leeds, Dewsbury, Leigh	1944–61	1,559
9	Lewis Jones	Leeds	1952–64	1,478
10	Bernard Ganley	Oldham	1951–61	1,398

David Watkins playing for Salford in 1978. He holds the record for the longest-scoring run of 92 consecutive games (August 1972–April 1974) and for most goals in a season (221 in 1972–73).

JIM SULLIVAN – RUGBY LEAGUE'S GREATEST GOALKICKER

Cardiff-born Sullivan joined the professional game after a successful spell playing rugby union for his home-town team. He was also quite useful at baseball, representing his county, and was a low-handicap golfer, but it was to rugby that he turned his sporting attentions. Wigan tempted him north in 1921, ahead of Wakefield Trinity who were also keen to sign him. The first of his record-breaking 2,867 goals in the professional game were on his debut in the 21–0 win over Widnes; Sullivan successfully converted five kicks that day. He spent his entire playing career at Wigan. He was appointed player–coach in 1932 and, after 31 years at Central Park, he left in 1952 to take over as St Helens' coach. He also had a spell at Rochdale before returning to Wigan in the summer of 1961. But ill-health meant he sat on the bench only for one game before his retirement in October that same year, a month after suffering a stroke. Sullivan died in 1977.

THE TOP 10 TRY-SCORERS IN A CAREER

	Player	Club(s)	Years	Tries
1	Brian Bevan	Warrington, Blackpool	1946–64	796
2	Billy Boston	Wigan, Blackpool	1953–70	571
3	Alf Ellaby	St Helens, Wigan	1926–39	446
4	Eric Batten	Wakefield, Hunslet, Bradford, Featherstone	1933–54	443
5	Lionel Cooper	Huddersfield	1947–55	441
6	Johnny Ring	Wigan, Rochdale	1922–33	416
7	Clive Sullivan	Hull, Hull Kingston Rovers, Oldham, Doncaster	1961–85	406
8	John Atkinson	Leeds, Carlisle	1966–83	401
9	Eric Harris	Leeds	1930–39	396
10	Tom van Vollenhoven	St Helens	1957–68	395

Ellery Hanley (Leeds) is the best placed of all current players – in 17th position with 328 tries to his credit at the end of the 1991–92 season.

BRIAN BEVAN

The game's leading try-scorer, Brian Bevan was born in Australia. While serving as a stoker with the Australian Navy he docked at Portsmouth in 1945 and wrote to Leeds asking for a trial. They were not impressed with what they saw – which was to prove to be one of the club's biggest errors. Bevan joined Warrington and spent 17 seasons with the Cheshire club before ending his career at Blackpool on 22 February 1964 at the age of 39. One of the inaugural members of rugby league's 'hall of fame', Brian Bevan died at Blackpool on 3 June 1991.

Brian Bevan, rugby league's leading try-scorer of all time.

THE 10 PLAYERS WITH THE MOST APPEARANCES IN A SENIOR RUGBY LEAGUE CAREER

	Player	Club(s)	Years	Appearances
1	Jim Sullivan	Wigan	1921–46	928
2	Gus Risman	Salford, Workington, Batley	1929–54	873
3	Neil Fox	Wakefield, Bradford, Hull Kingston Rovers, York, Bramley, Huddersfield	1956–79	828
4	Colin Dixon	Halifax, Salford, Hull Kingston Rovers	1961–81	738
5	Paul Charlton	Workington, Salford, Blackpool	1961–81	728
6	Jeff Grayshon	Dewsbury, Bradford, Leeds, Featherstone, Batley	1970–92	702
7	Graham Idle	Bramley, Wakefield, Bradford, Hunslet, Rochdale, Sheffield, Doncaster, Nottingham	1969–92	700
8	Joe Ferguson	Oldham	1899–1923	691
9	Brian Bevan	Warrington, Blackpool	1945–64	688
10	John Wolford	Bramley, Bradford, Dewsbury, Hunslet	1962–85	683

Appearances in senior representative matches are included, as are all substitute appearances.

THE TOP 10 GOALKICKERS, 1991–92

	Player/club	Goals
1	Frano Botica (Wigan)	161
2	Steve Carroll (Bramley)	138
3	Deryck Fox (Featherstone)	115
4	Lee Crooks (Castleford)	113
5	David Hobbs (Bradford)	110
6	Chris Vasey (Dewsbury)	109
7	Paul Eastwood (Hull)	108
8	Steve Parrish (Batley)	106
9	Mark Aston (Sheffield)	104
10	Jonathan Davies (Widnes)	99

THE TOP 10 TRY-SCORERS, 1991-92

	Player/club	Tries
1	Shaun Edwards (Wigan)	40
2	John Devereux (Widnes)	35
3=	Greg Austin (Halifax)	33
3=	Iva Ropati (Oldham)	33
5=	Vince Gribbin (Whitehaven)	31
5=	Graham Steadman (Castleford)	31
7	Martin Offiah (Wigan)	30
8	David Myers (Wigan)	29
9	Paul Newlove (Featherstone)	28
10	Mark Preston (Halifax)	27

THE 10 PLAYERS WITH THE MOST INTERNATIONAL APPEARANCES*

	Player	Years	Appearances
1	Jim Sullivan	1921–39	60
2	Mick Sullivan	1954–63	51
3	Roger Millward	1966–78	46
4	Alan Prescott	1950–58	42
5	Ernie Ward	1941–52	41
6	George Nicholls	1971–79	40
7	John Atkinson	1968–80	38
8	Ken Gee	1943–51	37
9	Gus Risman	1931–46	36
10=	Joe Egan	1943–50	35
10=	Ellery Hanley	1984–91	35

*To end 1991–92.

THE 10 CLUBS WITH THE MOST FIRST DIVISION WINS SINCE 1973–74*

	Club	Seasons	Wins
1	Widnes	19	350
2	St Helens	19	348
3	Wigan	18	323
4	Leeds	19	318
5	Warrington	19	298
6=	Bradford Northern	18	287
6=	Castleford	19	287
8	Hull Kingston Rovers	17	276
9	Hull	14	230
10	Featherstone Rovers	17	221

*To end 1991–92 season.

THE TOP 10 POINTS-SCORERS IN INTERNATIONAL MATCHES*

	Player	Years	Points
1	Jim Sullivan	1921–39	329
2	Neil Fox	1959–69	237
3	Lewis Jones	1953–57	190
4	George Fairbairn	1975–82	187
5	Mick Sullivan	1954–63	135
6	Garry Schofield	1984–91	126
7	Ernie Ward	1941–52	120
8	Roger Millward	1966–78	110
9	Eric Fraser	1958–61	109
10	James Lomas	1904–12	98

*To end 1991–92.

The two-division system was re-introduced in 1973–74. Since then a total of 30 clubs have appeared in the top division, with Castleford, Leeds, St Helens, Warrington and Widnes being the only ones to the end of 1991–92 to maintain a continuous presence. During that period, the only clubs to spend every season in the Second or Third Division were Batley, Doncaster and Highfield (ex-Huyton and Runcorn Highfield). Carlisle had just one season in the First Division and their two wins is the smallest total of all 30 clubs to have appeared in Division 1.

RUNCORN HIGHFIELD'S 10 BIGGEST DEFEATS DURING THEIR 75-MATCH SPELL WITHOUT A WIN

Between October 1988, when they beat Fulham, and 3 March 1991, when they beat Dewsbury, Runcorn Highfield spent 28 months and 75 matches without a win – the longest winless streak in rugby league history. During their run they suffered some hefty defeats, of which the following were the 10 biggest in terms of most points conceded:

	Opponents (home/away)	Date	Competition	Score
1	Rochdale Hornets (a)	5 Nov 1989	Division 2	0–92
2	Wigan (a)	13 Nov 1988	John Player Trophy	2–92
3	Leigh (h)	15 Jan 1989	Division 2	2–88
4	Halifax (a)	14 Oct 1990	Division 2	8–82
5	St Helens (a)	17 Sep 1989	Lancashire Cup	10–78
6	Halifax (h)	6 Jan 1991	Division 2	0–62
7	Barrow (h)	16 Apr 1989	Division 2	0–60
8	Oldham (a)	18 Mar 1990	Division 2	2–60
9	Chorley Borough (h)	1 Jan 1989	Division 2	2–56
10	Carlisle (a)	3 Sep 1989	Division 2	14–54

THE 10 CLUBS WITH THE MOST PLAYERS SENT OFF, 1991–92

Club		Sendings-off
1=	Batley	7
1=	Featherstone Rovers	7
1=	Highfield	7
1=	Sheffield Eagles	7
5=	Barrow	6
5=	St Helens	6
5=	Trafford Borough	6
5=	Warrington	6
5=	Workington Town	6
10=	Chorley Borough	5
10=	Oldham	5
10=	Whitehaven	5

There were a total of 127 dismissals, with only one club – Salford – not having anyone sent off.

The 1990 Challenge Cup final: Wigan's Kevin Iro is about to be tackled by Mike Gregory of Warrington. The match resulted in Wigan's biggest-ever Cup final win, 36–14.

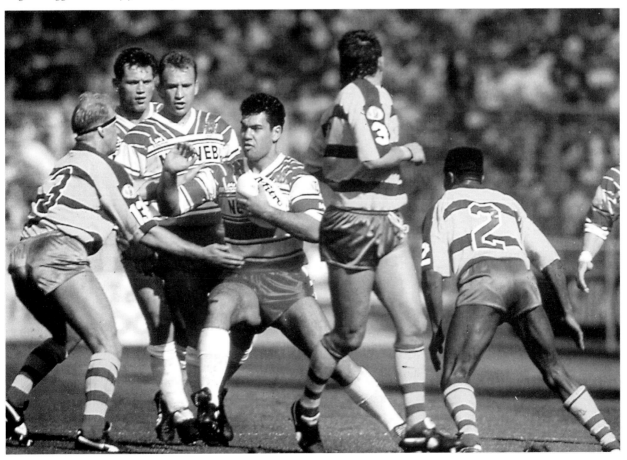

THE TOP 10 WINNERS OF THE CHALLENGE CUP

	Club	Years	Wins
1	Wigan	1924–92	13
2	Leeds	1910–78	10
3	Widnes	1930–84	7
4	Huddersfield	1913–53	6
5=	Halifax	1903–87	5
5=	Warrington	1905–74	5
5=	Wakefield Trinity	1909–63	5
5=	St Helens	1956–76	5
9=	Bradford Northern	1906–49	4
9=	Castleford	1935–86	4

The first Challenge Cup final, then known as the Northern Union Cup, was held at Headingley, Leeds, on 24 April 1897, with Batley the first winners, beating St Helens 10–3 in front of a crowd of 13,492.

WIGAN'S 10 BIGGEST CHALLENGE CUP FINAL WINS

	Opponents*	Year	Score
1	Warrington	1990	36–14
2	Halifax	1988	32–12
3	Hull	1959	30–13
4	Castleford	1992	28–12
5	Hull	1985	28–24
6	St Helens	1989	27–0
7	Oldham	1924	21–4
8	Hunslet	1965	20–16
9	Dewsbury	1929	13–2
10	St Helens	1991	13–8

All wins were at Wembley, except 1924 v Oldham, which was played at Rochdale.

Wigan have won the Challenge Cup a record 13 times, three more than their nearest rivals, Leeds. In addition to the 10 wins above, their other three successes were in 1948 when they beat Bradford Northern 8–3, in 1951 versus Barrow, which they won 10–0, and in 1958 when Workington Town lost 13–9.

THE 10 CLUBS WITH THE MOST WINNERS OF THE LANCE TODD AWARD

The Lance Todd Award is presented to the Man of the Match in the Challenge Cup final at Wembley. The award is made by members of the Rugby League Writers' Association and was first given in 1946 to Billy Stott of Wakefield Trinity. The trophy is named after New Zealander Lance B. Todd who made his name as a player with Wigan before World War I, and later played for Dewsbury. Following his retirement as a player he became secretary of Blackpool Golf Club before returning to rugby league as manager of Salford, who he guided to Challenge Cup success at Wembley in 1938. He was also the first rugby league expert behind the BBC microphone. Lance Todd died as a result of a car accident on his way back from a match at Oldham in 1942, at the age of 58. The clubs providing the most winners of the cherished trophy are:

	Club	Winners
1	Wigan	10
2	St Helens	6
3=	Wakefield Trinity	5
3=	Widnes	5
5=	Bradford Northern	3
5=	Castleford	3
5=	Featherstone Rovers	3
5=	Warrington	3
9	Leeds	2
10=	Barrow	1
10=	Halifax	1
10=	Huddersfield	1
10=	Hull	1
10=	Hull Kingston Rovers	1
10=	Hunslet	1
10=	Leigh	1
10=	Workington Town	1

The Wigan and Hunslet totals include one for the shared award in 1965 when Ray Ashby (Wigan) and Brian Gabbitas (Hunslet) were joint winners of the award. The only dual winners of the trophy are Gerry Helme (Warrington, 1950 and 1954) and Andy Gregory (Wigan, 1988 and 1990).

THE LAST 10 TEAMS TO BEAT WIGAN IN THE CHALLENGE CUP

Since losing to Oldham in the first round in 1986–87, Wigan have won 25 consecutive Challenge Cup ties, including the trophy on five occasions, thus making them the tournament's most successful team. Here is a list of the last 10 teams to beat them in the Cup:

	Opponents (home/away)	Round	Score	Date
1	Oldham (a)	1	8–10	4 Feb 1987
2	Castleford (h)	3	2–10	16 Mar 1986
3	Widnes	Final	6–19	5 May 1984
4	Castleford (h)	1	7–17	16 Feb 1983
5	Widnes (h)	2	7–9	28 Feb 1982
6	Halifax (a)	1	2–3	15 Feb 1981
7	Hull Kingston Rovers (h)	1	13–18	9 Feb 1980
8	Widnes (a)	2	5–21	24 Feb 1979
9	Bradford Northern (h)	2	10–22	11 Mar 1978
10	St Helens (h)	2	4–9	27 Feb 1977

THE 10 BIGGEST TEST MATCH WINS BY GREAT BRITAIN

	Opponents	Venue	Year	Score
1	France	Leeds	1991	60–4
2	Papua New Guinea	Wigan	1991	56–4
3	France	Leeds	1987	52–4
4	New Zealand	Auckland	1910	52–20
5	France	Leeds	1985	50–4
6	France	Leeds	1959	50–15
7=	France	Bradford	1972	45–10
8=	France	Perpignan	1991	45–10
9	France	Leeds	1957	45–12
10	France	Wigan	1957	44–15

Great Britain's record win against Australia is 40–17 at Sydney in 1958.

THE TOP 10 INTERNATIONAL ATTENDANCES

	Match*	Date	Attendance
1	Australia v Great Britain	6 Jun 1932	70,204
2	Australia v Great Britain	9 Jun 1962	70,174
3	Australia v Great Britain	14 Jun 1958	68,777
4	Australia v Great Britain	19 Jul 1958	68,720
5	Australia v Great Britain	17 Jul 1954	67,577
6	Australia v Great Britain	12 Jun 1954	65,884
7	Australia v Great Britain	17 Jun 1946	64,527
8	Australia v Great Britain	29 Jun 1936	63,920
9	Australia v Great Britain	23 Jul 1966	63,503
10	Australia v Great Britain†	25 May 1968	62,256

*All matches were played at the Sydney Cricket Ground.
†World Cup.

The highest attendance outside Australia was at Wembley Stadium on 27 October 1990 when Great Britain beat Australia 19–12 in front of a crowd of 54,569.

THE TOP 10 AUSTRALIAN TEAMS

The Winfield Cup is Australia's leading event, culminating in the Sydney Premiership Grand Final each September. The teams winning the final the most times have been:

	Team	Wins
1	South Sydney	20
2	St George	15
3=	Balmain	11
3=	Eastern Suburbs	11
5	Canterbury-Bankstown	6
6	Manly-Warringah	5
7=	Parramatta	4
7=	Western Suburbs	4
9=	Canberra	2
9=	North Sydney	2

RUGBY UNION

THE 10 MOST-CAPPED PLAYERS

	Player	Country	Years	Caps
1	Serge Blanco	France	1980–91	93
2	Philippe Sella	France	1982–92	83
3	Mike Gibson	Ireland/British Lions	1964–79	81
4	Willie John McBride	Ireland/British Lions	1962–75	80
5	Roland Bertranne	France	1971–81	69
6	Fergus Slattery	Ireland/British Lions	1970–84	65
7	David Campese	Australia	1982–91	64
8=	Michael Crauste	France	1957–66	63
8=	Benoit Dauga	France	1964–72	63
8=	Gareth Edwards	Wales/British Lions	1967–78	63
8=	J. P. R. Williams	Wales/British Lions	1969–81	63

THE 10 MOST-CAPPED ENGLISHMEN

	Player	Caps
1	Rory Underwood	55
2	Paul Winterbottom	52
3	Wade Dooley	50
4	Rob Andrew	48
5	Tony Neary	43
6	John Pullin	42
7	Peter Wheeler	41
8	Brian Moore	40
9=	Will Carling	36
9=	David Duckham	36
9=	Gary Pearce	36

THE TOP 10 POINTS-SCORERS IN AN INTERNATIONAL CHAMPIONSHIP SEASON

	Player	Country	Year	Points
1	Jonathan Webb	England	1992	67
2	Simon Hodgkinson	England	1991	60
3	Jean-Patrick Lescarboura	France	1984	54
4=	Ollie Campbell	Ireland	1983	52
4=	Gavin Hastings	Scotland	1986	52
4=	Paul Thorburn	Wales	1986	52
7	Peter Dods	Scotland	1984	50
8	Michael Kiernan	Ireland	1985	47
9=	Ollie Campbell	Ireland	1980	46
9=	Ollie Campbell	Ireland	1982	46
9=	Didier Camberabero	France	1991	46

Mike Gibson of Ireland, the most-capped player of all four home nations.

THE 10 MOST-CAPPED SCOTSMEN

	Player	Caps
1=	Colin Deans	52
1=	Jim Renwick	52
3	Andy Irvine	51
4	Sandy Carmichael	50
5	Alan Tomes	48
6	Roy Laidlaw	47
7=	Alistair McHarg	44
7=	Iain Milne	44
7=	Keith Robertson	44
10	Ian McLauchlan	43

THE 10 MOST-CAPPED IRISHMEN

	Player	Caps
1	Mike Gibson	69
2	Willie John McBride	63
3	Fergus Slattery	61
4	Phil Orr	58
5	Tom Kiernan	54
6	Donal Lenihan	52
7	Moss Keane	51
8	Jackie Kyle	46
9=	Len Kennedy	45
9=	Brendan Mullin	45

THE 10 MOST-CAPPED WELSHMEN

	Player	Caps
1	J. P. R. Williams	55
2	Gareth Edwards	53
3	Gerald Davies	46
4	Ken Jones	44
5	Robert Jones	42
6	Graham Price	41
7	Mervyn Davies	38
8	Paul Thorburn	37
9	Denzil Williams	36
10	Dickie Owen	35

THE 10 BIGGEST WINS IN THE INTERNATIONAL CHAMPIONSHIP

This Top 10 is based on the winning team's score, not margin of victory. However, where two nations share the highest score, then margin of victory is used to separate them. The biggest victory by margin is England's 37–0 win over France at Twickenham in 1911.

Ireland's biggest win is 26–8 against Scotland at Murrayfield in 1953.

	Match (winners first)	Venue	Year	Score
1	Wales v France	Swansea	1910	49–14
2	France v Ireland	Paris	1992	44–12
3	England v France	Paris	1914	39–13
4	England v Ireland	Twickenham	1992	38–9
5	England v France	Twickenham	1911	37–0
6	France v England	Paris	1972	37–12
7	Scotland v Ireland	Murrayfield	1989	37–21
8	France v Wales	Paris	1991	36–3
9	England v Ireland	Dublin	1938	36–14
10=	Wales v France	Swansea	1931	35–3
10=	England v Ireland	Twickenham	1988	35–3

THE TOP 10 POINTS-SCORERS IN MAJOR INTERNATIONALS*

	Player	Country	Years	Points
1	Michael Lynagh	Australia	1984–91	691
2	Grant Fox	New Zealand	1985–91	525
3	Gavin Hastings	Scotland	1986–92	410
4	Didier Camberabero	France	1982–91	328
5	Michael Kiernan	Ireland/British Lions	1982–91	317
6	Paul Thorburn	Wales	1985–91	304
7	Andy Irvine	Scotland/British Lions	1972–82	301
8	Naas Botha	South Africa	1980–89	268
9	Jean-Pierre Romeu	France	1972–77	265
10=	Ollie Campbell	Ireland/British Lions	1976–84	246
10=	Jonathan Webb	England	1987–92	246

*Full International Board countries and British Lions.

THE TOP 10 TRY-SCORERS IN MAJOR INTERNATIONALS

	Player	Country	Years	Tries
1	David Campese	Australia	1982–91	49
2	Serge Blanco	France	1980–91	38
3	Rory Underwood	England	1984–92	35
4	John Kirwan	New Zealand	1984–91	32
5	Philippe Sella	France	1982–91	25
6	Ian Smith	Scotland	1924–33	24
7	Christian Darrouy	France	1957–67	23
8=	Gerald Davies	Wales	1966–78	20
8=	Gareth Edwards	Wales	1967–78	20
8=	Patrick Lagisquet	France	1983–91	20

Australia's David Campese about to score the first of two tries against Ireland in the quarter-finals of the 1991 World Cup.

THE TOP 10 TRY-SCORERS IN THE 1991 WORLD CUP

	Player	Country	Points
1=	David Campese	Australia	6
1=	Jean-Baptiste Lafond	France	6
3=	Tim Horan	Australia	4
3=	Brian Robinson	Ireland	4
3=	Ivan Tukalo	Scotland	4
3=	Rory Underwood	England	4
7=	Tony Stanger	Scotland	3
7=	Martin Teran	Argentina	3
7=	John Timu	New Zealand	3
7=	Terry Wright	New Zeland	3
7=	Yoshihito Yoshida	Japan	3

THE TOP 10 POINTS-SCORERS IN THE 1991 WORLD CUP

	Player	Country	Points
1	Ralph Keyes	Ireland	68
2	Michael Lynagh	Australia	66
3	Gavin Hastings	Scotland	61
4	Jonathan Webb	England	56
5	Grant Fox	New Zealand	44
6	Didier Camberabero	France	32
7=	Diego Dominguez	Italy	29
7=	Takahiro Hosokawa	Japan	29
9	Jean-Baptiste Lafond	France	26
10	Matthew Vaea	Western Samoa	25

THE 10 HIGHEST-SCORING MATCHES IN THE COURAGE LEAGUE DIVISION 1, 1991–92

	Match	Score	Total points
1	Leicester v Rosslyn Park	51–16	67
2	Saracens v Harlequins	37–21	58
3	Bristol v Rugby	48–4	52
4=	Leicester v London Irish	36–13	49
4=	Rugby v Harlequins	29–20	49
6	Bath v London Irish	26–21	47
7=	Bath v Saracens	32–12	44
7=	Gloucester v Bristol	29–15	44
7=	Leicester v Rugby	22–22	44
10=	Bath v Leicester	37–6	43
10=	Leicester v Wasps	31–12	43
10=	Northampton v Wasps	28–15	43
10=	Nottingham v Rosslyn Park	34–9	43

THE TOP 10 POINTS-SCORERS IN FIRST-CLASS BRITISH RUGBY, 1991–92

	Player	Club	Points
1	Jonathan Newton	Dundee HSFP	527
2	David Johnson	Newcastle Gosforth	450
3	John Steele	Northampton	425
4	Alistair Donaldson	Currie	394
5	John Liley	Leicester	356
6	Paul Grayson	Preston Grasshoppers	353
7	Aled Williams	Swansea/Bridgend	349
8	Andy Finnie	Bedford	331
9	Byron Hayward	Newbridge	327
10	Neil Jenkins	Pontypridd	319

THE 10 HIGHEST-SCORING VARSITY MATCHES*

	Winners	Season	Score
1	Oxford	1909–10	35–3
2	Cambridge	1975–76	34–12
3	Cambridge	1925–26	33–3
4	Cambridge	1984–85	32–6
5	Cambridge	1926–27	30–5
6	Cambridge	1934–35	29–4
7	Oxford	1988–89	27–7
8	Cambridge	1978–79	25–7
9	Oxford	1910–11	23–18
10=	Cambridge	1989–90	22–13
10=	Cambridge	1927–28	22–14

Based on score of winning team.

The first Varsity Match was played at Oxford in 1872, when the home side won by one goal and a try to nil. The following year Cambridge played host and duly won. From 1873–74 to 1879–80 the match was played at The Oval before a seven-year spell at Blackheath. Queen's Club was its home between 1887–88 and 1920–21, and it then moved to Twickenham, where the match has remained and is played each December. To date Cambridge have won 50 times, Oxford 46, and 13 matches have been drawn. The winning team receives the Bowring Bowl.

THE 10 CLUBS WITH THE MOST APPEARANCES IN THE JOHN PLAYER/ PILKINGTON CUP FINAL

	Club	Finals*
1=	Bath	7(7)
1=	Leicester	6(3)
3=	Bristol	4(1)
3=	Gloucester	4(3)
5=	Gosforth	3(2)
5=	Harlequins	3(2)
5=	Moseley	3(1)
7=	Coventry	2(2)
7=	Rosslyn Park	2(0)
7=	Wasps	2(0)

Figures in brackets indicate wins.

Gloucester and Moseley shared the 1982 final.

THE TOP 10 WINNERS OF THE COUNTY CHAMPIONSHIP

	County	Titles
1=	Gloucestershire	15
1=	Lancashire	15
3	Yorkshire	11
4	Warwickshire	9
5=	Durham	8
5=	Middlesex	8
7	Devon	7
8	Kent	3
9=	Cheshire	2
9=	Cornwall	2
9=	East Midlands	2
9=	Hampshire	2
9=	Northumberland	2
9=	Surrey	2

The Durham total includes two shared titles, and the Surrey and Devon totals each include one shared title.

THE TOP 10 WINNERS OF THE MIDDLESEX SEVENS

	Team	Wins
1	Harlequins	13
2	Richmond	9
3	London Welsh	8
4	London Scottish	7
5=	Loughborough Colleges	5
5=	St Mary's Hospital	5
7	Rosslyn Park	4
8	Wasps	3
9=	Blackheath	2
9=	St Luke's College	2

First played in 1926, the Middlesex Sevens, though declining in popularity, still holds a special place in rugby history. The winners of the final, which is played at Twickenham each year, are awarded the Russell Cargill Trophy.

THE TOP 10 WINNERS OF THE SYDNEY FIRST GRADE PREMIERSHIP

	Team	Wins
1	Randwick	23
2	University	21
3	Eastern Suburbs	9
4	Glebe	8
5=	Manly	6
5=	Northern Suburbs	6
7	Gordon	5
8=	Newtown	3
8=	Parramatta	3
10	Western Suburbs	2

The Sydney Grade Premiership was first contested in 1900. Rugby union is played mostly in New South Wales and Queensland.

THE 10 PLAYERS WITH THE MOST TEST APPEARANCES FOR THE BRITISH LIONS

	Player/country	Appearances
1	Willie John McBride (Ireland)	17
2	Dickie Jeeps (England)	13
3=	Mike Gibson (Ireland)	12
3=	Graham Price (Wales)	12
5=	Gareth Edwards (Wales)	10
5=	Tony O'Reilly (Ireland)	10
5=	Rhys Williams (Wales)	10
8=	Andy Irvine (Scotland)	9
8=	Syd Millar (Ireland)	9
10=	Dewi Bebb (Wales)	8
10=	Phil Bennett (Wales)	8
10=	Gordon Brown (Scotland)	8
10=	Mike Campbell-Lamerton (Scotland)	8
10=	Mike Colclough (England)	8
10=	Mervyn Davies (Wales)	8
10=	Ian McGeechan (Scotland)	8
10=	Ian McLauchlan (Scotland)	8
10=	Bryn Meredith (Wales)	8
10=	Noel Murphy (Ireland)	8
10=	Alun Pask (Wales)	8
10=	J. P. R. Williams (Wales)	8

Willie John McBride (Ireland) made a record 17 appearances for the British Lions and is the second most successful tour captain.

THE 10 MOST SUCCESSFUL BRITISH LIONS TOUR CAPTAINS

	Captain/country	Tour	Year	Games played	won	Percentage
1	Bill MacLagan (Scotland)	South Africa	1891	19	19	100.00
2	Willie John McBride (Ireland)	South Africa	1974	22	21	95.45
3	Finlay Calder (Scotland)	Australia	1989	12	11	91.67
4	John Hammond (England)	South Africa	1896	21	19	90.48
5	John Dawes (Wales)	Australia/New Zealand	1971	26	23	88.46
6	Rev. Matthew Mullineaux (England)	Australia	1899	21	18	85.71
7	Darkie Bedell-Sivright (Scotland)	Australia/New Zealand	1904	19	16	84.21
8	Bill Beaumont (England)	South Africa	1980	18	15	83.33
9	Phil Bennett (Wales)	New Zealand/Fiji	1977	26	21	80.77
10	Ronnie Dawson (Ireland)	Australia/New Zealand	1959	31	25	80.65

The Lions' first-ever tour was to Australia and New Zealand in 1888. The tour captain was Robert Seddon but he was tragically killed in a boating accident on the Australian leg of the tour. Andrew Stoddart took over as captain and uniquely had the distinction of captaining the Lions and the England Test cricket team. Willie John McBride's team was undefeated on their 1974 South Africa tour, drawing the fourth and final Test 13–13. The least successful skipper was Mark Morrison who led the Lions to 11 wins from 22 matches on their 1903 tour of South Africa.

THE TOP 10 POINTS-SCORERS FOR THE BRITISH LIONS ON TOUR

	Player	Year	Points
1	Barry John	1971	188
2	Andy Irvine	1974	156
3	James Byrne	1896	127
4=	Phil Bennett	1977	125
4=	Ollie Campbell	1983	125
6	Dave Hewitt	1959	112
7	Bob Hiller	1971	110
8=	Terry Davies	1959	104
8=	Bob Hiller	1968	104
10	Phil Bennett	1974	103

No other players have scored more than 100 points.

QUIZ

RUGBY UNION RECORD-BREAKERS

1 Which side caused Wales to suffer their biggest-ever defeat in July 1991 on their Australian tour?
2 Who, in 1990, eventually ended the All Blacks' run of 23 international matches without defeat?
3 Place the five International Championship nations in the correct order according to championship wins, starting with the nation with the most titles.
4 Who scored a record 34 points in an international against Japan in 1975?
5 Who appeared in a record 34 internationals as captain of one of the Five Nations teams between 1979 and 1984?
6 The highest score in the inaugural World Cup in 1987 was New Zealand's 74–13 demolition of which team?
7 Who scored a record 462 points for Gloucestershire in his county career?
8 Which is the oldest club in Scotland, founded in 1857?
9 Record points-scorer Dusty Hare played for two English club sides. Name them both.
10 Who was the first man to be sent off in an international match?

THE 10 CLUBS PROVIDING THE MOST PLAYERS FOR BRITISH LIONS TOURS

	Club	Players
1	Cardiff	25
2	Newport	19
3	Swansea	14
4	Llanelli	13
5=	Oxford University	10
5=	Queen's University, Belfast	10
7	Blackheath	9
8=	Cambridge University	8
8=	Harlequins	8
8=	Leicester	8
8=	London Scottish	8
8=	London Welsh	8

A total of 97 British Lions players have been Welsh internationals at the time of their Lions debuts, while a further 71 were from England, 67 were Irish internationals, and 59 Scottish caps. One Australian international (T. J. Richards, 1910) has played for the Lions and 21 players were uncapped at the time of playing in their first Test for the Lions.

THE 10 MOST POPULAR SURNAMES OF BRITISH LIONS

	Surname	No. of players
1=	Davies	9
1=	Jones	9
1=	Williams	9
4=	Evans	6
4=	Smith	6
6=	Morgan	5
6=	Young	5
8	Richards	4
9=	Griffiths	3
9=	Price	3
9=	Taylor	3
9=	Thomas	3

SHINTY

Shinty is the popular name for *camanachd* which is played largely in the Scottish Highlands. It shares a 2,000-year history with hurling and was introduced to Scotland by the Irish Gaels. It was originally seen as a good form of practical training by the battling clansfolk but today it is a very popular sport which continues to flourish thanks largely to the many youngsters who play the game. The sport's premier tournament is the Camanachd Cup which was inaugurated in 1896 and has been contested every year since with the exception of the war years. The winners have been:

THE TOP 10 WINNERS OF THE CAMANACHD CUP

	Team	Wins
1	Newtonmore	28
2	Kyles Athletic	19
3	Kingussie	12
4	Oban Celtic	5
5	Ballachulish	4
6=	Beauly	3
6=	Inverary	3
8=	Caberfeidh	2
8=	Oban	2
10=	Fort William	1
10=	Furnace	1
10=	Glasgow Mid Argyll	1
10=	Inverness	1
10=	Kilmallie	1
10=	Lovat	1

SHOOTING

THE 10 MOST SUCCESSFUL OLYMPIC COUNTRIES

	Country	gold	silver	bronze	Total
1	USA	44	25	19	88
2	USSR/CIS	22	18	20	60
3	Sweden	13	23	19	55
4	Great Britain	13	14	19	46
5	France	12	16	13	41
6	Norway	16	8	10	34
7	Switzerland	11	9	10	30
8	Germany/ West Germany	8	8	5	21
9	Greece	5	7	6	18
10=	Denmark	3	8	6	17
10=	Finland	3	5	9	17

O ne of Sweden's 13 gold medallists was Oscar Swahn who holds the distinction of being the oldest-ever Olympic gold medallist in any sport. Swahn was aged 64 years and 258 days when he was in the Swedish team that won the Running Deer team title in 1912. Eight years later he collected a silver medal in the same event.

THE TOP 10 INDIVIDUAL OLYMPIC MEDAL WINNERS

	Medallist/nationality	Medals*
1	Carl Osburn (USA)	11(5)
2=	Otto Olsen (Nor)	8(4)
2=	Konrad Staheli (Swi)	8(5)
4=	Willis Lee (USA)	7(5)
4=	Einer Liberg (Nor)	7(4)
4=	Gudbrand Skatteboe (Nor)	7(4)
4=	Lloyd Spooner (USA)	7(4)
8=	Alfred Lane (USA)	6(5)
8=	Ole Lilloe-Olsen (Nor)	6(5)
8=	Louis Richardet (Swi)	6(5)

*Figures in brackets indicate gold medals.

M orris Fisher (USA) also won five golds, but no other medals. One of Alfred Lane's gold medals was won in the Military Revolver Team event at the 1920 Antwerp Games. One of his team-mates was James Snook who achieved notoriety in 1929 when he was arrested for the murder of his mistress after beating her with a hammer following a violent sexual act. In February 1930 Snook went to his death in the electric chair.

SKIING

T he Alpine Skiing World Cup was launched in 1967 and points are awarded for performances over a series of selected races during the winter months at meetings worldwide. The downhill, slalom, giant slalom, and overall titles were all instituted in 1967. The super-giant slalom, known as the super-G, was introduced in 1986.

THE TOP 10 WINNERS OF MEN'S ALPINE SKIING WORLD CUP TITLES

	Skier/nationality	Overall	Downhill	Giant slalom	Super-G	Slalom	Total
1	Ingemar Stenmark (Swe)	3	0	8	0	8	19
2	Pirmin Zurbriggen (Swi)	4	2	2	4	0	12
3	Marc Girardelli (Lux)	4	1	1	0	3	9
4	Gustavo Thöni (Ita)	4	0	2	0	2	8
5=	Jean-Claude Killy (Fra)	2	1	2	0	1	6
5=	Phil Mahre (USA)	3	0	2	0	1	6
7=	Franz Klammer (Aut)	0	5	0	0	0	5
7=	Karl Schranz (Aut)	2	2	1	0	0	5
7=	Alberto Tomba (Ita)	0	0	3	0	2	5
10=	Peter Müller (Swi)	0	3	0	0	0	3
10=	Jean-Noël Augert (Fra)	0	0	0	0	3	3

THE TOP 10 WINNERS OF WOMEN'S ALPINE WORLD CUP TITLES

	Skier/nationality	Overall	Downhill	Giant slalom	Super-G	Slalom	Total
1	Annemarie Moser-Pröll (Aut)	6	7	3	0	0	16
2	Vreni Schneider (Swi)	1	0	4	0	3	8
3=	Michela Figini (Swi)	2	3	1	1	0	7
3=	Erika Hess (Swi)	2	0	1	0	4	7
3=	Maria Walliser (Swi)	2	3	0	1	1	7
6	Lise-Marie Morerod (Swi)	1	0	3	0	2	6
7=	Carole Merle (Fra)	0	0	1	4	0	5
7=	Hanni Wenzel (Lie)	2	0	2	0	1	5
9=	Nancy Greene (Can)	2	2	0	0	0	4
9=	Tamara McKinney (USA)	1	0	2	0	1	4
9=	Petra Kronberger (Aut)	3	0	0	0	1	4

THE 10 SKIERS WITH THE MOST WORLD AND OLYMPIC TITLES*

	Skier/nationality	Years	C	D	GS	S	SG†	Total
1	Christl Cranz (Ger)	1935–41	5	3	0	4	0	12
2	Toni Sailer (Aut)	1956–58	2	2	2	1	0	7
3=	Marielle Goitschel (Fra)	1966–68	3	2	1	0	0	6
3=	Jean-Claude Killy (Fra)	1966–68	2	2	1	1	0	6
3=	Erika Hess (Swi)	1982–87	3	0	1	2	0	6
6=	Gustavo Thöni (Ita)	1972–76	2	0	2	1	0	5
6=	Vreni Schneider (Swi)	1987–91	0	0	3	2	0	5
8=	Stein Eriksen (Nor)	1952–54	1	0	2	1	0	4
8=	Annemarie Moser-Pröll (Aut)	1974–80	1	3	0	0	0	4
8=	Hanni Wenzel (Lie)	1974–80	1	0	1	2	0	4
8=	Pirmin Zurbriggen (Swi)	1985–88	1	2	1	0	0	4

*Men and women.
†C = Combined; D = Downhill; GS = Giant Slalom; S = Slalom; SG = Super Giant Slalom.

The first World Championships were held in 1931 and now take place every two years. There are no championships in Olympic years but the Olympic champions are classed as world champions in those years.

Jean-Claude Killy of France, top men's skier of the 1960s.

SNOOKER

THE 10 YOUNGEST WORLD PROFESSIONAL CHAMPIONS

	Player/nationality	Year	Age* yrs	months
1	Stephen Hendry (Sco)	1990	21	3
2	Alex Higgins (NI)	1972	23	1
3	Steve Davis (Eng)	1981	23	8
4	Joe Davis (Eng)	1927	26	0
5	John Parrott (Eng)	1991	27	0
6	Terry Griffiths (Wal)	1979	31	6
7	Cliff Thorburn (Can)	1980	32	3
8	John Spencer (Eng)	1969	33	7
9	Joe Johnson (Eng)	1986	33	10
10	Fred Davis (Eng)	1948	34	9

If a player would appear in the list twice, only his youngest age is included.

THE 10 OLDEST WORLD PROFESSIONAL CHAMPIONS

	Player/nationality	Year	Age* yrs	months
1	Ray Reardon (Wal)	1978	45	6
2	Joe Davis (Eng)	1946	45	0
3	John Pulman (Eng)	1968	44	4
4	Walter Donaldson (Sco)	1950	43	2
5	John Spencer (Eng)	1977	41	7
6	Horace Lindrum (Aus)	1952	40	0
7	Fred Davis (Eng)	1951	37	9
8	Dennis Taylor (NI)	1985	36	3
9	Joe Johnson (Eng)	1986	33	10
10	Alex Higgins (NI)	1982	33	1

If a player would appear in the list twice, only his oldest age is included.

Alex Higgins celebrates becoming world champion in 1982 with his wife Lynn and daughter Lauren. Exactly 10 years earlier he had won the world title to become the youngest-ever champion, a record which stood for 18 years.

THE 10 PLAYERS WITH THE MOST WORLD TITLES

The World Championship was launched in 1926 after Joe Davis and Birmingham billiard hall owner Bill Camkin put pressure on the Billiards Association and Control Club to organize such an event. The first-ever match was between Melbourne Inman and Tom Newman at Thurston's Hall between 26 November and 6 December 1926. The first final, which was played at Camkin's Hall, started on 9 May 1927 and was won by Joe Davis who beat Tom Dennis 20–11. Davis won every final up to 1940 and again in 1946 when the championship was revived after the war. Between 1952 and 1957 the professionals formed a breakaway group from the BACC and organized their own championship known as the Professional Match-Play Championship. Although some sources regard matches played under its aegis as World Championship games, we do not. However, the challenge system which was in operation between 1964 and 1968 is accepted as being relevant to the World Championship because it was under the auspices of the BACC and is included in this table.

	Player*	Titles
1	Joe Davis	15
2	John Pulman	7
3=	Steve Davis	6
3=	Ray Reardon	6
5=	Fred Davis	3
5=	John Spencer	3
7=	Walter Donaldson	2
7=	Stephen Hendry	2
7=	Alex Higgins	2
10=	Terry Griffiths	1
10=	Joe Johnson	1
10=	Horace Lindrum (Aus)	1
10=	John Parrott	1
10=	Dennis Taylor	1
10=	Cliff Thorburn (Can)	1

British unless otherwise stated.

THE TOP 10 WINNERS OF RANKING TOURNAMENTS

Ranking tournaments are those which carry points towards the annual ranking system which is re-calculated after the World Championship each year. The 1991–92 ranking tournaments were: Embassy World Professional Championship; Rothmans Grand Prix; Asian Open; Dubai Duty Free Classic; UK Professional; Mercantile Credit Classic; Pearl Assurance British Open; European Open; Regal Welsh Open; Strachan Professional Snooker Championship. Events like the Benson and Hedges Masters and Irish Masters, which are invitation-only events, are not ranking tournaments.

	Player/nationality	Wins*
1	Steve Davis (Eng)	24
2	Stephen Hendry (Sco)	14
3	Jimmy White (Eng)	7
4=	Ray Reardon (Wal)	5
4=	John Parrott (Eng)	5
6=	Tony Knowles (Eng)	2
6=	Doug Mountjoy (Wal)	2
6=	Dennis Taylor (NI)	2
6=	Cliff Thorburn (Can)	2
10=	Bob Chaperon (Can)	1
10=	Neal Foulds (Eng)	1
10=	Silvino Francisco (SA)	1
10=	Terry Griffiths (Wal)	1
10=	Mike Hallett (Eng)	1
10=	Alex Higgins (NI)	1
10=	Steve James (Eng)	1
10=	Joe Johnson (Eng)	1
10=	Tony Jones (Eng)	1
10=	Tony Meo (Eng)	1
10=	John Spencer (Eng)	1
10=	Willie Thorne (Eng)	1
10=	James Wattana (Tha)	1

To end 1991–92 season.

Steve Davis has won more ranking tournaments than any other player.

THE TOP 10 RANKED PLAYERS, 1991–92 AND 1981–82

	1991–92		1981–82*	
1	Stephen Hendry (Sco)	1	(126)	Ray Reardon (Wal)
2	Steve Davis (Eng)	2	(120)	Alex Higgins (NI)
3	Jimmy White (Eng)	3	(36)	Cliff Thorburn (Can)
4	John Parrott (Eng)	4	(2)	Steve Davis (Eng)
5	Gary Wilkinson (Eng)	5	(27)	Eddie Charlton (Aus)
6	Neal Foulds (Eng)	6	(58)	Kirk Stevens (Can)
7	Steve James (Eng)	7	(10)	Doug Mountjoy (Wal)
8	Mike Hallett (Eng)	8	(74)	David Taylor (Eng)
9	Dennis Taylor (NI)	9	(146)	Bill Werbeniuk (Can)
10	Doug Mountjoy (Wal)	10	(3)	Jimmy White (Eng)

Figures in brackets indicate 1991–92 rankings.

In compiling the 1991–92 rankings, performances in eight tournaments over the previous two years were considered, but in 1981–82 only performances in the previous three years' World Championships were taken into account.

THE TOP 10 RANKED PLAYERS, 1992–93

1	Stephen Hendry
2	John Parrott
3	Jimmy White
4	Steve Davis
5	Neal Foulds
6	Terry Griffiths
7	James Wattana (Tha)
8	Gary Wilkinson
9	Nigel Bond
10	Steve James

British unless otherwise stated.

THE TOP 10 MONEY-WINNERS, 1991–92

	Player	Winnings (£)
1	Stephen Hendry	645,300
2	Jimmy White	491,120
3	Steve Davis	361,420
4	John Parrott	281,020
5	James Wattana	209,000
6	Gary Wilkinson	172,540
7	Mike Hallett	157,570
8	Neal Foulds	128,740
9	Terry Griffiths	120,590
10	Steve James	107,010

These sums are for tournament earnings only. All the above are British except James Wattana, who is Thai.

THE TOP 10 RANKED NON-BRITISH PLAYERS, 1992–93

	Player/nationality	Ranking
1	James Wattana (Tha)	7
2	Alain Robidoux (Can)	14
3	Dene O'Kane (NZ)	18
4	Ken Doherty (Ire)	21
5	Tony Drago (Mlt)	24
6	Peter Francisco (SA)	25
7	Silvino Francisco (SA)	28
8	Eddie Charlton (Aus)	29
9	Cliff Thorburn (Can)	36
10	Brady Gollan (Can)	39

THE 10 BIGGEST FINES IMPOSED ON ALEX HIGGINS

The 12-month ban on Higgins and the deduction of 25 ranking points, together with £5,000 costs imposed in 1990 was, by far, the biggest punishment dished out to the temperamental but once brilliant Irishman. The following is the list of biggest fines that the sport's governing body has imposed on Higgins over the years.

	Offence	Year	Fine (£)
1	Headbutting an official, and other offences	1987	12,000*
2	Refusing to attend press conference, assaulting a journalist, foul and abusive language to journalists and WPBSA officials	1989	3,000
3	Bringing game into disrepute	1986	2,000
4=	Swearing during Benson and Hedges Masters	1985	1,500
4=	Failing to take a drug test	1988	1,500†
6	Incidents at Irish Masters and World Championship	1982	1,000
7	Being abusive to tournament director at Irish Masters	1989	500
8=	Abusive language and bringing game into disrepute	1980	200
8=	Improper behaviour at two events	1980	200
8=	Ungentlemanly conduct at an exhibition match	1981	200‡

*Plus five-tournament ban.
†Suspended fine.
‡Plus two ranking points deducted.

The first fine imposed on Higgins was £100 for misconduct during the 1973 World Championship. He was the reigning champion at the time.

THE 10 HIGHEST BREAKS IN THE WORLD PROFESSIONAL CHAMPIONSHIP*

	Player	Year	Break
1=	Cliff Thorburn v Terry Griffiths	1983	147
1=	Jimmy White v Tony Drago	1992	147
3	Doug Mountjoy v Ray Reardon	1981	145
4=	Willie Thorne v Alex Higgins	1982	143
4=	Bill Werbeniuk v Joe Johnson	1985	143
6	Bill Werbeniuk v John Virgo	1979	142
7	Stephen Hendry v Terry Griffiths	1989	141
8=	Steve James v Rex Williams	1988	140
8=	John Parrott v Cliff Thorburn	1990	140
8=	Jimmy White v Neal Foulds	1991	140

*At the Crucible Theatre, Sheffield.

THE TOP 10 FIRST PRIZES, 1991–92

	Event	prize (£)
1	Embassy World Professional Championship	150,000
2	Benson and Hedges Masters	105,000
3=	Pearl Assurance British Open	75,000
3=	Rothmans Grand Prix	75,000
5	Coalite World Match-play Championship	70,000
6	Mercantile Credit Classic	60,000
7	Dubai Duty Free Classic	40,000
8	UK Championship	35,000
9	Asian Open	30,000
10=	European Open	25,000
10=	Regal Welsh Open Professional Championship	25,000

CLIFF THORBURN'S 147

The first maximum break in World Championship history came in the fourth frame of Cliff Thorburn's second-round match with Terry Griffiths in 1983. The break started with a fluked red which was directed at one of the bottom pockets, but which missed, hit the jaws of the pocket and rolled along the cushion into the opposite bottom pocket. After that it was relatively plain sailing for the Canadian, who took 15 minutes and 20 seconds to compile the historic maximum. The feat was not achieved again until Jimmy White did so in 1992.

The highest break in the pre-Crucible days was 142 made by Rex Williams in his challenge match against John Pulman in 1965.

THE FIRST 10 OFFICIALLY RATIFIED MAXIMUM BREAKS

	Player/nationality	Venue	Date
1	Joe Davis (Eng)	Leicester Square Hall, London	22 Jan 1955
2	Rex Williams (Eng)	Prince's Hotel, Newlands, South Africa	22 Dec 1965
3	Steve Davis (Eng)	Civic Centre, Oldham	11 Jan 1982
4	Cliff Thorburn (Can)	Crucible Theatre, Sheffield	23 Apr 1983
5	Kirk Stevens (Can)	Wembley Conference Centre, London	28 Jan 1984
6	Willie Thorne (Eng)	Guild Hall, Preston	17 Nov 1987
7	Tony Meo (Eng)	Winding Wheel Centre, Chesterfield	20 Feb 1988
8	Alain Robidoux (Can)	Norbreck Castle Hotel, Blackpool	24 Sep 1988
9	John Rea (Sco)	Marco's Leisure Centre, Glasgow	18 Feb 1989
10	Cliff Thorburn (Can)	Hawth Theatre, Crawley	8 Mar 1989

S teve Davis's maximum was the first to be recognized in tournament play; the 147 achieved by both Joe Davis and Rex Williams were in exhibition matches. Steve Davis's was also the first to be televised. However, a 147 made by John Spencer in the Holsten Lager tournament at Slough in 1979 should have been the first to be seen by a television audience but the camera crew were at lunch at the time and missed the opportunity of the first televised 147. There was double disappointment for Spencer because his break was never officially ratified by the B&SCC. The first witnessed maximum was in Australia in 1934 when New Zealander Murt O'Donoghue compiled a 147 but his achievement was never officially ratified.

JOE DAVIS'S FIRST MAXIMUM BREAK

T he first maximum break officially recognized by the Billiards Association and Control Club was Joe Davis's 147 in an exhibition match against Willie Smith on 22 January 1955. However, it was two years before they gave official approval to the achievement. At the time the professional players adopted a rule not recognized by the BACC – allowing a player to make his opponent play again after a foul (now very much part of the rules). Because of this the governing body would not accept the break as being official under their rules. Davis unsuccessfully applied for the break to be officially recognized but it was not until March 1957, at the third time of asking, that the BACC eventually succumbed and officially acknowledged his achievement.

THE PROGRESSION OF OFFICIALLY RATIFIED SNOOKER RECORD BREAKS

Player*	Year	Break
Tom Newman	1919	89
Joe Davis	1925	96
Joe Davis	1928	100
Joe Davis	1930	105
Joe Davis	1933	109
Joe Davis	1933	114
Horace Lindrum (Aus)	1936†	131
Sidney Smith	1936†	133
Joe Davis	1937	135
Joe Davis	1938	137
Joe Davis	1938	138
Joe Davis	1947	140
Joe Davis	1949	141
George Chenier (Can)	1950	144
Joe Davis	1954	146
Joe Davis	1955	147

*British unless otherwise stated.
†Records set on the same day.

THE 10 TOURNAMENTS WITH THE LONGEST CONTINUAL SPONSORSHIP

	Tournament	Years staged	Total years
1	Pontins Championships	1974–92	19
2	Benson and Hedges Masters	1975–92	18
3	Embassy World Professional Championship	1977–92	16
4	Benson and Hedges Irish Masters	1978–92	15
5	News of the World Tournament	1950–59	10
6	Winfield Australian Masters	1979–87	9
7=	Coral UK Championship/Open	1978–85	8
7=	Rothmans Grand Prix	1984–91	8
7=	Mercantile Credit Classic	1985–92	8
10	Lang's Scottish Masters	1981–87	7

THE TOP 10 ATTENDANCES AT THE BENSON AND HEDGES MASTERS

All the top snooker attendances in Britain have been at the Wembley Conference Centre in London, home of the Benson and Hedges Masters since 1979, four years after the launch of the tournament which is regarded as the most prestigious annual non-ranking tournament. A total of 17 matches have attracted crowds in excess of 2,500, six of which have included Alex Higgins.

	Match	Year	Attendance
1	Alex Higgins *v* Bill Werbeniuk	1983	2,876
2	Ray Reardon *v* Cliff Thorburn	1983	2,693*
3	Steve Davis *v* Doug Mountjoy	1983	2,690
4	Steve Davis *v* Doug Mountjoy	1982	2,686
5	Alex Higgins *v* Tony Knowles	1988	2,593
6	Alex Higgins *v* Doug Mountjoy	1984	2,580
7	Doug Mountjoy *v* Cliff Thorburn	1985	2,569*
8	Terry Griffiths *v* Alex Higgins	1982	2,567
9	Steve Davis *v* Alex Higgins	1985	2,566
10	Steve Davis *v* Terry Griffiths	1982	2,563*

Final.

THE ORIGIN OF SNOOKER, AND HOW IT GOT ITS NAME

The origin of snooker is known precisely, unlike many sports, and was chronicled in detail by the eminent writer Sir Compton Mackenzie. In 1875, Neville Bowes Chamberlain, an officer in the Devonshire Regiment stationed in India, used to play Black Pool in the officers' mess at Jubbulpore. Black Pool was played with 15 reds, a black, and a white cue ball and was primarily a potting game. However, the officers added three more colours: yellow, green and pink, and then added the brown and blue soon afterwards, thereby establishing the current complement of 22 balls.

The addition of the extra colours made the game more interesting and Black Pool continued to be played – but with an extra five coloured balls. Nobody had considered giving it a new name until the day one of the officers missed an easy pot like a novice. One of his fellow officers called him a 'right snooker', a snooker being, at that time, the name of a first-year recruit at the Woolwich Military Academy. Chamberlain added that as they were all novices at the new game they were all 'snookers' and it was agreed that the game should be so named.

SPEEDWAY

THE 10 WINNERS OF THE MOST WORLD TITLES

	Rider/country	I	P	T	LT*	Total
1	Hans Nielsen (Denmark)	3	6	9	0	18
2	Erik Gundersen (Denmark)	3	5	7	2	17
3	Ivan Mauger (New Zealand)	6	1	4	2	13
4	Ove Fundin (Sweden)	5	0	6	0	11
5	Peter Collins (England)	1	4	5	0	10
6	Ole Olsen (Denmark)	3	1	3	1	8
7=	Tommy Knudsen (Denmark)	0	2	5	0	7
7=	Jan Pedersen (Denmark)	1	2	4	0	7
7=	Malcolm Simmons (England)	0	3	4	0	7
10	Barry Briggs (New Zealand)	4	0	2	0	6

*I = Individual; P = Pairs; T = Team; LT = Long Track.

Hans Nielsen of Denmark, winner of 18 world speedway titles.

THE 10 COUNTRIES WITH THE MOST WORLD CHAMPIONS

	Country	I	P	T	LT*	Total
1	Denmark	10	8	9	3	30
2	England	5	7	5	4	21
3	Sweden	8	3	6	1	18
4	New Zealand	12	1	1	2	16
5	West Germany/Germany	1	0	0	10	11
6	USA	3	2	2	1	8
7	Poland	1	1	4	0	6
8	Australia	4	0	1	0	5
9	Great Britain	0	0	4	0	4
10	Wales	2	0	0	0	2

*I = Individual; P = Pairs; T = Team; LT = Long Track.

The first World Championship was in 1936 when Lionel Van Praag of Australia won the individual title. The team event was added in 1960 and the pairs in 1970 (after two unofficial championships in 1968 and 1969) and in 1971 the long track championship was inaugurated. All of Denmark's titles have been won since 1971 when Ole Olsen became their first champion after capturing the individual crown.

THE 10 WINNERS OF THE MOST INDIVIDUAL WORLD TITLES

	Rider/nationality	Years	Titles
1	Ivan Mauger (NZ)	1968–79	6
2	Ove Fundin (Swe)	1956–67	5
3	Barry Briggs (NZ)	1957–66	4
4=	Ole Olsen (Den)	1971–78	3
4=	Erik Gundersen (Den)	1984–88	3
4=	Hans Nielsen (Den)	1986–89	3
7=	Freddie Williams (Wal)	1950–53	2
7=	Jack Young (Aus)	1951–52	2
7=	Ronnie Moore (NZ)	1954–59	2
7=	Peter Craven (Eng)	1955–62	2
7=	Bruce Penhall (USA)	1981–82	2

The individual title was the first world speedway title, first contested in 1936 when Australian Lionel Van Praag won the title ahead of Eric Langton and Bluey Wilkinson.

THE 10 TEAMS WITH THE MOST BRITISH LEAGUE TITLES

Since its formation as the National League in 1932, the British League has undergone many changes in both format and name. This list is a Top 10 of the most successful teams in the 'first division' of the British League, irrespective of what it was called at the time:

	Team	Years	Titles
1	Belle Vue	1933–82	10
2	Wembley	1932–53	8
3	Wimbledon	1954–61	7
4	Coventry	1978–88	5
5	Oxford	1964–89	4
6=	Reading	1973–90	3
6=	Ipswich	1975–84	3
8=	West Ham	1937–65	2
8=	New Cross	1938–48	2
8=	Swindon	1957–67	2
8=	Cradley Heath	1981–83	2

SQUASH

THE TOP 10 WINNERS OF THE BRITISH OPEN

	Player/nationality	Wins
1	Heather McKay (*née* Blundell) (Aus)	16
2	Jahangir Khan (Pak)	10
3	Janet Morgan (GB)	9
4=	Susan Devoy (NZ)	8
4=	Geoff Hunt (Aus)	8
6	Hashim Khan (Pak)	7
7=	Abdelfattah Amr Bey (Egy)	6
7=	Jonah Barrington (GB)	6
7=	Margot Lumb (GB)	6
10=	Abdelfattah Aboutaleb (Egy)	4
10=	Vicki Cardwell (*née* Hoffman) (Aus)	4
10=	Mahmoud Karim (Egy)	4
10=	Azam Khan (Pak)	4

The British Open was first held for men in 1922 and for women in 1930. Until the arrival of the World Championships in 1976 it was the world's premier event and has continued to maintain its prestigious position in the squash world.

Heather McKay's 16 titles were in consecutive years (1962–77), as were Jahangir Khan's (1982–91).

SWIMMING

THE 10 MOST SUCCESSFUL OLYMPIC COUNTRIES

	Country	gold	Medals silver	bronze	Total
1	USA	215	164	134	513
2	Australia	39	34	41	114
3	East Germany	40	34	25	99
4	Germany/West Germany	22	31	42	95
5	USSR/CIS	24	32	37	93
6	Great Britain	18	22	29	69
7	Hungary	26	22	17	65
8	Sweden	13	20	21	54
9	Japan	15	18	17	50
10	Canada	10	15	17	42

This table includes medals for the diving and water polo events which form part of the Olympic swimming programme.

THE 10 FASTEST TIMES FOR THE MEN'S 100 METRES FREESTYLE AT THE OLYMPIC GAMES

	Swimmer/nationality	Event	Year	Time (secs)
1	Matt Biondi (USA)	Final	1988	48.63
2	Alexander Popov (CIS)	Final	1992	49.02
3	Matt Biondi (USA)	Heat	1988	49.04
4	Chris Jacobs (USA)	Final	1988	49.08
5	Chris Jacobs (USA)	Heat	1988	49.20
6	Alexander Popov (CIS)	Heat	1992	49.29
7	Stephan Caron (Fra)	Heat	1988	49.37
8	Gustavo Borges (Bra)	Final	1992	49.43
9	Gustavo Borges (Bra)	Heat	1992	49.49
10	Stephan Caron (Fra)	Final	1992	49.50

When he won the 1976 final in 49.99 seconds, Jim Montgomery (USA) became the first man to swim the 100 metres in under 50 seconds.

Perhaps better known for his film roles as Tarzan, Johnny Weissmuller was also the first man to swim the 100 metres in under a minute back in 1924.

THE TOP 10 INDIVIDUAL OLYMPIC GOLD MEDAL WINNERS

	Swimmer/nationality	Years	Gold medals
1	Mark Spitz (USA)	1968–72	9
2=	Matt Biondi (USA)	1984–88	6
2=	Kristin Otto (GDR)	1988	6
4=	Charles Daniels (USA)	1904–08	5
4=	Johnny Weissmuller (USA)	1924–28	5
4=	Don Schollander (USA)	1964–68	5
7=	Henry Taylor (GB)	1906–08	4
7=	Pat McCormick (USA)	1952–56	4
7=	Murray Rose (Aus)	1956–60	4
7=	Dawn Fraser (Aus)	1956–64	4
7=	Roland Matthes (GDR)	1968–72	4
7=	Kornelia Ender (GDR)	1976	4
7=	John Naber (USA)	1976	4
7=	Vladimir Salnikov (USSR)	1980–88	4
7=	Greg Louganis (USA)	1984–88	4
7=	Krisztina Egerszegi	1988–92	4

Spitz holds the record for winning the most gold medals at one Games – seven in 1972, which is the most by any competitor in any sport. His gold medals came in the following events and, remarkably, all were won in world record-breaking times:

Event	Time min : sec
100 metres freestyle	51.22
200 metres freestyle	1:52.78
100 metres butterfly	54.27
200 metres butterfly	2:00.70
4 x 100 metres freestyle relay	3:26.42
4 x 200 metres freestyle relay	7:35.78
4 x 100 metres medley relay	3:48.16

TABLE TENNIS

THE 10 PLAYERS WITH THE MOST WORLD TITLES

	Player/nationality	Singles	Men's doubles	Women's doubles	Mixed doubles	Total
1	Maria Mednyánszky (Hun)	5	0	7	6	18
2	Viktor Barna (Hun/Eng)	5	8	0	2	15
3	Angelica Rozeanu (Rom)	6	0	3	3	12
4	Anna Sipos (Hun)	2	0	6	3	11
5=	Gizi Farkas (Hun)	3	0	3	4	10
5=	Miklós Szabados (Hun)	1	6	0	3	10
7	Bohumil Vána (Cze)	2	3	0	3	8
8=	Ichiro Ogimura (Jap)	2	2	0	3	7
8=	Ferenc Sidó (Hun)	1	2	0	4	7
10=	Ivan Andreadis (Cze)	0	4	0	1	5
10=	Richard Bergmann (Aut/Eng)	4	1	0	0	5

Viktor Barna demonstrates the agility which brought him 15 world table tennis titles.

TRIATHLON

THE 10 FASTEST WINNING TIMES FOR THE HAWAII IRONMAN

	Winner/nationality	Year	Time hr:min:sec
1	Mark Allen (USA)	1989	8:09:15
2	Mark Allen (USA)	1991	8:18:35
3	Mark Allen (USA)	1990	8:28:17
4	Dave Scott (USA)	1986	8:28:37
5	Scott Molina (USA)	1988	8:31:00
6	Dave Scott (USA)	1987	8:34:13
7	Scott Tinley (USA)	1985	8:50:54
8	Dave Scott (USA)	1984	8:54:20
9	Paula Newby-Fraser* (Zim)	1989	9:00:56
10	Paula Newby-Fraser* (Zim)	1988	9:01:01

*Women's race winner.

This is perhaps one of the most gruelling of all sporting contests, in which competitors engage in a 3.9-km/2.4-mile swim followed by a 180-km/112-mile cycle race, ending with a full marathon. The first Hawaii Ironman was held at Waikiki Beach in 1978 but since 1981 the event's home has been at Kailua-Kona.

Dave Scott has won the men's race a record six times while the only woman to have won the ladies' race more than once is Paula Newby-Fraser (three wins).

Mark Allen of the United States on his way to the second fastest winning time for the Hawaii Ironman in 1991.

WATER SKIING

THE 10 WINNERS OF THE MOST MEN'S WORLD TITLES

	Skier/nationality	Overall	Slalom	Tricks	Jump	Total
1=	Sammy Duval (USA)	4	0	0	2	6
1=	Patrice Martin (Fra)	2	1	3	0	6
3=	Bob La Point (USA)	0	4	1	0	5
3=	Alfredo Mendoza (USA)	2	1	0	2	5
3=	Mike Suyderhoud (USA)	2	1	0	2	5
6=	George Athans (Can)	2	1	0	0	3
6=	Guy de Clercq (Bel)	1	0	0	2	3
6=	Wayne Grimditch (USA)	0	0	2	1	3
6=	Mike Hazelwood (GB)	1	0	0	2	3
6=	Ricky McCormick (USA)	0	0	1	2	3
6=	Billy Spencer (USA)	1	1	1	0	3

	Skier/nationality	Overall	Slalom	Tricks	Jump	Total
1	Liz Shetter (*née* Allen) (USA)	3	3	1	4	11
2	Willa McGuire (*née* Worthington) (USA)	3	2	1	2	8
3	Cindy Todd (USA)	2	3	0	2	7
4	Deena Mapple (*née* Brush) (USA)	2	0	0	4	6
5	Marina Doria (Swi)	1	1	2	0	4
6=	Maria Victoria Carrasco (Ven)	0	0	3	0	3
6=	Natalya Ponomaryeva (USSR) (*née* Rumyantseva)	0	0	3	0	3
8=	Leah Marie Rawls (USA)	1	0	1	0	2
8=	Vickie Van Hook (USA)	1	1	0	0	2
8=	Sylvie Hulseman (Lux)	1	0	1	0	2
8=	Jeanette Brown (USA)	1	1	0	0	2
8=	Jeanette Stewart-Wood (GB)	1	0	0	1	2
8=	Christy Weir (USA)	1	0	0	1	2
8=	Evie Wolford (USA)	0	2	0	0	2
8=	Kim Laskoff (USA)	0	2	0	0	2
8=	Dany Duflot (Fra)	0	0	2	0	2
8=	Ana Marie Carasco (Ven)	1	0	1	0	2
8=	Nancie Rideout (USA)	0	0	0	2	2
8=	Renate Hansluvka (Aut)	0	0	0	2	2
8=	Karen Neville (Aus)	2	0	0	0	2
8=	Tawn Larsen (USA)	0	0	2	0	2

WEIGHTLIFTING

THE 10 HEAVIEST WEIGHTS EVER LIFTED BY A MAN

	Weightlifter/nationality	Date	Lift (kg)
1	Leonid Taranenko (USSR)	26 Nov 1988	266.0
2	Anatoly Pisarenko (USSR)	16 Sep 1984	265.0
3	Sergey Didik (USSR)	31 Jul 1983	261.0
4	Viktor Marchuk (USSR)	19 Dec 1982	260.0
5	Vasily Alekseyev (USSR)	1 Nov 1977	256.0
6	Gerd Bonk (GDR)	11 Apr 1976	252.5
7	Yuri Zacharevich (USSR)	30 Apr 1988	250.5
8	Stefan Botev (Bul)	13 Mar 1988	250.0
9	Viacheslav Klokov (USSR)	30 Oct 1983	247.5
10	Alexandr Kurlovich (CIS)	4 Aug 1992	245.0

Anatoly Pisarenko of the Soviet Union, three times world super-heavyweight champion (1981–83), lifted a mammoth 265.0kg in September 1984.

A ll 10 lifts took place in the jerk section of weightlifting competitions.

THE 10 HEAVIEST WEIGHTS EVER LIFTED BY A WOMAN

	Weightlifter/nationality	Date	Lift (kg)
1	Li Yajuan (Chn)	3 Jun 1990	142.5
2	Han Changmei (Chn)	26 Sep 1990	140.0
3	Maria Urrutia (Col)	22 Jun 1991	138.0
4	Li Hongling (Chn)	26 Nov 1989	137.5
5	Milena Trendafilova (Bul)	1 Jun 1990	135.0
6	Karyn Marshall (USA)	3 Jun 1990	130.0
7	Li Chia Ping (Chn)	1 Jun 1990	127.5
8=	Shi Wen (Chn)	25 Sep 1990	125.0
8=	Carla Garrett (USA)	26 Apr 1991	125.0
10	Erika Takács (Hun)	19 May 1991	123.0

All 10 lifts took place in the jerk section of weightlifting competitions.

THE 10 MOST SUCCESSFUL OLYMPIC COUNTRIES

	Country	gold	Medals silver	bronze	Total
1	USSR/CIS	44	25	3	72
2	USA	15	16	10	41
3	Bulgaria	10	13	5	28
4	Poland	4	3	18	25
5	Germany/ West Germany	6	4	12	22
6	Hungary	2	7	8	17
7=	France	9	2	4	15
7=	Italy	5	5	5	15
9	China	4	5	5	14
10=	Austria	5	5	2	12
10=	East Germany	1	5	6	12
10=	Japan	2	2	8	12
18=	*Great Britain*	*1*	*3*	*3*	*7*

Britain's only gold medal was won by Launceston Elliot in the one-handed lift event at the 1896 Games. A versatile athlete, Elliot also took part in the wrestling competition at the same Olympics.

WRESTLING

THE 10 MOST SUCCESSFUL OLYMPIC COUNTRIES

	FREESTYLE				
	Country	gold	Medals silver	bronze	Total
1	USA	41	33	20	94
2	USSR/CIS	30	16	16	62
3=	Japan	16	9	7	32
3=	Turkey	15	11	6	32
5	Bulgaria	6	15	9	30
6	Sweden	8	10	8	26
7	Finland	8	7	10	25
8	Iran	3	8	11	22
9	Great Britain	3	4	10	17
10	Hungary	3	4	7	14

	GRECO–ROMAN				
	Country	gold	Medals silver	bronze	Total
1	USSR/CIS	37	22	13	72
2	Finland	19	19	18	56
3	Sweden	19	16	18	53
4	Hungary	15	9	11	35
5	Bulgaria	8	14	7	29
6	Germany/ West Germany	5	15	8	28
7	Romania	6	8	13	27
8	Italy	5	4	9	18
9	Turkey	9	4	2	15
10	Poland	2	7	5	14

Great Britain has never won a Greco-Roman medal. Their three gold medals in the freestyle event were all in 1908.

YACHTING

THE 10 MOST SUCCESSFUL OLYMPIC COUNTRIES

	Country	gold	Medals silver	bronze	Total
1	USA	16	18	13	47
2	Great Britain	15	8	9	32
3	Sweden	9	11	9	29
4	Norway	15	11	2	28
5	France	10	6	9	25
6	Denmark	9	8	4	21
7	Germany/ West Germany	5	5	6	16
8=	Holland	4	4	5	13
8=	USSR/CIS	4	5	4	13
10	New Zealand	6	3	3	12

Denmark's Paul Elvström, the first person to win yachting gold medals at four successive Olympics.

Yachting has provided one of the Olympics' most durable competitors: Paul Elvström of Denmark. The first person to win gold medals at four consecutive Games (1948–60), he went on to compete in a further four Games, in 1968, 1972, 1984 and 1988, when he was partnered by his daughter in the Tornado class.

ABBREVIATIONS USED FOR COUNTRIES

Arg	Argentina	GB	Great Britain and Northern Ireland	Pan	Panama
Aus	Australia			Phi	Philippines
Aut	Austria	GDR	German Democratic Republic (East Germany)	Pol	Poland
Bel	Belgium			Por	Portugal
Bra	Brazil			PR	Puerto Rico
Bul	Bulgaria	Ger	Germany	Rom	Romania
Can	Canada	Haw	Hawaii	SA	South Africa
Chi	Chile	Hol	Holland/Netherlands	Sco	Scotland
Chn	China	Hun	Hungary	SK	South Korea
CIS	Commonwealth of Independent States (formerly USSR)	Ina	Indonesia	Spa	Spain
		Ire	Ireland	SR	Southern Rhodesia
		Ita	Italy	Sri	Sri Lanka
Col	Colombia	Jam	Jamaica	Swe	Sweden
Cub	Cuba	Jap	Jap	Swi	Switzerland
Cze	Czechoslovakia	Ken	Kenya	Tan	Tanzania
Den	Denmark	Lie	Liechtenstein	Tha	Thailand
Dji	Djibouti	Lux	Luxembourg	USA	United States of America
Dom	Dominican Republic	Mal	Malaysia	USSR	Union of Soviet Socialist Republics
Egy	Egypt	Mex	Mexico		
Eng	England	Mlt	Malta	Ven	Venezuela
Est	Estonia	Mor	Morocco	Wal	Wales
Eth	Ethiopia	Nam	Namibia	WI	West Indies
Fij	Fiji	NI	Northern Ireland	Yug	Yugoslavia
Fin	Finland	Nic	Nicaragua	Zim	Zimbabwe
Fra	France	Nig	Nigeria		
FRG	Federal Republic of Germany (West Germany)	Nor	Norway		
		NZ	New Zealand		
		Pak	Pakistan		

INDEX